Standing at the Water's Edge

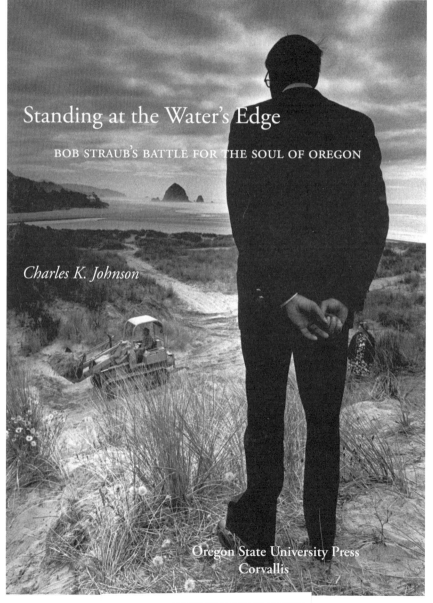

Standing at the Water's Edge

BOB STRAUB'S BATTLE FOR THE SOUL OF OREGON

Charles K. Johnson

Oregon State University Press
Corvallis

The paper in this book meets the guidelines for permanence and durability of the Committee on Production Guidelines for Book Longevity of the Council on Library Resources and the minimum requirements of the American National Standard for Permanence of Paper for Printed Library Materials Z39.48-1984.

Library of Congress Cataloging-in-Publication Data
Johnson, Charles K.
  Standing at the water's edge : Bob Straub's battle for the soul of Oregon / Charles K. Johnson.
      p. cm.
  Includes bibliographical references and index.
  ISBN 978-0-87071-669-0 (alk. paper) -- ISBN 978-0-87071-670-6 (e-book)
  1. Straub, Robert W. 2. Governors--Oregon--Biography. 3. Oregon--Politics and government--1951- I. Title.
  F881.35.S77J64 2012
  979.5'043092--dc23
  [B]
                                              2012015120

 Oregon State University Press
121 The Valley Library
Corvallis OR 97331-4501
541-737-3166 • fax 541-737-3170
http://osupress.oregonstate.edu

For Ken,

and for all those like him, who put their heart and soul into public service.

Ken Johnson, Bob Straub, and Robert F. Kennedy, Seaside, Oregon,
May 24, 1968. Photo by Michael B. Conard, UPI

Why don't we learn in Oregon? We should be planning for the future, the long-range future, not just for today and tomorrow. The strength and success and best hope for Oregon's future economic development and well-being lies in our ability today to clearly foresee, plan for, and protect long-range needs. Our beach resource is a limited resource. The demand for it, the need for it, the value of its beauty is stronger and stronger every day...

A few individuals, a few shortsighted promotional type organizations... are beating the drums for this beach route as a way for them to make a quick dollar and destroy, in the process, their most valuable asset, which creates these business values. Gentlemen, they would sell out too quickly and too cheaply. They would use up an irreplaceable capital resource for the immediate income that it would produce. I can only say that I know of no successful business that operates on this short-sighted principle that'll long survive.

—State Treasurer Robert W. Straub

Recorded Testimony before the Oregon State Highway Commission Hearing on the Cape Kiwanda – Neskowin Section Improvements to the Oregon Coast Highway, November 29, 1967, Tillamook Elks Club Social Hall, Tillamook, Oregon

Contents

Foreword by Governor Victor G. Atiyeh   x

Introduction   xii

Chapter 1: *Lessons of the Prune Orchard*   1

Chapter 2: *The Road Less Traveled*   17

Chapter 3: *Answering the Call*   36

Chapter 4: *Jumping in with Both Feet*   55

Chapter 5: *Get Our Money Out of the Mattress*   76

Chapter 6: *Nature's Warrior*   95

Chapter 7: *From State Street to Wall Street*   108

Chapter 8: *A Line in the Sand*   120

Chapter 9: *From Backwater to Vortex* 145

Chapter 10: *A Darkened Victory*   167

Chapter 11: *Utopian Dreams, Economic Realities*   194

Chapter 12: *Fighting Against the Tide*   220

Chapter 13: *A Graceful Departure*   254

Chapter 14: *The Arc of Bob Straub's Life*   277

Epilogue by Mark Henkels   284

Notes   291

Acknowledgments 329

Index   332

Foreword

This is a book about a fascinating man that a few Oregonians really knew and so many of us *thought* we knew. It is a long overdue biography of Governor Bob Straub.

Bob was a doer, not a talker. He had a vision for Oregon. He knew what needed to be done and he just went about doing it—with no fanfare, no study groups, and no blue ribbon committees. I guess that was one of the reasons I grew to like him so much. He was, in his style anyway, a conservative.

My first awareness of Robert W. Straub was when I became a freshman Republican member in the Oregon House of Representatives in 1959. Bob was already established over in the State Senate. He was a Democrat but not part of the power structure over there; however, this did not mean he was a shadow in that body. He made his presence known!

His star, however, really came into full light in 1964 when he upset incumbent State Treasurer Howard Belton, who was a highly respected figure in Oregon politics. Bob ran a very aggressive campaign promising to invest the state's money better and Oregonians came to his side.

Bob Straub was an exceptional state treasurer. He set the bar very high for those who came after him. He came up with the concept of investing state money in the stock market, which was considered risky in those days. In the 1960s, that was a bold step but it has paid off handsomely for our state funds. It made it possible for state employees to have secure pensions during times when the state budget was very restricted and, in turn, saved money to the benefit of all Oregonians. That took political courage and rare foresight.

Bob was a sincere and passionate advocate for the environment and led Governor Tom McCall on those issues in the early years. He was more in touch with the environmental concerns of Oregonians, such as protecting the beaches and cleaning up the Willamette River. He had so many innovative ideas including, for example, the Willamette Greenway plan. Tom McCall skillfully grabbed these concepts and made them his own, but it must be known from whence came the seed.

Bob and I ran against each other twice for governor. While we always remained personally cordial and respectful during those races, there was no mistaking his desire to win. He believed in himself and in his vision of Oregon, and he knew the frustration of watching government from the sidelines. A fearless competitor, he also understood and respected the difference between hard campaigning and destructive politics. I appreciate the deep civility with which he conducted himself in his campaigns and as a man. There are so many memories. Among them: during debates Bob would say that he "chose to *come*" to Oregon and I would reply that I "chose to *stay*" in Oregon.

Bob handed me my first, and only, political defeat, in the race for governor in 1974. As I said at the time, the people gave me a mandate to go back into the family rug business. He was just too well known and popular and his style of government activism was in favor with the voters.

I would not have run again in 1978 if I had not felt Bob was vulnerable. From the first, he didn't seem to be getting very good press as governor, maybe in reaction to the very different style he had from Governor McCall, and the public, the press, and even his supporters were having trouble getting access to him. Bob also had a full plate of difficult and controversial issues during his tenure, including a major drought and the continuing energy crisis, along with a lot of fighting over land-use planning and timber harvesting. Plus, years of government activism had left people feeling overtaxed.

My campaign positions on the issues matched the public mood better in 1978 than they had four years earlier. People were ready to slow down and put Oregon's house in order. I defeated former Governor McCall in the primary and Governor Straub in the general election. It was the end of an era.

A marvelous thing about Bob Straub was that he was who he was—he could never be someone else. At times, he might have wanted to have Tom McCall's way with words. Nevertheless, his warmth, great sense of humor, and frankness charmed people. It's a mystery to me why it took so long for his campaign to realize that. I do not think I could have defeated him if he had allowed people to see him as he was.

After the election, I appreciated Bob's mature approach in helping our administration make a smooth transition to office. Though there were things that I set out to change, I found state government in good shape from Straub's stewardship. My unofficial slogan was, "If it ain't broke don't fix it." For the most part, our agencies were serving the people very well.

As I said at the beginning, Bob Straub was a doer, not a talker. He has passed on to all of us the priceless inheritance of his life's work. I always sensed that Bob and his family understood what an important contribution he made to the state and that he succeeded in making a lasting mark for both our finances and our livability. Oregon is fortunate that Bob Straub took the plunge into politics, and his successes are our legacy.

Victor G. Atiyeh
Governor of Oregon (1979–1987)

Introduction

Robert W. Straub is best remembered today as a warm and genuine human being, a first-rate state treasurer, and an average governor. He served a four-year term as governor after what are generally viewed now as the eight glorious years of Tom McCall. McCall was, without a doubt, the toughest act to follow in Oregon political history, so it is easy to see why these impressions linger.

But these generalizations do not do justice to Straub and what he has meant to Oregon. For one thing, Bob Straub was more than merely first-rate as state treasurer; he was a national leader and the best that Oregon has ever seen. His investment reforms were revolutionary and vigorously opposed by the state's large banks, which had profited from the previous system. Under Straub's persistent leadership, Oregon was an early pioneer of state investment using the "prudent man" approach, as it was called in those days. Government funds were invested as any prudent investor would his or her own money in stocks, bonds, real estate, mortgages, and private loans. Straub was a state investment innovator. To keep political favor from influencing investment decisions, Straub had the good sense to establish an appointed Oregon Investment Council, which selected private money managers from throughout the country, based on their performance, to invest Oregon's money. The system of using outside money managers was unique to Oregon at the time and, as carefully implemented by Straub, his fellow members of the state's investment council, and their successors, worked extraordinarily well for decades.

Straub's reforms have saved Oregon taxpayers billions of dollars over the last forty years and helped tens of thousands of state and local employees to retire comfortably. The investment program was so successful that it was imitated in states, counties, municipalities, and school districts across the country and is accepted as standard government financial policy today.

Mark Hatfield, as a partisan Republican governor when Democrat Straub upset fellow Republican State Treasurer Howard Belton in 1964, was not an early fan of the brash newcomer. But he came to appreciate Straub's financial vision and, in later years, frequently referred to him, without irony or hyperbole, as "the Alexander Hamilton of Oregon."[1]

Regarding Straub's alleged leadership failings, the Tom McCall we know today—a heroic figure who, to reverse his own hilariously self-effacing quote to the contrary, *is* viewed as a "giant statue framed against a red sky"[2]—might not have reached his epic potential without his rival Bob Straub aggressively pursuing a strong environmental agenda and pressing McCall hard in their two gubernatorial races. When looking back on those heroic days, admiring the "giant statue" of McCall etched against a flaming sky, a discerning eye can see, looming on the edge of the light, another enormous figure. It is upon these twin pillars of Tom McCall and Bob Straub that the Oregon Story of the 1960s and '70s is built.

During their first campaign in 1966 and throughout McCall's first term as governor, Straub repeatedly took the initiative with environmental proposals. From supporting preservation of public beaches to the Willamette Greenway proposal, Straub frequently had McCall playing catch-up—which the veteran television commentator and his crack staff did brilliantly. The popularity of environmental protection as an issue grew stronger as each man tried to better the other in their battle of ideas.

We can never know whether McCall would have shown the same level of environmental leadership without his rivalry with Straub. McCall's legacy culminated in the development of Oregon's crowning achievement of the period: the creation of a system of statewide land-use planning designed to protect farm and forest land. Governor Straub, succeeding McCall, had the thankless and very complex task of implementing this groundbreaking legislation. Bob Straub weathered the backlash of developers and other aggrieved landowners. He and his administration firmly established many of the environmental gains made during the McCall years, while preparing the state for its transformation from a timber- to a high-tech-based economy. One thing we know for certain is that the Straub-McCall rivalry, and bipartisan agreement on environmental values and wise economic growth, helped make these achievements possible.

And this leads to the final element of Straub's legacy. Bob Straub always kept the goal of a better state first and foremost in his mind. He was an intensely competitive man and not above petty thoughts, but when it came right down to it, his goal was to have good public policy regardless of public credit or partisan advantage. During the fourteen years that Straub was the Oregon Democratic Party standard bearer, he did not stoop to low political tactics. Even during his extremely aggressive younger days in politics, when the political campaign was over he did his best to make government run efficiently and well. What some felt was a weakness for Straub—his directness and lack of political guile—was in fact one of his greatest strengths. It is easier to appreciate now, after years of watching the tragic destructiveness of government leaders making decisions based on popular gimmicks that will help them, or hurt their opponents, in their next political campaigns, that honesty and bipartisan cooperation are essential for good government to flourish. Honest discourse with the public is difficult when office holders know that unpopular honesty will be used as a lever against them, regardless of the consequences to good government.

In these pages I hope to show you a man who was decent, kind hearted, and strong willed; a frequently awkward political figure who had to overcome stuttering in public speaking; a man who periodically suffered from severe bouts of depression, yet always earnestly did his best for his dearly loved wife and family, his friends, and his chosen state; a visionary whose modest manner and rough-hewn exterior sometimes caused more polished contemporaries to underestimate him. Bob Straub was an Oregon original, in good company with the other charming oddballs and unlikely prophets who have made the politics of this state so creative and interesting.

Please allow me to make one final admission: I am not an impartial observer. I was raised a Bob Straub believer.

My father, Ken Johnson, was Bob's unofficial campaign manager on his first statewide campaign to become Oregon's state treasurer in 1964 and was appointed Straub's deputy after he won. Dad was Straub's chief strategist in his first two (bitterly disappointing, from my young perspective) races against Tom McCall for governor and his pro forma reelection as treasurer. I learned much of the political history of that period from the savvy, but clearly biased, perspective of my father during dinner table conversations.

Being involved in politics at this optimistic and exciting time hooked me forever. Our family hobby, other than some summer backpacking and mountain climbing, was distributing literature for Straub and other Democratic candidates or gathering signatures for ballot measures. My brother and I went to political rallies at an age when other kids in Oregon were learning how to ski, or hunt, or fish. We believed we were changing the world for the better. And we were.

This book is my attempt to recapture some of those feelings and remind all of us just how important it is that we act on them. Bob Straub's life is an example of how one person with good ideas, a good heart, and tremendous determination, working with other like-minded people, truly can change at least one small corner of the world for the better.

Bob Straub stood at the water's edge of Oregon politics, and casting aside his fears and personal difficulties, dove in. We honor him and those like him, each in our own way, by doing the same.

CHAPTER I

Lessons of the Prune Orchard

You cannot dream yourself into a character; you must hammer and forge yourself one.

—James A. Froude, English historian (1818–1894)

Watching Bob Straub striding through the mud in his work boots on his farm in the West Salem hills in Oregon, you had no clue that he began his years as a city boy.

Pounding in fence posts, cutting firewood with his chainsaw, or planting trees on his land further west, in Willamina, were Bob's meditations, reflecting a work ethic and a love of the outdoors he learned from his parents and carried as a personal touchstone throughout his life.

Bob Straub chose to see himself as a simple man of the soil, but the maze of fascinating contradictions that make up any person's life seem particularly complex in his case. Growing up the youngest in a rough-and-tumble household of competitive, prankster brothers, a father who was "a disciplinarian," who "insist[ed] on a high level of performance," and a loving, "very religious … but tolerant" mother,[1] Straub's upbringing was, on its surface, not atypical for the son of a self-made professional in the early part of the 1900s. But the hurts he suffered growing up, both physically and emotionally, and how he succeeded in overcoming them are a compelling story made even more so by his becoming an important public figure.

Given Straub's rural predilections, it is somewhat ironic that he was born and spent his first nine years in the civilized, "citified" household of an eminent San Francisco lawyer. When their youngest son, Robert William, was born on May 6, 1920, Thomas and Mary Straub and their family lived in a pleasant row house on the corner of 11th Avenue and Anza Street, in the Richmond District. Thomas Straub, a stern father and respected attorney, represented Pacific Gas & Electric, a rapidly growing Northern California utility company, eventually serving as their chief counsel. Mary Tulley Straub sustained home and hearth for Thomas and their five children with a flourish and a kind heart. The infant Bob already had three brothers: Thomas, Jr., referred to as "Tom" or "TJ" to distinguish him from his father, age nine, Frank, age six, and Jim, age two, and, a sister—the apple of her father's

Thomas Straub

eye—Jean, age four. Young Jean promptly named him "Bib," a childish mispronunciation that stuck with him as his friendly nickname within the family for the rest of his life.

It was a close-knit family and the years in San Francisco were good, Jean recalled: "My earliest memories in childhood were of bicycling and skating with my brothers on the hilly San Francisco streets. We used to sail down the hills through intersections and we almost always took our dog Jack," an energetic and friendly old-style cocker spaniel with a curly brown coat and a docked tail. "We enjoyed the city—going to the zoo, swimming in an enormous pool. Every Saturday our parents would take us to Luca's, an Italian restaurant. It had wonderful Italian pasta and sourdough French bread. I spent a lot of time with my little brothers Jim and Bob."[2]

But life wasn't always idyllic for the kids. A disturbing incident when Bob was around four years old, and an older brother's reaction to it, illustrates the tenacity of the family character. One day Jean and Jim, eight and six at the time, with little "Bib" tagging along, were out roaming with Jack and came to the Fleischmann pool, a huge indoor public saltwater pool perched on a cliff over the Pacific, at the end of Golden Gate Park, about a mile and a half from home. As Jean remembers it, "We wanted to go in, but we couldn't bring our dog. A man, who was very nice, said, 'I'll keep your dog for you, kiddies. You go in and have fun.' So we left Jack with the man while we went inside to look around. When we came back out, the man was gone. He stole our dog."[3]

The children were crushed. But older brother Frank just couldn't accept that Jack was gone. He spent every afternoon and all day on weekends on his bike combing the city looking for the dog. Frank continued this personal mission for several months.

One Saturday morning, Frank called home to his father and said, "I found Jack!" He had spotted the dog with a man he didn't know and followed them to a second-story flat. Frank was calling from a pay phone on the corner, keeping the dog thief's place in sight.

"I'll be right there," Thomas said, and hopped into their 1916 Cadillac touring car. It was the same car they took on camping trips, with running boards, folding panels, racks and curtains on the inside—a sort of early prototype of the minivan. Jack liked to lie on the running board and put his head on the front fender, feeling the wind whip past him. Leaving Frank waiting below, Thomas walked up to the second floor and knocked on the door. When the man opened the door, Jack clearly recognized Straub, jumping up and barking with friendly excitement. Thomas Straub said, "I've come to pick up my dog." The other man stared back at him and said, "That isn't your dog; it's ours."

Straub took Jack's new family to court. The alleged dog thief told the judge that Jack was a rare and expensive breed that he'd imported from Italy a few years before. The dog disappeared and now they had finally found him. Thomas Straub told the judge that he had rescued Jack from the pound and had him for several years. The judge quickly pronounced his verdict. He told the other man, "I'm sorry sir, but I've known Mr. Straub for many years and if he says that the story he told me is true, then I believe him."[4]

Thomas Jefferson Straub had grown up in a family where honesty, and a lot of hard work, was expected of children from a very early age. He was born in 1879 in Liberty Township, Montgomery County, Kansas and raised there in the "poor God-forsaken, dry wheat land country" around Cherryville.[5] This is in the southeast corner of Kansas, to the north of what is now Oklahoma, then Indian Territory. Thomas' father, Francis Straub, was a Civil War veteran from Wisconsin, born in 1846 of immigrant Swiss-German parents.[6] Francis had suffered permanent damage to his feet from frostbite at the notorious Andersonville Confederate prison camp. After the war, Francis settled on the free land offered veterans, in the Kansas prairie.

Francis Straub met Elizabeth Wilkinson, a Canadian of Scots-Irish descent, in Kansas and they married in 1871. Thomas the third of four children—the second son, with a twin sister, Catherine. Francis Straub was said to be a severe father, who wasn't afraid to dole out physical punishment to his boys if they didn't obey him.[7] Thomas appears to have been a diligent student, a very hard worker, and someone who learned by the example of his hard-working parents to be prudent with money.

In May of 1898, at age nineteen and fresh from high school, Thomas followed in his father's footsteps and enlisted in the Army for the Spanish-American War—joining the 20th Kansas Volunteer Infantry. The country was responding to the drumbeat in the newspapers calling for "freedom for Cuba" from corrupt Spanish rule. Many young men joined to become part of the liberating force. The 20th Kansas Regiment's fate was not to liberate Cuba, however. Instead they languished for months in San Francisco, with poor supplies and, for a time, without uniforms. The daily newspapers of San Francisco referred to them facetiously as "Kansas scarecrows," and reporters wrote "humorous" pieces about them.[8] Though Camp Merritt's conditions were squalid, the lengthy stay allowed Thomas to fall in love with the city and he vowed to come back and live there some day. Eventually, he went with several regiments of soldiers who were shipped through Hawaii to occupy the recently surrendered Philippines. Arriving on December 6, 1898, they soon discovered that the Filipinos were not nearly as delighted to see them as they might have expected. The Spanish had surrendered to the Americans to avoid being defeated by Filipino forces that had them pinned in the garrison within Manila. It soon became clear that the Americans weren't going to allow the Filipinos self-rule—that didn't happen until forty-eight years later, in 1946.[9] A couple of months after he arrived, a Filipino insurrection began.

Caught up in this suddenly fierce fighting, the 20th Kansas Regiment proved brave under fire and distinguished itself as the most aggressive of the American forces. Their commander, Colonel Frederick Funston was made Brigadier General when the 20th Regiment left the Philippines in September 1899, "after eight months in the trenches, on the firing line and leading charges over swamps and through jungles on the other side of the globe."[10] On a much less heroic note, General Funston was charged by Private Charles Brenner, also with the Kansas Regiment, with ordering the killing of all Filipino prisoners after one battle. The Army chose not to investigate further because "it is not thought that his charge is very grievous under the circumstances then existing, as it was very early in the war, and the patience of our men was under great strain." In addition to these charges, there were reports of village burnings, civilian massacres, and widespread civilian death from disease and starvation in unsanitary detainment camps.[11]

It is unclear exactly what Private Straub saw and participated in outside of the recorded battles during his nine months in the Philippines since he almost never spoke of it, but toward the end of his life he told his grandson he had been a member of "Funston's raiders." He had "tramped through the jungles" trying to catch the nationalist leader Aguinaldo. "We went into villages and we did things you can't even imagine," Thomas said.[12] The "Fighting 20th" Kansas Regiment returned home to a hero's welcome. They had fought in nineteen battles and lost 68 men from fighting and illness, with 129 wounded.[13] Thomas Straub no doubt benefited from the good feelings the people in his community had for the returning soldiers, though soon after he returned, he suffered another shock when his twin sister, Catherine, died from typhoid during an epidemic. At twenty-one, Thomas J. Straub had seen and felt the effects of the death of friends, family, and nameless strangers firsthand both overseas and at home. His life experiences had already forged a very hard and determined young man.

Not long after returning from war, Thomas became acquainted with the Tulley sisters, taking an instant liking to Mary—and she to him. Mary, three years his junior, had just finished high school and planned to get a degree at Baker University to become a school teacher.[14]

Mary Ellen Tulley was born in Coffeeville, Kansas, and raised in a well-established family in Independence. Her father, Mark Tulley, was a merchant, known for his integrity and honesty, who sold fine china, silverware and crystal. In a curious foreshadowing of Bob Straub's future career, Mark Tulley, was later elected State Treasurer of Kansas in 1906, serving three two-year terms. The Tulleys, like the Straubs, were staunch "Kansas Republicans," meaning, according to Bob Straub's later description "they were unyielding, unbending, undeviating, conservative, consistent Republicans," and they raised their children to be the same.[15]

Thomas also decided to study to become a teacher, completing two years of "History, English, and Plane Geometry" at Kansas State Normal School (now Emporia State University), but he never taught and instead began saving money to go to law school. He "was very lucky to get a job" as a registrar of property deeds "that paid him some good money."[16]

In 1907, when Thomas had saved enough money, he enrolled in the Bachelor of Law degree program at the University of Michigan Law School -the largest law school in the country, with a sterling reputation.[17] During his three years there he supplemented his savings in both typical and unusual fashion—as a law clerk and as a semi-professional boxer. He exchanged letters regularly with Mary Tulley, who was teaching elementary school, wooing her with words from nearly a thousand miles away.[18]

After completing Law School in 1910,[19] undaunted by the massive earthquake that had struck San Francisco three years earlier, Thomas was still determined to move there. He traveled by train to the Bay Area to look for work. As a thirty-one-year-old law graduate, with years of work experience and a strong level of self-possession, he was soon hired as an associate counsel for the newly merged private utility company, Pacific Gas & Electric. He telegraphed Mary to come out and join him. She telegraphed back, "If you want me, I'm in Kansas. You come here."[20] Thomas knew better than to question such a plain message. He went back to Kansas and they were married in Independence.

The chief counsel at Pacific Gas & Electric, a Mr. William Bradford Bosley,[21] took Thomas under his wing and was soon grooming him to be his successor. PG&E was growing rapidly and expanding its system of gas and electricity throughout Northern California, providing an array of complicated legal challenges for their law department. Straub proved thorough, exacting, and efficient.

Because Thomas had been stimulated by his education and had always been a compulsive and inquisitive reader, he began to develop friendships with some of the intellectuals who were part of the San Francisco landscape. He became friends with the Hermann family, whose daughter, Rena, had married one of the most notorious radicals in the country—Tom Mooney—a leading organizer of the International Workers of the World, also known as the "Wobblies." Thomas Straub may have been offering the Mooneys legal advice, which they desperately needed during those years, as both Tom and Rena Mooney were charged with participating in a highly publicized railroad bombing during a labor dispute. The family argued Tom Mooney's innocence for years and many prominent Americans agreed and joined in the campaign for clemency.[22] Straub didn't see his unofficial involvement with this legal issue as in conflict with his private sector employment. He was intellectually curious and open to discussing ideas with anyone—and was displaying a central Straub family trait: an admiration for "pluck" or "toughness," as Bob Straub would later describe it, even in, or perhaps especially in, defiant or independent ways. But when Mr. Bosley, a staunch conservative member of the local legal establishment, caught wind of Straub's involvement with Tom Mooney, this didn't sit well with his boss.

Bosley told Thomas Straub to be very careful with associating with the wrong kinds of people—that it could lead him to trouble.[23] The time, especially during and shortly after the First World War proved to be hazardous for radical thinkers, with over ten thousand people rounded up and imprisoned during the infamous Palmer raids, merely for expressing what were deemed by the US government as treasonous beliefs and sedition against elected officials.[24]

Straub took Bosley's warning seriously and was much more careful after that. Thomas Straub nevertheless continued to read voraciously and remain informed, a characteristic he successfully instilled in all of his children. He was particularly fond of the writings of nineteenth-century social theoretician and philanthropist John Ruskin,[25] something that revealed Thomas' appreciation of the aesthetics and harmony of nature, and a noblesse oblige sense of duty toward the well being of all people. In addition to the Mooney case, Straub seemed notably affected by the legal unfairness of the infamous Sacco and Vanzetti case, in which two anarchists were executed in Massachusetts on extremely flimsy evidence, which became an international *cause celebre*. Thomas would occasionally offer the opinion, even years later, that the court decision was a travesty and a miscarriage of justice.[26] With these conversations and personal opinions, the attorney for Northern California's largest private utility company nevertheless passed along to his children his personal egalitarian belief that America's justice system should be fair and impartial for all and that it was, at times, desperately in need of reform.

Aside from this slight brush with radicalism, young Thomas Straub took an interest in more traditional civic service. Emulating his mentor Bosley's continued association with the Hastings College of Law, Straub became a lecturer for the San Francisco Law School, established in 1909 as a night school for working students. As someone who had to work his way through law school, he appreciated the chance to give back to others in the same position.[27] Straub served on a number of boards and commissions of various types, both substantial and ceremonial, from local school boards to state societies, throughout his life, setting an example of public service that Bob Straub, no doubt, took to heart.

The Straubs epitomized the prominent, solidly upper-middle-class American family of the early part of the twentieth century. "Mother and father loved to host parties and worked closely together to entertain dinner guests."[28] They worked beautifully and effortlessly as a team and followed the common pattern of division of labor by gender. Stern and cool with his boys, Thomas was expansive and understanding with others and well respected and admired in the community.

As a new bride in San Francisco, Mary had given up her career as a schoolteacher and became an outstanding homemaker and loving mother. She was "famous for unbelievably delicious cooking."[29] She not only enjoyed entertaining friends and neighbors, but also "never missed a beat to be worthwhile" with her children as well. She was careful and elaborate in creating unique birthday celebrations, writing personalized jingles and doggerel poetry for everyone at the party and leaving notes at each person's place setting.[30] She never failed to send birthday cards and thank you letters. Mary was careful with money, keeping close track of every single amount spent on groceries.[31] Thomas was more given to making grand expenditures,

Mary Tulley Straub

though for a reason, such as his tailor-made suits, which were essential to creating a masterful image in court. Mary did have a fondness for beautiful china, something she learned to appreciate from her father's store in childhood. Mrs. Straub embroidered and crocheted, did a lot of sewing and was, all in all, an accomplished homemaker. She was also a loving mother, much more emotional with her children than her more distant husband. When Thomas was home, everything went exactly as he said. When he was gone, the house was full of laughter and fun.

Though Mary was not as strict in disciplining the children as her husband, she was very religious. She was raised and remained a faithful Methodist all of her life. Thomas was not in any way religious and would not join her at church. They left the decision up to the children, from an early age, as to whether they would go to church themselves. As they grew older, most of the children, including Bob, "took the pattern of Father, but would go to church occasionally because they loved Mother and wanted to keep her company."[32] Thomas and Mary generally encouraged their children to be independent and develop their own ideas of how they wanted to live.

Straub children in San Francisco
from left: Jean, Tom (above), Bob (below), Jim, and Frank

In 1929, after the stock market crash and bank foreclosures caused upheaval for the entire country, Thomas and Mary made a drastic decision. Mary's sister Margaret and her husband Sam Urner were in trouble. They owned a prune and apricot orchard on San Antonio Road in Los Altos, California. Unfortunately, it would be more precise to say that the bank owned the orchard and was about to foreclose on them. To help them, the Straubs decided to buy the farm and move their family out of the city and forty-seven miles south into what was then farm and forest country.[33]

The decision wasn't just a humanitarian gesture, but reflected Thomas and Mary's desire to breathe fresh country air again—and get out of the chilly San Francisco fog. During their time in San Francisco, they had continued to enjoy outings in the country, including camping in Redwoods out of their Cadillac touring car. In fact, just before moving to Los Altos the family spent two summers in the mountainous woods of nearby La Honda, camping in big tents the first year and then cabins the next. Thomas had a side job outside of PG&E representing a railroad tie company based there, so he arranged for his family to stay in the forest camp, along with the Urners, and even the kids' ill-tempered old grandfather, Francis, who came out all the way from Kansas. Those summers were idyllic and became legendary within family lore.

The kids ran through the woods, playing in the creek and chasing each other around with salamanders, which they called mud puppies or waterdogs. They picked blackberries and huckleberries and ate outdoors, at great long tables to accommodate everyone. Jean fell in love with a baby pig from a neighboring ranch and adopted him, naming him Louie after the farmer, Louie O'Neill. Louie—the pig, not the farmer—would wander under the table and bite people's toes.[34]

Thomas saw another major benefit to moving to the farm, even though it meant a significant new commute for him. He was concerned that his boys were growing up too soft. Having worked physically hard in his younger years, he felt it would be good for his sons do the same. The orchards required many hours of strenuous toil. After contracting with a local family to tend to the apricots, he relied on his sons to work in the larger prune orchard. And it was hard, sweaty, backbreaking work, on top of their regular house chores and school work: pruning trees; picking, packing and drying fruit; hoeing weeds; and irrigating the orchard in the dry months.

That first year was a major adjustment for the boys, but the harvest was extremely important, as the Straubs were able to send large bags of prunes and apricots to family members throughout the country, who greatly appreciated having the food at a time when many were going hungry.[35] As time went on and the food value of the crop became less critical, Thomas had the boys replace the dead trees with native redwoods—a conservation lesson that Bob later followed himself on his own property.[36]

When they first arrived, they found the farmhouse was a little small for the large family, so Thomas decided the boys should live in the garage, which was a large, separate two-story building that they split into rooms for them. It was part of his scheme for having them become more independent. The boys loved it. They could hatch their own plots out there and slip out undetected for mischief at all hours of the night. Thomas took a sly pleasure in knowing they were up to no good; as long as their chores were done, they weren't directly disobeying his or Mary's wishes, and he didn't know the details.[37] He felt it was a sign of their independence, which, along with the healthy dose of hard labor in the orchards, was helping them develop the "pluck" they would need to be successful men.

He was most concerned about his eldest son, Thomas J. Straub Jr., known as Tom or T.J. T.J. rarely found favor from Father and could do no wrong with Mother, who would console him if his feelings were hurt.[38] Of all the children, T.J. was the most disrupted by the move to Los Altos. He had been attending a good private college prep school in San Francisco and was now missing his senior year, forced to finish at the local rural public high school in Mountain View. The sibling rivalry the other boys felt toward Tom didn't

The Straubs' "garage," in Los Altos, converted into a separate dwelling for the four Straub boys

help matters. He could be high-handed with his brothers and they resented him for it.[39] They were quick with the "smut talking," as they called it— talking bad about someone, not necessarily swearing or using foul language— and the "high and mighty" Tom was the butt of a lot of it, especially from his nearest brother in age, Frank, who was the master of under-the-breath sour comments. Jim could do a fair imitation of Tom's "sissy" talking, giving the younger boys hours of guilty enjoyment at Tom's expense.[40]

Tom's prize possession was a Model T that he had bought with money he earned. One day he was very excited about a big date he had that night with a really special girl. Frank decided to play a nasty prank on him. He organized his younger brothers to join him in peeing on the engine block. For good measure, he smeared limburger cheese all over it. Once it heated up it is said to have made quite a stench.[41]

Other than in exacting envious revenge on his older brother, or, perhaps because of it, Frank was the model child in following his father's wishes. He always completed his chores on time, without complaining, did his schoolwork, and was generally the most dutiful of all the Straub children. He is the one who seemed to take his father's dictums of hard work and tough-mindedness most to heart.

The younger three kids, Jean, Jim, and "Bib" continued to be something of a happy pack when they first moved down to Los Altos. Her task was to look out for her little brothers, who, at Jim's instigation, were looking for ways to get into trouble. Jim, two years older than "Bib," was the family layabout and mischief maker. Everyone agrees he was very intelligent, but he resisted discipline and frequently found his father's disfavor and punishment. He and Bob used to have great fun with a go-cart they built. They and their friend, Ordway Manning, who was Bob's age, would pull it to the top of a big hill

Christmas card photo from Los Altos, featuring this note from Mary Straub: "A Merry Christmas to you all, from My Darling Tom, my five angel children and the old lady, who, as you see, is fast getting to the foot of the line. Lots of Love, Mary. N.B. Won't fail to notice Jack, our good old faithful dog."
From left, Thomas, Thomas Jr. (T.J.), Frank, Jean, Mary, Jim, Bob,
and (below) Jack.

on their way to elementary school each day and then ride it back down on the way home.[42] They found even more challenging and dangerous precipices to plunge down and frequently had to repair the cart, and themselves, after crashes. As the children got older, Jim remained incorrigible—refusing to do his chores and skipping school.[43] He and Bob used to spend hours hanging out with a hobo at the back of the ranch. Though Jim was the widest reader in the family, he also learned to like drinking, leading to more run-ins with his father and more disapproval. Eventually, his drinking became a serious problem.

One infamous incident of Jim's wild behavior as a boy involved the Straubs' Slovenian neighbors, the Janovics, who were hired to manage the Straubs' apricot orchard. During one Sunday in apricot harvest season, Helen Janovic, the mother of the family, burst into the local Methodist Church where Mary was attending the morning service. Hurrying over to her, she said urgently and loud enough for others around her to hear: "Miss Mary, come quick. Mr.

Jim, he drive fast. He no stop. Go 'round corner." Jim had been driving the farm truck crazily through the orchards, spinning out in the soft, squishy dirt and coming really close to the people on ladders harvesting the fruit. No one was hurt, but Jim was in serious trouble—again.[44] Bob enjoyed Jim's pranks and wild behavior and took part in some of it, but he was mostly cautious about initiating anything and couldn't completely enjoy doing things he knew would get them into trouble. He was responsible and conscientious, though not as much as Frank, who didn't partake in Jim's shenanigans.

Bob was a thinker. He thought about what he wanted to do and who he wanted to become. As his sister, Jean, said years later, "He came into life being a thoughtful person."[45]

His reflective nature didn't stop him from demonstrating that much-admired Straub spunk from time to time. Shortly after they arrived on the farm, young Bob, all of ten years old, showed a little entrepreneurial spirit. Mary Straub found out about it from Mrs. Parker, a proper old gal who owned a Cadillac Victoria and looked as formidable as the car she drove. The Straubs' house was about four hundred yards from the main road. Mrs. Parker came to the door one sunny day, saying, "Mary, I don't know if you know what is going on outside. Your youngest son has a stand under the almond tree," she continued. "He's selling your apricot jam and it's very popular." Bob had struck gold with his mother's massive jam hoard in the basement, giving an early clue to his future knack for business.[46]

After they moved to Los Altos, Bob developed a problem with a corneal ulcer in his eye, probably from irritation from the dust and dirt of the orchards. He spent a lot of time by himself, being home schooled by his mother for long stretches.[47] She and Bob became very close and he absorbed a lot of her good, warm qualities. Like all of the children, he was encouraged to read, and he derived great pleasure and learned much from books on a wide variety of subjects. It was something he continued to do for the rest of his life. But it was also during this time that his natural shyness increased and he began stuttering—a speaking problem that he struggled to overcome throughout the rest of his life.[48]

When Bob began attending Mountain View High School, a wonderful caring English teacher, Carolyn Woods, took an interest in the tall, shy boy in her classroom. She could see from his writing that he was a deep, clear thinker. She saw tremendous potential in Bob and suggested he tackle the stuttering problem head on, encouraging him to join the debate team. He did and, with painstaking hard work, drilling and recitation, he became very successful in competitive debating.[49] This was an enormous accomplishment and made real the family advice that he could find success in life with persistence.

Bob, like his brother Frank, took to the hard physical work and chores of the ranch, deriving pleasure and a sense of accomplishment from completing difficult labor. The boys didn't get paid for the work they did on the ranch, so had to look for employment elsewhere to earn money. As a youngster Bob worked as a sub-contractor for future U.S. Senator Alan Cranston, six years his elder, on a paper route in Mountain View.[50]

Bob got a job working digging ditches and moving pipe for PG&E's Gas Department in Grass Valley, California the summer after he turned sixteen. He was lonely there away from his family, but felt the accomplishment of surviving the demanding labor and making it on his own. While in Grass Valley, he wrote a touching, and telling, letter to his mother:

> *Friday P.M.*
> *Mamma, I have been trying to think of some way, some sure concrete way, to assure you of my ever deep love and adoration. I realize now, by writing it is impossible to make you believe just what you mean and in how many ways the thought of you is the strongest influence. The only way you will ever be able to know what good you have done is for me to so act and live that you can <u>see</u> the impression you make.*
> *Lovingly, Bob[51]*

Bob was already thinking about service to the community. What would be the most useful thing for him to do? He acknowledged later that, though his parents were both Republicans, he became interested in politics in high school and went in a different direction. Bob was influenced by the New Deal, as he acknowledged later: "I was impressed with the involvement the government took under Roosevelt's leadership to deal with the very obvious, terrible economic and social problems that existed all over the country and I've been a Democrat ever since."[52]

As Bob mastered his stuttering problem and gained confidence in his public speaking through his time on the debate team, his grade point average showed marked improvement. He was earning mostly As by his senior year.[53] This upswing in self-confidence was so dramatic that Bob decided to run for student body president that year—and won.[54] Miss Woods, his English teacher, suggested he consider getting a degree at a top university somewhere in the East, where he could further establish his independence. He chose Dartmouth College in Hanover, New Hampshire, because of its bucolic setting and its Ivy League reputation. Much to his surprise, he was admitted.

In the summer of 1937, after his senior year in high school, Bob's sister, Jean, was graduating from Stanford and preparing for a trip with two girl friends to Europe. As was understood in the Straub family, girls received different treatment from boys. "I had a 'Kings X'," Jean said later. "I wasn't favored by my mother, but I was by my father."[55] In addition to having college paid for, she also received a car to drive and piano to practice upon, Jean had already taken two ship cruise trips with her older cousin Bernice: one on the Inland Passage to Skagway, Alaska (playing a lot of pinochle), and another through the Panama Canal to New York City.[56] This time, Bob was the designated driver for Jean and her friends Harle Garth and Ruth Given, across the country to New York City, where their ship awaited. It was Bob's first big road trip and he planned to make the most of it. After taking the young ladies to their berth, Bob drove Jean's car, nicknamed "Judy," to Colorado, where his brother Frank was finishing a degree in chemistry from the University of Denver. Together they drove south, through the mountains of the Sierra Madre in Mexico, though neither knew more than a few words of Spanish. Bob was very impressed by the Indians, dressed in pure white, walking for miles along the dusty roads. He and Frank made it to Mexico City, with its centuries-old Spanish buildings tilting sideways, built upon the ruins of the Aztec capital. They returned north along the Pacific Coast, back to Los Altos. Bob was mesmerized by his experience. It was the beginning of his life-long love of Mexico and its people.

Knowing he would have to pay his own way, Bob needed to earn some money for college, so he took a job in a logging camp in Camino, California, in the foothills of the Sierra Nevada. It was hard work and a little lonely— Bob wasn't much of a roughneck or a hard drinker, like many of the men up there. Complaining about the maniac driving of his coworkers in one letter home to his parents he confesses:

I think I feel the qualms of homesickness more and more as I grow older. It normally should be the other way I suppose. But the older I get, the more of life I learn. And the more I learn the greater is my love for home.[57]

A later, unintentionally self-revealing letter to Jean, responding to her word that she had sold her car, was both whimsical and poignant.[58] Lamenting the loss, young Bob reflects:

Upon thinking it over, I wonder if it wasn't better you sold Judy. Remember Judy had lived a pretty hard life and maybe she had wanted to just break down for a long time but simply couldn't do it—to you. Now that she is out of your hands she can act as she feels and not feel bad about breaking down. You know the way sometimes something will be just tearing you apart internally and yet you carry on and never let anyone know it. But if you could break down when you feel that way, you feel much better. So with Judy, it must be. Remember the time we went about 100 miles to Paso

Robles over lonely mountain roads in Judy without any gas? You even slept you were so sure she would make it. No—it is probably for the better.

In the same letter to Jean, Bob apologizes for not writing more compellingly:

I realize, Jean, that my letters are completely lacking in interest and suspense and everything else which should be embodied in a good letter. For all that I'm sorry but it's awfully hard to write anything up here. It's dark about 7 p.m. now so I have little time to write or read anymore. I think though that in a week or two I'm going to Sacramento and get a secondhand Coleman lantern. Then I'll completely ignore my roommate's ignominious (sic) looks. It worries me to think that I'm slipping mentally like I feel I am. Also if I read at night I can have something to occupy my brain all next day.[59]

From the forlorn tone of the sensitive eighteen-year-old Bob Straub's letters, one might assume this was one of the worst times of his young life. At the time, it may have been. Later he looked back with pride at the toughness of enduring the camp, its hard work and its deprivations, both physical and mental. It was from his forest work camp employment, the discipline he learned in the prune orchard, and other similar experiences that Bob Straub discovered his core of inner strength and the endurance to persevere for the rest of his life.

CHAPTER 2

The Road Less Traveled

Two roads diverged in a wood, and I
I took the one less traveled by,
And that has made all the difference.

—Robert Frost, from "The Road Not Taken"

More than strength or perseverance, Bob Straub always credited his success in life to good luck.

"I've had a lot of good luck, and the best luck I've probably had in my whole life was meeting my wife on the top of a mountain in New Hampshire, having the chance to go to a good college like Dartmouth, and then having the good luck of having a good family and good jobs—and there's nothing more to it than that. Even getting into politics was luck and even getting elected state treasurer was luck. It's been luck so much."[1]

Surely it seemed that way to him as a young man and perhaps even more so years later. Looking in from the outside, one could ascribe his growing successes partly to good fortune, but just as much to following heartfelt choices. It was in enduring his setbacks and overcoming his difficulties and recognizing his opportunities that Bob, like any successful person, moved forward when times got difficult.

But Bob was right. Without a doubt, the luckiest break Bob Straub ever got in all his years was a chance meeting in August of 1941 with a camp counselor, an incoming freshman at Smith College named Patricia Stroud, and her brood of young campers on a steep path in the mountains of New Hampshire. Straub was a sophomore at Dartmouth College by then, working for his second summer at Dartmouth's Summit House on the top of Mt. Moosilauke.

Straub cut a striking figure, six foot four, tanned, in terrific shape from working hard all summer, and carrying a large, impressive pack board. Describing the scene years later, while fingering that pack, a striking object—easily mistaken for a Native American artifact—which he had made by hand by bending soaked hickory wood and fitting it with canvas, he would laugh, "Pat didn't know that the box I had lashed to the back didn't have anything in it." He had carried his laundry down to a woman in nearby Glencliff and was walking back with an empty pack up to the lodge.[2] It may not have been love at first sight, but she couldn't help being impressed. He shyly noticed her as well. Little did either of them know that this chance meeting would lead to a lifelong love and a close marriage.

Prior to that sunshine-dappled day in 1941, Straub had spent two productive and exciting years in Hanover, studying with some of the country's brightest and best-prepared students. Though Dartmouth, like other Ivy League schools, attempted to broaden its student body, it was mostly made up of young men from the better East Coast preparatory schools. Dartmouth, like many colleges of its day, was not coeducational in the fall of 1939, and unlike many of the Ivy League schools, it didn't have a sister institution for women nearby. This environment of privileged young men was a new one for Straub, but his year off working and traveling had toughened him to new experiences and he soon found he was able to compete well enough, receiving better than average grades, in the company of his more socially advantaged peers.[3]

Straub was unsure what to specialize in initially, though he thought, even then, he might pursue a career in politics, or in the law, as his father had done.[4] He soon found himself involved in the campus' Roosevelt Club, supporting President Franklin Roosevelt's second reelection bid in 1940 against Republican Wendell Willkie. This was Straub's first overt political action and would have been something of a traitorous act to his diehard Republican mother, had she known about it.[5]

Straub continued to hold tight to his egalitarian beliefs. On October 29, just before Roosevelt's landslide victory, Dartmouth's student newspaper published a barbed letter from Straub, chastising a previous writer, a Mr. Barstow. Barstow, an opponent of military conscription, made reference to the "extreme prevalence" of prostitutes and venereal disease, making the military "draft highly undesirable," and calling soldiers "robots instead of men."

Straub chided, "surely Mr. Barstow doesn't feel it would be more contaminating to live with the sons of the lower third than the sons of the upper two thirds." He went on, "I have a spent a year with each now—those who spend their days in the classroom and those who spend their days in the woods. My honest conclusion is that the way men spend their nights is unaffected by the way they spend their days. ... A year in a military camp doesn't necessarily mean goose-stepping all morning and lying on a cot all afternoon thinking of what to do that night." Straub concludes by urging the writer and others who object to military conscription to "offer some positive [alternative] plans" for service to the country.[6]

Such articulate outspokenness lent itself well to Straub's main extracurricular activity during the school year: continuing his high school passion of competitive debate as a member of the Forensic Union at Dartmouth. Once again, he excelled, with no evidence of his previous stuttering problem, and soon was winning awards for Dartmouth. On April 10–12, 1941, Straub took first place in the Lincoln Oratory Finals, had two second places in other individual competitions, and along with fellow student Edward Ferbert, was undefeated in four affirmative arguments at the Grand Eastern Debating Tournament held at Winthrop College in South Carolina, in competition with fifty colleges.[7] In May, Straub took second in Dartmouth's annual "Class of 1866" prize, discussing "What More Can America Do This Time?"[8] The following year, he was named co-president of the Forensic Union in recognition of his continued skill and leadership in debate.[9]

The only sign of trouble for Straub that can be gleaned from his records during his college days was his suspension of library privileges from January through May of 1941. He probably owed late library fees and was caught in a general crackdown on lax student behavior by the administration.[10] The lack of access to the library may help explain why Bob received his worst grades at Dartmouth that quarter, with a D in Physics and 3 Cs, balanced by an A in Political Science.[11]

Like a growing number of classmates and Americans of every stripe, by 1941 Straub supported preparations for entering the growing world war. Calling isolationism "nothing more than a hangover from the 18th century days," he believed that "when Hitler … builds a machine that will only live on war, conquest, destruction, and victory, it is as much the concern of America as any other country."[12]

Straub took advantage of the many opportunities to meet remarkable people who came to the college to give lectures. He cherished the memory of picking up the poet Robert Frost, a frequent Dartmouth lecturer, from the train station and the thrill of talking with him. Straub, for the rest of his life, could recite "The Road Not Taken," a poem whose instruction he aspired to follow—to take "the road less traveled by." These experiences gave him the sense throughout his life that he could seek out famous people who inspired him or who might have insights into problems he was facing.[13] Looking through Straub's records at Dartmouth, a portrait emerges of a passionate, politically engaged young man.

Despite his active scholarly and political interests, of all the experiences Bob Straub had in his undergraduate years, by far the most meaningful were his summers working for Dartmouth on Mt. Moosilauke. He had deliberately chosen Dartmouth because of its rural location, close to the woods and mountains. Founded in 1769 by Congregational evangelists, originally "to bring the blessings of the Christian Gospel to the Indians," the college's motto, *Vox Clamatis in Deserto* (voice crying out in the wilderness),[14] still seemed appropriate when Straub walked alone in the White Mountains nearby. In the solitude of the rugged, wild lands, he felt peace.

In April 1940, Straub's first year at Dartmouth, he was hired as part of the eight-man summer crew on the mountain, serving under Hutmaster Lincoln Wales and Assistant Hutmasters Dave Heald and Harry Bond.[15] He spent most of that summer rebuilding trails along the mountain's flanks. After a day of hard work, the crew was "on top of the world," enjoying, according to Straub, "the finest panorama in New England" from Moosilauke's Summit Lodge, with views of "the broad Connecticut Valley below, the Green Mountain ranges and several peaks of the Adirondacks in the west and the Presidential Range in the east."[16]

Bob developed his closest college friendships during this and the following three summers, which was typical of those who had the opportunity to work on the mountain. Bob's boss that first summer, Linc Wales, whom Bob and his friends had affectionately nicknamed "the Whale," remembers this as the best time of his young life, spending days in "pleasant spontaneous association with people who immediately became friends."

"Bob was big and strong," Linc recalls,

> *nobody worried about his ability to carry a pack. He had a quiet, delightful sense of humor—everybody who saw him liked him. When the girls came up to visit Bob never lacked attention. He was just a real solid person who could always get things done.*
>
> *I remember having delightful discussions with him. He had a manner of speaking and explaining things that caused you to listen to him—it might have been a slight affectation in his speech, but added to his likeability.*[17]

There were many permanent matches made on the mountain—Dave Heald met his future wife Gretchen on Mt. Moosilauke as well. Linc Wales' teenage sister, Ellen, visited her brothers Donny and Linc and experienced the thrill of socializing with college men. She had a particularly exciting time on the mountain that first year Bob worked there. Every night after dinner, if the weather was good, some of the people working and staying there would gather outside to watch the sunset. One gorgeous evening in the summer of 1940, a group of them were playing a game of hide and go seek outdoors and Bob was "it." Squealing with delight, Ellen ran toward the kitchen door with Bob chasing close behind. Unfortunately, instead of grabbing the knob, she put her forearm straight through a small windowpane in the door, giving herself a horrible, bloody gash.

"Bob turned white as a sheet," Ellen recalls. "He felt helpless. Lincoln took over, being a pre-med student. Everybody crowded around and Bob kind of disappeared." Later, after Lincoln had wrapped the wound and staunched the bleeding, "Bob reappeared, and he had changed out of his bloody shirt and was wearing a nice, fresh clean one," Ellen remembers with great glee. It is story she has delighted telling for many years, and would tease Bob about it every time she saw him thereafter. Her wounds required surgery and hospital time in Hanover, where she was visited by Bob and several of the other Dartmouth men, bringing cards, flowers, candy, teddy bears, and other gifts. It may have been the highlight of her teen years to have such earnest attention from these impressive college men.[18]

The next summer, on that "lucky" August day, Bob was striding up the hill with his empty backpack and met camp counselor Pat Stroud and her girls, coming for a visit from their lakeside camp in Vermont, on their way to Mt. Moosilauke's Summit Lodge. The kids asked, "Miss Pat, can we go on with him?" Pat was having trouble keeping up and was leaning on a rock. She told them yes and came along afterward at her own pace.[19]

What happened next is a matter of some dispute. One thing is certain: Pat Stroud and her girls were treated to a hearty dinner and the obligatory nighttime ghost story—a hair-raising tale of "Doc Benton," who learned the secret of eternal youth while studying in Heidelberg, Germany, became a lonely lunatic back home in New Hampshire, and, even now, wanders the mountain, nabbing an occasional victim, human or animal, to supply himself with a secret life-giving elixir, leaving only a dead body with a mysterious pinprick behind the left ear. The story was told in the great hall around the huge crackling fireplace and was usually enhanced by summit workers in the attic rattling chains and crying out in the darkness. It was a story guaranteed to scare the ever-loving daylights out of souls both young and old.[20]

The next morning, Pat and her girls would have been treated to the famous, special recipe, Mt. Moosilauke pancakes. Here is where the stories diverge. One version, found in a manila folder in Bob Straub's files, seemingly intended as the beginnings of his memoir, tells of how he conspired to help Pat break the record for hotcake eating, to entice her to stay another night. The lodge had a rule that anyone who could break the record for the number of plate-sized, three-inch-high stacks of flapjacks eaten at one sitting could stay the next night free. "In Pat's case, it was different," Bob wrote. "The more she ate, the smaller I made them. She broke the record eating hotcakes about the size of a [silver] dollar." Another guest was angry with him for cheating, telling him later, "[N]othing good ever comes from cheating." Bob wrote, "I don't know about that, because in the year 1993, Pat and I celebrated our golden wedding anniversary."[21] Pat Straub doesn't remember this version, though wouldn't it be nice if it were true?[22]

A more likely account goes something like this. It seems that when Pat arrived at the Summit Lodge, Bob wasn't the only one who noticed her. As Bob described it in an interview, "another guy on the summit crew, a guy by the name of Harry Bond, one year older than I, really was taken with Pat and I guess I was too tired from going down the mountain and up the mountain the same day, so he followed through on it." Staying in touch with the young Patricia Stroud, Bond invited her to come up from Smith College, in Northampton, Massachusetts, around a hundred miles away, to Dartmouth in the fall to an annual event called Green Key weekend.[23]

"Harry was a very intellectual guy and I was not," Pat recalls. "We didn't really hit it off. I stayed with a chaperone up there, which was how it was done in those days." Bob saw her at the Ice Festival Dance that first night and was suddenly struck by his error in not staying in touch with her in the first place. He arranged to meet her at her chaperone's house at about six in the morning the next day, to take her out for breakfast.[24]

"Harry was kind of a typical spoiled professor type that slept till nine o'clock in the morning," as Bob recalled later.[25] Sour comments aside, Bond certainly deserves credit for an invaluable, if inadvertent, assist to Bob and Pat's courtship and marriage. After Green Key weekend and Pat's return to Northampton, Bob and Pat began writing one another. But, to Pat, it was unclear how Bob really felt about her.

Pat Stroud, whose full name was Lana Laine Patricia Stroud, had grown up in a privileged family with a tragic history, in a grand home in the suburb of Villanova, Pennsylvania, across the street from the campus of Villanova University, northwest of Philadelphia. Her father, Morris Wistar Stroud, Jr., was an investment banker who "had a brokerage firm of his own called Stroud & Co.," and was the son of a successful businessman and pillar of Philadelphia society.[26] In 1927, when Pat was three years old, her father committed suicide.[27] Her mother, whose maiden name was Willa Boulton Dixon, continued to raise her five children, but suffered from a weak heart, due to a bout of rheumatic fever she had contracted as a child. As time passed, Mrs. Stroud became weaker. In 1934, she decided to marry a dear friend, R. Sanford Saltus, manager of the Camden, New Jersey, airport,[28] so that her children would have someone to look after them. Willa Stroud Saltus passed away two years later, when Pat was thirteen. Her kindly stepfather, "Uncle Sandy," did his best to be mother and father to the children, but Pat remembers being "rather wild and a bit of a handful."[29] Nevertheless, she succeeded in graduating from the exclusive Shipley School in nearby Bryn Mawr and was accepted at Smith College.[30]

Her eldest brother, Morris III, became a heart surgeon and eventually was associate editor of the *Journal of the American Heart Association* and a pioneer in the field of gerontology. In the 1940's, Dr. Stroud "was among the first physicians to form teams of professionals, including counselors, to work with the family to improve a patient's life."[31] To Pat, though, Morris was much older, rather aloof, and they were not close.

She was much closer in age and temperament to her brother Dickie— William Dixon Boulton Stroud—who continued the family business tradition. Dickie was very successful, though he assiduously followed the "old money" dictum of modesty in displaying his wealth.[32] After graduating from Princeton, he worked for many years as a representative in a number of Nelson Rockefeller's international endeavors, including an Italian fashion and merchandising company and a cattle operation in Colombia, and pursued a personal interest in environmental issues.

Dickie and his wife, Joan, "were co-founders of the Stroud Water Research Center on farmland they donated, and through which a branch of the White Clay Creek flowed. The center, in Avondale, Pa., has made profound contributions to the world's understanding of streams, rivers, and their watersheds, championing the restoration of forests along stream banks and on steep slopes. On his dairy farm, 'Landhope,' he also became an innovator in land management."[33]

Pat adored Dickie. She also remained close to her sisters Peg and Cassie, who, like Pat, in time, broke away from East Coast society. Peg eventually moved west to a ranch in Reno, Nevada, and Cassie ran a bookstore in Philadelphia for years before moving west to Southern Arizona to run a small ranch and store.[34]

Pat Stroud was from a totally different world than Bob Straub, a petite debutante to his gangly lumberjack. But they shared a love of nature, and both sensed a natural, genuineness in the other—they were both plainspoken and down to earth in their approach to life.

In the spring of 1942, Bob wrote a letter inviting Pat to come in June to help get the Mt. Moosilauke Lodge into shape for the visitor season. It was Bob's turn as hutmaster. He relished the responsibility, demonstrating the business shrewdness and talent for organization that were apparent throughout his career. One example of his frugality and understanding of the trade-offs involved in planning a public work project is demonstrated in a memo he sent to the Trustees of the Dartmouth Outing Club, regarding the

options for repairing the rain-damaged Carriage Road, which allowed a horse
and buckboard to deliver supplies to the summit:

> *[Charlie Andrews] estimated $1,000 and one month of time for five men
> to fix the road again. I do not dispute the innate perspicuity of a native of
> these parts, but I feel that he is thinking of a different kind of road repair
> job than I. I feel that the road can be fixed so it is usable for three or four
> years at half of Charlie's estimate both in time and expense. A temporary job
> will serve several purposes. It will fulfill our end of the bargain with Charlie
> Andrews for this summer, and it will serve until the War is over and we
> have a chance to see if Moosilauke still has the financial basis of operations
> it had before: private summer camps, and whether the expansive tendency of
> the Summit Camp continues to swell at the War's end as it has in the past.[35]*

Straub's caution proved prescient. His final report even showed additional
foreshadowing: "This summer has been marked by adversity. The wrongs
of the past years have been accumulating and God's wrath has at last been
consummated. First was the bolt of lightning that shook the house and
knocked Linc Wales's brother into the kitchen garbage can," Straub began, in
his mock litany of woes.[36] Real disaster came on October 23, 1942. When no
one was around, lightning struck the lodge again, this time "setting a fire that
burned evenly and steadily down through the house."[37] Sadly, Bob Straub
was the last hutmaster on Moosilauke. The Summit House was never rebuilt.

Not knowing of the Summit House's impending demise, in June of 1942,
Bob was full of energy and plans and he wanted Pat to share some time with
him in his favorite spot. His feelings for Pat were growing, but he didn't lay
his cards on the table. "I was up there for a week and brought a friend with
me. I still didn't realize that Bob liked me," Pat recalls.[38] One wonders when
Bob would have let her know how he felt, but as it was for so many people
living in this time of war, life suddenly began to speed up, and previous plans
were quickly tossed aside.

Bob had attempted to enlist in the Army as soon as war was declared in
December of 1941, but was rejected for poor eyesight—the long-ago ulcerous
eye condition from the farm in Los Altos had, essentially, blinded him in
one eye. Seeking another sort of adventure, he had succeeded in getting
permission to complete his coursework at Dartmouth with an independent
study in Guatemala researching the effect of the country's labor law on
workers, especially focusing on the problems of the large Indian population.
Inspired by a class he had taken from Professor Jose Arce, Straub impressed
his advisors at Dartmouth as "a lanky and engaging young man (not all lanky
men are engaging but this one is)" deserving a chance to pursue this unusual

course of study.³⁹ Straub planned to leave for Guatemala after his time as hutmaster was completed, and was hoping to have documents of approval from the U.S. government. He didn't get the documents but he did get some sound advice about pursuing a careful approach with the Guatemalan government, run by dictator Jorge Ubico.

"If the matter is handled delicately, I think Guatemala will be highly complimented to have someone study their labor law," but "the following points should be borne in mind:

> *The present regime in Guatemala is very suspicious of anything which smacks of Labor as such; it has a morbid fear of Communists and anyone who might be considered a labor agitator.*
>
> *Mr. Straub should be cautioned against mentioning such things (as he does in his petition) as pressure groups, or possibilities that the law is not working perfectly (although of course it isn't). His attitude should be that the law has awakened such admiration in the United States that he has come to Guatemala to make a thorough study of it. He can still accomplish his purpose on this basis.*⁴⁰

We can only speculate how different Straub's life might have been had he been able to follow through with his Guatemalan plans.⁴¹ Instead, word came on August 1 at Mt. Moosilauke Summit Camp that Uncle Sam needed him after all. He wrote a quick letter thanking Mr. Dickerson in President Hopkins' office, explaining that men classified "I-B are to be used for stenographic and clerical work" and that he was expected to report for duty in the fall.⁴²

On October 12, 1942, Robert W. Straub formally enlisted in the U.S. Army in Manchester, New Hampshire. He was initially stationed at Fort Devens, Massachusetts, about fifteen miles south of the New Hampshire state line, along with all men from New England serving as one-year draftees. It was there that Private Straub received his basic training.

Training for war was something Straub wanted to do, "which was not unusual," Bob recalled later; "every young person thought that." Like others of his generation, he did not talk a lot about his years in military service. As he recounts it, it was not a case of suppressing a horror but rather a reticence in discussing what "was an interlude, an interference with my normal progression," as he said later, "but there wasn't anything traumatic, nothing heroic, nothing self-sacrificing."⁴³ The records of Straub's activities during his ten months of military service are scanty.⁴⁴ His son Jeff remembers others telling him that his father served as a prison guard for Italian and German civilian prisoners during that time,⁴⁵ and, indeed, there was a program that is little remembered today (in contrast to the much larger and more well-

Lieutenant Robert W. Straub

known internment of Japanese Americans) in which German and Italian foreign nationals—and some American citizens of Italian and German descent—were rounded up and put into camps throughout the eastern and southern United States. One such camp was at Fort Devens, where young Straub was stationed, though Jeff believed his father served as a prison guard in Tennessee, where there were three camps. Son Mike recalls that Bob had kept an MP (Military Police) armband from the war and that he may have been some sort of prison guard.[46] If Straub did serve in that capacity, no one now knows if he had any qualms over civil liberty questions this alien internment program raised, or over his own participation in it.

During his early months in the Army, Straub continued to write Pat Stroud, but was not able to see her, due to his training schedule and duties. That changed when the summer of 1943 approached and Straub, possibly at the urging of his superiors, applied to Officer Candidates School and was accepted. Anticipating his graduation from that program, he began more eagerly corresponding with her. That summer, on break from Smith College, Pat went to Michigan to stay with her grandparents in a rural part of the state, and to visit another young man who wanted to marry her. "I didn't take this young man too seriously," she says. She appears to have had the pick of her suitors. From there she moved on to Madison, Wisconsin, for summer school at the University of Wisconsin.[47]

Straub reported to Officer Candidates School (OCS) at Camp Lee, near Petersburg, Virginia, for an accelerated training course. He knew that this training meant his impending entry into the theater of war and it focused his mind, as it did for so many young men in those days. He contacted Pat Stroud in Madison, asking her to come by train to his OCS graduation and dance. She said yes. He wired her through Western Union with instructions:

1943 *AUG 8 - 8 AM – Petersburg, VA*
Miss Patsy Stroud
Delta Gamma House 103 Langdon St. Madison Wis

GOOD GIRL. WIRE TRAIN ROUTE. CHICAGO OR CINCINNATI. GO TO USO WILL LEAVE WORD DON'T WANDER AND GET LOST. BRING PICTURE. NO FANCY HAIRSTUFF. I LOVE YOU BRING SWIMMING SUIT DANCE FORMAL.
STRAUB
USO[48]

All ambiguity about Bob's feelings toward Pat were now officially gone. Though this meeting was a formal affair and they only were able to meet for a short time due to military constraints, it was clear to Bob that a major decision was on the horizon. Pat returned to Madison and Bob was transferred to quartermaster school at Fort Sam Houston in San Antonio, Texas. Bob knew it was time to talk seriously with Pat since he was now in preparation to go overseas. Less than a month after the OCS dance, "he called me collect to propose," Pat laughs.[49] "I told him I'd have to think about it, then I went out to a park and sat down and wrote down my thoughts, pro and con, on a sheet of paper."[50]

I. Considerations:
A. Love (it's there!)
B. Children (predicted 3-5)
C. Religion (essentials in both)
D. Education (can be worked out between us)
E. Money (manageable)
F. Family (they can't help liking him) me?
G. Ideals (the same essentials with different approaches)
H. Manners (the darling)
I. Home (God knows for a while)
<u>*Summary*</u>*: general practicality (posit.)*

II. A. Pros
1. good time for it
2. good start
3. good for Bob

4. good for me
5. eventual good for more, we trust
  B. Cons
1. would like family to know him 1st (not essential)
2. would like to be sure his family approved me (not essential)
3. should have def. plans (they are intrinsic in us both)

III. Sidelights
previous disagreements (because of misunderstanding—do not take long to
  be cleared up)
future disagreements will only contribute to us both if we both continue as
  we are (open minded)
faith ever so much in Bob and hope for me if he's there too
personalities superficially different enough to be complementary

IV. Discussion
If I am rationalizing it must be because I am very in love. If I am very
  in love and Bob is (enuf to say what he has) then that is ALL THAT IS
  NECESSARY.

V. Act   Final question: Am I sure in my mind of the rightness of all this?
!! I AM!!!!!![51]

Though she claims that she thought it over for a week before calling him to say yes, it is clear from her list, in both text and subtext, that she was already convinced.[52]

Bob followed up his call Pat with a telegram:

1943 SEP 6 PM 9 47 — SAN ANTONIO, TEX
MISS PATSY STROUD — 103 LANGDON ST. MADISON WIS
REQUEST FORMAL CONSIDERATION CHANGING NAME OUD TO AUB TIME IN
NEAR FUTURE PROMISE ROSES LOVE ORANGE JUICE TIL DEATH DO US PART
LOVE
STRAUB

Pat consulted her stepfather, Sandy Saltus, and quickly got his blessing, then sent the following telegram to Bob.

1943 SEP 8 2 20 PM
LT ROBERT W STRAUB—815 GRAYSON ST SAN ANTONIO TEX
DARLING I HAVE NEVER CONSIDERED SO MUCH IN MY LIFE DECISION COMING
OUD

Later in the day she thought better of her previous message and sent the following one:

MADISON WISC

LT ROBERT W STRAUB—815 GRAYSON ST

BOBBY LAST TELEGRAM INFERRED STILL THINKING. NO DOUBT WHATEVER LEFT. PLEASE CALL DARLING COLLECT THURSDAY EARLY OR LATE. LOVE UNTIL DEATH US DO PART

PAT

By September 11 she was sending him a telegram announcing her arrival that evening:

1943 SEP 11 1 17 AM

ST LOUIS MO

LT ROBERT W STRAUB SA TEX

ARRIVE SEVEN SUNDAY MORNING BOBBY YOU ARE NICE

STROUD

And another en route:

CHICAGO ILL

LT RW STRAUB – 815 GRAYSON

DARLING FAMILY REACTION GOOD SURE LOVE YOU SEEMS ONE COMING GIVE STROUD AWAY SILLY I'M YOURS

PAT

Meanwhile, Sandy was keeping in touch by telegram that he was on his way to give away the bride:

SEP 10 11 38 AM – PHILA PA

MISS PATRICIA STROUD= CARE LIEUT ROBERT STRAUB = 815 GRAYSON

ON MY WAY COUNTING ON YOU TO WAIT FOR ME LOVE=

SANDY.

Dick Stroud sent an urgent message for Lt. Straub to contact him collect in Washington, DC, though it is not clear whether it was to congratulate him or give him a quick grilling—or both. Straub's mother and dad sent their "blessings on you both," and "deepest love." Bob's sister, Jean, by now married to Ike Russell and living on a ranch in Benson, Arizona, wrote to "bring her over right away. Let's take a gander." In pen, next to this telegram in Pat's handwriting is the word, "Nice!" Various and sundry other messages flowed in from friends and relatives near and far.[53]

Newlyweds Bob and Pat (Stroud) Straub in front of the Alamo, San Antonio, Texas,
September 12, 1943

On Sunday, September 12, Lt. Robert W. Straub, QMC, wed Lana
Laine Patricia Stroud at the home of the Rev. and Mrs. Samuel Orr Capers,
with Rev. Capers officiating. Stepfather R. Sanford Saltus of Villa Nova,
Pennsylvania, was there to joyously give the bride away.[54] "Sandy was so
supportive," Pat remembers. Bob had one of his lieutenant classmates serve
as best man. Pat wore a beige suit with matching accessories and Bob was
in Army dress uniform. There were no other witnesses. What the wedding
lacked in elegance it made up for in humorous spontaneity. "We used a taxi to
get to the church and Bob worried about the cost of it being there waiting for
us, with the meter running," Pat chuckled remembering early signs, for her,
of Bob's legendary frugality. "We had a breakfast of chicken sandwiches."[55]

The newlyweds stayed in San Antonio for a month, while Bob finished
his training there; then he was sent back East, and Pat went with him. They
went by train and saw some places they'd never seen before—including New
Orleans and Atlanta—on their way to an apartment in northern Virginia,
while Bob did more training, this time at Military Intelligence School, at
Fort Washington, just across the state border in Maryland and south of DC.
Through November and December of 1943, Lt. Straub was trained to be a
censorship officer to "examine communications of all kinds to see that secret
or confidential information was not sent."[56]

During this time, the couple was able to use Bob's leave time to go up to Pennsylvania and meet Pat's other family and friends. After that, Bob was sent to New York City to await transport to Europe and they rented a room over a tavern, which had flashing neon lights through the night. Quickly tiring of that, they moved to a hotel at the south end of Central Park. "I wanted to be with him as much as possible," Pat says. "I went with him early for breakfast every morning. Coming back one morning I was stopped by the desk clerk who wanted to be sure I had a room here. That was her way of checking to make sure that I was not a hooker. Bob was furious when he heard about this!"[57] They were in New York City for three weeks before he was sent to London as an officer. It was a very romantic time, very emotional, and very sad for both of them. Though they didn't know it yet, Pat was already pregnant with their first child, Jeff.

In London, Bob went to work initially as a censorship officer, checking the mail of soldiers sending messages home to make sure their letters did not contain war-related information. In addition, according to his discharge papers, Lt. Straub "examined photographs for valuable information"— possibly aerial reconnaissance photographs for the many bombing missions that were being flown from Britain into Germany.[58]

Being quartered in London was not completely hazard-free while Straub was there. The Royal Air Force had won the Battle of Britain, so U.S. and British aircraft ruled the skies. Unfortunately, shortly after D-Day, the German development of the V-1 and V-2 rockets kept the air raid sirens going at night and the public jittery about the chances of random death at all hours of the day or night. Nonetheless, Bob used his time off to do a little sightseeing in London and the areas nearby.

As the Allies began to push further toward Germany, Bob was moved to the European mainland and put to work using his quartermaster training. Lt. Straub was stationed in charge of what was then referred to as a Negro trucking supply troop, in America's segregated army, which was involved in moving provisions and personnel and was based in Dijon, France. It is a city in northeast France's Burgundy region best known today in the United States for its flavorful mustard, and to cognoscenti of fine wine, as the heart of pinot noir country—ironically, now viticulturally paired with Oregon's Willamette Valley wine country, including the Eola Hills just beyond Bob Straub's future West Salem home.

Mustard and wine aside, with winter coming on in 1944, Dijon was strategically located as a staging area between the South of France and Paris to supply American and British troops fighting the Nazi forces in Alsace and southern Germany. Straub generally enjoyed his few months there, and it was his first extended experience with black people, having grown up in predominantly white communities in Los Altos and at Dartmouth. It was certainly an awkward introduction, considering that he was a young, white, Ivy-league-educated first lieutenant, commanding a segregated unit. It probably helped with his command credibility that he had worked so many years in physical labor situations in the California forest camps and at the Summit House of Mt. Moosilauke. "It wasn't a hazardous job because we were behind the lines quite a bit," Bob recalled. "It was just really a relatively easy situation. We had a good crew of black drivers … and there weren't any problems that I can remember with the fellows."[59]

When Bob went overseas, Pat went home to Villanova, Pennsylvania, and lived with her stepfather, Sandy. A Scottish friend of Sandy's, who was in charge of the British submarines stationed off the East Coast, was also living there. "I was pregnant—it was exciting, but also scary," Pat remembers. "I told my stepfather and his friend that I would be their housekeeper. I was pretty hit or miss with my duties."

"During my pregnancy they tried to give me some sort of shot in my back, but it didn't work for me," Pat recalls. "It was some sort of curative. My aunt and uncle came into the house to help me and they were there when I was getting ready to give birth." On August 10, 1944, Pat gave birth to a healthy young boy—Jefferson Tully Straub. "In those days, they didn't want you to get out of bed in the hospital for ten days after you gave birth," Pat Straub remembers. "I lost a lot of muscle strength, so it took a long time to recover. I had a nurse that helped me."[60]

In Dijon, working in rough conditions with a lot of dust flying around, Bob's eye ulcer flared up again. It caused a lot of pain and he had to be hospitalized and then shipped home. He had been gone eighteen months when he returned. Jeff was already a year old.[61] "It was kind of emotional," Bob said trying to recall his feelings later. "I can't remember any more about it because the overwhelming thing was seeing and rejoining up with Pat at her home in Philadelphia."[62]

When Bob got back he was really ill and needed to stay in the veterans' hospital in Valley Forge. He was there for a month and the doctors had great difficulty figuring out how to heal the eye ulcer. As Pat remembers, "Bob was quite depressed, but he wouldn't talk with me about it." This was the first time she had experienced one of Bob's dark moods and his stammering speech that sometimes came with it, but it became something that she learned would come and go over the years. Finally, Bob's eye became well enough that the government hospital officials decided to allow him to move to Los Altos, where he could muster out of the Army.

On the way west, they stopped to visit Bob's sister, Jean Russell, and husband Ike and their three boys, Luke, Bob, and Dave, who were living on a ranch in the southern Arizona desert near the Mexican border. "There were coyotes at night," Pat remembers. "It was a new experience for me. We'd go out riding with Ike and he'd try to shoot crows. Jean couldn't come along because she was not well from having just given birth."[63] Bob was surprised and delighted to see that his dog, Bismarck—a friendly, not-so-bright black lab that he'd had at Dartmouth and which he had left with Jean and Ike to care for during the war—was still there.. "'I didn't realize you'd still have him,' Bob told me," Jean remembers. "He thought for sure we would have given him to someone else after all those years, but, of course, we wouldn't do that." Bismarck happily rejoined the growing Straub family, quickly remembering and warming to Bob.[64]

Continuing on to Los Altos, Bob, Pat, little Jeff, and their reclaimed dog, Bismarck, crammed themselves into their Ford convertible with all their belongings. They were frustrated to discover that many hoteliers would allow the dog, but not children, in the rooms. Bob was fuming mad about it. "That so soured us, I mean up to that time we were fairly normal people as far as traveling goes," said Bob, "that when we got to Los Altos … I bought a little trailer, a cargo trailer, and built a little covered wagon thing over it and we bought equipment—a Coleman stove, folding table, sleeping bags, and air mattresses. Then, when we went back to Hanover [New Hampshire], we slept out almost every night. A lot of our meals, not all of them, we cooked … out and we got to enjoy traveling that way." They continued to travel that way for decades, especially after they began their regular trips to Mexico twice a year. The snobby rules of the hotel owners after the war inadvertently led them to discover one of the ways that they came to love the open road and, as Bob pointed out, it cost "motels … many thousands of dollars."[65]

When they arrived in Los Altos, Pat met Bob's parents for the first time. She found Bob's father, Thomas, to be "on the strict side" and not terribly friendly. Fortunately, shortly after they arrived, Bob's brother Jim and his wife, Denny, came to stay, along with Wally Miller, Denny's half-brother. Jim's arrival, and his crazy kidding around, helped soften Thomas up a bit.

Bob's mother, Mary, did what she could to teach Pat how to be a better homemaker. As a young girl from a wealthy family with servants, and even after taking care of Sandy and his houseguest during the war, Pat had not learned many home-making skills. Mary never said anything mean about Pat's bad cooking at the time. According to Pat, the worst thing Mary ever said to her was, after a kitchen disaster, that she "didn't know anyone who could manage to make Jell-O not jell."[66]

Still receiving medical care for his eye, Bob was released from the Army at Dibble General Hospital in Menlo Park, California, on April 29, 1945,[67] and arranged to enroll in the Dartmouth Masters of Business Administration program for winter term 1946. To support his family until school started, he returned to work at the logging camp in "Hang Town" in the Sierras, where he'd been employed after high school. Bob worked there until the snow started.

"He and Jeff and I lived in a little cabin with a woodstove to heat water," Pat remembers. "It was rough, but really nice. We would buy food once a week. There was a camp cook there who would cook chicken wings and give them to me to take home sometimes. Mostly, though, I had to learn how to cook. It was a very basic kitchen."

After that, Pat recalls, "we went back to stay with Bob's folks in Los Altos and got ready for Bob to go back to Dartmouth for winter term." They caravanned, with their newly built trailer and camping gear, back to Hanover, New Hampshire, with a brief stopover in Philadelphia, where Bob once again had his eye examined. The report was encouraging: in a very few days of "fever therapy with penicillin … the eye cleared up remarkably and we were able to let him go back to Dartmouth with a fairly quiet eye."[68]

Arriving in Hanover, the little family temporarily lived in a dorm. "I had to go down to the next floor to have privacy to take a shower," Pat recalls. Soon after that they moved into a new complex south of Hanover called Sachem Village, which had just been built for married couples after the war.[69] When they moved into the house, Bob decided to buy a brand new three-quarter-ton Chevrolet truck. He was already planning to take a job in the plywood industry, wanting to continue to work with forest products, and thinking that these sturdy building materials were economically promising. He and Pat thought they'd like to live in the Pacific Northwest, and at the time, he was looking at Olympia, Washington, as a place to settle. Pat had inherited a great

Dartmouth College MBA student Bob Straub conducted a brisk side business of trash hauling.

deal of furniture from her mother so, after pricing the cost of using a moving company to move it up from Villanova to Hanover and then to Olympia, Bob realized it was cheaper to buy the truck and move it himself. Once he had the truck Bob began using it to haul other people's furniture and then people's trash from around the village to make some extra money.[70] "Because of this trash hauling business, we learned very quickly who was and wasn't a friend," Pat remarked, "but it helped a lot financially."[71] Bob Straub may be the only garbage-hauling MBA candidate in the Tuck School's history.

While Bob was earning his masters degree, their second and third children, Mike and Jane, were born, eleven months apart, keeping Pat very busy and increasing her steep maternal learning curve.

In 1947, Bob finished school. He enjoyed his studies, though it was a strain to work, study, and be a father and husband. Bob retained his interest, beginning with his youthful admiration for Roosevelt and the New Deal and continuing through his college studies, in issues of economic justice. His masters' thesis reflects that continued interest. It was about the factors that determine wage scales. He described it later as "what sets wages in society—why doctors are paid at a certain level, why construction foremen are paid at a certain level, what determines where wages are set, the influence of unions, and so on."[72]

Newly graduated, Bob used Dartmouth links to get a job with Weyerhaeuser, directly contacting its executive, Charlie Ingram, another Dartmouth alum. Ingram originally arranged for Bob to work at their plant in Longview, Washington. "We wanted to live somewhere that was close to the woods, away from too many people," Pat said. "We both loved hiking and being in the outdoors. The Northwest seemed like a good part of the country for that kind of lifestyle." So off they went across the country once more: Bob, Pat, Jeff, Mike, Jane, and Bismarck. This time they also gave a ride to an Italian man named Giulio Puntacarlo, who wanted to explore the West. Arriving in Longview, and looking at the gargantuan lumber, plywood, and pulp mills and a rather barren-looking town, the Straubs decided they didn't like what they saw. "It seemed too built up," Pat said.[73]

Bob drove up to Weyerhaeuser's Tacoma headquarters and told Charlie Ingram "it really wasn't what I thought I wanted to do and I wondered if he had anything else. Ingram said, 'yes, we're just starting a new mill in Springfield [Oregon], why don't you go down there and work. See how you like it.' So that's how we got to Springfield."[74]

They went there and they liked it.

In the end, the road less traveled led to Oregon. It was another lucky break for Bob Straub and his family—and for the new state he would call home.

CHAPTER 3

Answering the Call

Youth's natural idealism sometimes tends to shrink from the grim realities of present-day politics. A thirty-one-year-old ex-bomber pilot from World War II, who was practicing law in a small town in California, said to me, "I'd run for the legislature in a minute if I thought I could vote just as my conscience dictated, without having to worry about campaign contributors or the bosses of my party."

This was how I replied to him: "Maybe a whole lot of young men like you will have to run first, in order to bring about the conditions which you seek. When you don't even put your name on the ballot, you leave the business of state government to the political hacks."

—Richard L. Neuberger, from *Adventures in Politics,* 1954
Chapter 2, "Give the Young Folks a Chance"

The Straub family arrived in Springfield, a small but growing mill town next to Oregon's second-largest city, Eugene, at the southern end of the fertile Willamette Valley, in the summer of 1947. They moved into a cramped little trailer in a small trailer park—Bob, Pat, three little children (Jeff, Mike, and Jane, who was just a few weeks old), and Bismarck, their black Labrador dog. It wasn't the most promising beginning. A couple of weeks after they arrived, someone began poisoning dogs in the neighborhood. "Boy, I wanted to get out of there fast," Bob recalled.[1]

With this imperative to relocate, Bob found a five-acre plot in the Thurston area, east of Springfield. They immediately bought it and moved the small trailer onto it, relieved to escape the fear of losing their family dog, and happy to be making a start on their own land. Bob was working as a supply clerk for Weyerhaeuser, as the company finished construction of the new mill. After the first year, when the mill began operation, Bob shifted jobs and ran the personnel department. On weekends and evenings Bob worked to build their new family home. He started with the garage first, then moved on to the kitchen and utilities. When those were done, he sold the trailer and, with the money from the sale, was able to finish the rest of the house.[2]

"Our daughter Patty was born in Thurston," Pat recalled, "while we were living in the garage of the home that Bob was building." With two adults, four kids, and Bismarck, managing that household was quite a challenge. Pat planted and grew a large vegetable garden. Pat had certainly come a long way from her days of comfort and understated luxury in the Villanova suburbs of Philadelphia. Living in the Oregon countryside was a *very* different life. But, with Bob busy working, she didn't have much choice. Pat was in charge of raising the family and she relished it. "She kept us all with clothes and happy and kept the house up," Mike Straub remembers, "At first she didn't know much about cooking and child rearing so she had some stuff to learn. But she really worked at it and we really had a happy childhood."[3]

The two boys developed what Pat eventually concluded were allergic reactions to some foods, forcing her to begin looking for dietary answers. She began reading books and articles written by such organic food and gardening pioneers as J. I. Rodale, publisher of *Organic Gardening* and *Prevention* magazines. Pat experimented with different food combinations and became knowledgeable about organic gardening and cooking with whole, unprocessed foods—going against the prevailing postwar American belief in, as chemical giant Dupont advertised it: "better things for better living … through chemistry." Bob respected Pat's opinions on these matters and followed her lead,[4] including drinking such unpalatable combinations as brewer's yeast in his morning orange juice. Pat's efforts bore fruit, as her sons and the rest of her children went from being "thin and sickly" to healthy and vital into their adulthood, though they dumped the nasty-tasting brewer's yeast concoctions down the toilet whenever they could get away with it. "All of a sudden we started eating all this awful, nutritious stuff, but we stayed healthy forever," Mike Straub recalls. Her newly acquired abilities and interests would provide Pat with a lifetime of joy and sharing—and her family, including her future grandchildren, with a lifetime of healthy, (mostly) delicious eating.[5]

The young Straub children loved living out in the country, playing on the hillside and roaming on the thousand or so acres surrounding their property. The shingle mill across the road from their property had a log pond, and the kids would try to roll the logs on it—and that wasn't the only hazardous mischief they got themselves into. One time, Jeff and Mike hid behind some mammoth tree roots, watching the log trucks go by and, since their dad worked for Weyerhaeuser, they ignored the Weyerhaeuser trucks, but took some pot shots with their BB guns at the "bad guys" driving the Booth-Kelly trucks. Thank God, for them, their father never knew about that!

A man with a hook for a hand—a lot of men who worked in the wood products industry were missing hands, arms, or fingers in those days—was the guard at the shingle mill. He drank a lot of beer, so "between the beer and the hook, he was kind of an interesting guy," Mike Straub remembers. "We learned where he threw his beer bottles out the window of the little shack he

Bob and Pat's children on their land in Thurston, outside of Springfield, Oregon.
From left, Jane, Patty, Mike, and Jeff.

lived in and we'd collect them all and take them down to the little store on the corner and turn them in for cash so we could buy goodies." There was a big, wigwam burner for waste wood at the shingle mill, but the factory itself smelled wonderful because they split the wood right there and it gave off a delicious cedar scent.[6] Overall, the kids remember growing up in Thurston as being idyllic and filled with innocent monkey business, a little like a scene from a slightly dank, forested version of a Norman Rockwell painting.

Meanwhile, in the process of building the house, their restless father had made an interesting discovery. "I hired a carpenter who helped me quite a bit and showed me how to do stuff," Bob remembered. "How to frame, how to cut rafters, but it was something I was able to catch onto quickly."[7] In the course of that building project, learning each step of the process as he went, Bob found he truly enjoyed home construction. In fact, his spare-time building project brought him more satisfaction than working at the mill. Bob preferred doing the work himself—and, since he wasn't paying himself for his time, he knew he was getting better value for his money.[8] As Straub was putting the finishing touches on the family home, he began to envision building more homes. With that in mind, he seized an opportunity that presented itself, making a bid on some homes that Weyerhaeuser had to move as part of building their new plant. Straub got the houses dirt-cheap; he hired a surveyor from Weyerhaeuser to plat a subdivision of around ten acres of land he had purchased about a mile away from the site. Then he hired a few workers to help him build new foundations and move the houses. Straub sold some of the houses for $800 a piece and turned the others into rental properties.[9] Almost before he knew it, he had created a significant side business for himself.

With his growing first-hand experience in construction, and knowledge of local home prices, Bob realized he could make more money as a homebuilder than he could make by working for George Weyerhaeuser, the company owner's son, who was now running the Springfield mill. "I thought there would be more opportunity and I'd be able to get ahead a little faster," Straub figured, "so I felt it was worth the risk to see if I could make a go of it."[10]

Bob figured right. He left his job at Weyerhaeuser in the summer of 1949 and continued building on his original subdivision and then moving on to new ones in the growing Springfield area. As before, he built a mixture of rental housing and homes for sale. Straub put together a good crew of people, eventually led by a skilled carpenter named Floyd Konold, who had been working on a dam nearby. Konold had experience in heavy construction and was a problem solver. Straub gradually let Konold take over as an unofficial superintendent. This allowed him to quit worrying about building, because Floyd was so competent and responsible. To assist his burgeoning building enterprise Straub built a cabinet shop and a lumberyard on land in his original subdivision.[11] They built "pretty basic houses" with plans they drew up themselves without a lot of architectural assistance.[12] "Dad used to say that one of his nightmares was that he would have to live in one of those houses," Mike Straub remembers, "because one of the things that he always hated about those houses is that they didn't have any overhang on the end of the rafters," so there was no extra protection from the elements.[13]

In the late '40s and early '50s, the American economy was growing. Rebounding from World War II and the Depression, the U.S. was dominating world markets. Prosperity was increasing with the population, as more people could afford and wanted new homes. The new mill in Springfield and other growing businesses brought an influx of people into the area. Within a few years Bob's business was prospering. "It was what they call spec building, and again, I was lucky because that was about the time of the Korean War and a big demand for housing and it was easy to sell your properties," Straub recalled.[14] Bob had a good head for business and, with his homebuilding business as a platform, he continued to look for opportunities to make money, doing things he enjoyed.

In those days, like many men during this era, Bob Straub worked hard during the week and rarely had time on weekdays to spend with his children, but he took his family life on the weekends, and on occasional weeknights, very seriously. "In nice weather we'd be playing games outside—hide and seek, different games," Mike Straub recalls, "and often on weekends we were off camping." Frequently, Bob combined a work trip with some family recreation. "He had a cow and some horses there in Thurston, and on weekends we'd take an old truck and go over to Sisters and buy hay and stop at Scott Lake and go swimming," Mike remembers, "We did a lot things as a family." They would go hiking, in those early days with a lot of small children, rather than backpacking. "We'd camp near a lake or a stream and then we'd have these organized hikes," Mike says. "Dad always had to be on the go, so we'd hike to a lake or hike to a cave. It was fun. We'd go out maybe for a couple of hours, and then we'd come back and maybe swim." Bob Straub was drawn to the mountain forests, his old love from days in the California woods and the mountains of New Hampshire. Living on the eastern edge of Springfield was a convenient jumping-off point for weekend family adventures in the Cascade mountain forests, though they occasionally went further east into the dry areas of Oregon that Bob was also developing a deep appreciation for—camping in the Steens Mountains, or the Ochocos, and enjoying the windswept vistas.

Bob helped his eldest brother, Tom, get established in Oregon—a somewhat unusual role for the youngest child in the family. He had given Tom a job in his cabinet shop when his brother first got to Springfield. Tom bought some property up on Fall Creek and later published a small-circulation newspaper, really more of a newsletter, called *The Lane Reporter*, which sometimes was critical of his younger brother—contrarian Straub that he was—once Bob entered politics.

As Bob became more successful, his brother Jim also came north to visit and soon convinced Bob to stake him and his wife, Denny, and Denny's stepbrother Wally, with a farm in Central Oregon outside of Sisters—Bob's first property on the dry side of Oregon. Bob purchased the farm and Jim managed it for him. Of the brothers who joined Bob in Oregon, Jim Straub, in particular, lived an eccentric, complex life. Shortly after high school, he had gone to the University of Michigan to attend Law School, following in his father's footsteps, but didn't finish. After that he joined his brother Frank at Denver University, but didn't last long. Much later he moved down to live with his sister Jean Russell in Tucson to go to University of Arizona Medical School, but never completed his studies there either. Nevertheless, according to some in the family, Jim was something of a legal and medical scholar. "Jim had major problems with depression and with alcohol," his sister, Jean, remembers. "He got a medical discharge from the Army because of his depression."[15] It was a problem he shared with Bob, who continued to have his occasional dark periods, but in Jim's case the episodes completely debilitated him at times. During his 'up' periods, Jim was an irrepressibly charming prankster, though sometimes he got completely out of control. Bob felt an obligation to look out for his brother by providing a place to live and an opportunity to get ahead.

Pat Straub recalls, "Denny seemed to be jealous of me for having so many children when she wasn't able to have any. Jim wasn't very friendly to me, either. They had a tough time making a success out of the ranch up in Sisters."[16] "It was a disaster," Mike Straub, Bob's second son, remembers. "Mostly they just made their own beer and drank it before it was ready. Jeff and I thought it was great to go up there and visit them, though."[17]

Another story illustrates Jim Straub's intellect and contrarian sense of humor. Because of Mike's closeness to Jim, Bob asked Jim if he could help Mike with his academics—specifically, reading and spelling—as he had a great deal of difficulty in that area. Jim decided that Mike should start "reading Artemus Ward," Mike Straub recalls, "which was full of all this terrible spelling and kind of crazy writing." Artemus Ward was the pen name of Charles Farrar Brown, a nineteenth-century American humorist, admired by Abraham Lincoln, and a role model for a young Mark Twain. Ward was extremely intelligent and literate but wrote frequently in a vernacular style with a lot of intentional misspellings and commonly used bad grammar.[18] "That was Jim's answer to help Dad parent," Mike laughs, "but Jeff and I really had a good time and had a totally different exposure by being around Jim and Tom and the other hangers on."[19]

As time went by, Bob Straub was successful enough in business that he started looking for new challenges, particularly if they would help his community. His first major volunteer activity was as part of a large group of men, eventually numbering around one hundred, who, through 1953 and '54, went door-to-door soliciting funds to build the new McKenzie-Willamette Hospital in Springfield. Severe floods in 1949, which temporarily blocked access to the only regional hospital, in Eugene, had driven home the need for a new facility, and the project became a point of civic pride for the expanding Springfield community.[20] "We'd gather at seven o'clock for breakfast, then the teams would go out all over the city asking for donations," Clayton Anderson, then Springfield's park and recreation director, recalls. "It was a very successful event—great for the town, great for the people involved in it." This group of Springfield movers and shakers became very close, and some, like Anderson and Mayor Ed Harms became Bob Straub's lifelong friends.[21]

Bob retained his interest in politics. Early on, just after arriving in Oregon, "Bob decided to join the local Democratic Party organization, because he had some ideas about government that he wanted to support," Pat remembers. "He was always interested in improving society."[22] Straub later described his motivation for getting involved in politics as stemming from his childhood, growing up during the Great Depression, being "sensitive to the fact that there are a lot of people who suffer hardships that don't have much going for them and have bad times and have little kids that are hungry—and that has permeated my political activity. I think government should be very active in doing things to equalize people's condition in life."[23] These egalitarian beliefs were not diminished by his own personal accomplishments as an Ivy League MBA graduate and successful businessman. Despite his parents' staunch Republicanism, the Democratic Party—the party of Franklin D. Roosevelt from his youth—was the place Straub wanted to be.

It turned out that becoming an active member of the Democratic Party organization in Lane County in the late 1940s wasn't that easy. Bob contacted the county party chairman, "a squat, portly veterinarian,"[24] Dr. Jay C. "Doc" Hicks, to tell him, "I want to be active in the Democratic Party," Straub recalled, "and he said, 'Well, we don't know who you are. Do you have anyone that can vouch for you?' And I said, 'No, I'm new here.' 'Well,' he said, 'Don't you know anyone so that we know a little bit about you?' Then it occurred to me that one of my professors at Dartmouth was chairman of the Democratic Party in New Hampshire." Hicks told Straub that a letter from Herb Hill, Straub's former professor, "would be very acceptable to us." Straub received a letter from Professor Hill which stated that Bob was "a good, upstanding, responsible person and could be depended on," Straub remembered. "So Doc Hicks called me and with great joy he said, 'well, you'll be awfully happy to know you're in.' And he said 'we got that letter, good letter,'" Straub laughed.[25]

He never knew exactly why they were so particular about who might join the party organization, though, at the time, growing competition with the Soviet Union, and an enhanced atmosphere of fear in the United States about communist infiltration of organizations put everyone under suspicion. The mere association with socialist or communist organizations ruined the reputations and careers of a number of artists, academics, union activists, and political leaders.

Soon after he'd become a local party committee member, Straub experienced an even more ludicrous example of Doc Hicks' tight control. "After I became an 'in' member of the party organization in Lane County," Straub related, he discovered that "the organization consisted of about two or three people who sort of ran everything." One time, Doc Hicks called Straub at work and invited him to meet the Democratic candidate for governor in the upcoming 1948 special election. The candidate was scheduled to speak later that evening and Hicks wanted Straub to meet him, at Eugene's Osborne Hotel, in advance of the speech. Straub remembers it like this:

*So I was there and the candidate's name was Lew Wallace, in those days
a well-known and likeable Democratic candidate, a very conservative
Democrat with a real estate business in Portland. Wallace had run for
office several times and always lost. Well, I went up to the room when I was
supposed to be there and here was Doc Hicks and his right hand man, his
henchman, a guy named Gene Beroux, and that was it, and me, and I'm
brand new!*

*So after a little bit, Lew Wallace came in and he's very friendly, very
affable, and I just remember so clearly Lew Wallace turning to Doc and
saying, "Well, Doc, all set up for the meeting tonight?"*

*And Doc Hicks says, "Yes, Lew. I got a room out at the University for you.
Everything's lined up."*

*Lew thought a minute and he said, "Have you gotten the publicity out to
the radio and newspaper about it?"*

And Doc said, "No, Lew, I didn't."

And Lew said, "Well, Doc, why didn't you?"

*And Doc Hicks said, "Well, Lew, if I put out a news release about it you
wouldn't know who might turn up."*

Straub couldn't believe his ears: "As I think back on it, it was the funniest
thing I ever heard."[26] Younger Democrats, led by attorneys Charlie Porter
and Keith Skelton, eventually eased Doc Hicks out of the chairmanship,
as the first step to revitalizing the local party.[27] But the story explains in a
microcosm why the Democrats who, a few years later, in 1954, only trailed
the Republicans by around two thousand registered voters statewide, still
continued to lose consistently in state and local elections.[28]

In the 1953 Oregon State Legislature, for example, there were only
fifteen Democrats out of the state's ninety senators and representatives. State
Senator Richard "Dick" Neuberger pointed out, "Some counties haven't sent
a Democrat to the Legislature since the railroads crossed the Great Divide!"
Neuberger, his wife Maurine, who was a state representative, and other active,
liberal Democrats, such as Democratic National Committeeman Monroe
Sweetland and State Party Chairman Howard Morgan, were organizing
throughout the state, trying to revive a party that had the potential to be
competitive, yet was sleepy and cowed from years as the "out" party in a
one-party state. As Dick Neuberger explained it, "Oregon's most recent
Democratic United States Senator was elected in 1914. The last Democratic
Legislature sat in 1878. Of the ten past Governors of Oregon, eight have
been Republicans." The pro-Republican bias was so ingrained that Maurine
Neuberger was challenged as a member of the board of the League of Women
Voters for being a Democratic precinct committeewoman, contrary to

their "impartial principles." As described by her husband, Maurine "smiled sweetly across the table at the objector. 'Aren't you a Republican precinct committeewoman, Frances?' she asked. 'Well, yes,' admitted Frances, 'but I don't think that's exactly the same thing.' The board of the league hurriedly moved on to the next order of business."[29]

In addition to the prevalent assumption by many "proper" Oregonians that the default position in the state was Republican, some liberal Democrats also believed there was some Republican skullduggery involved in the lopsided election results. As Straub described it later: "Somebody in the party, it might have been Howard Morgan, I heard say repeatedly that in the Democratic Party in those days, the Republicans picked the Democratic candidate [for governor] and agreed to finance them. I mean, they would find someone, I don't say this happened but this is what was told me, and they would say, 'Now you're a well-known Democrat. We've got ten thousand bucks that will go into your campaign, if you want to run for governor and it's not going to hurt your business any with the publicity you're going to get.' They would pick somebody that they knew couldn't win and they'd run the guy. The Republicans picked the Democratic candidate year after year for the major statewide offices. I don't know whether that's true or not, but I don't have any understanding why anyone running a political party would try to close the ring and keep people out."[30] Keith Skelton, another of the young Democratic activists, shared Straub's suspicions, observing that Doc Hicks "exhibited no desire to build Democratic strength in the area but rather contented himself with accepting a minimal flow of Republican patronage."[31] Straub's and Skelton's views reflect their own, perhaps biased, position on the conservative-liberal divide within the Democratic Party—with the insurgent liberals accusing the conservatives of being too cozy with business interests and of, essentially, being in league with the Republicans. It was certainly true, for whatever reason, that some of the candidates representing the Democrats statewide put little money and effort into running a statewide campaign.

Monroe Sweetland and Howard Morgan hoped to change the Democratic Party's sluggish ingrained patterns by pushing out the conservative leadership and beating the bushes for likely young Democrats to run for elected office and to fill the local party central committees' ranks. Sweetland was already an experienced activist who had cut his teeth in the 1930s and early '40s as a leader of the socialist-leaning Oregon Commonwealth Federation, challenging the conservative Democratic leadership who, as he put it, "tried to operate the political party really against the wishes and needs of the unemployed and working people, and the working farmers of the state."[32] The conservative Democratic governor at the time, retired Brigadier General

Charles H. Martin, referred to the Commonwealth Federation as a "gang ... of young Jew[s,] ... Communists, C.I.O.'s and crackpots." The Commonwealth Federation's candidate, Democrat Henry Hess, defeated Martin in the 1938 primary, preventing his reelection.[33] Hess lost badly in the general election to Republican moderate Charles Sprague, but Sweetland and others felt Sprague's administration was an improvement over what was likely to have come from a second Martin administration.[34]

Years later, the Republican-leaning *Oregon Voter* could not help itself in admiring the tenacity and effectiveness of Monroe Sweetland: "We differ so considerably in political philosophy ... but recognize in him such ability in public affairs with some ideas and ideals in public service from which we cannot differ, that we frankly lean over backward in appraising him for the benefit of our readers ... He's smart as a whip in espousing vote-getting causes; is a work-horse for the issues he believes in and can fight about the best rear guard action in defeat that we have seen. He's been down often but never out and persistence often rewards him."[35] In short, the underdog Democrats were fortunate to have such a committed and skilled leader working for their cause.

Sweetland's younger colleague, Howard Morgan, had been President of the Reed College Liberal Club and had invited Sweetland to speak for the Oregon Commonwealth Federation there in 1940. The two stayed in touch during the war years. When the war ended, Sweetland, then serving as the head of Red Cross operations on Okinawa, sought out Morgan, jumping on an air transport plane and flying nearly three thousand miles to Kwajalein, in the Marshall Islands, where Morgan, a naval officer, was stationed. He rousted Morgan out of bed in the middle of the night, and, as Sweetland described it later, the two men "spent from 2 a.m. until daylight in the offices there, discussing Oregon politics—what our ideas were for when we got back there, and how we could revitalize and reorganize the Democratic Party of Oregon. We were assessing various political figures, Dick Neuberger and his speeches—because he was already very important—the existing conservative establishment in the Democratic Party, and who we might be able to work with. From then on I felt I had a very strong ally in Howard."[36]

Beginning with that partnership, formed over strong coffee in a Kwajalein barracks office, the two men began rebuilding the party from the ground up, while attracting strong, charismatic candidates to run for positions at the top of the ticket. Richard Neuberger, just such a compelling leader, had a particular interest in bringing more viable candidates on board. In 1954, Neuberger was running for the U.S. Senate against very strong opposition in the person of two-term Republican incumbent Senator Guy Cordon, a highly respected moderate. Neuberger came to a Lane County Democratic Central

Committee meeting in January 1954, with an agenda to recruit Democrats to run for local office in Lane County. Bob and Pat Straub were there. Even before coming to Oregon, Bob had been reading and admiring Neuberger's articles in national magazines for years, as Neuberger was published regularly in many publications, including *The Saturday Evening Post, American Magazine, This Week, Coronet, Harper's, Redbook,* and *Collier's.*

At the meeting, Bob asked him if there was anything he could do to help the campaign. Neuberger replied, "If you young people would run for city and county offices, it would really help me get out voters."[37] Neuberger "was a very smart strategist," Bob recalled, "and he was encouraging people all around the state that he had any influence with to run for a local office. The idea was that the friends of that person would come and they'd be liberal fellow travelers and also vote for Dick Neuberger. I told him, 'Christ, Dick, I've got five children'"—daughter Margaret (Peggy), had been born the year before—"'I'm making good money. I'm not ready for it. I don't have any business running for a political office now.' And he said, 'You don't have to worry. I looked up the record and they haven't elected a Democrat in Lane County for eighty-two years.' So, on that basis, I ran" for Lane County Commissioner.[38]

Given Bob's competitive nature, he ran all out. "He couldn't help but try his hardest; that was the way he was," Pat recalls. "He jumped into it with both feet and the whole family was involved, including Bob's brother Jim and his wife, Denny. I was all in favor of it. Everyone in the family and everyone we knew was out carrying the message door to door."[39] It wasn't just Bob's family that got involved, but a large number of the Springfield McKenzie-Willamette Hospital boosters that Bob had volunteered with who began wearing out their shoe leather on Bob's behalf. "There was a lot of enthusiasm for Bob from that Springfield group," remembers Clayton Anderson, who became Bob's campaign manager.[40]

At the statewide level, campaigns were becoming more sophisticated and required increasing amounts of cash for advertising. Long gone were the days when, as in 1910, Oswald West could be elected governor spending $3,000, funded by himself and one friend. Back then most campaigning took place at town rallies in an era before other entertainments and distractions, such as radio and television, even existed. "Today $3,000 would just about buy you half an hour on a state-wide radio hookup," the then eighty-year-old Governor West, still an active Democrat, observed in 1954.[41] However, at the local level, it was possible to run a strong grassroots campaign with very little money. Straub was ideally suited for retail politics, organizing an energetic campaign relying on face-to-face contact. Bob and his family and friends covered a lot of ground.

Bob and his campaign also developed some cute and catchy visual gimmicks. Straub's message was that county government was too sleepy and needed some vigorous new leadership to get it moving toward providing better service to its citizens. "The campaign was that the county government was too slow, too stodgy," Bob recalled, "so I bought an old model 'T' Ford pick-up for a hundred bucks and I put a big sign on it and it said, 'County Government Can't Continue at This Pace, Vote for R. W. "Bob" Straub.' I thought it was pretty clever, and I drove that old model 'T' all over the county. It was wonderful."[42] The brash young Straub "unhooked one or two of the spark plugs" of the car, his son Mike remembers, "so it would make more noise and draw more attention, because it really ran awfully well. We'd see a parade going on and we'd slip into the parade between cars and drive down it so people would see his sign."[43] In the last month of the campaign, a friend of Bob's had his dog pull a cart with the same sign up and down the sidewalks on the Ferry Street bridge, a major traffic link into Eugene's downtown. Needless to say, this dogcart attracted a lot of attention. One of Bob's nephews, Jean and Ike Russell's eldest son, Luke, came up from Arizona and wore a sandwich board in front of an eating establishment with a sign that said, "Eat whatever you like, but vote for R. W. 'Bob' Straub."

Bob did personally spring for the cost of a radio ad, which Clayton Anderson had put together for him. A friend at a local radio station allowed Anderson to record the spots at the studio for free, and he located a high school barbershop quartet "who were just pleased to do it to be on the radio," Anderson recalls. "Maybe we paid them five bucks or something, but they were very good."[44] The words that went with the jingle were "Robert W. Straub is the man for the job. He'll work for you and work for me. He'll benefit the entire county!"[45]

The general election in 1954 was crowded with many important high-profile races, but it would also decide who would fill two of the three positions on the Lane County Commission, for which two Democrats and the two incumbent Republicans, Kenneth Neilsen and Robert Maclay, were on that November's ballot. The top two vote getters, countywide, would win.

Road construction and jurisdiction, funding for the Lane County Fair, and a proposal for county leasing of city jail space were the sorts of issues the Lane County Commission concerned itself with in that election year, and Straub and his supporters were contesting some of these decisions in the press. In late September, Straub showed his political feistiness, lighting into the commissioners for cutting funding for the Lane County Fair, which was considered an important annual celebration and agricultural showcase in those days. Straub praised "the sound business management" of the fair's manager, Hallie Huntington, saying she deserved "more support," including a small tax levy to "allow the fair board to make capital improvements." County Commissioner Robert Maclay defended the cuts as a "budget committee decision" not made by the commissioners themselves and implied that Straub was coming off half-cocked saying, "perhaps Mr. Straub is not fully aware of the finances of the county."[46]

Undeterred, a week later, Straub's friend, Springfield Mayor Ed Harms, continued the public questioning of the Lane County Commission's decisions. Harms sharply criticized the commission's support for state highway funding of the proposed Q Street extension, from 19th Street in Springfield to the McKenzie Highway, as "wasteful" and a "duplication of services." Calling it "a bypass to bypass a bypass," Mayor Harms also complained that the City of Springfield "wasn't consulted" by the Lane County Commissioners.[47]

With Straub and his supporters working hard, using every means and angle they could come up with, and with a vast number of high-profile races on the ballot, both Republicans and Democrats focused a lot of their attention on registering voters and maximizing their voter turnout.[48] As registration closed, the momentum was with the Democrats, who crept within 1,397 votes of the Republicans in voter registration countywide a month before the vote.[49]

The Eugene *Register-Guard*, Lane County's leading newspaper, took notice of Straub and his energetic campaign. Stepping away from its customary Republican leanings, the paper endorsed Straub, describing him as "a young man who has made a success of his home construction business and has a yen for public service," concluding "we'll gamble on youth and zeal." This was a major coup for a young, previously untested candidate and may have been a decisive factor in the election. The only two Democrats the *Register-Guard* endorsed that fall were Straub and his former Dartmouth Tuck School classmate (and future Oregon Speaker of the House) Dick Eymann, who was running for the state House of Representatives.[50] To illustrate what a rare pleasure it was to be a Democrat endorsed by the *Register-Guard*, a letter published in the Eugene paper, written by state legislative candidate (and Democrat) Keith Skelton, complained that the newspaper did not deserve to carry on its masthead the banner that read "an Independent Newspaper." He cited, with year by year totals, the endorsement of ninety-six Republicans versus eleven Democrats in the elections between 1936 and 1952—roughly a nine to one ratio.[51]

When the last ad was placed, the final speech given, the last door knocked on, and the last voter called and offered a ride to the polls … finally, the election came. It was quickly clear on election night that Bob Straub had won a decisive victory. Bob emerged as the top county commission vote getter, with 23,896 votes, followed by incumbent Republican Kenneth Neilsen, also elected commissioner, with 20,831. The other incumbent Republican, third place finisher Bob Maclay, received 20,523 votes. Bob had beaten both his Republican rivals by over three thousand votes and became a member of the Lane County Commission.[52]

Statewide, in a cliff-hanger election that looked to be going in the other direction on election night, Richard Neuberger narrowly won his race for the United States Senate, turning Oregon voters into Democratic Party darlings as Neuberger's vote, along with Oregon's then Independent Senator Wayne Morse, provided the 49-47 margin to wrest control of the US Senate from the Republicans.[53]

Democrats made gains throughout the state, upping their numbers in the State House of Representatives from eleven to twenty-four of sixty and from four to six in the thirty-member State Senate. And, in Oregon's Third Congressional District centered in Multnomah County, Democrat school teacher Edith Green bested Republican radio reporter T. Lawson McCall— better known to future generations as Tom McCall—by a healthy margin, 102,551–93,400,[54] after a scorched-earth campaign. Democratic Party mastermind Ken Rinke, Green's campaign manager, had painted the Boston-accented McCall, descendant of the wealthy and powerful, as an effete fop in contrast to the no-nonsense schoolmarm Green. McCall was left a beaten man, absolutely convinced he would never again run for public office.[55] Considering McCall's future dominance of his political rivalry with Straub, it

From left, Lane County Commissioner Bob Straub, Judge George Woodrich (standing), general contractor Gale Roberts, and fellow commissioner Ralph Petersen sign the contract for a new county courthouse.

is ironic to consider the vastly different campaigns and results of Bob Straub's and Tom McCall's first political forays in the 1954 elections.

Though Republicans still easily controlled the three other congressional seats that year, the tectonic plates of Oregon politics were shifting toward the Democrats after several rough and tumble—and extremely competitive—campaigns.

Analyzing the vote, Straub clearly led the ticket in Lane County. Statewide, Neuberger had 285,775 votes to Cordon's 283,313—50.2 percent to 49.8 percent—a margin of 603 fewer votes statewide than Straub's margin of victory in Lane County. As for Neuberger's theory about Straub bringing out voters to help provide the difference in his race, it, no doubt, had an effect, but it is hard to gauge: Neuberger lost to Cordon by 1,953 votes in Lane County and also lost in most of the rest of the state, but his big numbers in his home of Multnomah County and neighboring Clackamas County helped carry the day.[56]

Starting in January of 1955, Bob rolled up his sleeves and began his new career as an elected official. At the time, the county was in the midst of making a number of road improvements. According to Straub, at times the commissioners spent little time in the office and were "homeless, because we were on the road most of the time, looking at roads, and I loved it. The road master would call up in the morning and say, 'Well, I'm going to go down to Noti, just wondering if you'd like to look at that bridge that we're going to replace.' I'd say, 'Yes, you bet, Fred, come on over,' so he'd come over and pick me up and off we'd go."[57]

"Bob was proud of the water level route he worked on for logging trucks between Florence and Eugene," Pat recalls. "They put a tunnel through a large rock as part of the excavation. The County started planning a number of other roads, including the Belt Line around the northern part of Eugene and Springfield while Bob was Commissioner." Pat also remembers a small controversy when "the county paved 57th Street near our property and some people said Bob was just doing it for himself. They harassed us. For a while we stopped answering our phone."[58] But the neighbor kids on the school bus told the Straub children to "thank their dad" for paving 69th Street, "because up until then it had always been gravel and pretty rough."[59]

George Hermach, a friend and business partner of Bob's—in a fiberglass building materials enterprise that ultimately fizzled—remembers County Commissioner Straub as "not afraid to speak out and take positions. He wasn't a follower, he was a real leader." Straub spearheaded building the modern new Lane County Courthouse and Public Service Building and was generally "very productive."[60] Commissioner Straub inserted his opinion and influence into many aspects of county life and its burgeoning development. For example, Bob's insistence that the Fall Creek Dam, constructed during this time by the Army Corps of Engineers, include public boat access, camping, and day-use sites helped create "a premier recreational facility for local residents."[61]

Being a political family was a new experience for the Straub family. In 1955, Straub's first year as Lane County Commissioner, the family welcomed their newest member, William McKenzie Straub (Billy), into the fold. With Jeff (eleven), Mike (nine), Jane (eight), Patty (seven), Peggy (two), and now, Billy, it was quite a full household. In addition to occasionally taking heat from enraged constituents phoning in, they felt obliged to present a cheery family portrait to the world, which had a few strange moments. One Thanksgiving, the Eugene *Register-Guard* sent photographers to the Straubs' house to shoot a photo-spread feature for the newspaper. They brought along a giant plastic turkey in order to create a faux turkey-carving ceremony. Here was Bob, poised with his carving knife in hand, and his family looking on adoringly, their grins almost as plastic as the turkey itself. "We thought that was stretching things just a little," Mike Straub remembers.[62]

In reality, their family life was evolving during that time to reflect the maturation and development of Bob's children. Much as his own father had, Bob Straub felt it was his duty to make certain that his boys learned the value of hard work. Bob and Pat and the six children moved to a larger farm on Seavey Loop in Goshen, south of Springfield and east of Eugene. There, the boys' chores became more arduous. Jeff was old enough, in his father's eyes, to shoulder cow-milking duties in Thurston, but now that he and Mike were entering junior high they were expected to handle a growing herd of cattle in Goshen and, later, on land Bob purchased in Creswell, further to the south. Mike, showing an aptitude for car repair, became the family mechanic. As if this was not enough, Bob had already purchased additional land to the south and east up Fall Creek, a tributary to the Willamette as it descends from the Cascade Mountains. On this forested property, Bob "kept his hand in the timber industry," falling trees, cutting brush and firewood, and planting a commercial crop of Christmas trees, and his sons were his primary work hands,[63] though, often, friends like Clayton Anderson would come and enjoy the work party camaraderie.

Anderson, the Willamalane Park and Recreation District manager, would frequently reward the Straub family for their hard work by opening up the Springfield public pool to them on Sunday, when the pool was normally closed. Straub and Anderson were unselfconscious about this privileged perk, but it fit with Straub's belief that hard effort and recreation went hand in hand.[64]

Maintaining the traditional rules Bob had grown up with, the older girls, Jane and Patty, were expected to help their mother with cooking, cleaning, and gardening, but, as had been the case with Bob's sister, Jean, in his household growing up, they were mostly exempted from the heavy work reserved for the men folk. Peggy and Billy, a toddler and an infant when the family moved to Goshen and several years younger than the rest, were left to play and to charm their parents and siblings—which they both were exceedingly good at.

Jane Straub remembers those early years in Lane County. "Dad tried to make work fun. He'd put on Souza marches on the record player to wake us up in the morning. [Eldest brother] Jeff found it obnoxious." Bob was in charge of the whole family show. "Dad was nurturing toward the girls," Jane recalls. "He would wake Patty and me and fix us breakfast. I wanted to help in the fields, but Dad thought there were things that boys should do and things that girls should do. I had to beg to use the tractor. Dad was harder on Jeff and Mike as far as having expectations."[65] His attitudes, formed in childhood, about male and female roles had remained fixed in this way.[66]

The boys responded as Bob and his brothers had years before to their father, by working hard when Dad was looking and playing hard when he wasn't—much to Bob's satisfaction. Bob took the position his father had taken that, as long as you were getting the job done, you were allowed to push the boundaries on your off time—it was part of the joy of country life. "Dad sort of liked it when we got a little out of line as long as no one was hurt, but it was sometimes hard to know where the line was," Mike Straub recalls. "You could cross the line and then it wasn't okay."[67]

As Straub expanded his land-based business operations with the help of his sons, his brother Jim convinced Bob to exchange the ranch he'd bought for his family, near Sisters, for a new parcel on the west side, in Douglas County, just south of the Lane County border, near Curtin. Jim and his family weren't any more efficient at ranching in Curtin than they had been in Sisters, but the property was closer by and soon became another important locus of Straub family activity. Curtin proved to be a perfect, wooded summer retreat for the family. As his father had when they summered in La Honda, Bob drove during the workweek up to his office in the Lane County Courthouse in Eugene, and then back down to Curtin at night to be with his family. They were joined in Curtin by Bob's sister, Jean, and husband, Ike Russell, their three boys, and Jay and Robin Thomas, identical twin brothers who were the children of friends of the Russells. The Thomas boys had already spent some time up in Oregon a couple of years before, when the family was still in Thurston, helping maintain the Christmas tree farm in Fall Creek. Their father, Robert Thomas, was a medical doctor whom Ike, a bush pilot who frequently contracted with University of Arizona professors and others interested in traveling to remote areas of Mexico, used to fly down from Tucson in his plane to treat the Seri Indians who lived in villages along the Gulf of California in Sonora, Mexico.[68] Ike had been working in Southern Oregon that summer, so it was natural that he and the rest of his family and friends would come up from Arizona and stay. Bob put people to work. "Dad had a bulldozer there," Mike Straub remembers, "and we were clearing brush and tried to dig a pond. Always that thread of work went through these family occasions and kind of tied the family together."[69] In Curtin, hard work combined with large communal meals outdoors and fresh, clean air made for family memories that have lasted a lifetime.

In time, Jim Straub's already chaotic family life completely fell apart, and his wife, Denny, eventually needed to be institutionalized for several years at the State Mental Hospital in Salem for schizophrenia. Jim and Denny's brother, Wally, moved in with the Russells in Tucson. The Russell and Thomas boys frequently stayed with the Straubs on one of their properties, working and living as extended family members. As time went on, the Thomas boys, in particular, became essential to running the operation in Curtin and were considered part of the family. Little did they know that first summer in Curtin that Jay Thomas would later marry Patty Straub and, a few years after that, his twin brother, Robin, would marry Peggy.

Also during Bob's term as Lane County Commissioner, Ike Russell suggested a big family vacation on a pristine Mexican beach on the Gulf of California north of the town of Guaymas. From 1955 onward, the Straubs, Russells, and a regular crew of friendly families, twenty to thirty people in all, began caravanning down to Mexico during Christmas break to enjoy the sunnier weather, swimmable water, outdoor living, and unspoiled Mexican culture of San Carlos Bay and Guaymas, where, for many years until tourism eventually found its way there, they were the only gringos for hundreds of miles.

On the way down, they would usually camp in farmers' fields or orchards, just off the main roads, as had been the Straubs' traveling habits for years. Just before that first trip to Mexico, the family had gone down on a road trip to Disneyland when it first opened and camped for several days in an orange grove about five blocks from the entrance. "We woke up each morning and ate oranges, and then went down to Disneyland," Mike Straub remembers, "Nobody ever bothered us."

When down in Mexico, the adults and the children separated and allowed each other to have their own separate spaces. This freedom suited both the parents and their kids very well. It was truly a vacation in which they let their hair down and became very close with the friends and family members who joined them each year. Bob was particularly expansive, trying his best to converse with the local people.[70]

Clayton Anderson remembered one time when Bob was trying to have a conversation with a Mexican fisherman who lived close by, while drinking tequila, sitting on the beach. "They would each take a drink of tequila, and Bob would ask, '*Esta ciego*, Ramon?' '*Si*,' was the reply. And then Ramon would ask '*Esta ciego*, Roberto?' And Bob would say, '*Si*.'" Clayton recounted, "and this conversation went on pretty much all afternoon—not much more than that. They sat there in the sun, talking back and forth without much progress, but having a good time, I guess."[71] Bob found he could completely relax in the alternative reality he experienced when in Mexico. He enjoyed every aspect of these trips and really liked meeting the local people and sharing meals with them. He loved bartering for fish with the fishermen, getting a good price, bringing them back for the women to cook on Coleman stoves, and sitting around big bonfires on the beach, talking and laughing late into the night.

In many ways, the four years from 1955 to 1959, when Straub was Lane County Commissioner, was a period in which his business, political, and family life were all extremely active and yet were relatively in balance with one another, but this equilibrium was beginning to shift further in the direction of politics. Straub was becoming increasingly fascinated with politics on the statewide stage, where a lot of interesting changes were happening and his fellow Democrats were on the move. Bob's restlessness compelled him to get more closely involved.

In one of his first statewide forays, while Straub was county commissioner, he helped reorganize the Association of Oregon Counties (AOC), which he and some other county commissioners around the state felt needed to become more active as a group, to share ideas and try to influence state government. They started by holding annual meetings in different parts of the state.[72] By 1958, Straub's last year as commissioner, the AOC moved its headquarters from The Dalles to Salem, hired a full-time executive secretary, Kenneth Tollenaar, and began to exert itself more forcefully in representing the counties in state matters, including legislative issues.[73]

In 1958, Straub decided he could not resist getting more personally involved in statewide politics and decided to file for a seat as a state senator from Lane County, rather than for reelection to the county commission.

CHAPTER 4

Jumping in with Both Feet

I'm tired of hearing it said that democracy doesn't work. Of course it doesn't work. We are supposed to work it.

—Alexander Woollcott, writer and critic (1887–1942)

Bob Straub's seduction into state politics was probably inevitable, given his driven nature and the exciting developments happening in Oregon for Democrats.

Midway through Bob Straub's term as Lane County Commissioner, in the 1956 election, the Democrats built upon their successes in 1954 and managed a tremendous breakthrough, winning the governorship for the first time in twenty years with their candidate Robert Holmes, from Gearhart, on the northern Oregon coast. The Democrats also picked up three of the four congressional seats, and retained U.S. Senator Wayne Morse's seat after his conversion from Independent to Democrat. This change meant that, with Senator Neuberger, Oregon Democrats now held both U.S. Senate seats. Oregon's 1956 political transformation included the Democrats winning control of the State House of Representatives and a fifteen–fifteen split in the State Senate.[1] Democrats now held an advantage of more than thirty-seven thousand registered voters, statewide.[2] The utter rout of the Republicans was alleviated only by election of a young, charismatic State Senator Mark O. Hatfield as secretary of state, narrowly defeating the Democratic Party mastermind, State Senator Monroe Sweetland in the otherwise very Democratic year.

A confluence of fortuitous and unfortunate events led to Holmes' victory and the Democratic sweep. The fact that there was a governor's race in 1956 was due to the untimely death of Oregon's popular Republican governor. Governor Paul Patterson had decided in January of 1956 to challenge U.S. Senator Wayne Morse.[3] Two days after Governor Patterson's announcement that he would run against Morse, on January 31, 1956, the governor died of a massive heart attack.[4] The president of the State Senate, Elmo Smith, a Republican from Ontario, along the Idaho border, became governor under Oregon's laws of succession, but was also required by state law to run for the right to complete the final two years of Patterson's term. Had Patterson lived, the Republicans would have retained the governorship whether he had won or lost in his race against Senator Morse. Patterson would have either served out the final two years of his term or appointed his successor to do the same before leaving for Washington, DC.

Democrat Robert Holmes announced his candidacy for the special election shortly after Governor Patterson's death and the state's newly emboldened Democrats rallied behind him. Holmes was a respected state senator from Clatsop County, who managed local radio station KAST in Astoria. Holmes had a distinguished record, including being entrusted by the Senate Republican majority, like his friend Dick Neuberger before him, to chair the Senate Education Committee; he won statewide acclaim for his work to improve the state's system of public education.[5]

The Democrats had two major issues in their favor. The first, and probably the most decisive, was that the Republican-dominated state legislature had championed a very high-profile 3 percent sales tax measure in the 1955 State Legislative Session. After the bill had passed the House of Representatives, Senator Holmes led a dramatic Senate floor fight on May 3, the day before the end of the legislative session, which blocked the bill from being sent to the voters. In addition to the Senate Democrats, Holmes picked up enough skeptical Republicans, including rising Republican star Mark Hatfield, to win the critical vote that day by a twenty–ten margin. Though future Governor Smith, as president of the state senate, ultimately voted against the sales tax referral, he was tarred with the Republican pro-sales-tax brush.[6]

Historically, Oregon voters have looked unfavorably upon attempts to tax commercial sales transactions and the Democrats rode this issue hard in all the state races. Their main argument against this proposal, as it would be for all broad sales tax measures, was that it taxed at a higher percentage the disposable income of those who earn less, but who still need to purchase basic necessities. The Republicans' pro-sales tax argument was that the 3 percent tax would be used to fund public schools.[7] For this reason, they found support among school advocates and many newspapers. Holmes, and the Democrats, who were generally in favor of spending more on education argued that the sales tax was not the way to do it. Oregon voters were with them, having consistently turned down, by large margins, any sales tax proposals put before them. Holmes and Democrats hammered the Republicans with this issue.

The second notable election controversy was federal and one that the Eisenhower administration had initiated. During their two decades in exile from the presidency, Republicans throughout the country had fumed over Franklin D. Roosevelt's New Deal policies. They were determined to roll back as many of his social welfare systems and public works projects as they felt were politically prudent. In the case of their approach to the

Pacific Northwest's Bonneville Power Administration system, along with the South's Tennessee Valley Authority, the Republicans no doubt took a step beyond what was politically wise—they explored the idea of selling these systems to private utilities. In charge of Eisenhower's new energy policies was his secretary of the interior, former Oregon Governor Douglas McKay, who was given the name "Giveaway McKay" by the opponents of his friendly attitude toward private contractors on public lands and his rejection of New Deal policies. While much of Oregon's electricity was provided by private utilities, Oregonians were fearful of having future large dams or any of the existing federal infrastructure owned by private, profit-making interests. They understood that much of the Northwest's postwar economic boom had been fueled by cheap hydroelectric power and opposed attempts to disrupt it.

In March of 1956, Interior Secretary McKay decided to take on the renegade U.S. Senator Morse, making the Oregon's Senate race a high-profile battle both locally and nationally. *The New York Times* assigned two reporters to cover the story.[8] Having a heavyweight new Democrat like Morse in their corner helped energize the Democrats throughout the state, as he lit into his opponent over the Republicans' public land and public power policies.

When the smoke cleared in November, Robert Holmes beat Governor Elmo Smith by a narrow 369,439 to 361,840,[9] and dozens of Democrats were swept into legislative office.[10] And, despite a national Eisenhower re-election landslide—Ike beat Adlai Stevenson in Oregon 55-45 percent— Senator Morse prevailed over McKay 54-46 percent,[11] bringing with him new Democratic Congressmen Al Ullman in the 2nd District, and Charles O. "Charlie" Porter in the 4th District to join Edith Green of the 3rd District in Congress.

Bob Straub supported Holmes, Morse, and Porter and the legislative candidates in Lane County and was particularly impressed with Senator Morse, who, when he wasn't in Washington, was a fellow Eugene-Springfield resident and became a close friend. The Senator was an avid breeder of cattle and horses on his properties on the edge of town in Eugene and in Poolesville, Maryland. Since Bob's business interests now went well beyond home construction to include raising cattle on his land in Creswell and in Goshen, they had something in common besides an interest in politics. The senator convinced Bob to buy one of his prize Devon cattle, and several more thereafter. "Bob and Wayne liked to get together and talk about cattle breeding and livestock," Pat remembers. "Morse knew a lot about the genetic inheritance of cattle. He was a wise, bright man."[12] Mike Straub remembers, "Morse used some political pressure on his friends to buy, in the way that he sold his livestock, but it was fairly natural for Dad to buy cattle and get interested in Morse's Devons because we were raising cattle already. I remember Morse as kind of stiff and worried about appearances." Mike wasn't too thrilled about the fact that he had to clean the stalls and thoroughly scrub both his Dad's and Morse's cattle during the annual agricultural shows, such as the Oregon State Fair. "Morse and Dad had a really good time together. They would get together and laugh and joke a lot."[13]

However, Wayne Morse wasn't nearly as friendly with the junior U.S. Senator, Richard Neuberger, the other Democratic Party luminary, whom Bob Straub admired a great deal. The Morse-Neuberger rivalry was below the surface going back many years, but after the 1956 Democratic victory, it became more generally known and was increasingly divisive within the party, involving nearly every active Democrat in one way or another, pressuring them to choose sides, and causing lasting rifts in political relationships that had repercussions for the party for many years.[14] The two had once appeared to be so close that the press sometimes referred to them with a single moniker: "Morseberger." As the fight continued they began attacking one another on an almost daily basis, taking the air out of the recent Democratic electoral victories and depressing their supporters. In time, the two leaders became, according to Morse biographer Mason Drukman, "engaged in American history's most extraordinary public feud between two senators from the same state and the same wing of the same party."[15]

The reason why Morse and Neuberger didn't like each other went back to 1934, when young Neuberger decided to leave his studies for a bachelor's degree after his junior year and enter law school at the University of Oregon, something that was not uncommon at the time. Morse was the dean at the law school, and knowing its rigor and Neuberger's tendency to ignore studies in favor of his political and commercial writing work, was concerned that he might not be ready. He thought Neuberger might benefit from attending the University of Washington's law school for a year to get away from his built-in distractions in Eugene. Up until that point, the precocious Neuberger, who as an undergraduate journalism student was already regularly published in national magazines, and the brilliant and much admired Law School Dean Morse were very close. Neuberger was almost sycophantic, comparing Morse's legal mind to those of Justices Oliver Wendell Holmes and Louis Brandeis in his descriptions of him in the student newspaper, the *Oregon Daily Emerald,* which he edited. The older man, who famously loved flattery, was genuinely taken with Neuberger's political passion and entrepreneurial writing genius. By all accounts, the two had almost a father-son bond, which may explain the depth of the bitterness that came later. Despite his admiration for his mentor, Neuberger ignored Morse's warnings and entered law school in Eugene.

In the course of participating in campus politics, Neuberger had offended the university's fraternity leadership with his advocacy of a low-cost dormitory/meal plan system to help lower-income Oregonians afford college. When a fraternity brother student assistant discovered that Neuberger's answers on weekly work for the required legal bibliography course were identical to those of other, more diligent, students, he pounced, charging him with cheating. A professor moved to have Neuberger expelled. Neuberger was lazily doing what others had done in this rote-learning course—he "compared" his answers with others in the class before turning them in—but that didn't stop the accusers from seeking to make an example of him.[16]

In the course of lengthy appeals, Morse was a lone vote in Neuberger's favor, while being privately scourged by the desperate young man for not doing more to defend him. Eventually, the political influence of Morse and of Neuberger's parents protected him from expulsion, but the relationship was forever changed. Morse tried to get Neuberger to withdraw from law school, but Neuberger wouldn't hear of it. When Neuberger complained about a D that Morse gave him in criminal law the following term, Morse, upon reviewing Neuberger's work, changed his grade to an F. His most unforgivable act, to young Neuberger, was writing to his father in Portland, urging him to cease paying for his son's legal education. Neuberger withdrew from school shortly after that with neither a bachelor's nor a law degree. He never went back and, according to close friends, nursed a permanent grudge against his former mentor. Instead, he pursued his already highly successful career as a journalist and rising political star.

Now, more than twenty years later, with both men ensconced in the U.S. Senate, at the zenith of the resurgent Democrats' power in Oregon, their differences came out in an increasingly angry tit-for-tat petty squabbling that was harming both men's effectiveness and squandering their party's victory. Neuberger applied the thinly disguised needle, and Morse the enraged, and vicious, retort.[17]

Meanwhile, the Democrats in the incoming Holmes administration struggled to make its transition after twenty years out of power. Dozens of brand new administrators were appointed by Governor Holmes, each requiring time to learn their job and all in a rush to prove, before the next election two years later, that they could run state government better and more efficiently than the other party. It was a heady time at the state level for the Democrats, who had visions of becoming the dominant party in the years to come.

Bob Straub was inspired by this vision, and was anxious to join the action at the state level. In 1958, instead of running for reelection to the county commission, he decided he would try for a state senate seat from Lane County.

With four successful years of governing Lane County behind him, Bob was well known, had strong volunteer support, was favored by the newspapers, and won easily.[18]

Would that Governor Holmes had such an easy path for reelection. Unfortunately for the Democratic standard-bearer, he was challenged by newly elected Secretary of State Mark O. Hatfield. Hatfield was a handsome, young moderate Republican, who was staffed by a group of clever young tacticians. In a time when the state's party registration shifted from Republican to an increasingly Democratic majority, Hatfield was what would become the prototype for a successful statewide Republican candidate in Oregon.[19]

Against this attractive, well-funded opponent, Governor Holmes had only a two-year gubernatorial record to stand on. His campaign was not nearly as focused as Hatfield's and he had two memorable stumbles at the end of the campaign that sealed his fate. First, in mid-October, the Forestry Department and Game Commission convinced the governor to shut down deer-hunting season due to extremely dry conditions in the forests that, they felt, would lead to many fires. Despite the fact that hunters, in those days, made up a significant percentage of Oregon's working men, who ordinarily tended to vote Democratic, Holmes felt obligated to back up the department's unpopular recommendation only two weeks before the vote, sparking statewide fury and condemnation.

"It rained heavily a couple of days after Dad made that decision," Robert Holmes' son Denny recalls. "On Saturday we went to the University of Oregon – USC football game at the old Multnomah Stadium [now JeldWen Park] in Portland, and they introduced Dad over the public address system—and he was booed by thirty thousand people! I'll never forget that feeling. That was something else."[20]

To add to Holmes' woes, Senator Morse, trying to help Governor Holmes win, in his typically blunt style, went to the news media with a story that Holmes himself had rejected: it seemed that years before, a teenaged Mark Hatfield had accidentally struck, with his automobile, and killed a young woman walking on a dark country road one night. This last minute revelation completely backfired with the press, who vilified both Morse and the Holmes campaign as exploiting a tragic story and engaging in dirty campaign tactics, and the public seemed to agree. Hatfield won comfortably, and Democratic control of the state executive branch ended after two short years.[21]

Bob Straub entered a state senate in January 1959 that was ostensibly controlled by the Democrats led by two very conservative Democrats, Senate President Walter Pearson, from Portland, and Majority Leader Harry Boivin, from Klamath Falls. In reality, liberal Democrats like Straub were a minority,

Governor Mark Hatfield (left) greets Pat and State Senator Bob Straub.

and most issues were decided by a coalition of conservative Democrats and Republicans. Straub was intemperate in his criticism of the status quo and was "rewarded" by Pearson with appointment to no committees. After complaints from the Eugene *Register-Guard*, among others, for this blatant unfairness, Straub was put in charge of the Committee on Military Affairs. Straub remembers that "this was a joke, since there wasn't much that the state was responsible for with regard to the military."[22]

While in the doghouse of the Senate Democratic leadership, Bob linked up with a young press aide, Ken Johnson, whom the State Democratic Party had hired to help get media coverage for Democrats during the 1959 legislative session. Johnson was a "refugee" from the Holmes administration, having served as deputy director of the State Department of Motor Vehicles until the incoming Hatfield administration gave all politically appointed Democrats their walking papers. Prior to that, Johnson had been very active in state party politics as the managing editor of the *Coos Bay World* newspaper, one of the few papers in Oregon with a liberal Democratic slant at the time.

Because Ken Johnson was also on the "outs" with Pearson, Boivin, and the rest of the Democratic conservative leadership who didn't trust his closeness to the State Party, which was run by the liberals, Johnson found common cause with Straub and began helping to generate press around the senator's pet issues: cleaning up the Willamette River and establishing a summer forest work camp for what would now be called "at risk" teenage boys.[23] Straub successfully passed funding for the work camp both in 1959 and the following session in 1961.

Straub also recognized that he now had more time, since he "wasn't popular with the powers that be" to "get into helping others with political races," as Pat Straub remembers. "He was friends with other liberals in the legislature, like Beulah Hand and Monroe Sweetland," who were both from Clackamas County. "Our family became very close to Monroe and his wife, Lill, and their daughter, Becky. We used to go camping with them in Central Oregon," where the Sweetlands gathered greens to ship East for Christmas wreaths, which was "a pretty lucrative side business for Monroe."[24]

Even before that first legislative session was over in the spring of 1959, Ken Johnson and Straub were already planning Bob's next political move. "I saw a lot of leadership potential in Bob and wanted to do all I could to help him," Johnson recalls, "we were already talking about the possibility of him running for governor."[25]

Not everyone saw Straub's potential in the same way. Veteran newsman Floyd McKay remembers the first time he met County Commissioner Bob Straub in 1958, when McKay was a "fresh from journalism school" reporter for the *Springfield News* covering a county park district meeting. McKay came home and told his wife, Dixie, "That guy will never do well as a politician. He stutters so badly." McKay also noticed that Bob also seemed uncomfortable with the social amenities, which may have been related to his speaking problems.[26] Straub's stuttering problem, which had come and gone since his youth, was back again in high-pressure situations, such as public meetings and speeches. He sought training from Dr. Kenneth Wood, a University of Oregon speech professor who was a "pioneer in speech pathology and audiology" and helped found a training center and clinic in Eugene.[27] "If you saw the movie, *The King's Speech*, well, that was sort of like my father," remembers Wood's daughter, Margie Goldschmidt. "My dad worked with Bob Straub quite a bit and he did eventually overcome his stuttering."[28]

Later, as Straub became more involved in state politics, Ben Padrow and Frank Roberts—who, in addition to being active Democrats, were speech professors at Portland State University—also worked with him to improve his public speaking, including his stuttering problem. "Ben said it wasn't a stutter. He called it something else," Ken Johnson remembered. "Whatever it was, it was that his ideas were running ahead of his tongue. It sounded like stuttering, but it wasn't."[29]

Johnson may have been referring to "cluttering," a fluency disorder that Winston Churchill is believed to have suffered from, which can sometimes sound similar to a stutter. Straub exhibited some signs of cluttering, such as difficulty in regulating the tone of his speaking voice and getting stuck on scrambled word combinations, for example, repeatedly referring to bumperstickers or bumperstrips as "bumperstrippers," much to the alarm, in this case, of housewives leaving a Salem Payless drug store to whose cars Straub eagerly offered to affix the aforementioned "strippers."[30]

Nevertheless, Bob's primary problem was probably stuttering, based upon the fact that he knew he had the problem; that it came and went depending upon his moods or the situation; and that he could successfully follow techniques and memorize speeches in order to improve his fluency.[31] Ultimately, Straub's strong will was probably his biggest asset in eventually overcoming this impediment to his success. By the mid-1960s, as Floyd McKay noted, "he had basically conquered the stuttering."[32]

After the 1959 legislative session was over, Straub's ally Ken Johnson was hired as managing editor of the *Capital Press*, a Salem-based weekly newspaper that specialized in Northwest farming issues. The owner, Dewey Rand, Sr., was an earthy, Roosevelt New Deal Democrat, who thoroughly approved of Johnson and Straub's politics and gave Johnson carte blanche, during or after working hours, to volunteer for Democratic Party politics.[33]

In October 1959, Bob was elected the state Democratic Party chairman. "Ken Johnson recruited him for that," Pat remembers.[34] "We thought it would raise his profile statewide and give him a platform to talk about the issues," Johnson recalled, "The campaign was very basic. Bob just went out around the state and met with all the county leaders. He beat State Representative Berkeley 'Bud' Lent from Multnomah County quite easily, taking their county delegation by complete surprise."[35] Lent was Congresswoman Edith Green's candidate for the position, and this ambush, as she saw it, may have been one of the reasons for her unfriendly attitude toward Straub. She never warmed to him.

As Straub's statewide role grew, he and Johnson began meeting on weekends in a small outbuilding near the Straubs' farmhouse in Goshen, sitting around a pot-bellied stove, drafting press statements and political schemes. The two men decided that it would behoove the Democratic Party to have a recognized state platform, something that clearly outlined for the public the party's beliefs. They decided to organize a state platform convention, "something that hadn't been attempted by either party since 1910."[36] The convention was held in Salem's Marion Hotel with great fanfare in January of 1960, just prior to the buildup to the May primary election. They had the event so completely "wired" that the robustly liberal document passed unanimously "without one word changed" from Johnson and Straub's draft.[37] Of course, as with most later Democratic documents passed at the local and national levels, it was ignored by the more conservative Democrats running for office.

As Bob shifted his attention more fully into statewide politics, he had less time for hands-on parenting, leaving that responsibility to Pat. Jeff and Mike Straub, as they entered their late teens, took on more and more farming, ranching, and forestry duties. All of the children missed their father's attention at times, but were proud of his dedication to public service. On the plus side, Bob's absence also gave them more chances for mischief.

Pat used to go up to Salem sometimes when Bob was in the State Senate, and spend the night with him there. She would leave Jeff and Mike in charge of babysitting. "Jeff's and my rooms were at the other side of the house," Mike remembers, "so we would sneak out after everybody was supposed to be asleep." Jane Straub remembers "one time coming into Mike's room in the middle of the night and seeing him curled up in bed and poking him, and it turned out it was just some blankets that had been rolled up to look like someone was in there. I called our folks in Salem and Mike got in big trouble for that."

Mike recalls, "I disconnected the odometer so it would seem like I hadn't taken the car out. One time, somehow Dad knew I had gone out and he asked me if I'd driven the car and I said 'no.' He said that the mileage had increased and he wondered if I knew anything about it. I was stuck because I couldn't say that wasn't true because I had disconnected the odometer."

Jeff and Mike, both star distance-runners in high school, "got to be in such good shape that one time we were able to run down some cattle that had gotten loose," Mike recalls. "We wore them out chasing them and were able to easily round them up after that." Jeff Straub, as first-born, perhaps felt the pressure of his father's expectations, and missed his presence more keenly. "It seemed to bother Jeff that Dad didn't come to our track meets, but it didn't bother me," Mike said later.[38]

Out on the political circuit, Bob Straub proved to be a bombastic, confrontational state Democratic chairman—unabashedly liberal. He began aggressively attacking Governor Mark Hatfield's "woeful lack of leadership," claiming "if Hatfield had been a pioneer wagon master, the pioneers would have settled on the east side of the Platte River instead of overcoming obstacles to come to Oregon."[39] U.S. Senator Richard Neuberger liked Straub's aggressive tone and hailed the election of his fellow liberal as "a party leader with character, personality, and courage."[40] Sadly, Neuberger, battling cancer, died of a brain hemorrhage a few months later, while campaigning for reelection, at age forty-seven. His wife, Maurine, replaced him on the campaign trail and, eventually, in office, only the third woman, up to that time, elected to the U.S. Senate.[41] Governor Hatfield chose to appoint Oregon Supreme Court Justice Hall Lusk as U.S. senator until the campaign season was over and Maurine Neuberger had won the seat in her own right.[42] The death of an appealing leader like Dick Neuberger made the development of younger leaders, such as Straub, even more important for the health of the Oregon Democratic Party.

Straub took his leadership role seriously and continued to approach it with gusto. He went after Governor Mark Hatfield at a speech in Coos Bay, chastising Hatfield for advocating forced sterilization of unwed mothers at a meeting of the State Welfare Commission, prompting Hatfield aide Warne Nunn to call Straub a "liar" in the press.[43] Straub maintained that, while without seeing the minutes from the closed meeting he could not be sure that Hatfield advocated it, "the mere fact that he discussed the idea of sterilization of unwed mothers to save money demonstrates a shameful lack of concern and compassion for the deeper involvements of the problem." Hatfield explained himself by saying "We have opened up welfare from every approach. I have never advocated sterilization but certainly feel it bears discussion."[44]

At a joint appearance with State Republican Party Chairman Peter Gunnar at Willamette University on March 26, 1960, *Oregon Statesman* reporter Tom Wright wrote that "each politely knifed the other and the party each represents." Straub touted his recently organized state convention and the county conventions that led up to it as "providing new ideas and plans for meeting long-range problems" developed by the "'percolate up method,' rather than 'trickle down.'" Gunnar promised that the Republicans would hold their own state convention in the summer and attacked the Democrats for paying campaign workers—accusing the party of using the "discredited … techniques of the eastern Democratic machine politicians"—in contrast to the Republican volunteer-based system. Straub countered with a swipe at Governor Hatfield for traveling on the east coast "praising Oregon's tax situation, which resulted from the same Democratic Party legislation he had condemned two years ago," and of not offering "a single positive effort" in "his approach to welfare problems."[45] Yet Straub didn't feel it obligatory, as an opposition party leader, to oppose everything that Governor Hatfield did. For example, Straub pledged his "full and active support" to a state government reorganization plan the governor was proposing for the 1961 state legislature.[46]

In the November 1960 general election, John F. Kennedy triumphed nationally, but, even with a statewide Democratic Party registration majority, Oregon again favored the Republican presidential candidate as it nearly always did, with Richard Nixon winning by a vote of 408,060 to 367,402. By contrast, however, the voters elected Democratic Party majorities in both houses of the Oregon State Legislature. Democrats held a slim thirty-one to twenty-nine majority in the House, but had a twenty to ten majority in the Senate. Curiously, it was during organizing the leadership in the overwhelmingly Democratic state senate that the split between the liberal and conservative wings of the Democratic Party blew up in public, with Bob Straub right in the middle of it.

The Democratic Party's platform convention, which Straub had orchestrated earlier in the year, had decreed that Democrats elected to the state legislature should caucus as a party and select their leadership by majority vote. Conservative Democratic senators shied away from such a rule. While thirteen of the twenty Democrats were prepared to support liberal Multnomah County Senator Alf Corbett as senate president, seven conservative Democrats, along with all ten of the Republican senators, opted to support a coalition candidate, conservative Democratic Senator Harry Boivin, from Klamath Falls. This move demonstrated why Senator Boivin was nicknamed "the Fox" for his successes as a parliamentarian.

Naturally, Boivin's coalition maneuver left the liberals hopping mad, but without immediate recourse. Senator and State Party Chairman Straub asserted, "Only by the majority party exercising this responsibility for organizing the Senate will the voters of Oregon be able to accurately judge the performance of Democratic leadership." Portland Senator Tom Mahoney, a Boivin supporter, retorted, "It is no business of the Democratic executive committee whom I vote for so long as he is a Democrat."[47]

Adding insult to injury, outgoing Senate President Walter Pearson, never a fan of his party chairman, wrote a critical letter to Straub, "speaking in his capacity as President of the Senate," which somehow got leaked to the press. In addition to disputing the right of the state party to dictate how the senate elects its leaders, Senator Pearson contended Straub had done a "poor job" in "getting the Democrats only a 31-29 edge in the State House," given "the large Democratic edge in registration," and that Straub should resign.[48]

Straub, who had not read the letter before he was asked by the press to comment on it, said, "I would be disappointed if Pearson has done this, but I would not be surprised. Pearson has opposed what I attempted to do both in my job in the Oregon Senate as well as my job as state chairman of the Democratic Party. We are two different kinds of Democrats." Straub continued, "He stands for the conservative, cautious wing of the party and I identify myself with the wing of the party that attempts to develop programs which are adequate for the needs of the people." Straub cited Pearson's lack of support for "any increase in basic school support money" or "any salary increase for state employees," along with his opposition to the state party convention, as evidence of their differences. Straub claimed that he "was acting with the broad approval of the majority of the Democrats in the state of Oregon" and had no intention of resigning.[49]

After this Democratic imbroglio, the 1961 legislative session that followed left Senator Straub out of favor with state senate leadership, much as he had been in his first session, but his work with the state party garnered respect among the more liberal members. His major political accomplishment that session came when he led the fight to strengthen Oregon's poorly enforced water pollution laws. "No one ... has the right to use the state's water unless it is returned to the stream as clean as when he got it," Straub declared.[50] Senate coalition leadership, at the behest of pulp mills and other polluters, attempted to add "three little words—'if economically feasible'"—to a bill Straub and others introduced requiring the State Sanitary Authority to force compliance with environmental laws. Straub lost the vote in the senate, but followed the bill to the House, where he worked with his friends and colleagues to successfully knock the offending three words out of the bill, which eventually passed both houses.[51]

Senator Straub also was able to maintain funding for his summer work camp program for youth, a pet project of his that spoke to his own experience of the value of hard physical labor in molding his personality during his teen years. "Part of the problem of young people lies in their inability to find work during the summer months," Straub said. "We are unusually fortunate in Oregon in that so much of our forest lands are publicly owned and that a vast amount of economically rewarding work of a non-hazardous nature can be done by these boys." The forest work camps were for boys between the ages of fifteen and nineteen and were not part of the criminal justice system, but were to provide job opportunities doing useful work, such as "pruning young trees, thinning, working to control insects and disease ... stream clearance, and building and maintaining fire trails."[52]

Still, Senator Straub, as party chairman, continued to differ in the press with some members of his own party. In June of 1961 Straub joined recently elected U.S. Senator Maurine Neuberger in chastising Congresswoman Edith Green for failing to consult with them over the Kennedy administration's appointment of Portland attorney Sidney Lezak to be Oregon's U.S. Attorney. Senator Neuberger even threatened to delay Lezak's confirmation until she

State Senator Straub.

and Green reached some understanding. Congresswoman Green was close to President John F. Kennedy and his brother Robert, the attorney general, and she jealously guarded her access. Green did not see fit to inform fellow Democrats of the advice she gave to the new president. Straub called it "a difference of opinion as to what role state party officials should play in matters affecting Oregon."[53] Opposition to the respected, avuncular Lezak was short-lived and he went on to serve as U.S. Attorney until 1982.[54]

Continuing to agitate on issues he thought were important, Straub announced in July that he was launching a citizen's initiative petition for the next year's general election ballot to require mandatory automobile insurance in Oregon. A bill, first proposed by Governor Bob Holmes in 1959, which Straub had reintroduced in the 1961 legislature, had failed to get out of committee after "the insurance lobby killed it for their own selfish reasons," Straub said, "so I am taking it to the people." No doubt the insurance industry were opposed to the provisions in Straub's bill requiring insurers to base their rates on driving records, "rather than on age, sex, marital status, color of skin and other unfair yardsticks."[55] Straub felt it was "completely unfair" for insured motorists to cover the costs incurred by the uninsured. Straub said, "in effect, my 'fair' bill would place the burden for insurance in the pockets of drivers who cause accidents."[56]

The insurance industry countered Straub's claims through the press, claiming that the $5 million annual cost of covering the uninsured only amounted to "around $2 and $3 per year," and that states that required mandatory insurance had much higher insurance rates.[57] They also charged "setting rates would become a political football which would drive insurance companies out of business."[58] Refuting these charges was difficult enough for Senator Straub, but he soon discovered that, when it came to "political football," the insurance companies knew some trick plays. The Oregon Association of Independent Insurance Agents delayed signature gathering on his ballot measure for several months by challenging the ballot title in the state supreme court. Straub railed against "this picayune approach," which, to his mind, indicated their fear of the measure's popularity with the voters.[59] As time passed and enthusiasm waned among the measure's supporters in the Oregon State Grange and the Labor movement, Straub ended up dropping it.

As political decision making for the 1962 races approached, Straub's personal time was consumed by a new opportunity that he was deciding to pursue—a seat in the 4th Congressional District of Oregon then held by a freshman Republican, which many considered vulnerable.

One casualty of the 1960 election had been Oregon's fiery radical congressman from the 4th District, Charles O. Porter. Elected in the 1956 Democratic "revolution," Charlie Porter proved to be too hot for the voters to handle by 1960. Among other things, the congressman had visited Cuba after Fidel Castro's successful overthrow of the Fulgencio Batista dictatorship in 1959 and initially declared himself foursquare behind the new Marxist leader—a difficult position to take in Communist-phobic America. The *Roseburg News-Review* editorialized in 1958, after the congressman was warmly received in Venezuela, that "Porter's speeches sound as if they were made by [Soviet Premier Nikita] Krushchev."[60]

Porter was also well remembered for a 1952 incident, before he was elected to Congress, in which he led a small group of young Democrats to aggressively picket a Richard Nixon campaign train whistle stop. One of them, a U of O graduate student, was standing in front, just below the vice presidential candidate, in a spot perfect for photographs, with a sign that Charlie had created making reference to the accusation that the famously anti-Communist Nixon maintained an illegal campaign slush fund. "NO MINK COATS FOR NIXON – JUST COLD CASH," the sign read on one side and "SHH DON'T SPEAK OF THE $16,000 OR YOU'RE A COMMUNIST," on the other. This sight so enraged local Republicans at the event that they began catcalling, right in the middle of Nixon's speech. The angry candidate pointed an accusing finger at the sign-bearer, complaining, "I know why they're doing this. They are trying to make me pull my punches on these people I've been exposing." As Nixon's train left the station, an ugly melee ensued, as some of the crowd shoved the picketers and tore up their signs. One of them grabbed the sign from the graduate student's hands and hit him over the head with it. Charlie, a lawyer, collared the man, making a 'citizens arrest,' and handed him over to the police, who booked him into the city jail, though Porter later dropped the charges.[61]

By 1960, the voters in the 4th District decided that the more sedate Republican candidate, State Senator Edwin R. Durno, a Medford medical doctor and former University of Oregon basketball player, was a safer choice for them.[62]

Because Congressman Durno was not yet firmly established, Bob Straub now saw a chance to advance his expanding political career. Lane County, where Straub lived, and was well known and admired, was the largest county in the congressional district. The 4th District consisted of Coos and Curry counties on the southern Oregon coast; Jackson, Josephine, and Douglas counties in southern Oregon, and Lane and Linn counties in the southern Willamette Valley. With regard to other Democrats considering the race, Straub knew that Speaker of the Oregon House Bob Duncan from Medford, who was highly thought of, was thinking of running, but Straub believed he could defeat him in a head-to-head race. The key was convincing former Congressman Charlie Porter to stay out of a rematch with Durno. Porter would likely split the Lane County vote with Straub in the May 1962 primary. Straub believed that Porter could be persuaded not to run if he was in the race.[63]

Senator Straub announced to the press in August of 1961 that he would resign as state Democratic Party chair in September, to file for Congress. Straub promised to make economic issues the central theme of his campaign and that he would "assure party workers who had encouraged him to run that he would make a strenuous effort to win the seat."[64] With his connections as state party chairman, he set up local campaign committees and began personally making the rounds of cities and towns throughout the district.

A young Medford lawyer at the time, Jim Redden—himself a brand new candidate for the state House of Representatives—remembers one of Straub's campaign forays into Jackson County, House Speaker Bob Duncan's home turf, pursuing votes. Straub stopped by Duncan's campaign office in Medford to say hello and ask for some brotherly advice. Redden was there, alone in the office, supporting his friend Duncan. This was the first time he'd met Bob Straub, but he and the recently resigned state party chairman quickly struck up a friendly banter. Jim Redden remembers, "Straub said, 'I've got to do some campaigning down here, where should I go?' I told him to go to the 'Big Y' grocery store and that he probably should also go down to Ashland to the big grocery store there and do the same thing." Straub came back later and said that "he'd gotten a good reception in Medford, but that in Ashland all the people there were shoppers who had come up from California to avoid the sales tax. He accused me of setting him up," Redden laughed, "but it was all in good humor."[65]

In October, Straub took on Congressman Durno directly at a congressional hearing over the Kennedy administration's plans for creating recreational and wilderness areas in the 4th District in what are now the Oregon Dunes National Recreation Area and the Waldo Lake Wilderness Area in the Cascade Mountains. Straub allied himself, again, with U.S. Senator Maurine Neuberger, who was attempting to get greater protection for wild areas "away from chains saws, motor boats, and house trailers," while "lumbering interests" supported "multiple-use areas" that would give them access to additional timber lands to cut.[66] Straub, who remained an avid hiker and camper, was especially focused on the Waldo Lake proposal for a twenty-thousand-acre wilderness area around the crystal-watered alpine lake in the Cascade Mountains east of Eugene. He had actually taken a long backpacking trip through that unspoiled area with his family and George and Ruth Hermach and their sons that previous summer. Now that their kids were a little older, the Straubs and the Hermachs went on numerous trips together, using two burros to pack most of the food and tents, and leaving clothing and less burdensome items in their backpacks. They mostly used army surplus gear—"simple, not fancy," George Hermach remembers. "Bob was a genuine outdoorsman, who enjoyed the natural setting and the hardships that went with it."[67]

Understanding that the commercial value of the timber at the higher elevations around Waldo Lake was small, Straub spoke in praise of "conservation groups and people concerned with recreation" as "reasonable and far-sighted in their proposals for the Waldo Lake area," saying that the "highest and best use" would be to have it "preserved in a primitive state for the enjoyment of the increasing number of people who are availing themselves of the out-of-doors for their relaxation and recreation."

In contrast, Congressman Durno criticized President Kennedy's new Secretary of Interior Stewart Udall for attempting to "double the acreage of national parks." Durno asserted that "we feel the [Waldo Lake] area can best fill the needs of all the people through application of multiple-use principles of land management, insofar as possible." Representing the views of many lumbermen, W. D. Hagenstein, Executive VP of the Industrial Forestry Association, angrily charged that "we have been so barraged with propaganda for the last five years urging the conversion of the Western Federal Estate into a vast outdoor playground, 'before its too late,' so that one would think

State Senator Bob Straub (right) with U.S. Senator Estes Kefauver (D-TN).
At the time, Oregon was one of the few states with a presidential primary, so figures
such as Senator Kefauver—the vice presidential standard-bearer for the party
in 1956—were frquent visitors.

that there wasn't any opportunity on federal lands, or on any other lands, for people to pursue their outdoor pleasures."[68]

As was his style, Bob Straub didn't avoid the hot button issues, in this case, taking on the powerful timber industry. For someone who had originally come to Oregon to work for Weyerhaeuser and who harvested timber on his own lands, Straub was definitely not turning into a timber company favorite.

Later in October, Senator Straub once again stung the Hatfield administration for its insensitivity to the poor—in this case, elderly medical care recipients. It seemed that Dr. Ennis Keizer, chairman of the Oregon Welfare Commission, had told the Oregon Nursing Home Association that, as an example of a poor use of resources, an eighty-three-year-old welfare recipient had received a hernia operation "when, in Dr. Keizer's judgment, this person would have been just as well off with a truss, at considerably less money." Straub fumed that "the inference which can be drawn … is … that a hernia operation for an elderly person is something of a luxury to which welfare patients are not entitled." The governor's office claimed that Straub had "misinterpreted Dr. Keizer's remarks." An unnamed source, presumably also on the governor's staff, asserted that Dr. Keizer's hernia-truss case was an illustration and was a "hypothetical situation."[69] This testy political exchange over medical care to the elderly was an especially sensitive subject. It took place a few years prior to President Lyndon Johnson signing the Social Security Act of 1965, creating Medicare and Medicaid. With roughly half of the population over sixty-five uninsured in the 1960s, and 30 percent living below the poverty line, defending the elderly from Republican "cost savings" under the inadequate welfare medical care then available to the poor was a popular position for the Democrats to take.

Shortly after this row, Straub again goaded the governor, asking him to convene a special session of the Oregon State Legislature to deal with a $2.7 million shortfall in the state's Higher Education budget, due to "an unanticipated fifteen percent fall term enrollment increase at state supported colleges and universities." Straub felt the shortage could be dealt without raising taxes by using unexpended monies in other state budget areas.[70] Because Hatfield could not agree with legislative leaders over the scope of a special session, he ended up choosing not to call one. A few months later, Straub dinged the governor once more in the press on a higher education issue, terming Hatfield's executive decision to create the Oregon Graduate Center in Portland, independent of the State Board of Higher Education, "a serious mistake." Straub claimed "the result would be of higher quality if the effort and funds were made available to the *present* system."[71]

As 1962 began, in one of those surprising moves in the "musical chairs" world of politics, Congressman Durno decided not to run for reelection to the U.S. House in order to pursue what turned out to be an ill-fated challenge to Senator Wayne Morse. Durno lost in the Republican primary to former State Treasurer Sig Unander, who eventually lost to Morse. In addition, former Congressman Charlie Porter decided for certain to stay in the race. This was a particular problem for Straub, because both he and Porter were considered liberals, while Representative Bob Duncan, with his southern Oregon base, was considered more conservative. "I was probably in the middle," Straub recalled later. "Charlie was more liberal and daring than I, and Bob Duncan maybe a little more cautious and laid back."[72] Porter was obviously well known throughout the district, having served as its congressman for four years, cutting into Straub's chances of picking up more liberal votes in the counties outside of his Lane County base.

Continuing to raise a wide variety of issues in the press, on March 30, 1962, Straub called for Governor Hatfield to order a special session of the Oregon legislature to "correct this confused and irritating situation facing Oregon this summer" on the varied establishment of Daylight Savings Time in different counties within the state. An effort in 1960 by the legislature to establish Daylight Savings Time statewide had failed with the voters. The legislature in 1961 had allowed Multnomah County and the counties neighboring it to choose to adopt Daylight Savings Time, which they had done, joining about half of the United States at the time. In addition, some communities had "unofficially" adopted Daylight Savings Time, leaving a crazy quilt of confusing time zones in the state.[73] Hatfield, again, rebuffed a special session because he believed legislators were likely to "advance pet projects. It was obvious there would be no end of cost to taxpayers nor the length of the session."[74]

The May primary loomed, and Straub traveled throughout the district, personally campaigning, trying to call upon his friends and contacts from the state Democratic Party to assist him, but found that loyalty to Bob Duncan in southern Oregon was strong and that former Congressman Porter remained a favorite of his most liberal supporters, who felt torn and unsure who to support. Only in Lane County could he count upon his previous supporters and friends to help him. On May 18, 1962, despite Bob Straub's best efforts, 35 percent of Democratic voters in the 4th Congressional District nominated Robert Duncan to be their candidate in the general election. Duncan beat Porter, at 33 percent, by just over a thousand votes, while Straub, at 27 percent, was another three thousand votes back. It had been a close race in much of the district, and Straub had won Lane County by nearly fifteen hundred votes over Porter, and nearly thirty-five hndred more than Duncan, but Duncan racked up huge margins in Jackson County, his home base, with more than 4,000 more votes than Porter and nearly 5,500 more than Straub.[75]

As Straub had feared would happen, he and Porter split the vote in Lane County and Duncan's southern Oregon support made him the winner. Straub said later, "It was very difficult to succeed where a person as well-known as Charlie was running for nomination. He was well liked and well thought of and, of course, Bob Duncan was a very well liked and able fellow. I lost the district, but at least I was pleased that I carried Lane County."

It was his first political defeat. Straub didn't realize it at the time, since he was primarily focused on career advancement—as he said later, he was "just anxious in advancing up the ladder"—but it was Bob Straub's and Oregon's good fortune that Charlie Porter and Bob Duncan spoiled his plans that year. Straub and his family wouldn't have been happy with him living in Washington, D.C., and traveling back to Oregon to campaign. Looking back on it, Straub said, "I'm glad I lost the election because I know now I would have been very uncomfortable in Congress. In trying to live in Washington, D.C.— it's not my nature; it's not my cup of tea. I've got to live closer to the earth, closer to my ranches and farms and timber."[76] Straub's temperament was much better suited to executive branch duties than the horse-trading of Capitol Hill politics. His frustrating four years as a liberal outsider in the state senate had shown that Straub bridled at following a more conservative leadership and pursuing insider political stratagems in a legislative setting. It is doubtful that his blunt, straightforward style would have fared well in the stuffy backrooms of Washington. [77]

Bob Duncan went on to win the seat for the Democrats in November 1962, bringing the Democrats back to a three to one advantage in Oregon's delegation to Congress.

As 1962 ended, State Senator Bob Straub was about to be out of elected office for the first time in eight years, yet he still had a political fire in his belly. Straub continued to issue press statements and challenge Republican policies, waiting for an inspiration or for some sort of break—something to make it clear to him what he should do next to advance his career and the causes in government that he cared about. As usual in his restless life, Straub was impatient to find his next opportunity and to aggressively pursue it.

CHAPTER 5

Get Our Money Out of the Mattress

Foul cankering rust the hidden treasure frets,
But gold that's put to use more gold begets.

—William Shakespeare, from "Venus and Adonis," 1593

No longer in office, Bob Straub was still active in Democratic Party affairs. He continued to consult Ken Johnson and Johnson's boss, Dewey Rand Sr. at the *Capital Press*, when he came through Salem. One day in early 1964, Bob came into the office and said, "Ken, I've decided to run for state treasurer." Johnson shook his head and said, "State treasurer? Now why would you do that?"[1] The two men had talked for years about a Straub run for governor. State treasurer was the lowest profile of the three major statewide offices, and not particularly glamorous. On the other hand, if Straub were successful, it could be a step up the ladder toward the governorship.

One thing that most Democrats didn't know about Bob Straub in those days, because he seldom discussed it, was that he had extensive experience in finance and investment. Straub had been successfully investing his money in the stock market for many years, beginning as a teenager.[2] His Dartmouth connection gave him ties to influential people in the world of finance, as did his marriage to the former Patricia Stroud, whose brother, Dixon, worked for a fellow by the name of Nelson Rockefeller. Straub's boldness when it came to pursuing his interests served him well in understanding the world of finance and investment. Because he was unafraid to pick up a telephone, Straub came to be on a first name basis with another Rockefeller brother, David, who was also a Dartmouth graduate, and who was the CEO of the Chase Manhattan Bank. If Bob needed advice from him, it was only a phone call away.[3]

This was one of the many interesting contradictions in Bob Straub's life— that a man could grow up in a family whose patriarch, Thomas Straub, was a staff attorney for California energy behemoth Pacific Gas and Electric; get a Dartmouth education; marry into a prominent family; successfully go into business for himself … and still retain an acute sense of duty to ordinary citizens to help them achieve a better life. Straub never forgot that he had had lucky breaks and privileges that others never had—and never got over the unfairness of the huge wage disparities he saw growing up in the Depression. Beginning in the prune orchard of his childhood, on through his college years, and as a man starting his own business, he had worked side by side with laborers who did not have those advantages and knew that they deserved whatever opportunities he, and the rest of those more successful in society, could summon up on their behalf.

Straub, as someone increasingly knowledgeable about the prudent investment of his own growing personal wealth, had been disturbed about the state's investment policies, or lack thereof, for years. The legislature had passed laws that restricted how surplus money and pension funds could be invested. About the only thing the state could invest in long term were AAA Blue Ribbon Bonds at about 3.25 percent interest. This extremely safe arrangement made good sense to many people, still remembering the stock market crash in 1929, which led the nation into the Great Depression. However Straub believed that the state could make two to three times that amount with wise investment in the equities market. Short-term money was held in banks paying even less interest, at substantial profit to themselves. These banks saw no reason to change this "safe" arrangement. Straub told Johnson that day, "Ken, there is only one sure way to lose money and that is to *not* invest it. It's as if we were hiding our money under a mattress."[4]

"Get our money out of the mattress" was Straub's initial theme in the state treasurer campaign, though it became only one of a wide spectrum of issues he raised to convince voters to break the Republican monopoly hold on Oregon's statewide offices. From the beginning of the race, Bob Straub was the decided underdog. His incumbent opponent, Howard Belton, was nicknamed "Mr. Integrity," and, as the name connotes, was widely respected, having unblemished service in state government for over thirty years.[5] Straub knew he needed an aggressive campaign to convince voters to turn out a respected sitting state treasurer, a position few Oregonians understood or cared much about. The treasurer's primary job was to serve as a central bank for all state agencies, manage retirement funds and other longer-term investments, and coordinate and manage the state's debt through its sale of bonds for various purposes. Straub publicly charged that Belton was barely keeping up with inflation in long-term state investments and was losing money by not receiving enough interest on the state's short-term funds.

In 1964, Straub was not the only one interested in this issue. State employees and the management of the Public Employee Retirement System (PERS) had introduced legislation in the 1963 session that would have created a position for a specialized state employee with the responsibility and the freedom to invest retirement long-term fund money more aggressively, including up to 50 percent of the fund in the stock market. That legislation failed in its first try, but, during the campaign, Straub promised to aggressively promote similar bills in the future. Straub promised state employees in an interview published in their union newsletter:

> *If I were State Treasurer, I would have supported the principle of the State Investment Council. Benefits would accrue both to the State of Oregon and to employees covered under the Public Employees Retirement System. A senior, professionally trained financial specialist could earn far in excess the cost of his salary and operation of his small staff. Such large sums of money are involved that increasing earnings on this money by a fraction of 1% can produce several million dollars more income per year.*

Straub claimed, "Employees covered by PERS should realize that a 1% higher return on PERS funds, assuming the normal period of 30 year pay in and 15 year pay back, will increase retirement benefits 27%." This assessment would later prove to have been extremely conservative.[6]

State Treasurer Belton's response, as summarized in the same issue of the state employee newsletter, was not positive: "I opposed that bill in its original inception because they were talking about going into equities up to 50% of the fund, and I certainly don't think that I would sanction that sort of an investment policy because there is just altogether too much risk involved." While saying, "you might better justify it by the Public Employees Retirement Fund," he cautioned, "when you go into equities, if you are going to assume the risk of loss, and it's there, you can't get away from it because it's inherent in the equity market." Belton finished with this jab at Straub and supporters of more aggressive investment: "now if you want to risk that kind of a game, you might play the roulette wheel or something else. Personally as a state administrator, and one who has followed the investment market to some extent, over a period of 30 years, I don't think that I would want to risk that chance with trust funds. Certainly not up to 50 percent of value."[7]

Straub's belief in investing state money in the stock market did draw many skeptics. Those skeptics had some historical reasons for questioning his plan. In 1964, the stock market had a nearly forty-year track record of spotty profitability, having gone through many down periods. In fact, the Dow Jones Industrial Average, a key indicator of stock market health, only first passed 1,000 in 1972, after rising and falling near that number for a decade or more. From 1961 to 1969, the market actually was negative in nominal terms, since inflation and interest rates continued to rise. Gold, government bonds, and nearly every other investment was safer than stock.[8]

Those making money in the stock market were people who were highly skillful in picking individual companies in which to invest. Straub's personal investments continued to be successful, and he believed that a properly structured committee, hiring the best fund managers in the country, could do much better than the state's current 3.25 percent earnings. Nationally, no other government body had dared invest public pension money in equities traded on the stock market, though in Straub's home state of California the State Employees' Retirement System (later known as CalPERS) had been, since 1961, seeking legislation to permit it to do so.[9] Similarly, some private pension systems were just beginning to invest in equities to improve their returns for their pensioners. Straub was up-to-date on these national private pension plan trends and believed they would be good for Oregon state employee pensioners as well. "Our missions," Straub observed later, "are the same—to provide for our beneficiaries in the best ways we know."[10] State Treasurer Belton and his supporters in the banking industry thought otherwise and termed Straub's ideas dangerous.

Straub's interest in the treasurer's office wasn't limited to state investment. He was also interested in two other aspects of the job: serving on the State Land Board and on the State Board of Control, with the secretary of state and governor. He knew that if he hoped to become treasurer he would need to raise more issues besides the arcane business of state investment policies.

With regard to the land board, he had noticed with frustration, as Lane County Commissioner, that state, federal, and private lands were often, for historical reasons, divided in a checkerboard pattern throughout the state. This unique pattern, frequently found in the western states, dated, in this particular case, to the period from 1862-1871, when the railroad companies were granted land by the federal government as an incentive for completing new rail and telegraph links in the west. The checkerboard pattern of public and private ownership was established on the theory that in order to improve their own land, the railroad companies would also add value to public lands adjoining theirs.[11] In the Oregon of the 1960s, Straub and others believed that the considerable acreage of lands retaining this historical artifact of checkerboarding made development difficult and uncoordinated, in many cases. He advocated that the State Land Board, responsible for managing all the state's land interests, "block up" these lands into larger, more manageable tracts, by trading land parcels with individuals and other government agencies.[12]

There were other environmental and populist reasons to serve on that board, as well. The State Land Board governs the use of the submerged and submersible lands under the state's navigable rivers and coastline, as well as the timber harvest on state lands, with funds deposited in the state's Common School Fund. Ken Johnson at the *Capital Press* had had the good fortune the previous year of scooping the rest of the state's press by exposing a cozy arrangement between the State Land Board (consisting of Governor Mark

Hatfield, Secretary of State Howell Appling, and State Treasurer Belton) and Shell Oil Company. It seems the land board planned on giving Shell an exclusive $5 an acre offshore oil drilling right. Even in 1963 dollars, that was a pretty good deal for the oil giant. When Johnson quizzed Hatfield's Chief of Staff, Warne Nunn, about the rumored deal, Nunn replied, "Well, that's a secret."[13] Johnson's exposé inspired the legislature to pass a law requiring a much more substantial fee, and putting additional environmental and other restrictions on state oil leases. In the end, Shell backed away from their bid. Straub was a vociferous opponent of sweetheart deals like the one originally proposed. It seemed clear that he would be a difficult person to keep quiet on any future "secret" deals the land board might entertain.

Straub also saw the land board as a platform for his goal of cleaning up the sewage- and industry-polluted Willamette River, an issue he had worked on as a state senator. He had succeeded during the 1961 legislative session in removing what he called "the three little words"—*if economically feasible*—from a bill giving the State Sanitary Authority additional power to enforce environmental cleanup. In 1964, Straub still found that the authority deferred to industry and municipalities rather than require pollution improvements.

Straub's ambitions with the State Board of Control stemmed from his long-time interest in the theory and practice of running penal and mental health institutions, which were governed at that time by that board. He had successfully advocated for the creation of forest work camps for teenagers as a way of encouraging healthy, productive outlets to what we would now call "at risk" boys. He also had a personal interest in the Oregon State Hospital, having seen his sister-in-law Denny, Jim Straub's wife, who had continuing mental health issues and was diagnosed with schizophrenia and briefly hospitalized there in the late 1950s. "He always cared about people who needed help—that's just the way he was," his son Mike remembers.[14] It hurt him to see the suffering at the state hospital and he wanted to see if he could make a difference there.

Straub savored the prospect of investigating Oregon's prisons and mental health facilities as a decision maker, and improving the lives of the people living in them. Appearing in press conferences around the state with such young reformers as Multnomah County's new thirty-year old sheriff, Don Clark, whose thinking was in line with his previous views,[15] Straub favored programs that emphasized hard work, education, and rehabilitation for prisoners, such as setting up day work release programs for convicts, which he said "worked well" in North Carolina. He harshly criticized Belton and the board of control for their "dark, dismal, unimaginative" theories about running state institutions.[16] Straub noted the needs for better treatment and living conditions for the mentally ill and expanding access to the Fairview Home for the Mentally Retarded.[17] Straub also favored "improved employment opportunities for our young people—through development of sound programs of education and training"—such as his successful Youth Forest Camp Program.[18]

Beginning in July of 1964, Straub launched a series of attacks in public speeches and press statements upon State Treasurer Belton and the other Republicans members' "political monopoly" of the board of control, charging "the lights have been off in the state treasurer's office for the past 12 years." "The crowded conditions in Oregon's institutions prevent an effective plan of rehabilitation," he said.[19] He also protested that he "was appalled, dismayed and shocked to learn that in the past two years the waiting list at the Fairview Home for the mentally retarded has grown from nothing to over 300." He further claimed "the office of state treasurer has shrunk in the minds of the people because of the inactive performance of the office in the past few years."[20]

Straub's proposals and brash attacks brought favorable response from fellow Democrats, including Senator Wayne Morse, who praised Straub, noting "many of us are not fully aware of the board of control's contribution to the administration of state government. He is doing a great service, a great political education, in this campaign, taking the facts to the public about the need for a change in policy for these public welfare institutions."[21]

Secretary of State Howell Appling wasn't running for reelection, but became the designated hitter in responding to Straub's many charges of Republican mismanagement of state policy. It seemed to some observers at the time that Appling was angling to become the Republican candidate for governor when Hatfield reached his term limit in 1966. Belton, who was not aggressive by nature, mostly ignored Straub and focused on making positive statements in his campaign, while Appling served as his self-appointed attack dog.

In addition to defending the Board of Control's actions from Straub and the Democrats, Appling was "masterminding a quiet campaign to insure the election of Republicans to the state Legislature, and to keep State Treasurer Howard Belton in office."[22] With a war chest of more than $20,000— serious money in those days—and with the help of a budding new political mastermind, State Representative Robert Packwood of Portland, Appling was attempting to influence the results of key races.[23] Control of the Oregon State House of Representatives was a precarious thirty-one to twenty-nine in favor of the Democrats, and Appling hoped to swing control back to the Republicans. Straub and Appling had a testy history dating back to 1960, when Bob was State Democratic Party Chairman, engaging in a war of words in the front pages of Oregon's newspapers over an obscure elections issue. Straub charged Secretary of State Appling "had committed a serious blunder" in not notifying county clerks of their need to hold elections for county coroners, a requirement that was being phased out by law, but was determined by Oregon's Attorney General Bob Thornton to still be in effect for the 1960 election. Appling shot back defensively that Straub demonstrated "his ignorance of Oregon elections," since "it is the county clerks, not the Secretary of State, who conduct the election of county coroners."[24]

Straub had gotten under Appling's skin once more with his series of new accusations, and Bob believed it was helpful to have Appling publicly responding, creating more publicity for his own underdog campaign and raising his name recognition.

In August, Appling's anger was past the boiling point: "If demagoguery were brains Straub would be a genius," Appling frothed. "By so fraudulently pitching his campaign medicine show on the basis of innuendos, half-truths and no truth at all, he is simply making the political silly season even more silly than it already was." Citing cooperation between "sincere Democrats and Republicans" in addressing the Fairview Home issue, Appling concluded with a flourish: "If he thinks Democrats … are going to join him in putting political demagoguery above sincere and effective effort … he is dumber than even I thought he was."[25]

Straub wasn't only irritating the secretary of state. Governor Hatfield derided what he termed as attempts at "character assassination" of Treasurer Belton by his Democratic opponent, calling them "dastardly examples of extremism," without naming either Straub, or his "examples."[26] Belton was more restrained in his replies: "In my many years of political campaigning I have consistently treated opponents with respect and courtesy. The kind of campaign Straub is waging for office … deserves neither."[27] Belton actually tried to get Appling and others to stop criticizing Straub and giving him more press coverage during the campaign.[28] He said, "I do not intend to be drawn into discussion with a man who so completely disregards accepted standards of political decency and integrity." When asked to respond more specifically to Straub's charges, he refused, saying, "The statement needs no elaboration. He has made any number of statements."

Straub and his press advisor, Ken Johnson, were delighted that they'd struck such a nerve and continued to stoke the fire, sending a rather obnoxious, tongue-in-cheek letter to Secretary of State Appling's director of elections, asking "whether there have been any unannounced withdrawals or substitutions in connection with the Republican nomination for state treasurer." Straub's letter, which he copied to the press, further explained, "it has been my understanding that the incumbent was running for re-election, but not having heard from him on any of the vital issues for the campaign, I am wondering whether he has retired from the race." Appling retorted to reporters, "[W]e don't waste our time or the taxpayers' money answering silly letters such as Mr. Straub's, which have no serious purpose."[29]

In August of 1964, Straub took a break from his own campaign to serve as a delegate to the National Democratic Party Convention in Atlantic City, New Jersey. President Johnson would be nominated by acclamation, but that didn't stop some of the Oregon delegation from getting involved in the biggest political issue there—civil rights, specifically, the civil rights of black people in Mississippi to participate in electing their government. Oregon Delegates Monroe Sweetland, Straub, Portland attorney Norm Stoll and his wife, Helen, a realtor who was co-chair of the delegation, joined those opposed to seating the segregated, all-white, Mississippi delegation, which had barred African Americans from participating. These Oregon delegates supported, instead, seating members of the mostly all-black Mississippi Freedom Democratic Party (MFDP), which had selected its members in open meetings throughout the state.[30]

To Straub and many other northern delegates, it was a simple question of fairness and a chance to make an important statement that the Democratic Party stood on the side of equality for all. Many white Americans today have forgotten the brutality and injustice of daily life for African Americans in those days, especially in the South, and particularly in Mississippi. Bob Straub was well aware of those facts, though his general sense of the unfairness of it had more of an intellectual quality than a personal one, since he had lived the majority of his life in nearly all-white communities in California, New Hampshire, and Oregon. His one interracial experience had been for a few months commanding an all-black trucking supply corps in the segregated U.S. Army during the Second World War, something he spoke awkwardly about later in life. But like many other white liberals in the country, by 1964 he was disgusted by the blatant ugliness of segregation in the South.[31]

Despite Johnson's decisive support for the Civil Rights Act, passed earlier in 1964, he and his vice presidential candidate, Hubert Humphrey, who was considered the liberal standard bearer at the time, offered a questionable compromise heavily slanted toward the segregationists whose support Johnson and Humphrey hoped to retain in November. In that deal, the MFDP would receive two token at-large seats in the delegation and the white segregationists would have all their members seated, but all would be required to swear loyalty to the ticket elected at the convention. For the MFDP, this was unacceptable. Fanny Lou Hamer, an outspoken leader of the group, spoke for nearly everyone when she said, "[W]e didn't come all this way for no two seats."[32]

Supported by Straub, Sweetland, and others in the Oregon Delegation, Oregon Congresswoman Edith Green, who was operating independently of Humphrey and Johnson, suggested a different solution: seat ALL delegates from both groups who would take a loyalty oath, in which they would pledge to support the party's ticket, and share the votes equally. The Mississippi "regulars" quickly vetoed this, and Humphrey, who resented Green's meddling,[33] and his negotiators, did not press them on it. The credentials committee went back to the original "compromise" without the approval of the MFDP.[34] Ironically, as the convention went forward, all but three of Mississippi's all-white delegation objected to the loyalty oath and, eventually, staged a dramatic walkout. MFDP delegates borrowed passes from sympathetic delegates from other states, symbolically occupying the vacated seats. Oregon Senator Wayne Morse was among prominent Democrats who "boasted of helping to smuggle MFDP members onto the convention floor." With "nearly two dozen MFDP delegates" having "passed security into the Mississippi section," the few remaining oath-signing "regular" Democrats disappeared for good.[35] Straub later proudly told others that he personally opened a side door that allowed the first MFDP delegates to take the segregationists' place in the Convention Hall.[36]

This ugly incident and its aftermath, which included the defection of the all-white Mississippi Democratic Party to Republican candidate Barry Goldwater and the alienation of young black activists from the Democratic Party, foreshadowed major shifts in the Southern electorate that would begin to favor Republicans in future national elections. But not in 1964. That year was owned by a master politician, Lyndon Johnson, at the height of his craft—and it was a very good year for a Democrat to run for elective office.

September began auspiciously, as Straub's entrant in the Devon cattle division of the Oregon State Fair, named "Morse-Melanie," defeated the prize cattle of perennial champion U.S. Senator Wayne Morse, who had introduced the breed to the fair, and to Straub. The event netted Straub a photo with Morse-Melanie and a smiling Senator Morse, which went statewide.[37] The senator's smile probably reflected that the champion animal was named after his granddaughter, Melanie Campbell.

Back on the campaign trail, Oregon Attorney General Robert Y. Thornton, a fellow Democrat, had raised yet another question about management at the state treasury, this time over the proper use of dedicated pension funds by the state treasurer's office. Treasurer Belton was having trouble dealing with an opinion Thornton had issued that summer that declared the long-time practice of depositing earnings from the pension fund into the general fund was illegal. The attorney general had been responding to questions raised by

Morse-Melanie, Bob Straub, and Wayne Morse

state employees about whether pension fund earnings were state funds, to be used as the legislature saw fit to cover state budget shortfalls, or if these funds were to be kept separately in trust for pensioners. Making the correction required by the attorney general's opinion could cost the general fund as much as $16 million. This announcement caught Belton, campaigning in Eastern Oregon, completely off-guard. With typical caution, he had no immediate comment, but "I'll have one some time this week," he promised.[38]

These August and September press stories proved to be the high points for the Straub campaign in the late summer and early fall, a very crucial time in a campaign that would end on the first Tuesday of November. Straub continued trying to lob grenades at the Republicans, but by then the news media had grown accustomed to his themes and were not as interested in covering what he had to say. He raised funds, organized volunteers, gave speeches wherever he could arrange them, but he still worried that his campaign wasn't really catching the fire needed in the last weeks. Then, Bob Straub caught his biggest campaign break yet.

Late one Friday, October 2, Straub called his advisor, Ken Johnson, at his home in Salem. He was in shock—shaky, and terribly distraught. "Ken, a terrible thing has happened," Bob said. Their art auction fundraiser, being held at the Eugene home of University of Oregon Economics Professor Robert E. Smith, had just been busted for serving liquor without a license. "Somebody must have tipped them off to this," Straub said. "It'll be all over the press." Johnson began laughing, reassuring Bob. "That's great!" he said. "It's more publicity and it is such an obvious frame up by the Republicans."[39]

Professor Smith was non-political, but had been convinced by some of Straub's friends on the UO faculty to hold the event. He had a large, beautiful house with a well-stocked bar. Accounts vary as to how bar service was arranged, either with scrip, or with a donation box that auction-goers could contribute to if they wished to help with the cost of the drinks. In any case, the Oregon Liquor Control Commission sent three men to Smith's home and, revealing themselves as agents, issued him a citation when one of the men received 50 cents change for a dollar offered to purchase a drink.[40]

Sure enough, Straub's supporters soon discovered that Lane County Republican Chairman Martin Brandenfels had called the state police, the sheriff's office, the mayor, the city police, and the liquor control commission trying to "organize a raid which he hoped would embarrass me at the home of a respected citizen," as Straub told the press when the news came out a few days later.[41] Brandenfels had apparently caught wind of the party and had some people crash it for him. He was shocked to hear that Straub was selling liquor without a license! Naturally, as a good citizen, he felt it necessary to inform the authorities.

The AP story that eventually emerged was front page news throughout the state on the following Wednesday—and Straub's supporters made sure that it was clear who had initiated the raid, with Straub's state chairman, Paul C. Hoffman, taking the lead in describing how the three agents "subjected some of our dearest friends to a stressful and terrifying experience," and "seized both the contributed money and the money collected from the art sale, and went through Smith's private stock of wines and liquor, seizing everything they could find."[42] Hoffman even managed to bring Howell Appling back

Pat and the kids—Bill, Jane, Patty, and Peggy—stuffing envelopes
for Straub's campaign.

into the fray by claiming Appling had prior "knowledge of this event before a complaint was filed," calling upon him to "promptly disassociate himself from any involvement in the affair." Appling couldn't resist serving up a couple of choice quotes: "The childish and desperate insinuation of Straub and his campaign manager that I am somehow to blame for his being caught in this predicament has the same flawed logic that characterizes much of Straub's demagoguery. There is not an ounce of truth in it. ... I am afraid he is going to have to explain this apparent violation of the liquor laws to the court and to the voters whose confidence he seeks without either help or hindrance from me," Appling sniffed.[43]

The next day, Straub telephoned Johnson. "Ken, you were right. Some guy in Albany that I'd never met stopped me on the street today to tell me how ticked off he was at the Republicans for their dirty tricks." Bob was feeling very encouraged as friends, and even strangers, seemed to be rallying to him.[44]

Lane County District Attorney Bill Frye, a Democrat, had attended the party, putting him in an uncomfortable position as the person in charge of prosecuting the alleged violation. It was an odd case, as no one could recall the state government raiding a private home for a liquor violation since the days of prohibition.[45] Frye dreamed up a creative, if somewhat tongue-in-cheek, solution. In a follow-up AP story that went around the state, he invited the local Republican Party Chairman Martin Brandenfels, who was an attorney, "to accept his appointment as a 'special deputy district attorney to work with one of my deputies' in prosecution of the alleged liquor code violation case." District Attorney Frye, in recusing himself, noted that his own presence at the party "could cause gossip among some folks about my interest in the case." He praised Brandenfels for "the diligence and resourcefulness you showed concerning the incident and the great amount of time you have expended on it, all as a private citizen and at a time when your energies are otherwise heavily committed as county Republican chairman, exhibiting an interest in law enforcement ... unparalleled in the tenure of this office."

Brandenfels told the reporter he hadn't decided whether to accept the offer. "This is not a very responsible attitude, making a big joke about it," he said sourly.[46] Unfortunately for the Republicans, most Oregonians treated it as such. The perceived cheapness of it may have helped convince some that Straub must be worth a look if he could inspire such a transparent scheme. The Great Liquor Bust of 1964 gave the race the visibility that Straub had been seeking all along—and that poor Howard Belton, with his wise strategy of tamping down the campaign rhetoric, was now unable to stop. Belton knew that a lot of voters still hadn't known who Bob Straub was. Well, now they did.

Straub's momentum was also caught up in the great Democratic sweep of Lyndon Johnson's massive victory over Barry Goldwater, which continued to build through the month of October. Still, though some had positive things to say about Straub's vigorous approach, most established voices in Oregon, including virtually every newspaper in the state, favored the incumbent Belton. Even Straub's hometown newspaper, the Eugene *Register-Guard*, concluded in its lead editorial five days before the election: "On the basis of his record and in the absence of any clear-cut evidence of inability, Mr. Belton merits re-election."[47]

On election night, the Straub campaign held their election night party in Salem. All eyes were glued to the television, which would sweep through the statewide and local races from time to time, displaying the picture of the person in the lead. Time after time, there would be Belton's campaign picture beaming back from the TV set. He continued to lead all night. By midnight everyone was getting discouraged. Other Democrats were leading, but Straub was still lagging behind. It seemed he just had too far to go to catch "Mr. Integrity." Finally, just as they were about to go off the air, the station's camera swept the list for one last time and there was Bob's picture.

The "lunch bucket" vote always came in late, particularly in Multnomah County, and it put Straub over the top by eighteen thousand votes statewide, a very close margin. That dirty trick the Lane County Republicans pulled may well have made the difference. It was a big victory and capped an almost complete Democratic Party sweep of state and federal offices— only Republicans Tom McCall, elected secretary of state, and Congressman Wendell Wyatt, reelected to Oregon's 1st District, bucked the trend among the high-profile races. In another noteworthy exception, Appling and Packwood *were* able, with their targeted campaign of funding and professional assistance, to take back control of the Oregon House of Representatives in this otherwise heavily Democratic year.

After taking the oath of office in January, joining McCall as one of two new members of the board of control and state land board, Straub launched himself just as energetically into his new role as treasurer as he had been campaigning for it.

State Treasurer Straub flew into his new task with the intensity and disregard for established wisdom that had typified his approach to politics. It became apparent to the Republican leadership that, even with their historic political advantages, he would be a formidable, or, at least, consistently irritating, opponent. Years later, former Governor and Senator Mark Hatfield came to appreciate Straub's legacy and observed regarding his revolutionary changes in the state's investment policy, "Bob Straub was the Alexander Hamilton of

Oregon."[48] At that moment, however, Governor Hatfield regarded Treasurer Straub as nothing but a royal pain in the assets.

As passionate as Bob Straub could be, he was dispassionate and fair in his dealings with the existing employees at treasury, long-time public servants and Republicans. This was not a given. When Governor Hatfield had taken the reins from his Democratic predecessor, Governor Robert Holmes, he had given the sack to all of Holmes' Democratic appointees. This was considered traditional patronage in those days. Instead, Straub, after carefully studying his staff structure, retained all of Belton's staff including his deputy, Gordon Barker, though he created a second deputy state treasurer position to help pursue his interests on the land board and board of control.

Straub began by touring all the state institutions he would be responsible for overseeing while on the board of control. All board of control members were required to do that, quarterly, under state law, but, according to long-time director of the state mental hospital, Dr. Dean Brooks, "Bob Straub, I think, was the only one who completely fulfilled that obligation. He never once missed." This regular practice helped him stay in touch with the staff and with the patients and inmates, whose welfare he spent many hours contemplating and trying to improve during his years in statewide office. As Dr. Brooks described it, "When he came to the hospital, Bob was not content to have a brief meeting with me, the superintendent, and then leave. He wanted to tour the wards, to talk with the patients, and to see first hand how they were faring. Bob Straub came to see, not to be seen."[49]

At the board of control meetings, Bob didn't hesitate to bring up concerns regarding what he had seen on his tours and, somewhat surprisingly, found a sympathetic ear in Tom McCall, the new Republican secretary of state. They frequently found each other on the same side of votes there and also on the State Land Board governing environmental matters. Straub and McCall were also at cross-purposes with the more secretive Hatfield on the issue of keeping meetings open to the press. McCall's independence infuriated Governor Hatfield, who felt betrayed by his Republican colleague. Hatfield frequently belittled McCall at the meetings, considering him a political "lightweight who had only won office through television fame."[50] It was during this turbulent period that Straub quipped, when viewing a new oil painting his secretary, Barbara Hanneman, had hung in the treasurer's office—a stormy ocean scene with lots of dramatic brush strokes by Corvallis artist Corinne Chaves—"It looks like a meeting of the board of control."[51]

Straub continued to use every opportunity to demonstrate the shortcomings of state policy. He was especially critical of the governor's management of the State Sanitary Authority, responsible for cleaning up the Willamette River.

Straub organized a press event in Portland on the Willamette River, at one of the sewer outfalls, demonstrating for the assembled reporters that the contamination was intense. As if to prove his point, as Straub lifted a large fish carcass from the river bank, its flesh slid off into the river, leaving the startled state treasurer holding the head and its bones. It may have been after this that Travis Cross, a key aide to Governor Hatfield, took to referring to him as "a sewer politician." As before, the inevitable leaking of such slights into the press simply gave Straub and his causes more publicity.[52]

When the 1965 legislature went into session in January, the new state treasurer was right there pushing HB 1347, which would create an Oregon Investment Council with the power to invest state funds in the stock market and other more potentially profitable ways. Even with a new majority of Republicans, Straub was able to get his bill, sponsored by newly elected Democratic Representative Cornelius Bateson of Salem, through the House of Representatives.[53] Straub borrowed language from the Public Employees Retirement System bill attempted in the 1963 session, but expanded it to allow investment of all long-term state funds, including PERS, all to be governed by a board made up of the state treasurer and four citizens appointed by the governor.

Straub not only faced opposition from banking interests and conservative legislators fearing the uncertainty of riskier investments, but also from PERS Executive Secretary Max Manchester, who was beginning to develop his own investment program at PERS, using the mandate given them by Attorney General Robert Thornton's August 1964 opinion. Manchester felt that the legislation PERS had requested to hire an investment manager, SB 199, "could do what this bill would accomplish," without the oversight of an appointed board and state treasurer. The Oregon Education Association also expressed reservations about the bill, fearing amalgamation of locally based government pension funds, which was included in Straub's bill.[54] Straub tried to accommodate his critics at PERS by having two of the four public members of the board appointed from the PERS board itself. In the end, despite these efforts at compromise, the combination of opponents succeeded in sidelining the bill in the Senate. On May 14, the Senate State and Federal Affairs Committee unceremoniously "tabled" it, the legislature's euphemistic term for ending further consideration of a bill. Straub would need to wait two more years for the next legislative session to try again in 1967.

Initially, Straub lived in Salem during the week in a small apartment he rented from the state in the downtown Capitol mall area, and joined his wife, Pat, and the rest of the family at their farm in Goshen on weekends. At the end of the school year, he and Pat made the permanent move to a modest ranch-style home in the Candalaria area of south Salem, along with their children who were still at home: Patty, Peggy, and Billy. This city living proved a temporary stop, as they moved a few years later to an 1860s farmhouse perched, among acres of forest and farmland, on a hillside on the edge of West Salem. The move to Salem was a major change for a family that was deeply and proudly rooted in Lane County. Bob and Pat's eldest, Jeff, left to attend Yale, becoming a Chinese linguist, and later served in Air Force intelligence. Mike and Jane remained in Lane County and eventually both graduated from the University of Oregon.

America's First Lady, Lady Bird Johnson, once remarked that "every politician should have been born an orphan and remained a bachelor." Unlike poor Lady Bird's spouse, Bob Straub's devotion and connection to his wife never wavered as he sojourned further into the political world, but his relationship with his children did suffer somewhat, due to the political demands for his attention. "I don't think they would necessarily express it this way themselves, but I think Bob's kids felt a little abandoned," family friend Tim Hermach remembers.[55] That may explain why, except for Jeff Straub's unsuccessful run for state senate in Jackson County, later in life, they mostly stayed away from politics themselves when they became adults. "One time cured me," Jeff observed later.[56] Of course, they helped out at every stage of Bob's political career, and as he got deeper into politics the more pressure they felt not to reflect badly upon his image. They realized that carrying the Straub name meant people paid closer attention to what they did.

Straub assembled a personal staff of four in his inner office. Deputy State Treasurer Ken Johnson was charged with the more political duties of the land board, board of control, and, unofficially, planning for Bob's expected future run for governor. His personal secretary, Barbara Hanneman, was an extremely talented and respected veteran of both the executive and legislative branches, who both spoke and typed at rates achieved by few, if any, living mortals. She was well connected and fiercely loyal. Johnson's personal secretary, Jean Birrell, another respected legislative veteran, with a wry wit and a sly grin, completed the inner office quartet.

Though Straub remained driven and focused, there was tremendous good humor and camaraderie around the office. One day, Bob invited Ken and Barbara over to his apartment for lunch, offering to cook them hamburgers. The impatient Straub, who was known to inhale his food, neglected to cook the patties longer than a little surface browning, giving his staff years of merriment recalling his attempt to give them food poisoning by feeding them raw meat sandwiches.[57]

From day one, Straub insisted on scrupulous honesty and thriftiness in the office, to the point of never claiming expenses for travel, with the exception of flights to New York City required by the state for bond signings, because he could never be sure what part of his work was political, what part was personal, and what part was business.[58] If being fiscally tight is the measure of a good manager, Bob's record at Treasury stands out as one of the best ever. His close control of that agency's budget was recognized throughout the capitol. Ken Johnson noted how, in Bob's last appearance before the legislature's budget committee, the treasury staff's assiduous preparations for the biennial grilling were rendered unnecessary:

As usual, the committee's fiscal officer (in this case, Jay Gould) made his recommendation. In words to this effect he said: Mr. Chairman and members of the committee, State Treasurer Straub has been in close touch with the legislative fiscal office through the biennium and has done everything possible to offer a tight budget. We are satisfied with it in its entirely and we recommend its adoption. The chairman lifted his gavel and said: Any objections? (plunk went the gavel) So ordered! And that was our budget hearing. We hadn't said a word. To the best of my knowledge that's the only time in history that such a thing has happened.

Johnson further commented:

Actually, it might have been set up by our previous budget, in which we wound up with a $25,000 surplus. Our office manager said: Great! Now we can get those IBM typewriters! No we can't, said Bob. We'll revert it to the state general fund. And we did. The standard practice for all department heads had been to spend up every surplus so the legislature wouldn't think they'd been given too much in the last budget. "Use it or lose it" was their guiding model. As a matter of fact, Bob concluded his eight-year term with a doubled workload and fewer employees than he inherited from the previous Treasurer.[59]

Some efforts at thriftiness on Straub's part were irritating at the time, and comical in retrospect. James George, who worked for the state investment programs in Straub's later years at treasury remembers that "Bob was so tight, he had a 'supply sergeant' lady and if you wanted a pencil you had to go up and turn in your old pencil to get the new pencil—I'm serious. She had all the writing pads and everything right behind her desk so you couldn't just help yourself; you had to ask for another twelve sheets of paper or whatever it was."[60]

Scrupulously careful with the state's money, Bob liked to take personal risks and do "thrifty" things, which even verged on the questionable. He was delighted to learn from Barbara and Gene Hanneman's twin daughters, Laurie and Linda, who were attending Columbia University in New York City, how to save subway fare by getting two people through the same turnstile on one subway coin. As he had since childhood, Bob took great pleasure in gaming the system like that, so here was Oregon's state treasurer squeezing through a subway turnstile with an attractive college girl and risking arrest from the New York City Transit Police. Bob was also a notorious, and terribly nervous, backseat driver. He frequently insisted that he drive instead of his wife, Pat, when everyone, except Bob, of course, understood that she was a much safer driver. Bob's eccentricities mostly delighted his staff and his family and certainly kept life interesting.[61]

In February of 1966 Straub was finally ready to formally announce what every politically aware person in the state already knew—that he was running for governor. He started the month by again charging that the State Sanitary Authority was not enforcing the state's laws against polluters, and announcing that he was hiring his own analyst to independently check for a variety of industrial and municipal contaminants.[62] Straub had samples taken in Salem and Portland near known polluters, eventually charging the sanitary authority with specific examples of dereliction for not requiring such companies as

"Should Liven Up the Town" Cartoon by Art Bimrose, from *The Oregonian*, February 10, 1966. © 1966 *The Oregonian*. All rights reserved. Reprinted with permission.

Portland's Chipman Chemical, for example, "to stop discharging phenols into the river."[63]

At his campaign announcement press conference at the Portland Hilton on February 7, Straub noted, in a not-so-veiled reference to his rival Tom McCall, "Republicans are beginning to talk more like Democrats. This puts a Democrat at a disadvantage, because a Republican is talking like a Democrat, but is still being financed like a Republican." This crack brought applause and laughter from the gathering of Democrats—candidates, office holders, and activists—who jammed the press conference. A reporter asked Straub if he thought he would be the "underdog" in a race against Secretary of State McCall. "Those betting on the race are betting quite comfortably and securely on my opponent winning. I don't think I would feel very comfortable in the race if I had a downhill pull." Straub continued, "I am used to rowing into the wind, and I believe that for the next eight months, until November 1, I will be running into a heavy wind."[64]

The question remained unanswered: could he surmount McCall's advantages of positive name recognition, charisma, and campaign cash to win? As in the treasurer's race, Straub knew his best—and only—chance was to dramatize the difference between his style of activist leadership and the more passive, establishment approach of his Republican opponent.

But how?

CHAPTER 6

Nature's Warrior

Great joy in camp. We are in view of the ocean, this great Pacific Ocean, which we have been so long anxious to see, and the roaring or noise made by the waves breaking on the rocky shores (as I suppose) may be heard distinctly.

—Captain William Clark, November 7, 1805

Straub's first opportunity to challenge McCall came within two weeks of the announcement of his race for governor. On February 2, 1966, newspaper reporter Jim Long from the *Oregon Journal* called Straub at home in the evening. Long was just back from attending a highway commission hearing in Coos Bay. He noticed an obscure item on the agenda for approval of bridge construction over the mouth of the Nestucca River, as part of a major highway diversion project.

The overall plan was to shift Highway 101 onto Winema Beach north of Neskowin, up over the headland, and the new four-lane bridge, across the Nestucca River estuary, and onto the sandy finger of the Nestucca Sand Spit on the other shore. From there the proposed highway would travel three miles due north along the first dune, then on up through Pacific City, passing Cape Kiwanda and Sand Lake, finally turning inland to Tillamook.

Long was looking for a quote—did he think it was a good idea? "No," said Straub. "I'm opposed to it." Long was looking for a better quote than that, so he suggested, "How about saying something like, 'it would harm the ecology of the bay?'" Straub said, "Let me get back to you." A half hour later Straub called Long back and gave him a brief statement, incorporating his suggestion. The quote and the story ran in the next day's paper.[1]

Seeing the news article, a group of Pacific City landowners requested a meeting with Straub to discuss their anger and frustration over the plan, which they felt would spoil a stretch of pristine ocean beach. He promised to look into it further. The more he looked, the more outraged he became. Destroying that beautiful beach was "unthinkable," Straub fumed. This was just exactly the sort of issue he could use to illustrate his style of leadership. Here in a nutshell was what was wrong, from Straub's point of view, with Oregon government's approach to preserving the unique beauty of the state.

State Treasurer Straub at the Oregon Capitol.
Photo by Gerry Lewin

The essence of the dispute was whether a highway should be located along several miles of beachfront for maximum efficiency of travel and ease of coastal access or whether the beaches in the highway's planned path should be preserved for recreational and ecological benefit in their natural state.

It is appropriate that the opening battle in the fight for control of Oregon's beaches was over a highway. Pacific coast beaches had served as a road for travelers since ancient times. And those early travelers must have marveled at its awesome beauty just as later visitors did, who recorded their thoughts in journals and books. Oregon's rugged coastline and thick undergrowth of rain-fed bushes and trees made inland pathways difficult to construct and sometimes dangerous to traverse. Coastal Native peoples used the beach—long, flat, and straight in many places—to travel up and down the coast to trade with other tribes. When fur traders and pioneers arrived in the Oregon Country, some settled near the ocean and along harbors and also found travel on foot, horseback, or horse-drawn vehicles along the beaches the most useful and practical option, especially using low tide to go around rocky headlands where path construction was difficult. So it wasn't too surprising that a long stretch of sandy beach in Clatsop County, Oregon's northernmost county, where many of the early coastal pioneers had settled, was named a state highway in 1899 by the Oregon Legislature.

More than a decade later, when horse travel was giving way to motorcars, the far-sighted and crafty young governor, Oswald West, used the Clatsop County precedent to convince the legislature in 1913 to declare the entire length of Oregon's beaches, up to the high tide line, as a public highway. As a progressive Democrat and an early conservationist with a spiritual connection to Oregon's coast, he saw this as a way to ensure that the public retained its rights to its beaches and that they not be chopped into inaccessible private lots by future land developers. "In administration of this god-given trust, a broad protective policy should be declared and maintained," Governor West wrote about the new law. "No local self interest should be permitted, through politics or otherwise, to destroy or ever impair this great birthright of the people."[2]

As Governor West intended, this is exactly how succeeding generations saw it—Oregonians had a birthright to access and enjoy their public beaches. Eventually, through the stewardship of wise public servants and with public support, Oregon's beaches, from north to south, became the crown jewels of a nationally renowned state park system. State highways linking the city dwellers from the Willamette Valley and out-of-state tourists to Highway 101, the Oregon Coast Highway, which was completed in 1932, facilitated access to the new parks. These new roads brought campers and hotel visitors quickly and efficiently to some of the most beautiful coastline imaginable.

Initially the highway and local roads were not built along the beaches or dunes because in many places these were too unstable for construction, though drivers could, at their own risk, find access to the wet sand and drive along the beach (and still are allowed to do this in a few locations today). Thus, the first automobile roads mostly avoided close proximity to the beaches. But the introduction of European beach grass and improved road-building techniques changed this equation dramatically. The beaches of today are quite different from those that existed before the 1930s, when European beach grass was introduced by the Civilian Conservation Corps, one of President Franklin Roosevelt's public improvement programs for unemployed workers during the Great Depression. The grass was well adapted to hold shifting dunes in place, allowing other vegetation to follow. It soon spread up and down the coast, radically changing the coastal environment and allowing for greater coastal land development on property that had previously been unstable sand.

Demand for coastal land was growing. As American migration continued westward, Oregon's population grew. By the 1960s, overcrowding and high land prices in California were causing some people to look northward for opportunities. The State of Oregon, as part of a national effort begun in President Dwight D. Eisenhower's administration, was engaged in highway improvement to serve its growing population. This included straightening the twisting course of the Oregon Coast Highway. By 1961, plans were being drawn up at the State Highway Department to cut as much as an hour off the lazily winding trip, in and around the steep hills between Neskowin and Tillamook. This would involve re-routing the coastal highway north of Neskowin along beaches and headlands, and over the Nestucca estuary, before rejoining the current inland route in Tillamook.

Pat Straub (right) and daughters Patty, Peg, and Jane (left to right), with the
Nestucca Sand Spit behind them

When the new highway route was publicly announced in August of 1965, it split the local community. Some saw it as evidence of progress, speeding the commute and bringing tourist dollars into town. But people who owned houses near the ocean, some local business owners, and dory fishermen were very concerned that the highway would choke their natural stretch of coastline with cars and destroy their peaceful way of life. They formed a group called Citizens to Save Our Sands (SOS) and testified against the route in a series of hearings.[3] By late February of 1966 they had initiated repeated contact with Governor Mark Hatfield, their congressional delegation, and local and national highway officials to no apparent effect. It seemed the highway officials already had their minds made up in favor of the route, which was supported by key local business interests and the three-member Tillamook County Commission. So it was in desperation that the small delegation of SOS members, led by vacation homeowner Gordon Guild, met with the feisty and energetic state treasurer in February of 1966. They asked him to champion their cause.

Straub decided to drive out to the coast the following weekend and see the highway route for himself, to get a real feel for the place beyond the maps and architectural drawings. His wife, Pat, and his three daughters accompanied him. One thing Straub noticed from looking at a map of the north coast was that building the highway across the Nestucca River and Sand Spit, as planned, seemed, logically, to lead to a whole series of highway beachfront leaps across waterways: from Netarts Spit across Netarts bay; Tillamook Spit over Tillamook Bay; and across the Nehalem River to the Nehalem Sand Spit —making for a long, smooth, scenic drive north up the coast to Seaside and

Astoria, but permanently spoiling the calm beauty of several long, undisturbed beaches. When he arrived at the site, Straub was shocked to see that the highway department had already pounded in yellow stakes marking where the highway would go, not only on the headland on the south side of the mouth of the Nestucca River, but on the north side right on the first dune. He could see that the highway department meant to build there … and soon.

Back in his office on Monday, Straub called everyone into his inner office to recount his trip. The proposal and the precedent it set disturbed him. "It's like a cocked arrow," he told his aides. Once the arrow "flew" it would destroy the scenic values and wreak environmental havoc on the entire north coast. He decided to make stopping this highway one of his top priorities in the coming months. He and his deputy, Ken Johnson, who was once again his campaign manager, saw its potential as a major issue in his campaign for governor. But Straub didn't just see it as a political issue. He knew he would need quite a head of steam to succeed in taking on the powerful highway department and, especially, Glenn Jackson, CEO of Pacific Power & Light and long-time citizen chairman of the commission. Straub was going to have difficulty winning over Hatfield and McCall. He was going to have a hard time even getting help from his old friend Wayne Morse, if it came down to it. [4] Jackson was connected in state politics like no one else.

It wasn't his efficiency and popularity as chairman of the highway commission that gave Jackson power, though it didn't hurt that he had early notice of where highways were to be located. Glenn Jackson is best known today for the I-205 bridge over the Columbia River named in his honor. In 1966, he was at the height of his political power and was, by far, the most influential business and civic leader in Oregon. Jackson was a crafty, likable businessman, son of the owner of the Albany *Democrat-Herald* newspaper, who worked his way up through the ranks to become chairman of the California-Oregon Power Company (COPCO), a small southern Oregon electric utility company. Creating a massive ranch from surplus land and equipment at the abandoned World War II Army base at Camp White in southern Oregon, Jackson merged his company with Oregon's second largest utility company, Pacific Power and Light, and soon became its chief executive officer. He alternated his time between an office in Portland and one in Medford so he could remain near his ranch in White City. A small, dapper man with a pipe perpetually hanging from his mouth, Glenn Jackson had a calm manner and quiet, but deep voice that commanded respect. Once Jackson decided to do something, one way or another, he got it done—and few had the nerve to cross him.

Running a private utility company in Oregon required excellent political skills. Since the development of electric power in the state, and especially during its widespread expansion in the 1930s, there was a constant battle over whether ownership should be public or private. Generally speaking, Republicans had favored private power, and Democrats, following the line of President Roosevelt, public ownership. In Oregon, bastion of Republicanism that it was, private power had mostly prevailed, garnering the most populous (and profitable) service areas. But the battle was never completely won. Public utilities, not required to turn a profit for stockholders, charged lower rates to their customers. And there remained, despite utility-inspired legislative meddling, a couple of different electoral processes to convert a locale from private to public utility service. Private utilities needed to remain constantly vigilant in politics to survive. For this reason, Jackson and other utility leaders were connected not just to elected officials of both parties but to local businesses and their statewide organizations, and to civic and charitable groups.

Glenn Jackson was a master of power politics and greatly respected. In time, he became the most respected businessman in the state, whose influence was so great he could even determine which statewide candidate would get business support in the Republican primary election. Yet his personal charm was such that even his political opponents liked him and felt he often had the state's best interest at heart. He subscribed to the philosophy that he and PP&L would do well by doing good. At least that is the image he wanted to project.

It would seem strange in later years to think of Governor Hatfield, in 1959, appointing the head of one of the state's leading private utilities to lead the agency that determined policy for the state highway system. But, by all accounts, Jackson did a masterful job; under his leadership, Oregon was one of the first states to complete its interstate freeway system—on time and under budget. He was now trying to apply his talents to improving the coastal highway. He hoped to bring more efficient access for businesses and, especially, for recreational users attracted to the beautiful coastline. State parks were always under the purview of the highway department, as parks and the highways that brought larger numbers of people to them developed together in Oregon. Jackson took that part of his mission seriously as well, continuing the tradition of stewardship of Oregon's parks, and public access, especially on the coast.

The state engineers had already sold him on the beach route for the highway, local business and political leaders agreed, and Jackson was ready to back them to the hilt. [5] For Glenn Jackson and the engineers at the Highway Department, straightening out the northern stretch of Highway 101 would cut an hour of travel time from the current winding inland route and get

Oregon and out-of-state tourists to Oregon's beautiful beaches much quicker. And, on top of all that, it would be a breathtakingly beautiful drive for motorists passing through. In an era when First Lady Lady Bird Johnson's Highway Beautification Program and anti-littering drives were considered major environmental programs, Jackson and the highway department can be forgiven for thinking that they were enhancing the public's enjoyment of nature by building a highway next to a beach. There was no such thing as an Environmental Impact Statement in those days, or an Endangered Species Act. The highway department planned to establish a state park on the Nestucca Sand Spit as part of the project, so believed they were actually making a beautiful beach more accessible.

Oregon's State Land Board, consisting of the governor, secretary of state, and state treasurer, governed decisions affecting estuaries, including the siting of highway bridges over them. With Straub's fellow members of the board, Republicans Mark Hatfield and Tom McCall, looking to Jackson for political support, it seemed impossible for Straub to win if Jackson dug in his heels. Straub's only hope was for McCall to side with him, since, to Hatfield's frustration, the former newsman agreed with Straub from time to time on issues before both the land board and the board of control. So far, on this issue, McCall was publicly hedging his bets.

This was just the sort of fight that Bob Straub sought when he entered politics. It was why he had become a Democrat—to be an agent of change, to challenge the establishment when it didn't get things right. If the powers that be were going to make a mistake, then someone had to stand up to them, and Straub relished the challenge of it. Here, also, was a chance, with McCall's reticence on the issue, for Straub to distinguish himself as a true environmentalist, rather than merely a good talker, as he and his supporters believed McCall to be.

Straub's allies at SOS certainly didn't lack for passion. One of them, in a letter to the editor to the *Oregonian*, wrote: "[On] the horizon is a colossus rearing its ugly head to devour this beach frontage. Its black asphalt serpent-like tongue will come careening down the beach, its venom desecrating everything in its path, covering the homes, the land, the dreams with a thick, black crust." Another suggested that the future would leave our beach front with a giant auto patio, where "we will have to set up a museum containing a few jars of sand so ... we can show our children what the beach was made of in the old days."[6]

In addition, increasing numbers of people were writing to the governor and State Highway Engineer Forrest Cooper in protest. They included Mrs. Douglas McKay, widow of the staunchly conservative former governor and

U.S. interior secretary, who wrote in a letter dated March 21, 1966: "My late husband and I have owned a home in Neskowin since 1944 and naturally I feel very badly about the new road which, I think, would ruin Neskowin as a family resort town. Please be assured, I am not opposed to progress, but I feel there is a better way to improve Highway 101 ... than to make the drastic changes now proposed."[7]

Straub knew this effort needed more support than a few coastal opponents, even well-connected ones like Mabel McKay, to stop the highway juggernaut. He turned to Janet McLennan, a Portland Democratic Party activist whom both Straub and his chief aide, Ken Johnson, greatly admired. They had tried unsuccessfully to recruit her to help with the 1964 state treasurer's campaign, but by the time they contacted her, she had already committed to coordinating the ballot measure to repeal Oregon's death penalty.[8] McLennan's strength as an organizer lay in her seeming tirelessness and her ability to integrate her political work within her married and family life. She often included her children in her political activities from a very young age. She and her husband, Bill, also an attorney and active in Democratic Party circles, were part of a group of politically active young attorneys and their spouses. As Straub had been initially, these young lawyers were inspired by U.S. Senator Dick Neuberger and loyal to his liberal causes. McLennan was filled with quiet purpose. McLennan made connection to other like-minded families in Portland, especially among Reed College faculty and their spouses in her neighborhood and, as time went on, throughout the state. The camaraderie of these idealistic, liberal families and their social network made the work fun for everyone and attracted others to join them. Whether it was organizing a door-to-door canvass, political rally, cocktail party, or backpacking trip to the mountains, these families worked and played together. Their children grew up as a tight-knit group of friends, reveling in a stimulating social world of their own. "We knew we were being used as props, you know, cute kids on the beach, and worker bees on campaigns," daughter Martha McLennan remembered later, "but there was a sense of nobility of purpose. We felt special to be part of it."[9]

By this time, McLennan was already very accustomed to campaigning, having run twice for the legislature and managed two successful statewide ballot measure campaigns. She was involved in local civil rights issues, including integrated housing, and the environmental movement, as an active member of the Sierra Club. She was part of the effort to create the Oregon Dunes National Park in the area south of Florence—with Dick Neuberger's name attached to it.[10]

In short, McLennan was a fighter for good causes and the ideal person to help spread the word against the proposed beach highway construction. When Janet McLennan, inevitably, said yes to Straub's plea for help to save Winema Beach and the Nestucca Sandspit, he, McLennan, and Ken Johnson knew they had to organize a campaign with press releases and speeches at service clubs and other venues, but they began thinking about doing something more dramatic to grab press attention.

McLennan, with her experience in organizing political events, came up with the idea of holding a march on the beach on Mother's Day, May 8. It was conceived as a festive affair, with people of all ages, songs, balloons, and a bonfire. She immediately began organizing the event. Due to Straub's leadership the previous year on Willamette River cleanup and other issues, a coterie of interested conservationists was forming "who identified with Bob and looked to him for leadership," McLennan said later. "I served as a sort of a go-between and 'factotum.'" To these groups she added the Pacific City 'SOS' highway opponents.[11] In addition to working with her Portland base, McLennan and Johnson activated Democratic Party loyalists throughout the state. Nancie Fadeley in Eugene, later a state representative, among others, was successful in getting people to commit to attend the Mother's Day event on the North Coast.

Mother's Day, May 8, was cloudy and cold, with a frigid breeze. But it didn't chill the enthusiasm of the three hundred people of all ages who showed up at the Winema Beach parking lot. The build-up to the march hadn't gone unnoticed by local proponents of the highway route. They held their own "welcoming committee" meeting prior to the marchers' arrival, hanging a figure of Bob Straub in effigy and leaving signs such as "you are being misled" on the march route. A local property owner, armed with a rifle, was reputed to be waiting for the marchers. When the reporters told Straub about this, he shrugged it off and urged his supporters to proceed with the march.

The entire Straub family was well represented there. Mike Straub, Bob's son, came up from Eugene and brought his future wife, Linna, on their first date. It was a unique introduction to the family, though she'd seen much more dramatic confrontations while attending high school in Berkeley, California.

A Straub loyalist wrote a song parody about the highway to the tune of "The Battle Hymn of the Republic" and passed out the lyrics beginning with: "Mine eyes have seen the misery of the coming of the road, it is blighting all the wonders and the joys that we have knowed." The crowd's enthusiastic rendition, if not exactly on key, did make the evening news with the chorus: "Sandy beach we're going to miss ya, cement's coming down to kiss ya, we're here trying to assist ya, 'cause somebody gives a darn ..." Was it corny? Yes, but it fit the homemade atmosphere.

The group marched along Winema Beach and arrived at the north end, next to the Nestucca River. People gathered driftwood and built a campfire, roasting hot dogs and marshmallows on sticks, and getting warm. Straub spoke briefly and passionately, saying he was glad they could see firsthand, as he had himself, "what a terrible folly it would be to destroy this beautiful, tranquil area by running a noisy, smelly, unsightly, four-lane highway through it."

Then, as people slowly began retracing their footprints back along the beach to the road head, collecting Japanese glass floats and seashells along the way, Straub noticed a man, "in true Western style," on the bluff above with a rifle. "Let's go up and talk to him," Straub said. His aide Johnson and others followed him, keeping a healthy distance behind and wondering if Bob knew what he was doing. After a spirited confrontation in which the man expressed his concern about not being able to use his property as he saw fit, they parted amicably.

Initial reaction to the Mother's Day march in the press was disappointing. Some editorial writers panned it as a publicity stunt, which, of course, it was.[12] And the opposition tactics received equal billing with the march in press reports. Nonetheless, Bob Straub was clearly energized by the event. A few days later he wrote McLennan, "[l]ooking back on our now-famous beach hike, I feel that the whole day was a thoroughly enjoyable, unqualified success, due in large part to your enthusiasm, hard work and superb organization. I look forward to many more enjoyable outings." Soon it became clear that the controversy and coverage had achieved the desired effect. Glenn Jackson and the highway commission decided the issue was too hot to handle in the middle of a governor's campaign and announced on June 1 that it was reconsidering its decision. "It may be some time before we weigh all the factors and come up with the final answers," Jackson told Straub. He said there were conflicting issues involved and the commission wanted to do "what is right."[13]

What Straub and the public didn't know was that Glenn Jackson had already received a commitment from Tom McCall to support the Sand Spit route in return for his support in the Republican gubernatorial primary.[14] McCall, with his high, positive visibility as a television newsman, was popular among the general public. But his liberal politics could have made him vulnerable in the Republican primary.

Yet the tactical victory of the highway commission's postponement was powerful fuel for Straub's campaign. Even the normally Republican-leaning *Oregonian* newspaper editorially praised Straub's "agitation … and the support he has obtained for preserving scenic and recreational values," and warned its readers that "the reprieve doesn't mean that an asphalt and concrete noose will not finally be dropped on the Pacific City beach and the Nestucca outlet" unless "people all over Oregon make it known they want the beaches saved for recreation." Finally, and most pointedly, the *Oregonian* editorial noted: "No new final decision is likely until after the November elections. Mr. Straub, incidentally, is the Democratic nominee for Governor."[15]

Once again, as it had in the treasurer's race two years earlier, Straub's aggressive campaign style was impressing Oregonians and disturbing the sleep of Republican strategists. A month later, he demonstrated further that if Oregonians wanted change, he was the man to deliver it. Sitting down with the editorial board at the Eugene *Register-Guard* on July 21, he unveiled a plan for what he called "the Willamette River Rediscovered,"[16] later known as the Willamette River Greenway proposal. Under the editorial title, "A Dream Too Thrilling for Politics," the *Register-Guard* rhapsodized:

> One thing about State Treasurer Robert W. Straub: He's got imagination.
> Or, if you prefer, vision. His newest idea—getting as much Willamette River
> frontage into public hands as possible—is more than just commendable;
> it's great. And it shows that he's thinking about Oregon not so much as it is
> today as the way it's going to be 20 and more years hence.

Straub's long-standing effort, as state senator and then treasurer, to clean up the Willamette River had convinced him that a longer-term vision for the river was needed. As the *Register-Guard* described it, he knew that "Oregon already has two magnificent north-south recreational strips, the Cascade Skyline and the Oregon Coast." He threw out a challenge to the state: Why not create a third, and turn the festering sewer of the Willamette River into a conservation and recreational sanctuary right in the midst of Oregon's most heavily populated area?

The scale of Straub's proposal took Tom McCall completely by surprise. Even in later years, McCall could never get over his jealousy in not having thought up the idea first. He endorsed it immediately, but in public speeches throughout the campaign pointedly made incorrect reference to the idea coming from University of Oregon professor and noted conservationist, Karl Onthank, and insisted on this version for the rest of his life. In fact, Straub had first shared his idea with Onthank, as the professor readily acknowledged, and Onthank, in turn, had passed the idea along to McCall.[17] On the stump, both Straub and McCall embraced the new "Willamette Greenway" proposal and promised to begin the hard work of achieving it in the coming legislative session.

Even with all the momentum building from his many environmental ideas, Straub still wasn't making headway against McCall in the opinion polls. Tom McCall had been on Portland television and radio for over a decade. He was a beloved institution, with his florid prose and distinctive Bostonian accent. McCall's views were already similar to Straub's on the environment and nearly

Tom McCall speaks, while Bob Straub waits his turn. Photo by Gerry Lewin

everything else. He and his campaign knew that if they stuck close to Straub on the issues, the voters would see no reason to change their opinion about whom they would prefer as governor. With a sizable advantage in fundraising over Straub and time running short in the campaign, McCall's advisors knew that only a major slipup could tip the race in Straub's favor. They knew their high-strung candidate was capable of collapsing under pressure. Straub realized his only chance was to significantly outperform the eloquent McCall in his debates. This seemed a long shot, given Straub's history of speaking problems and McCall's experience.

Exercising great discipline, Straub thoroughly prepared for the fall debates and began outperforming McCall at joint appearances. McCall appeared rattled and nervous at times, and in one televised debate at KATU, Channel 2 in Portland, appeared to have had a couple of drinks. He was dressed in a white suit that washed out his color in the television lights, making him look pallid. After a painful half hour for McCall and his team, during which Straub verbally ran circles around him, the program took a pause for a station break. McCall press advisor Ron Schmidt gave the station manager a finger across the throat signal, and the manager, Tom Dargan, announced the taped debate was now finished, instead of continuing for the full hour originally scheduled. Once again, it proved helpful for McCall to have friends in the press.[18]

At the September 30 debate at the Portland City Club, a key debate that was also broadcast on radio, McCall floundered, while Straub was in top form. Not long after that, fearing Straub would challenge him to another debate, McCall called his former employer, KGW-TV, Channel 8 in Portland, to preemptively challenge Straub himself. Already into October, still holding a strong lead, this was the last thing McCall's campaign wanted. Ron Schmidt pressed Ed Westerdahl, who had been assigned to keeping McCall in line during the secretary of state race, into service. With no debate details negotiated, McCall disappeared. Neither Straub and his campaign nor KGW-TV officials could find him to pin him down. In fact, Westerdahl checked McCall into Portland's Imperial Hotel where they ate, watched television, played cards, and waited out the election. As McCall said later, "they had me chained to a bed for the rest of the campaign."[19]

Frustrated, Straub and his campaign could only continue their campaign without the potential "knock-out" debate and wait to see the election returns in November. As expected, McCall won handily. There was just too much ground to pick up on someone as well known with the public and popular with the media. But Straub and his staff were content with having run a good, hard race against the odds and having raised important issues. Straub knew there was much work to be done to improve Oregon's environment and believed he'd get another chance in four years, if McCall didn't achieve enough to merit another term.

He and his staff knew they were going to be following up with at least two of the major issues raised in the campaign—opposition to the beach highway and supporting the Willamette Greenway proposal. What they didn't know was that a hotelier in Cannon Beach by the name of William Hay was already precipitating an even greater crisis over public access and preservation of Oregon's beaches.

CHAPTER 7

From State Street to Wall Street

October: This is one of the peculiarly dangerous months to speculate in stocks in. The others are July, January, September, April, November, May, March, June, December, August and February.

—Mark Twain, *Pudd'nhead Wilson's Calendar for 1894*

With his unsuccessful 1966 race for governor behind him, and not content to merely serve as McCall's foil on environmental issues, Bob Straub vowed to make good on some unfinished business—his most far-reaching campaign promise from his 1964 race for state treasurer.

Straub resumed lobbying key Oregon legislators to help him create what he called the Oregon Investment Council, whose members would preside over the expansion of the state's financial capacity to include investment of state funds in the stock market and other potentially more profitable ventures. Straub had managed the state's short-term money much more profitably than past treasurers, and this track record gave him credibility with knowledgeable government leaders as he took his second crack on the long-term investment issue.[1]

During the first go 'round, in the 1965 session, Straub had taken his lumps from both sides—from the banks and the business establishment *and* from his more natural allies, the public sector workers, whose pension money he was hoping to invest more wisely. The public employee lobbyists, particularly Max Manchester, who directed Public Employees Retirement System (PERS) for twenty years, along with the Oregon Education Association, representing most of the state's public schoolteachers (many of whom were members of PERS), were skeptical of Straub's "takeover" plan and were pursuing their own investment schemes. Since World War II, Manchester had taken the PERS fund from zero to $200 million in assets. Local governments had created their own versions of pension funds, though by this time most of the smaller ones had merged with PERS. Larger funds were thought to be better able to manage their own affairs and stayed independent.[2]

Using Attorney General Robert Y. Thornton's 1964 opinion that the retirement system funds were not state money but were owned by state pensioners, Manchester and PERS had already initiated a fledgling equity market investment program, hiring an investment manager to run the program. Manchester disagreed with Straub that combining with other state funds in an investment account would be the best policy, even considering that increasing the clout and diversity could create a higher capacity fund. Manchester preferred controlling PERS funds without outside interference.[3]

To accommodate state workers and pensioners, Treasurer Straub modified his legislative draft to incorporate some control and self-determination by the PERS board. The modification would allow the PERS board to choose two of its representatives to be members of the five-member Oregon Investment Council. The governor, who appointed members of the PERS Board, would also *directly* appoint another two members to the investment council, while the state treasurer would serve as the fifth member. Straub intentionally designed the board to prevent himself or future treasurers from taking control, in order to prove he was not attempting a power grab. He truly believed that a diffused authority among five members would make it harder for the pet projects or connected investment interests of any one board member to prevail against the better judgment of the full board. Straub's unique investment vision for Oregon was the creation of an independent body that could hire the best private investment managers from throughout the country based upon their track records. Straub knew that, for the system to work, it needed to be completely independent from political pressure and devoted solely to what was then called the "prudent man" rule: that is, investing only as a prudent investor would with his or her own money. He committed the investment council to the rule by making it the primary requirement in the proposed law.[4]

As in 1965, the House of Representatives in 1967 was controlled by Republicans and the Senate by conservative Democrats not naturally sympathetic to the more liberal Straub. A key to success was to convince more conservative members of the legislature that this investment idea would save the state money and improve the performance of state workers' pensions. Straub knew that the House Ways and Means Committee chairman, Stafford Hansell (R-Hermiston), a hog farmer from northeastern Oregon, was well respected and influential. He decided to meet one-on-one with Representative Hansell and make his pitch before the legislative session started.

As noted earlier, Straub's excellent early track record of running the treasurer's office worked in his favor, helping convince skeptics to consider his ideas. He had significantly improved earnings on short-term funds. He retained Howard Belton's previous deputy state treasurer, Gordon Barker, and assigned him to set up a system to aggressively collect and deposit payments held by state agencies. "Sometimes I found that our agencies had collected large sums of money, even the revenue department," Straub remembered. "Checks worth sizable amounts of money wouldn't be cashed for three weeks or a month."[5] Straub and Deputy Barker were so effective at collecting and investing the state's money that at any given moment they would frequently have more than 100 percent collected and invested. How could they do that? By having state offices from around the state report by phone the amounts of their deposits to the treasury in Salem, Barker could invest the "float" from the banks—the period of time it took to record the deposit in one city and have it appear in the treasury's central account a few days later.[6]

In addition, Straub discovered when arriving at treasury that some of the state's short-term money was being kept in non-interest-bearing bank checking accounts.[7] State Treasurer Straub reduced non-interest-bearing cash balances within the state from 20 percent of available funds to less than 1 percent by the time he left office.[8] Overall, the *Oregon Voter* publication in 1966 claimed that Straub "doubled the productive efforts of the Treasurer's staff without adding new people or spending additional money." He had, in fact, cut his work force "by 9 percent," through natural attrition, during those first two years.[9]

Straub was beginning to turn some of his Republican doubters into believers, even those who found it hard to imagine this reputed "wild liberal" was fiscally responsible. Norma Paulus, who served as a Republican legislator in the 1970s and later as secretary of state, noted that her husband's uncle, Fred Paulus, a died-in-the-wool Republican and respected long-time employee at the state treasury, who had retired as deputy state treasurer just before Straub arrived, eventually became one of those believers.[10] For "Uncle Fred" this was a long journey, as he had been deeply offended by Straub's bumptious and belligerent campaign against Paulus' former boss, Howard Belton.

Though Fred Paulus generally approved of the new treasurer's vigorous and fiscally sound approach with the short-term funds, he found fault with Straub's decision to allocate interest earnings back to funds from which the invested money originated, rather than consolidating it in the state's General Fund for expenditure in the state budget. With former Governor Charles A. Sprague, a pillar of the Republican establishment, as his as chief petitioner, Paulus aggressively sought the court's clarification on this issue shortly after Straub took office in 1965. The Oregon State Supreme Court ruled partly in Straub's favor and partly in Paulus' on March 22nd of that year, "ordering that interest from statutorily created funds be paid into the general fund, but that interest from a common school fund, a highway fund, and a state board of higher education fund all [established under state constitutional authority] be paid back into the respective funds."[11]

However, Paulus had more than a quibble when it came to Straub's plan to create the Oregon Investment Council and shift a portion of state money from long-term funds to the stock market. He shared his view with legislators and anyone else who would listen and he wasn't alone in his skepticism. Even by 1967, memories from the 1929 stock market crash were still fresh, and Paulus had taken great care to maintain Oregon's good credit standing by steering clear of risky investment. "At the time, no one was investing in stocks," remembers Jim George, who was managing PERS investments at the time. "Stock dividends were beating returns, people were mostly investing for those. Frequently, dividends might be 3 percent."[12] Paulus was not only concerned about that, but there were specific clauses in the state constitution that, he believed, prohibited Oregon from investing in the stock market. He took his positions and issues up with Representative Hansell, just as Straub had done from the opposite perspective.

Stafford Hansell, who described himself as a simple pig farmer, was actually an extremely shrewd agri-businessman and an early adopter of enclosed pen, indoor factory farming. He listened closely to Straub's reasoning. Straub was able to convince him that, even though the stock market overall was flat at the time and had been for several years, clever investors who understood the market were getting excellent returns on their investments. What was different about Straub's approach to state investment was that he believed the state should be maximizing profit for its agencies and its beneficiaries just as a prudent person would with his or her own money. Straub believed it was immoral to treat the money he was responsible for in any other way. Hansell, after studying and reflecting upon the issue, decided to support Straub's legislation. He and Straub worked with the Legislative Fiscal Committee staff to prepare legislation in advance of the session, incorporating some safeguards to make the bill more palatable to nervous legislators, including setting an initial limit of 10 percent on the amount of available funds that could be invested in common stock.

Chairman Hansell arranged to have Straub's revolutionary investment plan introduced by the Ways and Means Committee as HB 1076 at the beginning of the 1967 Legislative Session. To deal with Fred Paulus's concerns about constitutionality, Straub agreed to have language added to the legislation that would require a state supreme court ruling that stock purchases were constitutional before any would be allowed to proceed. With Hansell's endorsement helping reassure Republicans and conservative Democrats and Straub addressing the unions' concerns by adding PERS board members to the investment council, the legislation steadily worked its way through the legislature, passing in the House on April 24 on a fifty-three to one vote, and on May 9, in the Senate on a vote of twenty-four to four.[13]

Still, one final hurdle remained—Governor Tom McCall and his veto pen. Before the session started, Max Manchester at PERS warned his newly hired investment manager, Jim George, that "this guy Straub in Salem has been trying to take over our investments, but McCall has been on retainer with us. He probably realizes he owes us."[14] McCall, who struggled with personal debt throughout his life, had moonlighted from his television work as a part-time writer and publicist for PERS before taking statewide office. Nevertheless, the overwhelming vote in favor made HB 1076 difficult for McCall to veto, despite pressure to do so and his own misgivings. The governor signed it on June 1, 1967.

Though it wasn't apparent at the time, this was quite possibly Bob Straub's most significant political victory. Under Straub's leadership, the State of Oregon was the first governmental body in the nation to create an investment strategy that would actively implement the "prudent man" rule through an appointed investment council, which hired financial companies to invest government money. Contracting with outside money managers was a brilliant innovation that had the added benefit of reducing startup costs, because it would have been extremely expensive to set up the high quality investment staff Straub would have insisted upon. Instead, he sought to hire the best people available in the private sector.

The new state investment program would yield huge benefits for Oregon state funding and for the future course of local and state government funding throughout the nation. "It was truly an amazing visionary piece of legislation," Straub's future investment officer James George said. "Twenty years later other states were still trying to get similar bills passed."[15] Even today, the investment head start that Straub's plan gave Oregon is a major reason why Oregon's PERS fund is the twenty-third largest public or private pension fund in the United States, and Oregon's State Accident Insurance Fund has some of the lowest rates in the country.[16]

Typically, Straub gave credit to others, "We couldn't have done it without Staff Hansell," Straub consistently told people in later years. "He was an independent thinker and was so well respected. When he came over to our side, we had it won."[17]

Governor McCall chose to temper Straub's plan by appointing the treasurer's *bête noire*, former Secretary of State Howell Appling, along with Don Ellis, the Chief Financial Officer of Tektronix, to the council. The two PERS board choices were Max Manchester himself and W. Park Stalnaker, retired president of Standard Insurance, an experienced investor and conservative Republican,[18] who had served on the Federal Reserve's Western Insurance Voluntary Credit Restraint Committee."[19] Thus, with skeptical experts on board, progress could be slowed on Straub's investment program while Fred Paulus organized a legal challenge to the new law.

Paulus continued to believe that the state constitution prohibited Straub and the investment council from investing state money in the stock market. Article XI, section 6, of the state constitution says "the state shall not subscribe to, or be interested in the stock of any company, association, or corporation, but as provided by law, may hold and dispose of stock ... that is donated or bequeathed." In addition, section 9 of Article XI more explicitly did not allow a local government in Oregon to "become a stockholder in any joint company, corporation or association, whatever."[20] Rather than wait for the Oregon Investment Council to petition the state supreme court for an opinion, as required by the new law, Paulus, once again, recruited former Governor Charles Sprague, the editor and publisher of the *Oregon Statesman* newspaper, to join him in a lawsuit against the treasurer, soon after the legislative session ended. Straub's brash campaign to unseat Treasurer Belton in 1964 had also "rubbed Sprague the wrong way." By 1966, Sprague was beginning to find common cause with Straub on the issue of beach conservation, but he was readily convinced by Paulus to lend his name to the lawsuit, which they filed in Marion County Circuit Court.[21]

Straub's counter argument, backed by Attorney General Robert Y. Thornton, was that the state and local funds collected for employee retirement, along with the policy money collected for the Industrial Accident Fund— later called the State Accident Insurance Fund, or SAIF—was money held in trust for the account holders and was not the state's money.[22]

Despite the lawsuit, State Treasurer Straub assembled the first Oregon Investment Council meeting in September of 1967. The PERS funds were now formally under the jurisdiction of the new council. Straub recommended that the council begin the process of evaluating potential investment companies. He also announced that he had hired one new staff member in August to conduct the research and assist the investment council in its decision making. Having already retained Republican holdover Gordon Barker as a deputy to handle day-to-day financial management and the state's bonding portfolio, Straub, at Max Manchester's recommendation, kept Jim George, who had been hired only eight months before by Manchester to coordinate the small PERS investment program, mostly purchasing bonds.

Not surprisingly, before Straub decided to keep him on, George had to interview again for the new job. The two job interviews, eight months apart, could not have been more dissimilar. When Jim George, a native Portlander, first applied at PERS in 1966, he was a young, struggling stockbroker at Blyth and Company, one of Portland's top investment companies in those days and the largest locally owned firm. That year, the market was so slow that only three million shares were traded on average each day nationwide. He was on commission, so "slow trading meant slow rewards," George recalls. Thinking he had better explore other prospects, he noticed an ad in the *Wall Street Journal* for the PERS position in Portland. The first interview with Manchester was a "three martini lunch" (typical for many businessmen of the day) in which they discussed bonds. Having passed that test, George was invited to Manchester's house for the final interview. This mostly consisted of all the vodka he could drink and orange juice. "Thanks to my good Greek heritage and ability to hold my liquor with him for two or three hours," says George, "he hired me. Manchester said, 'Here's the phone: call your wife and tell her I'm offering you the job.' He figured if I could dial the phone after that, then I could still function after one of our three martini lunches."[23]

Eight months later, Bob Straub handled Jim George's job interview a little differently. George met the state treasurer in his office in the State Capitol and "there were no social niceties," George remembers. "Straub was gruff and not very friendly—his time was important." Straub began the interview by telling the young man, "I'm not really sure I need help" in staffing the investment council. After they talked about what sorts of work George might do, and Straub spoke passionately about the investment issues he felt were important, George went away not knowing where he stood. Apparently he impressed the treasurer sufficiently that Straub's office called a couple of days later telling George that he had been hired at an equal rank with Deputy State Treasurer Gordon Barker and would have the title of chief investment officer, a job that George held until his retirement.[24]

George's initial task was to find out what other states were doing, sending letters to the state treasurers of the other forty-nine states, to help establish the program, assuming the courts would allow them to proceed. He also arranged for the meetings of the Oregon Investment Council, which were held as needed. The lunch meetings were short. "Bob saw to that," George recalls. "By the time dessert was served the meeting was over." Since George had no additional staff, he typed his own letters and the council's minutes on an electric typewriter. He also assisted Deputy State Treasurer Barker in purchasing bonds.

Slowly, as the months went by, the investment council began to work through its processes for hiring investment contractors. Once Max Manchester and Straub began working together, Manchester became quite supportive. He understood investments pretty well, though not as well as the treasurer, and Straub gained his trust. Surprisingly, Straub's former sparring partner, Howell Appling, got along well with Bob in his new council role. "I never recall Appling and Bob having a cross word," said Jim George. George also noted that McCall's other appointee, Don Ellis, "was a money man himself at Tektronix, and was very interested and knowledgeable about stock." Park Stalnaker, the other PERS representative, "was a sort of 1920s era, button-down-collar gentleman, very old school," according to George. Stalnaker, like the rest, was quite comfortable with the new investment program at this stage, because the legislature had limited the amount of investment to 10 percent of available funds. The new council believed the risks were manageable and was eager to move forward.[25]

Then on the 29th of July, 1968, Marion County Circuit Court Judge Val Sloper ruled in favor of Sprague and Paulus, declaring the "said Investment Council Act violates Article XI, Section 6, of the Oregon Constitution, insofar as it purports to authorize the investment of Public Employees Retirement Fund and the Industrial Accident Fund in corporate stocks." Judge Sloper wrote that "the entire Act is ... invalid and unconstitutional" and that Straub and the investment council were "hereby restrained and enjoined from investing state funds, or any part thereof, in corporate stocks ... and from contracting with any other person or persons to do so."[26]

Since the Investment Council Act already required that the state supreme court rule upon the law's validity, Straub and the council were anxious to appeal the decision to the higher court and get their final answer. According to Jim George, neither he, Straub, nor members of the investment council were too perturbed at losing in the lower court. "We all felt the judge made a mistake," George recalls. "We were pretty confident about it."[27]

Attorney General Robert Thornton, representing Treasurer Straub and the state law, immediately appealed to the Oregon Supreme Court. Oral arguments were made on November 13, 1968, with Assistant Attorney General Peter Herman arguing on behalf of the Attorney General and the appellants. Portland attorney Randall Kester represented Governor Sprague. With him on the brief before both the Marion County Circuit Court and the supreme court, besides the ubiquitous Fred Paulus, was a young up-and-coming, Harvard-educated attorney named Bill Rutherford. Ironically, Rutherford later served as state treasurer from 1984 to 1987.[28]

A little more than two months after formal arguments, on February 26, 1969, the Oregon State Supreme Court unanimously reversed the trial court's decree. The court "concluded, not without difficulty, that Article XI, §6 constitutes a general prohibition against the purchase of corporate stocks by the state of Oregon." However, the court also concluded that the PERS fund and the Industrial Accident Fund were funds held in trust, and that "the state has no beneficial interest of any part of these funds." Because the act only authorized the purchase of stock on behalf of the PERS and Industrial Accident Fund beneficiaries, such stock purchases were *not* constitutionally prohibited. Rejecting the plaintiffs' argument that "a constitutional prohibition intended to protect public moneys from the vagaries of the stock market ought to apply with even greater force to moneys held by the state or its agencies in a fiduciary capacity," the court concluded that "the fact that the fund which the state holds is administered as a part of a law which affects the public at large is not enough to make the fund 'public' and thus entitle it to protection."[29]

Bob Straub was finally free to put his plan into action. While the drama of the court battles unfolded, Straub, Jim George, and the investment council had continued preparing for the day they got confirmation from the court. George had been busy evaluating firms. Tossing aside some of the contract forms he had reviewed from corporate retirement funds that were as much as forty pages long, George and Straub created an evaluation form of less than two pages. It asked who the firm was, what their business consisted of, and how successful had they been at doing it. Once the form was completed, George began contacting companies from around the country and set up files on a large number. There was pressure to hire local banks and brokers to be the state's investment managers, but this didn't fit into Bob's "prudent man" vision. "We discovered that the investment talent wasn't in the banks," Jim George remembers. "They were making loans to businesses instead." But that didn't stop local banks from pressuring Straub to keep the state fund money in Oregon.[30]

George had to develop some knowledge of the national investment firms. "We had to rank those," George says, "and we found some consultants who could help us." The treasurer's office didn't have travel funds to go visit the most promising firms, which would have been ideal, but they "invited many of them" to visit. As news spread of the new investment fund opportunity, "many came uninvited to Salem to interview."[31] Oregon was poised to become one of four states investing in the stock market, but would be the only state hiring outside private firms to handle the investment funds. Straub planned to reward the best performing funds after the initial investments with an increased share of the state's contracts. While the firms earned relatively small management fees, on a graduated scale from one-eighth of one percent to one-half of one percent, "the power that a $42 million package" gave them in the market "is a hidden inducement."[32] Oregon's new program intrigued many of the top management firms in the country, who sent their emissaries to Salem.

Visitors to the treasurer's office from out of state often suffered a bit of culture shock when they saw the humble quarters for this vaunted new fund. Their contact, Jim George, didn't even have a private office. Deputy State Treasurer Gordon Barker merited a semi-private cubicle and a secretary. "The rest of us were out in this big room of desks left over from World War II, with a linoleum floor," George remembers. "When these guys would come in from New York wearing their blue suits, they'd look around and they'd say 'are you really the guy that's going to work on this contract?' They'd see me there with my tie on but no jacket, because no one wore jackets in the office and they'd be in these tailored suits and be looking around at this guy with a typewriter on his desk."[33]

The two guys next to Jim George in the room were cashiers. More than once he had visitors come in at the beginning of the month, which was payday, so there would be a long line of state employees from around the Capitol Mall to cash their paychecks at treasury. "The cashiers were in cages, like in the old western movies, with iron bars," George recalls, "and on those days a state policeman would stand guard. My desk was tucked in around behind the cashiers, and these guys from New York would take a look at this whole process and shake their heads and say, 'What the hell's going on here? This isn't like Wall Street at all.'"[34]

Straub's political aide, Deputy State Treasurer Ken Johnson, tells a similar story about a time when some "slick" Wall Street guys "in their Brooks Brothers suits" came in to see Bob Straub seeking a contract during the early days of the Oregon Investment Council. "Bob was wearing a blue work shirt and a string tie, with his bad hair cut from the barber college, and you could tell that they really underestimated him. They were thinking they could really put one over on this 'rube,'" Johnson said, "and they started by trying to explain their proposal in very simple terms, thinking he wouldn't understand, After listening for a short while, Bob's eyes got really focused and he started peppering them with questions about their business and I had to laugh at the shocked look on their faces, when they realized that this guy really knew what he was talking about."[35] Hearing that story, Jim George laughed and said, "They didn't understand that Bob had an MBA from an Ivy League school."[36]

On May 6, 1969, with their green light from the Oregon Supreme Court, nearly two years of accumulated research, and very careful analysis of the track records of the investment companies, Straub and the investment council announced the selection of three companies to begin Bob Straub's grand experiment with public investment in the stock market.

Business Editor Gerry Pratt's column on the front page of the *Oregonian's* business section, under the headline "Straub Boldly Moves in Buying of Stocks," began:

> *Oregon's 49-year-old State Treasurer Robert Straub has never been accused of being a conservative, in politics or in how he runs the state's money. This*

week Straub was in form in announcing that the State Investment Council has selected three firms to handle the purchase of stocks for the Oregon State Retirement Fund and the Industrial Accident Fund. "We hope to be buying stocks by July and to be fully invested by 1970," Straub said, following the announcement.[37]

The three firms Straub selected were Transamerica Investment Counselors, Inc., of Los Angeles, led by George Bjurman; Capital Guardian Trust Co., also of Los Angeles, led by Robert Kirby; and Fayez Sarofim Co. of Houston, an energy investment company led by the company's namesake. None of these companies were located in Oregon and, though they had no way of knowing it then, all three principals of these companies would prove themselves successful and remain investors of Oregon Investment Council funds for decades.[38]

The stock news for that Tuesday was a good omen, "finishing in the plus column, despite profit taking," with the Dow Jones Industrial Average closing at $862.06, "another high for the year" and up more than 5 percent total over the previous seven days.[39] But Straub kept expectations modest: "We hope to have the value of the dollars invested in this retirement fund keep pace with inflation so we can keep the purchasing power as high ten years from now as it is today."[40] The annual inflation rate for the previous year, 1966, had been 3.01 percent and prior to that it hadn't even broken 2 percent annually since 1958.[41] The PERS and IAF funds were already earning "about 4.5 per cent" annually despite the fact that a "large segment" of the state investments had been placed several years ago in more cautious long-term investments and was dragging down the average, so Straub's goal of beating inflation was cautious.[42]

"It is wrong to try to predict what will happen in the stock market in the future," Straub told the *Oregonian*. But he admitted they had compared the state fund performance over the previous two years with the market, and he couldn't help telling the reporter: "Our judgment is that, during the past five years, if we had these three firms that have been selected managing our money based upon the performance they have obtained, we would have enjoyed about a 15 per cent annual growth compounded." "That would have about doubled our money in five years," Straub added. An extra $42 million would have gone toward increased payout for the fifteen thousand state and local government retirees and improved the future pensions of the seventy-two thousand current employees, not to mention reducing the cost of insuring workers for the businesses contributing to the Industrial Accident Fund. If all went well, he hoped to go back to the legislature for permission to increase the amount of funds invested in the stock market beyond the original 10 percent.[43]

"It is very important to have clearly in mind that these kinds of values are not going to generate overnight," Straub cautioned. "In fact, the performance over the next five years may be negative. The only justification is on a long-term basis."

"It could be very exciting," he admitted, "if the market goes to hell." As *The Oregonian* summed it up: "Straub realizes his neck is out," but "the state in now in the game."[44]

CHAPTER 8

A Line in the Sand

The edge of the sea is a strange and beautiful place. All through the long history of Earth it has been an area of unrest where waves have broken heavily against the land, where the tides have pressed forward over the continents, receded and then returned. For no two successive days is the shoreline precisely the same. Not only do the tides advance and retreat in their eternal rhythms, but the level of the sea itself is never at rest ... Today a little more land may belong to the sea, tomorrow a little less. Always the edge of the sea remains an elusive and indefinable boundary.

—Rachel Carson, from "The Edge of the Sea," 1955

While Bob Straub was assembling his revolutionary plan to put state trust funds into the stock market, he continued to press the new governor, Tom McCall, on environmental issues, sparking controversy and enlivening Oregon political life. As the two men grappled with one another, they propelled Oregon's environmental movement forward at an increasingly rapid pace.

When Tom McCall was sworn in as governor in Salem in January of 1967, few people suspected that, due to the beachfront property claims of a Cannon Beach hotelier, they were directly in the path of a tsunami that would crash over and swamp the coming legislative session, forever changing the course and the nature of Oregon politics. From that point forward , it became gospel for successful politicians to promise to vigorously protect Oregon's natural beauty—and increasingly clear that an aroused public would organize itself to make certain that they made good on their promises. In the process, the rivalry between Tom McCall and Bob Straub would broaden and deepen as their creative competition for leadership pushed Oregon into the forefront of a growing national environmental movement.

January of 1967 meant the renewal of another season of state legislative government. Farmers, businessmen, retirees, and housewives from around the state gathered for the once-in-every-two-years ritual of representative governance favored by Oregonians since statehood in 1859. The governor's office, nearly always the leading force in the legislative agenda, had its set of pre-filed bills to pursue. Included on the governor's agenda, and important

Left to right: Secretary of State Clay Myers, Governor Tom McCall, Treasurer Bob Straub. Republicans McCall and Myers and Democrat Straub worked remarkably well together, serving as the state's board of control. Photo by Gerry Lewin

enough for Governor McCall to feature it in his inaugural address, was a piece of legislation later consolidated into House Bill 1601, which came to be known as the "Beach Bill." Its significance would dwarf the arguments over the beach highway, riveting the public's attention to the actions of the Oregon State Legislature, and raising direct citizen lobbying and correspondence to levels rarely, if ever, seen in Salem.

The summer before, during the height of the 1966 gubernatorial race between McCall and Straub, a young graduate student in biochemistry named Lawrence Bitte was in Cannon Beach, enjoying a relaxing weekend digging clams and exploring the beach with his family and assorted other relatives, as was their custom. Bitte's aunt came back to their beach house with an amazing story: she had tried to walk through an area of the dry sand beach in front of a rather nondescript motel and was told she was trespassing. It was then that she noticed that driftwood logs had been placed to form an informal fence, outlining a square in front of the Surfsand Motel. Larry Bitte went to see for himself and confirmed that her story was true. He was dumbfounded, having grown up in Oregon believing that the public had owned the beaches since the time of Governor Oswald West in the early 1900s.[1]

Bitte, an ornery cuss by nature, wouldn't accept this land claim at face value, so he drove up to Astoria to check with the county clerk's office about the Surfsand's land claim. It turned out that Mr. William Hay did indeed own title to the land in front of his motel down to the sea. Bitte learned that Oregon's 1911 law establishing the beaches as a state highway was limited to the wet sand portion of the beach, even though, by common practice, people had been using the dry sand up to the vegetation line without private permission since the pioneer days. Until the summer of 1966 in Cannon Beach, that is. It turned out that the Bitte family was not the first to come across this issue. That summer, several visitors to Cannon Beach complained to the state and various elected officials.[2] Larry Bitte wrote a letter to Secretary of State Tom McCall, understanding that it was likely McCall would be the next governor.[3] He never received a response to his letter, but Highway Commission Chairman Jackson and his Parks Superintendent Dave Talbot were already aware of the discrepancy between the perception of public ownership of the dry sand and the reality of private deeds claiming it. William Hay's challenge, which they heard about from several sources, alerted them to the need to get the ambiguities resolved with legislation.

Talbot learned about this problem at the beginning of his tenure. He writes: "Shortly after I took over as superintendent [in 1964], I received a letter from John Yeon [a renowned architect and preservationist] congratulating me. Almost as an aside, he said, 'Oh, and by the way, be sure and look into the myth of public beaches.'"[4] Talbot investigated and discovered that "about 30 miles of beach land had been sold section by section by 1913" when Governor Oswald West convinced the legislature to put the wet sands off limits as a state highway. There was already "development down on the beach in Lincoln City and a few other places."[5]

HB 1600 and 1601, cleverly drafted along the lines of a recent Texas law that recognized in statute that the public use of private beach land gave the public permanent rights for continued use of those lands, were introduced at the Highway Commission's request with incoming Governor McCall's vocal support. The bill recognized public access to the state's dry, sandy beaches up to the vegetation line, to be administered by the State Highway Commission. It was referred to the House Highway Committee, where it sat for a couple of months, mostly out of the public eye. In an era when computer database searches and a well-organized environmental lobby did not exist, it seems that State Treasurer Straub and his supporters lost track of the Beach Bill legislation and may not have understood its significance.[6] In any case, Straub was absorbed with his efforts to change state investment policy and promote a strong Willamette Greenway bill.

At the Beach Bill's first hearing, on March 7, State Park Advisory Committee Chairman Loran "Stub" Stewart, the well-known principal of the large family-owned Bohemia Lumber company, who was also an avid advocate for state parks, urged quick passage of the bill to avoid the problem Californians faced in losing access to miles of coast line due to private development and beach fencing. We have "the finest beach recreation areas in the nation," Stewart claimed, and we must avoid the "impossible ... situation in California."[7]

The House Highway Committee, heavily stacked with business and private property-oriented Republicans and conservative Democrats from the coast, was much more sympathetic to the testimony presented by property owners and business lobbyists, who opposed the bill.

While the Beach Bill was quietly languishing , Governor McCall was trying to make good on his promise to create the Willamette River Greenway— turning his campaign "platitudes into reality … in a way that would not redound too much to the credit of his erstwhile rival," while still enlisting Straub's help and support.[8] Dave Talbot, state parks director at the time, remembers it like this: "I was asked to meet with Governor-elect McCall and Commission Chairman Glenn Jackson right after the election in McCall's secretary of state office in the Capitol. McCall was a little worried and said to Jackson, 'Gee, Glenn, I made this commitment during the campaign to support the Willamette River Greenway plan; what am I going to do now?' He had won the election, now it was time to follow through."[9]

In contrast to Straub's detailed plans for a "continuous greenway on either side of the river, complete with bicycle trails you could ride from Eugene to Portland,"[10] McCall's ideas were much less defined. Jackson and McCall agreed that a plan needed to be brought before the legislature. "McCall said, 'Who's going to do the plan?' to which Jackson replied, 'He is,' pointing at me," Talbot remembers.[11]

Talbot created the Willamette Greenway Task Force with volunteer experts and recreation planners who helped determine the extent of the greenway and the options for developing it. According to Talbot, "they left their jobs, lived in Salem, and put together a crash plan."[12] They were assisted in the effort by a steering committee of citizens led by University of Oregon Professor Karl Onthank, whom McCall credited, rather than Straub, with conceiving the greenway idea in the first place. The task force developed a paper demonstrating the need for the greenway and outlining some of the problems the state would encounter in creating it.[13]

In his January 9, 1967, inaugural address, McCall reiterated his support for the Willamette Greenway and announced he expected to have a plan to submit to the legislature by March 1. Talbot's task force was replaced by an executive order creating a broader, more formal Willamette Recreational and Greenway Committee, beginning a public discussion of how it should be implemented. At the new committee's first meeting, its membership quickly divided into two camps: one with a more aggressive approach and the other favoring a "soft sell," intended to keep conservatives and opponents in the farming community at bay. Naturally, Bob Straub, who was actively monitoring the work of the committee, favored the more muscular position, while McCall's sympathies were more in line with the incremental tactics. As would also be expected, the governor's approach prevailed.[14]

The overall plan had six elements: 1) a system of camps along the river (some accessible only by boat or on foot); 2) a series of boat launches and picnic areas accessible by automobile; 3) a network of recreational trails; 4) a system of scenic drives along some portions of the river; 5) several large tracts to be used for a variety of recreational activities; and 6) a conservation easement system to maintain the beauty of riverbanks in the areas not set aside for recreation and trail development. In line with McCall's wishes, the final report of the committee called for enabling legislation, but not for major financing from the legislature. Reflecting the bipartisan compromise involved in creating the plan, Straub took part in the formal dinner announcing the plan and was allowed to explain it to the assembled supporters and members of the press.[15] An advocacy group, the Willamette Greenway Association, was founded by the participants of the dinner to promote the new proposal. Reflecting favorable press coverage statewide, the *Oregon City Enterprise-Courier* opined: "It behooves us as individuals and as communities to support this project wholeheartedly and without stint."[16] It seemed the plan had a great deal of momentum.

Such an auspicious beginning didn't prepare Straub and McCall for the trouble they encountered in the legislative process. The greenway proposal was packaged in three bills: House Bill 1770, the basic implementing legislation, which set out the purpose and description of the Willamette River Greenway and allocated $800,000 to get it started; House Bill 1581, which established the rules defining the scenic easements that were part of the greenway plan; and Senate Joint Resolution 33, which would refer a $10 million bond issue to the voters to finance land purchase for greenway parks and camp grounds.

SJR 33, the bond measure, was in immediate trouble because, though Straub and his supporters heavily favored it and the need was clear, some within the pro-greenway camp felt it was premature to ask the voters for funding, fearing that a rejection might kill the proposal altogether. Onthank was among those skeptical of the value of the referendum. He suggested earmarking a one-cent-per-gallon state gas tax increase, an approach he felt would raise as much money without alienating as many people.[17] In the end, neither idea found favor with the legislature and no major funding plan passed.

HB 1581, the scenic easement legislation, was even more controversial. A number of Willamette Valley farmers were alarmed by the idea, in their worst case scenarios, of hordes of hippies floating down the river and landing on their farm property for orgies and pot-smoking parties, while wreaking havoc with their crops and water-intake systems. These farmers were generally concerned about the entire greenway plan, but the idea of the state acquiring even scenic conservation easements on their riverfront property made them furious. And it was not merely fear of trespass and vandalism that was of concern. Many farmers looked at the development potential of these lands for future high-value housing or some commercial activity as their retirement nest egg, and were outspoken about this value to them. HB 1581 did eventually pass, but required that any easement established must be purchased from a willing seller. Furthermore, such easements were limited to scenic conservation and did not enable the state to create trails, boat launching access, or picnic or camping spots. "It was not at all what Straub had envisioned," Dave Talbot remembers.[18]

HB 1770, the bill establishing the greenway concept, also passed, but similarly would not allow the state to condemn land for parks and did not authorize the originally envisioned trail system. The $800,000 funding authorization remained in the bill as a matching fund with local governments to buy land for the greenway over the next two years.

In the aftermath of this rather tentative start to the bold greenway proposal, the McCall-Straub rivalry flared as each man interpreted the results. McCall declared it was "more than just getting the camel's nose under the tent" and would give greenway advocates a start toward implementing their plan. Straub believed, and wasn't shy about saying it, that McCall hadn't pressed the legislature hard enough to enact the plan in its original form.[19] Later, in his autobiography, McCall blamed Straub's aggressiveness for the failure to make more progress in the 1967 legislature, describing having mollified the farmers through a series of meetings until "Bob Straub came in and jibed at us about what a puny effort we were making. His bull-in-the-china-shop approach turned the farmers against the Greenway. Instead of the moderate procedure we had followed, there was this setback."[20] Long-time Straub supporter and environmental advocate Janet McLennan remembered it a little differently. "The farmers were against the idea of the greenway from the get-go," she recalled, "and to try to get around their opposition, McCall and his allies decided to establish voluntary scenic conservation easements, which was a new and unproven method for preserving scenic beauty. The farmers had legitimate concerns about vandalism and crop theft that were hard to solve," McLennan continued. "To the extent that McCall placated the farmers, it was with the promise that no one would be allowed to condemn their lands. Of course, scenic conservation easements gave no right to use the land, which took away the idea of a trail network or abundant river access from the start."[21]

While the Willamette Greenway legislation wound its way slowly toward compromise, Lawrence Bitte, the self-appointed citizen activist, began to worry that the Beach Bill seemed to be stuck in the House Highway Committee. He had been following its progress in the newspaper but hadn't seen anything in quite a while. On the morning of May 2, "I got a hold of [Committee Chairman] Sid Bazett and he said, 'I'm holding the last hearing I can today. There's no interest in this.'"[22] Bitte had an exam that day as part of his doctoral studies at the University of Oregon Medical School in Portland (now Oregon Health and Sciences University) and could not leave for a hearing in Salem. He immediately went to the office of Robert Bacon, an M.D. who was also a trained marine biologist and was known to be an ardent environmentalist. Bob Bacon was so passionate about his "hobby" of marine studies that he and two colleagues had created a laboratory at his beach cabin in Depoe Bay, studying sea urchins and other sea creatures on weekends and whenever they had free time.[23]

Like most Oregonians, Bacon had not yet heard about the beach controversy, but when Larry Bitte brought him up to date the ordinarily mild-mannered academic was "enraged to hear about this threat to beach access." Dr. Bacon explained later. "I came from New Jersey and I used to have to put a coin into a gate to get to a beach. The coast over there was mostly unavailable and Oregon's beaches were one of the main reasons I chose to stay here," instead of taking more academically prestigious jobs elsewhere.[24] Bacon decided to jump in his car and drive to the state Capitol with Bitte's wife, Diane, to attend the hearing. They did not know the bill number or what time the hearing was to be held; they arrived just before noon and went to the legislative bill room and asked the clerk if there was anything regarding beaches on the docket. The woman at the desk told them no, after looking in the index under beaches and other possible headings. The actual title of the legislation, "Concerning public rights and lands," and its vague description didn't lend themselves to intuitive index searching.[25]

Overhearing the conversation, another worker in the back of the room piped up, saying, "I think there is a bill like that but they just finished the last hearing on it. The chairman of the committee might still be in the hearing room." Dr. Bacon and Diane Bitte rushed up to the hearing room and found it empty except for Representative Sidney Bazett, chairman of the House Highway Committee, quietly reading and writing at the front table reserved for committee members. Bazett was delighted to meet Bacon and Bitte, exclaiming: "I have been hoping some members of the public would attend these hearings—you are the first to show up."[26] Representative Bazett explained that the committee had just agreed to table the Beach Bill, which in Oregon legislative parlance means to kill a bill by agreeing not to use any more committee time to discuss or vote on it.[27] When the rest of the House

Highway Committee and assorted Capitol lobbyists returned to the hearing room after lunch, Chairman Bazett announced that citizens still wanted to testify on the Beach Bill and that he intended to hold another hearing the following week. He asked Dr. Bacon and Diane Bitte to stand up in the back of the room to be introduced. The lobbyists, many of them representing private property owners, turned around to look at them with baleful eyes.[28] "It was obvious they didn't like what they heard, to say the least," Bacon dryly observed later.[29] They were, no doubt, less than thrilled by the prospect of having to revisit an issue they thought they had already resolved in their clients' favor.

Sitting in the back of the hearing room, also, was an Associated Press reporter named Matt Kramer, who had been consistently writing stories about the bill's progress during the legislative session. He had coined the name, the "Beach Bill," and seemed to sense its importance before the other Capitol-based reporters. Kramer filed an article that night, quoting Representative Sid Bazett almost imploring citizens to come to Salem to voice their opinions on the bill. Building upon previous articles he had written, this story, which began, "Beach goers joined the battle for the Oregon beaches Tuesday—and lost," showed that the bill was nearly dead without additional citizen support.[30] The article, since it was an AP wire service story, was published the following day in nearly every newspaper in Oregon. Subsequent articles by Kramer and other reporters at Oregon's major dailies suddenly began to grab the attention of Oregonians throughout the state, and editorial writers magnified the story, assisted by State Treasurer Straub and by Governor McCall, who again weighed in on the issue.

Predictably, Bob Straub took a hard line.[31] He already had credibility in many circles as a passionate champion of Oregon's pristine beaches. At a May 5 press conference held in the treasurer's office in the state Capitol shortly after Matt Kramer's story broke, he forcefully exhorted the legislature:

> *The public playground area is on the dry sands area of the beach and this is what's being threatened by a few, by a very few, commercial developers down on the coast. We are at a crossroads in Oregon in regards to our beaches, and if the legislature turns its back on passing this needed legislation you won't recognize the Oregon coast four years from now.[32]*

Straub had good reason to believe this statement was not hyperbole. In addition to Hay's claim in Cannon Beach, at least four other projects were already moving forward rapidly, threatening Oregon's beach land: 20,000 yards of sand had been scooped up in front of Proposal Rock in Neskowin by a sand and gravel company; a massive new development, Pacific Riviera, was planned for a dry sand area along the mouth of the Necanicum River in Seaside; a property owner had begun building a road on the beach north of Neskowin; and pilings were already being pounded into the dry sand to stabilize the foundation of a new cliff-side hotel, The Inn at Spanish Head, in Lincoln City.[33]

McCall was equally forceful and, as a governor with press friendships going back decades, gained even more publicity for the cause. McCall had been in quiet support of the Beach Bill all along, his administration having introduced it in the first place. He was extremely irritated that House Republicans, led by Majority Leader and future Congressman Bob Smith of Burns, had stifled the bill. Cleverly, by prior arrangement, McCall wrote Chairman Bazett a stern letter, dated May 4, which the governor really aimed at the House leadership by leaking it to the press, saying "We cannot afford to ignore our responsibility to the public of this state for protecting the dry sands from the encroachment of crass commercialism." McCall's letter made front-page headlines and led the newscasts throughout Oregon, raising the visibility of the beach issue, and the political stakes.[34]

As if this letter from their fellow Republican governor did not bring enough public focus on the House Republicans' handling of the Beach Bill, a rare, incendiary television editorial from Portland's NBC affiliate, KGW-TV, two days before the next hearing, landed like a Molotov cocktail in the middle of the House Republican Caucus. KGW's General Manager Ancil Payne began his May 9 message with the ominous statement that "we well may lose our rights to freely use the beaches of our Oregon coast." Payne outlined a dismal future in which "fences and barriers bar you and your children from the present easy access to the water and clutter up and divide the beaches, ruining the magnificent view and penning up the people." Describing the Beach Bill as guaranteeing public access to beaches, Payne asserted, "There is no room for compromise in this simple bill, unless this is what you want your beaches to become," as artist-drawn fence lines down to the water's edge suddenly appeared on the screen, superimposed upon a beautiful photograph of iconic Cannon Beach near Haystack Rock. Payne capped his powerful statement with a call to action: "Do you want to save your beaches? You have but a few hours in which to act. The Highway Committee will meet in Salem Thursday afternoon. Attend that meeting or at least let your legislators know by letter, telephone, or telegram that you're angry about this and want House Bill 1601 passed with no compromise, no flimflam and no tricks," repeating the message again and giving viewers the address for letters and telegrams.[35] In an era in which local broadcast television news was respected and faithfully watched by many, this was powerful stuff.

Legislators in Salem were inundated with thousands of letters, telegrams, and phone calls. On May 11, not only Dr. Bacon and the Bittes but other conservationists and concerned citizens from throughout the state showed up and brought their friends to the hearing, overflowing the hearing room.

The politics of the Beach Bill were topsy-turvy, with Democrats and Republicans taking both sides of the issue. Certainly, the more conservative members—many of whom were Republicans, but including some coastal Democrats such as Clatsop County's Representative Bill Holmstrom, who was closely linked to developers in Seaside—were suspicious of legislation that appeared to roll back private property rights.[36] The battle lines were similar to those drawn in the fight over the Willamette Greenway proposal. Representative Paul Hanneman, R-Tillamook County (brother-in-law to Straub's office manager, Barbara Hanneman), who served on the Highway Committee, bemoaned the potential loss by private owners of their property rights, while they "retain the right to pay the taxes and the title." He opposed the bill and demanded that it at least be "amended to provide some compensation." But the public beaches issue touched a nerve with Oregonians of all stripes. "I don't know of any other issue that could ever raise Oregonians like that one did," Federal Circuit Court Judge Jim Redden observed later. Redden, who was a state representative from Medford during the 1967 session, remembers that "people who never even went to the coast were strongly for or against, but overwhelmingly for" the Beach Bill. According to Bob Bacon, "Sid Bazett came into the hearings with bushel baskets filled with letters and telegrams—somewhere between thirty and thirty-five thousand letters and telegrams. That was the largest public response to any legislative issue ever."[37]

On this issue, unlike the Greenway proposal, notable conservatives, such as Representative Sid Bazett himself—a Republican retired banker from Grants Pass—favored the traditional protection of Oregon citizens' "right" to enjoy the beaches, including the dry sands, whether or not private landowners had clear title to it. In reality, Bazett was not a typical small-town banker—he had been a San Francisco Bay-area financier and owner of an iconic house designed by Frank Lloyd Wright, among other things, in his peripatetic life prior to retiring in southern Oregon.[38] As committee chairman in the Republican-controlled House of Representatives, he was a critically important ally. "If he hadn't been willing to hold more hearings when no one else was paying attention to it, it would have been the end of the whole thing—no question," Bacon observed. The alliance of liberal public rights advocates with the businessman Bazett, mused Floyd McKay, who was then a political reporter, working at the Capitol for the *Oregon Statesman* newspaper, "was kind of a strange combination, and as a reporter, it was delightful to watch it unfold."[39]

Bob Bacon and Larry Bitte, though neither had any political experience, formed a new organization, Citizens to Save Oregon's Beaches (CSOBs for short), along with a few of their new-found friends, including long-time left-wing labor organizer and professional curmudgeon Ken Fitzgerald, who helped them learn the political ropes. They threatened to file an initiative petition if the legislature did not act favorably on the Beach Bill. Attempting to keep connections with both political camps, they decided to have Bacon, a Republican, and Bitte, a Democrat, serve as liaisons to McCall and Straub, respectively. Governor McCall quickly adopted Bacon as one of his unofficial advisors, while Bitte's relationship with Straub proved a little more problematic, particularly as the CSOBs' and Straub's views on the beach issue began to differ over time.[40]

With all this pressure from the public and the state's political leaders, state legislators "knew that they had to pass a bill," Jim Redden said. The devil was in the details. The Highway Commission's original language called for public access up to the vegetation line, but, as Representative Paul Hanneman warned, "it is going to be a problem in the courts to determine where a vegetation line is on the coast and beachfront property owners and those involved are fearful of that description." "Amendments were flying all over the place," remembers Bob Bacon.[41] Most of them attempted to set some arbitrary line at a set distance from the beach at high tide, within which the public would have the right to frolic, or in the colder months, walk along and shiver, as it traditionally had for generations.

Majority Leader Robert Smith proposed a boundary line of seven feet above sea level. This proposal infuriated Beach Bill proponents, as it put the boundary line closer to the sea than current law, giving away access to land already claimed by the legislature in 1913.[42] This proposal was ridiculed in the press. House Speaker F. F. "Monte" Montgomery proposed a compromise boundary line between public and private use at 200 feet above the normal high tide line. This plan also, in most places, would remove land traditionally used by the public from public use. Bob Straub, appearing before the Highway Committee Hearing on May 11, deemed the Montgomery plan "a real sell-out of the public right to enjoyment of the beach" and "the most scandalous giveaway of public rights in this country."[43]

Then on Saturday, May 13, 1967, Tom McCall with perfect newsman instincts, created the ideal photo opportunity, in time for a spread in the Sunday *Oregonian*, that helped bring the beach controversy in the legislature to a conclusion favored by the majority of Oregonians. Legend has it that he and his brilliant press secretary, Ron Schmidt, organized a helicopter tour of three sites on the north coast, bringing scientists from Oregon State University, legislators, and, especially, the press along with him. Measuring the effects of different heights from sea level, McCall appeared vindicated that the 16-foot level his advisors had urged him to support was approximately the level of the vegetation line named as the boundary to public access in the original bill. In Cannon Beach, one of the helicopter stops, McCall made sure to be photographed glaring defiantly across the log barricade erected by William Hay to protect his "private beach" in front of the Surfsand Motel. The entire day's events were a media grand slam, though not entirely choreographed as everyone assumed. In fact, filmmaker Tom Olsen recently discovered in interviewing a helicopter pilot who flew McCall that day that the pilots' participation was unplanned—they were on the beach when McCall arrived, invited him for a ride to the next stop on the tour, and the governor, the consummate ad-libber, hopped aboard.[44]

Straub was upstaged, but he appreciated that McCall's ploy was good for the cause he supported. "It was good theatrics and it was constructive as well," remembers long-time Straub associate Janet McLennan.[45]

Back in Salem, Highway Commission Chairman Glenn Jackson quietly strong-armed reluctant conservatives with not-so-subtle threats about future road projects. When asked why he switched his vote, Representative Bill Holmstrom told colleagues, "Glenn explained it to me."[46]

The House leadership was grateful for a solution when Representative Redden (D-Medford) and Representative Lee Johnson (R-Portland) pieced together a compromise preserving public access, and acceptable to all sides. Redden adjusted the language to reflect zoning restrictions "like you do in every city and every town and every suburb." As owners "you give up some of your rights to your property because it is zoned to prevent the property from going down hill."[47] The compromise also relieved property owners of liability for taxes or personal injury on their beachfronts, removing another stumbling block. Because the 16-foot designation was acknowledged as a rough estimate of the natural vegetation line, the bill now was written to be temporary until Highway Department engineers and OSU scientists had a chance to survey the entire coastline and establish the official property demarcations for the legislature to approve when they next met in 1969.

In one final bit of wheeling and dealing, the new bill allowed property owners a waiver procedure through the Highway Commission. As soon as the legislative session was completed, Glenn Jackson and the Highway Commission exempted the Inn at Spanish Head condominium project from the new law, allowing the cliffside development to build its foundation on what would have been a protected dry sand public area. Perhaps coincidentally, Peter Gunnar, a former long-time chairman of the state Republican Party, owned the multi-million dollar Spanish Head project.

With 'i's dotted and 't's crossed, the Beach Bill, as amended, sailed through the House by a fifty-seven to three vote and passed the Senate unanimously. On July 6, Governor McCall signed the bill, declaring it "one of the most far-reaching measures of its kind enacted by any legislative body in the nation."[48] But some people, including Bob Straub, felt the legislation didn't go far enough in protecting the ecology of the oceanfront by setting no limit on development overlooking the beach all along the coast. Lurking in the language, and soon to be before the Oregon courts, were fundamental questions about what, if any, rights the public actually had on these dry sand beaches.

The Beach Bill avowed that "over the years, the public has made frequent and uninterrupted use of the ocean shore and ... further, that where such use has been legally sufficient to create rights or easements in the public through dedication, prescription, grant or otherwise, that it is in the public interest to protect and preserve such public rights or easements as a permanent part of Oregon's recreational resources." Popular wishful thinking had the public owning these lands, but this was not yet legally established in the courts. The legislation left dangling such questions as: When and where had frequent and uninterrupted use of that ocean shore been legally sufficient to create rights or easement in the public? Are these rights of total or partial public ownership in some or all of these lands? Are these merely rights for some, or all members of the public, to use some or all of these lands for recreation, for some specific or perpetual future time?[49] No one doubted that answers to these and a myriad of associated legal questions would eventually be found in at least several and possibly a long continuum of court decisions.

The legislation's reference to "dedication, prescription, grant or otherwise" only hinted at the substantial variety of complex and arcane English Common Law doctrines, translated in a somewhat hit-or-miss fashion into the real property law of the different American states, which might be applicable to Oregon's beaches.[50] Among the dozens, if not hundreds, of lawyers involved in the Beach Bill controversy, were partisans for many different theories of how the public's rights might be best protected and magnified, or how the upland owners' rights might be best buttressed against massive and continual trespass.

Many of the lawyers advising Bob Straub feared that despite the Oregon public's historic use, courts when interpreting the new act would rule that the new law amounted to a "taking" of property rights, which would require owners to be compensated, either for loss of a portion of their lands the deeds of which went down to high tide line (and, in some cases, further) or for loss of the exclusive use of a portion of their lands.[51] Moreover, it was entirely possible that the legislation might give rise to a long string of upland owner lawsuits, reflecting somewhat different fact situations and initially litigated in different county courts. If not generally, certainly in some specific cases, highly desirable lands might only be secured by cash purchase. Along some portions of the shore, early deeds had granted title to low tide, and this further confounded achieving the goal of free public use of the beaches. Bob Straub was more bemused than caught up in the hours of legal strategizing and hypothesizing, but he recognized and took seriously the threat the lawyers identified, and moreover, he was concerned that the legislation didn't go far enough in protecting the ecology of the oceanfront.[52] It provided no tools for limiting development overlooking the beach, adding new parklands, or acquiring from upland owners needed access easements, so that the public might more readily get to the beach. And obviously, the legislation was only that; its protections could be amended or even abrogated by future legislatures. Whatever public rights the courts eventually confirmed, or the state otherwise acquired, could best be protected in perpetuity by inclusion in the Oregon Constitution, which no legislature could disturb without a vote of the people.

Straub met with conservation-minded supporters and began discussing how to proceed. They believed that the easiest and most democratic way to create land-purchasing legislation was to skip the legislature altogether and gather signatures for a ballot measure to be put to the voters in November 1968. Straub remembered Karl Onthank's idea of levying a penny a gallon gas tax to pay for parks on the Willamette Greenway. At first he proposed that the gas tax could be expanded to include both the Greenway and land purchases on the coast. The Greenway portion was later dropped as being too ambitious and costly for a short-term one-cent tax, and possibly too confusing to voters if combined with the more popular beach access issue. Straub estimated that the penny a gallon tax for four years would raise enough money to acquire beach lands and interests (such as easements) in land the courts might find not to be in state ownership. Unlike the Greenway situation, where he recognized the need for full compensation, Straub believed the public had existing rights to use the beaches, but he simply did not know what the courts would decide, and sought to guarantee the outcome of the issue by preparing for a court decision contrary to his hopes. Straub's initiative was designed to use any extra money, beyond what might be required to protect the public's existing beach access and use, for acquiring access to the beach, protecting key estuaries, and adding new parks, particularly along the southern coast, where there were fewer.

The Bob Bacon-Ken Fitzgerald-Larry Bitte group, Citizens to Save Oregon's Beaches (CSOBs), had studied the legal issues as well, and had a different take on the results of the legislature's Beach Bill. They were comfortable with the popular notion that the public owned these dry sand areas or at least prescriptive easements to use them, through the doctrine of adverse possession, and agreed with Governor McCall that it wouldn't be necessary to purchase what they thought Oregon owned. They disagreed with Straub and his supporters that any compensation money needed to be raised or ought to be paid to property owners, and they didn't find enough value in purchasing additional park land and access points through what they feared would be an unpopular tax. The CSOBs were drafting an alternative ballot measure whose purpose was to lock the legislative beach use and access laws into the state constitution.

While the Beach Bill coalition was beginning to show fissures and Straub and his allies contemplated next steps, another front in Oregon's "sand wars" reopened. Glenn Jackson and the engineers at the Highway Department had not forgotten, but merely postponed, their plans for a bridge and a highway up the narrow Nestucca Sand Spit through Pacific City. Jackson was biding his time until after the legislative session to approve it and begin work. The Beach Bill helped his argument by defining the narrow tuft of vegetation along the spine of the sand spit as outside the public beach area and, thus, perfectly appropriate for a new highway.[53] On July 7, Jackson convened the Highway Commission in Pacific City to reaffirm their support for the Nestucca Spit route for Highway 101. Straub was livid, attacking Jackson and McCall for supporting this route along the beach so soon after the Beach Bill controversy. He found a lot of sympathy in the public and the media, much to the embarrassment of the governor.

Then, Straub and the highway opponents noticed a flaw in the Highway Department's plans. Land ceded to the state by the federal Bureau of Land Management would be crossed in two places by the highway on the sand spit. This land had been given to the state with the proviso that it would be used for recreational purposes, that is, to create a state park. Could the Department of Interior, which manages BLM lands, be convinced that rerouting Highway 101 over these lands was a violation of the agreement? If so, the lands would revert to the federal government, blocking the road.

Secretary of Interior Stewart Udall was a lanky Arizonan of Mormon pioneer ancestry, with a love for the wild natural areas of the West. As secretary during the Kennedy and Johnson administrations, Udall, a former Arizona congressman, was a key link to the growing conservation movement. He was widely acknowledged as an early leader, completing his "call to arms" book on the need for stronger anti-pollution laws and the preservation of natural areas, *The Quiet Crisis*, in 1963, while a sitting cabinet secretary. In his book and through his actions as interior secretary, Udall found common cause with the land, air, and water conservation beliefs of Oregonians like Straub.

Straub got in touch with Stewart Udall through Senator Wayne Morse, who asked Udall if he would meet with Straub when the state treasurer was in the east signing state bonds in New York City in July. The curious practice of bond signing, which continues to this day, requires that bonds must be signed in person on massive contraptions allowing for multiple pens to work at once. It is cheaper to bring the treasurer to the bonds than to bring the bonds (and the contraption) to the treasurer, so Straub was able to go to the east coast from time to time and build many useful contacts in the financial and political worlds. He was careful to cover his own expenses for all activities not related to his bond-signing duties.

According to Morse, no doubt reflecting the influence of Morse's political ally Glenn Jackson, Udall thought it was strange to take up the secretary of interior's time with something as small as a highway route in Oregon, but he agreed to meet Straub. Straub did not know it, but he would have been better off without Morse's introduction, as the interior secretary did not much care for Oregon's senior senator.[54] When State Treasurer Straub met Secretary Udall on that July afternoon, the two hit it off right away. Both men shared a love of nature and Udall felt Straub's passion for the Oregon coast. He agreed that he would do his part to stop the highway.

Delivering on Udall's promise, in late August 1967 the Department of the Interior issued an order that "disapproved the application of the Oregon State Highway engineer for a variance to permit highway construction through the Nestucca Sandspit area in Pacific City, Oregon … which was vested to the State of Oregon exclusively for outdoor recreation purposes." Udall issued a press release announcing his decision and Governor McCall received the letter the next day. McCall complained bitterly to Udall. "You could have shown me the courtesy of informing me personally, rather than through the press," he fumed. In a letter to McCall, which he also released to the press, Udall wrote: "Quite frankly, it is my opinion that your aides have given you bum advice on this question. The old argument by highway engineers that it is 'cheaper' to route a road through a beach or a public park was always outrageous from a conservation standpoint … If the new route costs a little more, so what? In our time a wise resource use demands that we always search for the best solution for the long run—and never settle simply for the cheapest solution."[55]

Secretary Udall commented later "that was kind of a weird issue, kind of out of character for Tom." Udall had "worked with Tom McCall on conservation projects and liked him very much. He wanted to have a trail downriver all the way to Portland [the Willamette Greenway]. We matched $1 million to $5 million put up by the state to get it started. Bob Straub was cut out of the same cloth." Regarding the decision on the beach highway, Udall said, "I was always on the side of preservation. It was my bias and it was a strong bias."[56] McCall had never been comfortable in his bargain with Glenn Jackson, so, though irritated at being outflanked by Straub, he was also a bit relieved to be done with the issue, or so he thought. He issued a statement that the controversy was finished and that an alternative inland route would be pursued. "If I ever catch a highway engineer looking even cross-eyed at a sand spit, there will be the devil to pay," he told the press, ruefully.[57]

With this supposed victory in hand, Straub and his allies convened a meeting in August to discuss what would be the best next steps in preserving the state's beaches for ecological and public enjoyment purposes. Seven hundred people attended the gathering on the Portland State College campus and agreed to form a new group, the Committee to Save the Beaches, centering on Straub's proposal for a ballot initiative.

No one realized that Jackson and the state engineers weren't ready to quit fighting for the beach highway just yet. Though there is no sign of any personal financial interest, Glenn Jackson was a man who had never lost on a political issue. His reputation depended upon his invincibility and he took that reputation extremely seriously. When the BLM lands were closed to highway development, Jackson and the state engineers, unbeknownst even to Governor McCall, soon developed a back-up route. The new route also went along Winema beach, up over Cannery Hill, then skirted the tip of the spit, with the bridge landing midway up the bayside and heading northward to the east of the BLM plot, returning to its previously planned course at the north end of the spit and then on through Pacific City.

In September 1967, Glenn Jackson, in a rare display of political insensitivity, announced the new route without consulting the governor. By bizarre coincidence, both Straub and McCall were at the Hilton Hotel that day. An angry Straub caught the governor completely flat-footed, in front of television cameras no less, with the news of the new beach highway plan. Rarely at a loss for words, McCall stuttered and stammered as Straub pressed him hard for going back on his word, with the press recording it all. McCall had no good justification for the flip-flop, but, referring to Interior Secretary Udall's decision, angrily excused it: "Because the route was not eliminated in a democratic way." "You eliminated it, according to the papers," Straub retorted. McCall agreed to hold a hearing to consider the new plan, though he didn't succumb to Straub's pressure to hold it in Portland, "where most of the people are." McCall told him he'd be happy to hold it halfway between the coast and the valley. "For Christ's sake, that's in the middle of nowhere," Straub laughed. "Exactly," replied the governor, smiling as he regained his composure.[58]

The Highway Commission scheduled the hearing for Tillamook in November, so Straub and his allies arranged for a second, unofficial, hearing to be held the night before at Benson High School in Portland. Over a thousand people attended, nearly all opposed to the beach route for the highway. The governor's environmental advisor, Kessler Cannon, bravely appeared and was rather rudely booed when introduced. Janet McLennan, Straub's main environmental ally, had organized an "unofficial advisory petition" to the Highway Commission on an enormous scroll and she and her volunteers had been gathering signatures on it for a month. Everyone at the meeting signed it, bringing the total to 12,500 signatures, and many spoke at length about the need to protect the state's precious beachfront from all development, including highways. [59]

The next day at the official hearing in the Tillamook Elks Club, the crowd was evenly divided. Dave Talbot, director of the State Parks Division, and other highway supporters presented the new beach route as a natural complement to a new park they would establish on the sand spit, making it easier for campers and day-trippers to get to the beach from their cars. State Treasurer Straub was introduced early in the proceedings to a chorus of loud boos, duly noted in the official transcript, which Hearings Officer Victor Wolfe gaveled down saying, "I will not tolerate any of this type of action during this hearing."[60]

Bob Straub began his testimony with two pointed questions: did the highway as planned violate the new 16-foot elevation rule established by the Beach Bill along the beach in Winema in addition to the Nestucca Sandspit, and would the state park, described at the beginning of the hearing be developed without the highway? On the first question Mr. Wolfe promised to get back to the state treasurer and on the second he assured Mr. Straub that the park could be developed with or without the highway. State Treasurer Straub implored the commission to consider how few areas of coastline remained as unspoiled as the section they were considering. Citing a 1959 National Parks Service study, which reported, "The highway on the entire Pacific Coast closely paralleled the ocean for 90% of the distance," he asserted, "It is even more true today." Raising the lack of public access to beaches in southern California as Oregon's possible future as its population size grew, Straub said, "We will never have another foot of useable beach area in Oregon—never. Yet the demand for the beach, for recreation, for family outings, for safe, healthy, places for children to play, is increasing by leaps and bounds."

The proposed highway, Straub said, "would consume … a minimum of 320 acres of among the finest sections of beach and ocean view property that is left in Oregon." He pointed out that this was not a scenic highway, but a working highway with a lot of traffic, including large trucks, "one truck every 45 seconds, one vehicle every nine seconds—by the Highway Department's own statistics." Straub urged the commission and all Oregonians to plan for "the long-range future … the strength and success and best hope for Oregon's future economic development and well-being lies in our ability today to clearly foresee, plan for, and protect long-range needs." A positive future must include "places where the awe and the majesty of nature, the force and the reach of the ocean can be observed and contemplated without distraction and danger."[61]

Making an economic argument that was unusual in its day, the state treasurer, demonstrating his practical business background, made the case that, while "private economic considerations are not overriding," the high price paid at modern luxury developments like Salishan and the Inn at Spanish Head, which were "already all sold even before they had begun to build," indicate "a valid index of the value that people put on a resource— the price that people are willing to pay for a quiet view of the ocean and a peaceful enjoyment of the beach." This resource and value to Oregonians was threatened, Straub said, by "a few individuals, a few short-sighted promotional type organizations, like the Oregon Coast Association, [who] are beating the drums for this beach route as a way for them to make a quick dollar, and destroy in the process their most valuable asset, which creates these business values. Gentlemen, they would sell out too quickly and too cheaply."[62]

The rancorous, highly publicized, hearing, went all day and into the evening. Although there were balancing voices advocating the highway change, the massive turnout of over a thousand opponents from the valley and up and down the coast was an embarrassment to Governor McCall. When Mother Nature had her say in December, breaching the sand spit during a storm and tossing drift logs all over the proposed highway route, McCall informed Glenn Jackson that he was pulling the plug.[63] Today, the Nestucca Sandspit is also known as Robert W. Straub State Park, and Highway 101 in southern Tillamook County follows the same route it followed in 1967, minus a few curves that were eliminated when the Highway Department completed its work. None of the other four potential sand spit highway routes were pursued by the Highway Department as they improved Highway 101 northward to Astoria.

The detour that Bob Straub and his environmental supporters took to fight the beach highway plan reduced the amount of time they had to work on a ballot measure campaign to improve Oregon's Beach Bill. During that interim the first glimmerings of litigation respecting the Beach Bill began

Ethel and Senator Robert F. Kennedy walk with Bob Straub on the beach at
Seaside, Oregon, on May 24, 1968, before Oregon's presidential primary.
Twelve days later, Senator Kennedy was assassinated in Los Angeles. Photo by
Michael B. Conard, UPI

to take shape. A landowner in Neskowin, Lester Fultz, had begun work
on a private road seaward of the vegetation line in May 1967, before the
Beach Bill passed. After it was signed into law in July he sought a permit
to complete his road and build a revetment. Following a public hearing
in September, his permit was denied in November. Fultz then resumed
construction, relying on the advice of his lawyer that his fee title to the
beach was superior to the provisions of the Beach Bill. Within twenty-
four hours, Oregon Attorney General Robert Y. Thornton filed suit to
stop Fultz' project; Fultz counter sued and appealed the denial of his
permit, also asking the court to declare the Beach Bill unconstitutional,
based on alleged violation of the Fifth and Fourteenth Amendments
of the U. S. Constitution by confiscating private property. The suits
were consolidated for trial, which began May 7, 1968 in Tillamook."[64]
Meanwhile, the state highway engineer had written William Hay on March
21, 1968, requesting that Hay remove his barricade at the Surfsand Motel in
Cannon Beach. Hay countered with a request to set the barricade back farther,
which was denied. Thereupon, Hay sued the state in federal court, asking that
a three-judge federal court tribunal declare the Beach Bill unconstitutional

under the same amendments. He also sought in state court to enjoin the state from bringing suit against him to require removal of the barrier.[65] The initiation of these cases heightened the significance of the continuing division of beach activists over whether or not to pay property owners for purchasing their land rights. The Citizens to Save Oregon's Beaches (CSOBs) remained opposed to purchasing "prescriptive rights" from landowners. They believed the state would prevail in the lawsuits, but also advocated a constitutional amendment guaranteeing: 1) public free access and use of the dry sand areas; 2) placing the burden of proof of continuous use and, therefore, ownership of the disputed areas, on the landowner claimants; and 3) giving the state vague bonding authority with no mechanisms for repayment to purchase whatever minor easements or properties were needed to ensure adequate beach access.[66] Straub's attorneys thought this approach was as vulnerable to legal challenge as a "taking" as was the Beach Bill itself. Straub's group, now calling itself Beaches Forever, favored a constitutional amendment that also prohibited construction outside of the vegetation line, not the 16-foot line. It banned highway construction and authorized the state to purchase ocean beach land or rights to such lands found not to be in state ownership, and beach access, with money from the sale of bonds funded by 1 penny per gallon of gasoline tax for four years.[67]

It took months to hash through the legal details and make policy choices for both ballot measures and time was running very short—it was only six weeks before the July deadline for signature gathering by the time Beaches Forever received approval from the secretary of state's office to begin gathering signatures. The CSOBs had just filed their ballot measure as well. Mindful of the short time available to collect signatures, urged by a number of well-meaning community leaders to consolidate the two efforts, and attentive to the developing litigation, Straub, Janet McLennan and her husband Bill, a Portland attorney, arranged for a meeting with the CSOB leaders at Bob Bacon's home in Portland. Janet McLennan, who had managed successful ballot measure campaigns in 1962 and 1964 and the advisory petition signature gathering against the Sandspit highway, took the lead in laying out the challenges of signature gathering and ballot measure campaigns. She tried to persuade them to join forces with the Beaches Forever initiative rather than pursue what was likely to be a futile independent effort. She didn't succeed.

While both measures sought bonding authority, and both relied on the vegetation line to mark the upland boundary of the dry sand area, Larry Bitte and Ken Fitzgerald could not relinquish the notion that the public already owned prescriptive easements through application of the doctrine of adverse possession. This had been the state's position when the Highway

Commission's attorney first conceived the notion of what became the Beach Bill, Governor McCall had gone along with it, and they were unmoved by the many doubts and contrary legal theories advanced by interested attorneys as more thought and analysis were given the issues. They wouldn't support raising revenue for what seemed like a confession of judgment against their belief. Bitte and Fitzgerald were especially upset about paying landowners unnecessarily. They saw no point in it. Governor McCall supported their position, so they saw no reason to change their minds. The meeting ended with some frustration.[68]

Shortly after the meeting, attorney Bill McLennan, Janet McLennan's husband, filed a ballot title challenge to the CSOBs' ballot measure. The automatic delay for a court challenge doomed their chances of getting certified by the secretary of state's office in time to make the ballot. This hardball tactic left severely bruised feelings, but cleared the way for Beaches Forever to qualify for the ballot without the confusion of a competitive measure. As noted, Straub agreed that the public had established rights to use the beaches, but he felt there was too much legal uncertainty to leave things to the courts alone. A close review of his proposal, which became Measure 6, shows that Beaches Forever intended the state to get final resolution to their legal claims before proceeding to any purchases of remaining beach properties that the court found to have legitimate private ownership. Section 4 of Measure 6 states: "The State of Oregon … shall … define, establish and quiet its title to all ocean beach lands and easements and other means of public access thereto owned or claimed by it."[69] How the actual revenues would be spent would depend on the outcome of the court cases, with beach access and new

Jean Frost, Bob Straub, and Janet MacLennan campaigning for Measure 6.

parks being high priorities after ensuring basic ownership of the sand. Perhaps out of respect for Glenn Jackson's persistent character, Beaches Forever also included a ban on building highways on beaches.

In their pitch for Measure 6 printed in the 1968 *Voter's Pamphlet*, McLennan, Straub and Portland attorney Keith Burns claimed: "VOTE #6 YES! IT'S THE BEST BUY IN OREGON! How much will Measure #6 cost you? NOT MUCH! For the four years it is in effect, the cent-a-gallon gas tax will cost the average car owner less than 13¢ a week. When you consider what it will buy for you and your children forever, you bet it's worth it. And tourists will help pay for our, beaches, too. Remember—the longer we wait, the, more it will cost."[70] Although $30,000,000 sounded like a lot of money then (and still does today), it was certainly not enough to buy major stretches of beach from private owners, and the amount reflects Straub's assumption that the state would win most of the public's claim for use of dry sand beaches.

McLennan and key volunteers around the state contacted supporters from the massive list she and Ken Johnson, Straub's deputy state treasurer, had been collecting. With the beach victories of the past year, volunteers throughout the state were plentiful and enthusiastic. Beaches Forever, with a team of signature collectors preceding the parade, collected more than ten thousand signatures during Portland's Rose Festival alone. In the end they collected almost ninety thousand signatures, many more than the approximately forty-eight thousand needed to qualify as Ballot Measure 6.[71]

Coming into the fall election of 1968, public opinion polls indicated that Measure 6 would win handily—it was leading by 85-15 percent.[72] Clearly, remembering the Beach Bill furor from the previous year, the vast majority of Oregonians feared losing access to their beloved beaches, which overcame their ordinarily thrifty nature. It is rare for Oregon voters to favor raising any tax, let alone by such a large margin.

Bob Straub was running for reelection as state treasurer, but, facing only token opposition, he and his deputy, Ken Johnson, could focus their attention on the ballot measure. Beaches Forever had enthusiastic volunteers in place, a mostly favorable media, and there was no organized opposition to their ballot measure. Unfortunately, as we have seen, beach preservation advocates were not completely united. This disunity was the one really dark cloud on the horizon for what seemed to be a mostly popular ballot measure. Governor McCall continued to publicly agree with critics like Larry Bitte and Ken Fitzgerald that "we don't need to pay for what we already own." Bitte had been assured by Dave Rhoten, a well-connected attorney from Salem, that members of the state supreme court were favorably inclined toward the

Beach Bill and that beach property owners who objected stood no chance of winning in court.[73]

But what Bob Straub and his supporters truly didn't anticipate was that "hired gun" lobbyist Ken Rinke would see an opportunity to make some money and have some fun running a campaign to sink their ballot measure. Rinke was a veteran campaigner and the long-time Democratic Party chairman from Multnomah County in the 1950s and early 1960s. Tom McCall bitterly remembered him as the mastermind who helped Edith Green defeat him for Congress in 1954, mocking McCall, who at the time went by his radio name, T. Lawson McCall, as an upper crust blueblood. It had been a lopsided and humiliating defeat and kept McCall out of politics for a decade. Ken Rinke was a happy mercenary, "the Karl Rove of his day,"[74] who wore gold pinky rings and gleefully told whoever was interested "I'm a whore" when it came to his clients. He really didn't care who they were or what they did as long as they paid him well, styling himself as an honest rogue. Rinke told people he had always wanted to run a ballot measure campaign with the slogan "Beware of Tricks in Number Six!" and here was his opportunity, for which he would be handsomely paid.[75]

The penny a gallon gas tax turned out to be an easy target for Rinke. He contacted the big seven gasoline companies and got six of them—all except Texaco Oil—to give him enough money to advertise heavily on television and radio against Measure 6 in the last two weeks of the campaign. The thrust of the campaign was that this was an unnecessary tax, quoting Governor McCall, Lawrence Bitte, and other critics of the ballot measure in press statements, while running TV ads with a simple jingle and a cartoon rabbit jumping out of a magician's hat. The jingle, of course, warned voters to "beware of tricks in number six!"

Rinke's false front citizens' committee had the address of a house he and his wife had just purchased in Salem. When Bob Straub saw the press release announcing the mysterious committee's formation, he drove over to the house and found it completely empty with no one living there. Straub announced to the press that the opposition committee was not a true citizens' group since its headquarters was an empty home. This attack from Straub played into Rinke's hands as he was able to convince his friend, Marion County District Attorney Gary Gortmaker, to file a campaign ethics charge against Straub, accusing him of making false campaign statements. The more obfuscation surrounding Ballot Measure 6, the better, as far as Rinke was concerned. This charge against Straub came at a time when Attorney General Robert Thornton was claiming that his Republican opponent, State Representative

Lee Johnson, was illegally funding his campaign with his own private money, which, at the time, was against state law. Rinke must have felt that roping Straub and Measure 6 into another campaign circus would help to further confuse the voters.

Watching from the sidelines in horror, Governor McCall finally decided to weigh in on Straub's side ten days before the election. McCall couldn't stomach seeing Rinke buffalo his way through another election and he had to admit that the penny a gallon gas tax would help purchase park and access lands, which would greatly enhance the state's park system. But despite McCall and Straub's mutual campaigning, a yeoman effort from their corps of volunteers, and many editorials in favor, Measure 6 went down to defeat by a margin of 60 percent to 40 percent. This huge election reversal was crushing and disheartening for Straub and so many throughout the state who had worked on the campaign. Straub aide Ken Johnson recalls that Ken Rinke explained to him later the primitive psychology involved in defeating ballot measures: "the confused voter votes no."[76] That was Rinke's simple strategy, well funded and expertly executed.

Former State Parks Director Dave Talbot wistfully recalls: "Oh, what a missed opportunity. For very little money we could have settled the issue forever and we still to this day have large stretches of southern Oregon beaches that are inaccessible because there are no parks or access points to get to them."[77]

The election defeat was not the happy ending he had hoped for, but Bob Straub soldiered on, still strongly feeling the call to serve Oregon and to fight hard to preserve its natural heritage for all time. He believed he was a more decisive leader than McCall and that the times called for stronger medicine than McCall had the stomach to administer. Straub was more determined than ever to take McCall on again in two years time, in a rematch for the governorship.

CHAPTER 9

From Backwater to Vortex

This year it's "Give Peace a Chance." Remember love. The only hope for any of us is peace. Violence begets violence. If you want to get peace, you can get it as soon as you like if we all pull together.

—John Lennon, statement to the press, July 1969

At the beginning of 1969, it was apparent that Oregon's political landscape—indeed, Oregon itself—was undergoing a rapid transformation. The spacious natural landscape that Oregonians treasured was threatened by population growth and booming development. In addition to the changes brought on by rapid economic and technological growth, the nation itself was in the throes of a tectonic social shift. Though not located on a central fault line for these upheavals, Oregon could not avoid getting caught up in the national turbulence over civil rights and the Vietnam War.

Oregon contained a rich mixture of passionate, creative political activists giving voice to a local citizenry that had traditionally seen itself as living in an oasis, and was now feeling an even greater imperative to preserve and protect it from a lurching national chaos. By 1970, the year of the first Earth Day, Oregonians were, through some sort of public relations alchemy, on the verge of unfamiliar notoriety. Unbeknownst to the residents of this traditionally ignored state, Oregon was about to become the national media's "flavor of the month" at the forefront of a newly created international environmental movement.

The late 1960s in the United States was an extremely emotional time and highly politicized. Beginning in the 1950s with the historic, nonviolent struggle for civil rights, and continuing in the 1960s with the free speech movement and opposition to the Vietnam War, an increasing number of Americans became disillusioned with the national mythology and came to question authority generally on a vast range of topics. The nation became deeply polarized as people chose sides to passionately argue in favor of change versus the status quo, each claiming the mantle of true American patriotism. These arguments frequently spilled out into the streets and onto the campuses of America in the form of riots and protests, and by 1970, that included Vietnam War confrontations between police and youthful protesters in

Oregon that were as fierce and violent as any in the rest of the country. As was true in other parts of the country, something transformational was happening in Oregon, changing a sleepy, backwater state into one on the cutting edge of social change.

In the midst of this political turmoil, Bob Straub and Tom McCall prepared for their next collision in their upcoming gubernatorial rematch in the fall of 1970. State Treasurer Straub continued in the role of the aggressive insurgent, a provocateur pushing Governor McCall forward on a gathering host of environmental issues. But these two political leaders, who genuinely liked one another, managed to avoid the nasty, name-calling tit-for-tat political spiral that was tearing the rest of the nation apart. Rather, Straub and McCall's incessant competition clarified state issues and forged a new vision for Oregon, the result of which was the most fruitful period of environmental policy making in Oregon's history.

How does one understand and characterize the development of a healthy rivalry? What is it that allows certain competitions to make *both* of the competitors better, improving the quality of their work? In political combat, it is disturbingly frequent to watch candidates, bent on winning, gratuitously lay waste to one another, exposing and exaggerating their opponent's weaknesses, resulting in a triumphant, but scarred, winner and a bitter loser. It is rare to see two passionate politicians, scrapping in political campaigns over a number of years, actually force one another to develop strengths and blend their voices

Bob Straub campaigning for governor. Photo by Gerry Lewin

to express truths that benefit the greater society. Yet, this was the case with the political rivalry between Bob Straub and Tom McCall. For these two men, it started with mutual respect and the sense to understand what was fair game to raise as a campaign issue, and what was irrelevant. It was rooted in knowing that it is more important to serve the cause you believe in with honor than to disgrace yourself in order to gain an electoral advantage.

Bob Straub vividly remembered the first time he met Tom McCall. It was when Bob was state Democratic Party chairman in the early 1960s. Straub recalled, "I was from Eugene, and I took up a news release to the big city of Portland and went around to the news commentators to leave off my release and most of them said, 'Lay it over there.' … They paid it not the slightest bit of attention," Straub continued, "and here was this newscaster from Channel Eight that had the courtesy to ask me to sit down until he read it, saying 'he might want to ask me some questions,' and he was courteous, he treated me like a human being."

"That was Tom McCall. There was all the difference in the world between the way he treated a nobody and the way other big-shot newscasters treated a nobody," Straub said. "They treated a nobody like he was a nobody and Tom treated a nobody like he was a somebody. I can't say anything but complimentary things about Tom."[1]

McCall returned the admiration as he came to appreciate Bob's depth of character and keen analytical mind. As Brent Walth noted in his biography of McCall, "despite their rivalry for the governorship, there was more in Straub to respect than resent. Like McCall, Straub was a political oddity, whom few people took seriously" when the two men first came onto the statewide political scene.[2] There was this sense of being the outsider that the two men had in common, which helped each appreciate the fresh thinking of the other.

As far as Bob Straub was concerned, the first campaign for governor and his decisive loss to McCall were only round one of their political fight. Liking and appreciating Tom McCall never stopped Bob from believing that he could do a better job than McCall at running the state. Straub felt McCall was too cautious and accommodating to entrenched interests, too constrained by his Republican Party ties to business interests, to be the forceful leader Straub believed Oregon needed. Straub continually tried to find new ways to test McCall and prove his case with Oregon voters. Bob Straub continued to speak out on all the state's issues, especially the environmental issues near to his heart: beach preservation for public use, opposition to the Nestucca Spit Highway, the Willamette River cleanup, and the Greenway proposal.

The coming 1969 legislative session, with no immediate high-level crisis looming, seemed a lackluster candidate for political drama, when compared with the previous session's fight over the Beach Bill. That didn't prevent the state treasurer from attacking Governor McCall's budget proposals for the coming two-year budget cycle, when they were released in early December of 1968. Straub "blistered McCall," criticizing him for reversing a board of control decision to fund a psychiatric security unit for prisoners in the state system and critiquing McCall's proposed approach to reduce the burden of property taxes on homeowners and the business inventory tax. Straub wondered, "I don't know who in government has the power to countermand a board of control decision," referring to the three-member board consisting of governor, secretary of state, and treasurer that made executive decisions regarding state institutions. He further pointed out that the McCall budget had an additional $160 million available to spend in the biennium, some of which could be allocated for property tax and business inventory tax relief, and stated that he thought "the first order of business is to demonstrate good faith with the homeowner by reducing his proportionate share of the total tax burden" before considering such things as a new McCall sales tax or income tax plan, as "predicted in the press." Straub found fault with numerous aspects of the governor's budget, stating that he would favor giving "more state aid to schools, restore the veterans' home loan money, increase welfare programs to help recipients become more self-supporting, provide more money for mental health needs, put more into anti-pollution programs and provide for funds to acquire beaches and access corridors."[3]

The day after cataloguing the changes that he wanted in McCall's budget, Straub tore into the governor over what he believed was a "floundering Willamette Greenway project." He told the non-profit Greenway association during its annual meeting in Portland that, at its present rate of progress, the Greenway would take 840 years to complete. "To date, no money has been spent for land," Straub said, and "only 2,600 feet of river frontage of the more than 210 miles involved in the project has been approved. The people think that something magnificent is happening when nothing is happening at all." To get the plan moving, Straub suggested that authority for the program be given to the State Highway Commission and its parks department and, unlike during the Nestucca Spit highway controversy, he was backed up by his old opponent, Glenn Jackson, the powerful chairman of the Highway Commission. Jackson also attended the annual Greenway association meeting and told the group that he was concerned with escalating costs over time and thought action should be taken soon. He believed that "the project would cost $15 million if done now."[4]

Both Jackson and Straub believed that the legislature should bite the bullet, appropriate money, and use eminent domain to establish the network of parks

No votes here. Photo by Gerry Lewin

while public support was still strong. They were still getting strong resistance from the affected farmers and their rural Republican supporters, who again succeeded in blocking any major action during the 1969 legislative session.

The major legislation of the 1969 session ended up being another referral to the voters of a sales tax measure, intended in part to give relief to property taxpayers. McCall supported the new sales tax and Straub strongly opposed it. One common political thread in Oregon political life is a deep and abiding hatred of sales taxes. To this point, five attempts at passing state sales taxes had been referred to the voters and had all been defeated by better than two to one. Republican support for a sales tax had been a factor in Democrat Robert Holmes' victory in the governor's race, and a massive Democratic sweep across the board, in 1956, yet, little over a decade later, Republican leaders were back proposing a 3 percent sales tax.

In a debate before Portland's Commercial Club in April of 1969, State Treasurer Straub told club members, "Oregon now has a surplus of $43 million that could be applied immediately to property tax relief for homeowners," and he believed the state could raise an additional $100 million by eliminating the federal income tax deduction on state tax forms. His opponent that day, Representative Roger Martin, an up-and-coming Republican from affluent Lake Oswego, declared that Oregon had the fourth highest income taxes in the country and Straub's proposed increase would make the state number one. Straub decried the added cost of collecting a new sales tax and auditing businesses to make certain the tax was collected fairly. He asserted that the tax would shift the burden to homeowners, who would "pay $2 in tax for every $1 of relief," while businesses would "receive $2 in relief for every $1 in new taxes."[5]

Governor McCall supported the measure, which the state legislature sent to the voters at a special election on June 3, 1969, but he did not campaign very hard for it, knowing it had little chance of passage. Straub and the Democrats were brutally vindicated by the voters by a whopping 504,274 votes opposed to 65,077 in favor, a margin of nearly eight to one.[6]

Through 1969 and the beginning of 1970, Straub maintained that same intensity toward politics he had shown since his first treasury race in 1964. He came into the 1970 election year with confidence in his chances and a full head of steam. His advisors continued to raise money and collect volunteer commitments, and, as time passed, they were all encouraged by the early statewide polling numbers. By the spring of 1970, according to the *Oregonian's* public poll, Straub was actually leading McCall by one percentage point among registered voters. The headline on the Republican-leaning *Oregonian's* April 12 front page read: "McCall Grabs Hairline Lead for Governor" because the governor led among "potential voters" by 41 percent to 40 percent over Straub, with 19 percent undecided among all Oregonians surveyed. Nevertheless, the pollster, J. Roy Bardsley, acknowledged below the newspaper fold that "Governor McCall's tenuous advantage over Straub among all potential voters is due to his greater name familiarity among non-registered voters, many of whom will probably not turn up at the polls in November." Among registered voters Straub led 43 percent to 42 percent, with 15 percent undecided. Both these poll results were within the 3.4 percent margin of error, so the race truly was too close to call.[7]

Bardsley further stated that the "results represent a marked gain for Straub, who was defeated by McCall in the 1966 race for governor by a 55 per cent to 45 per cent margin. This gain is due to a greater loyalty to Straub by Democratic voters than was evidenced in the last gubernatorial election." Straub led McCall among Democrats by a 59 percent to 27 percent margin and only trailed him among Republicans by 22 percent to 60 percent. Bardsley foresaw danger for McCall in the coming race "since Democrats outnumber Republicans in Oregon by a 56 percent to 44 percent ratio, McCall is faced with the problem of maintaining the loyalty of his own party, and creating a sizable Democratic defection to his cause."[8]

That poll confirmed what a lot of political observers perceived: that Bob's consistent aggressive leadership style had shifted a significant portion of

Oregonians to his side, when contrasted with McCall's more careful, some said "wishy-washy," style. Contrary to the somewhat inflated legend that has since grown surrounding McCall, "there was a general feeling of a lack of leadership on his part," Straub recalled later. "That's hard to believe [now] because he is characterized as having very strong leadership, and he did, but … most of that occurred in the second administration," Straub remembers. "So when I opposed him … he was running on his performance, which was not too vigorous in the first [term]."[9] Even one of his closest advisers, Chief of Staff Ed Westerdahl, acknowledged later that "Tom was a wonderful policy maker and a wonderful man—but a lousy decision maker."[10] Governor McCall seemed to make decisions with an eye toward trying not to lose the election or offend anyone, which, as any sports fan watching their team sit on a lead can tell you, invites defeat.[11]

A sympathetic *Oregonian* editorial board explained the governor's slipping poll numbers in an editorial entitled "Starting Even" that "a governor makes news almost every day and thus is constantly in public view" and "may make more opponents than supporters … In the four years since their last race, Gov. McCall has been on the firing line on a lot of fronts, while Treasurer Straub has been relatively quiet, although politically active."[12] Straub and his supporters might have challenged their characterization of Straub as "relatively quiet" during the last four years, but certainly McCall's profile was much higher, for better or worse.

Encouraged by the *Oregonian* poll, Straub commissioned a poll of his own, which confirmed the *Oregonian*'s findings and their impression that voters viewed McCall as a weak leader. "We knew Tom was an accommodating, fair person," remembered Straub aide Ken Johnson. "He would wring his hands over issues in public. He hated to make decisions that were going to hurt anybody. It was either black or white and he'd always go with gray. And that left the impression of weakness."[13]

There is no better example of McCall's timid approach to controversy during this period than his wavering support for Oregon's iconic Bottle Bill. The innovative bill was introduced and energetically promoted by conservative Tillamook County Republican State Representative Paul Hanneman at the request of a self-starting citizen lobbyist named Richard Chambers. Chambers "was a frequent hiker who would often walk long distances," remembers his daughter, Vicki Berger, who was later elected a Republican state representative. "Dad was constantly picking up litter. He hated it." Chambers, who lived in Salem, but frequently spent time in Pacific City with his family at their beach cabin, came up with the idea of going back to the old system of returnable bottles that had been replaced in the early 1960s by "no deposit, no return."

The change had resulted in a lot more ugly and hazardous broken bottles. "The bottle bill wasn't really a new thing," his daughter recalls. "Dad wanted to go back to what we had been doing." Chambers also tried to get industry to agree to a standard bottle—making the "stubby" (a short-necked beer bottle common at the time) into the standard that would make reusing glass bottles easier. He was never able to get agreement from industry or the legislature. "Marketing drives the product," Berger observed.[14]

The Bottle Bill caught the interest of the media and became a signature issue of the 1969 legislature. Treasurer Straub supported the bill, but Governor McCall kept his counsel to himself, while the bottling companies and grocery chains organized against it. A key motion on the House floor sending the bill back to committee, presumably to keep it there indefinitely, passed by three votes. Hanneman and Chambers appealed to the governor for help. McCall's reply came in the form of a letter to a bottling company executive stating that he did not support a bottle bill this legislative session. Bottle Bill opponent Republican Representative Roger Martin of Lake Oswego distributed McCall's letter widely to his fellow Republicans, who were still in the majority in the House. The governor's opposition killed the bill.[15]

"McCall did not support the bill," Berger said. "Instead he went out and started Stop Oregon Litter and Vandalism (SOLV), the industry response," which they hoped would quell public support for bottle bill legislation in future legislative sessions. Given McCall's initial opposition, it is ironic that this legislation, which McCall endorsed and trumpeted in 1971 after successfully navigating his reelection, is frequently listed as one of his major achievements as governor. "Suddenly, a year later, he turned on a dime in a speech," Berger remembers, "which shocked everyone."[16] But coming into the 1970 election, Bottle Bill supporters were not impressed by what could be characterized as McCall's failed leadership on the bill, wondering why he would help create an organization that duplicated the existing Keep Oregon Green volunteer anti-litter group.

In fact, at the time, many suspected that McCall's show of support for environmental issues was, in fact, a less than heartfelt "triangulation" tactic, meant to appease an increasingly activist populace. Oregon's voting population had shifted in the late 1950s into majority Democratic registration, where it has remained as at least a plurality, to a greater or lesser degree, ever since. By 1970, Democrats outnumbered Republicans by over 110,000, with the tally running 521,662 Democratic, 410,693 Republican, and 23,104 Independents—a 55 percent to 43 percent to 2 percent split.[17] In this climate, Republicans running in statewide elections were challenged to differentiate themselves from their party. It became imperative to find ways to attract crossover voters—though years of supporting quirky, maverick politicians, such as U.S. Senator Wayne Morse, whose party affiliation went from Republican to Independent to Democrat, helped reinforce the common belief that Oregonians vote for the person, not the party, and will reward someone who cuts against the grain.

Therefore, it wasn't entirely surprising that Republican U.S. Senator Mark O. Hatfield, a pin-stripe wearing conservative on economic matters, was one of the nation's most renowned "doves" on the Vietnam War, running on an anti-war platform in 1966, before such a position became a majority crowd pleaser. In 1970, Senator Hatfield formally broke with President Nixon on the issue, co-sponsoring the McGovern-Hatfield Amendment, which called for a complete cutoff of funding for the increasingly unpopular war. Hatfield established his moderate credentials early. As a young State Representative, Hatfield, in 1953, sponsored and was the chief advocate on the House floor debate of a key civil rights bill, banning racial discrimination in public accommodations. This law helped expunge the shame Hatfield felt, as a student leader at Willamette University in Salem, of having to drive the great singer and humanitarian Paul Robeson from a performance at Willamette, up to Portland to one of the few hotels in the state that would allow African-Americans to spend the night.[18]

Oregon's other Republican U.S. senator, Robert Packwood, jumpstarted his statewide political career by publicly breaking with Goldwater conservatism after the 1964 Republican Presidential debacle. Packwood, after leading a successful effort to take back control of the Oregon House of Representatives in that heavily Democratic year, organized a highly publicized retreat of fellow Republicans, on April 9-12, 1965, at the Dorchester Hotel on the Oregon Coast. The invitation to the first of many annual "Dorchester" retreats proclaimed, "Far right wingers will be deliberately excluded."[19]

In fact, Senator Packwood was an economic conservative, and a war "hawk," but, as would seem ironic later, he was an early, steadfast champion of the growing women's rights movement. He showed his prescience in understanding the coming importance of women in politics in a "one hundred page campaign 'cookbook'" he authored in 1964. In it, in embarrassingly sexist language by today's standards, Packwood outlined how to best utilize an army of female campaign volunteers to win elections. He told his friend Jack Faust, "Women's talents are the greatest wasted resource in the country."[20] Whatever his motivations, Packwood was especially stalwart in supporting a woman's right to choose on the matter of abortion, introducing the Senate's first abortion legalization bill in 1970, and later successfully filibustering President Ronald Reagan's attempts to pass a constitutional amendment banning abortion.[21] Further proof of Packwood's successful political formula of cooption was provided by environmentalist Andy Kerr, who frequently observed with a combination of mirth and appreciation that Packwood could always be counted upon to support a new wilderness area every six years—in time to campaign for reelection.[22]

Governor McCall probably didn't need to observe these examples of Republican maverick behavior to understand good politics—and his public record reflects the opinions of a man significantly to the left of the Republican center. Nevertheless, he was somewhat constrained during his first term for fear of attracting more conservative opposition in a contested primary.

With Straub serving the role of firebrand, McCall sought to co-opt each environmental issue with more centrist solutions. As time passed, however, Tom McCall developed an additional motivation for cultivating his role as environmental leader. For McCall, the perception of Oregon's leadership on the environment, and the part he played in it, became the opening he had long sought for a national spotlight and another focus for his gadfly tendency to sting the national Republican establishment. Bob Straub, in contrast, never had the slightest interest in national attention and did not seek it. Though Straub and his supporters persistently sought to use environmental issues to promote his quest to become governor, Straub, in seeking to preserve Oregon's wild and scenic beauty, viewed environmental issues through a state and local lens, seeking federal help, as he had with Interior Secretary Stewart Udall on the Beach highway, only to accomplish a key local goal.

Oregon's isolation was the reason Straub had come to the state—to get away from the societal mainstream and walk a road less traveled. Most Oregonians shared Straub's love of the state for same reason. In a divisive era when many people were choosing sides on weighty national issues, Straub supported national civil rights legislation, as did most Oregonians, who were mostly blissfully unaware in the 1960s of a virulently racist past that had left the state with few black citizens. Oregonians, like most northerners, had a patronizing attitude toward the violent and strangely accented white southerners they saw fomenting hatred on television. Most of the legal impediments to racial equality had been removed during the 1950s in Oregon, so the issue was of national concern, but did not seem to have great personal impact upon the overwhelmingly white Oregon voters.

On the other major national issue of the day, under the influence of his good friend, the acid-tongued war opponent Senator Wayne Morse, Bob Straub came to view the Vietnam War as "a bottomless pit that we had gotten into."[23] Nonetheless, he saw no reason to advertise his opinions on federal issues. The Dartmouth College debater in Straub believed that, as someone who wanted to be governor of Oregon, his opinions on issues over which he would have no control were not germane to the voters. This sort of practicality—advocating action over symbolism—made Straub appealing to Oregonians on one level.

Paradoxically, McCall's grandstanding and growing national profile were essential to the governor's eventual second triumph over Straub, in their 1970 gubernatorial rematch. McCall's victory resulted from the lethal combination of a politically lucky bounce, in which national politics came crashing down upon Oregon's political life, and the masterstroke that he and his staff devised for dealing with it. This mixture would knock Straub completely out of the race in August, just before the final stretch of the election campaign. Governor McCall cemented his reelection when he sponsored Vortex I, a five-day Woodstock-style outdoor festival, with plenty of sex, drugs, and rock and roll.

In an ordinary year, sponsoring a marijuana- and LSD-saturated hippie love-in in a state park, and asking the state and local police to look the other way, wouldn't be the ideal way to open the fall reelection campaign for governor, but 1970 was no ordinary year.

By the beginning of 1970, it was clear that President Nixon's secret plan to end the Vietnam War was going to take a long time to develop. In the meantime America's young men died in the jungles by the thousands and protests against the war gathered steam throughout the country. After witnessing national leaders like Senator Robert Kennedy and the Reverend Martin Luther King, Jr. murdered in service to their cause, many Americans despaired at the unfulfilled state of equality and justice they saw in their country. Disillusionment became even more personal for eighteen-year-old men, subject to the military draft, who were expected to put their lives on the line for the hazy concept of freedom in Southeast Asia.

With news reports showing atrocities perpetrated by South Vietnamese and American soldiers, at the same time that our military commanders were consistently proven overly optimistic in their assessment of military progress, it became difficult for young men to trust government assurances that they were being called to fight for a noble purpose. Young people throughout the country, especially on college campuses where draft-age men tried to wait out the conflict, became cynical and began questioning the basic beliefs and principles their parents and other authority figures had taught them. This questioning led to a rejection of rigid traditional values of all sorts, including proper dress, grooming, hairstyle, and general behavior. The older generation looked on in horror as a mob of unruly, unkempt, disrespectful, pot-smoking, libertine, electric-music-worshipping heathens rapidly became the mainstream of youth culture.[24]

Oregon's college campuses reflected the rapidly deepening trend of youthful rebellion, especially at the University of Oregon in Eugene, with its traditional liberal arts focus. As Dennis Stovall, then a local Students for a Democratic Society (SDS) anti-war organizer, remembers, the movement started small but swiftly grew. "In 1966, we had six people in our group and the frat guys used to threaten to beat us up," Stovall recalls. "By 1968 we had five thousand people at the free speech platform outside of the student union and I began to count on the frat guys to help with rallies. I used to swing by the ATO house to pick up recruits."[25]

In April of 1970, hundreds of students listened on a public address system as the U of O Faculty Senate defeated, by a vote of 199-185, a resolution requiring "the Army and Air Force ROTC [Reserve Officers Training Corps] contracts be terminated as soon as possible. The outcome of the vote incited the students in attendance and they angrily spilled out onto the campus."[26] Whipped into a frenzy by organizers, they marched on the ROTC building, where about fifty people broke away from the main group and began trashing the place—breaking typewriters, smashing windows, and starting small fires in the wastebaskets. Eugene police intervened, forcing the mob out of the building. Later that night, an even larger group of students marched on the ROTC building with torches, some throwing them at the wooden structure, but were driven off again by police and national guard troops who, this time, fired tear gas. "The tear gas seemed to stir up a lot more activity," Stovall recalls, "It looked a lot like Berkeley or Chicago along University Avenue that night," as students went on a rampage around campus, breaking windows and throwing rocks at police cars, and quickly building a brick barricade on busy 13th Street on both ends of campus, which still remains closed to through traffic to this day.[27]

Despite a brief occupation of the administration building later that week, U of O President Robert Clark declined Oregon Attorney General Lee Johnson's advice to press charges against the students. President Clark's minor concessions to students' demands for greater self-governance brought an end to the major confrontations, and an uneasy truce descended upon the campus. The riots were largely a surprise to the rest of the state and its political leaders. Governor McCall placed state police and national guard units on alert, eventually deploying the state police on campus to reinforce local law enforcement officers and protect buildings from vandalism—and, according to Tom McCall's chief of staff, Ed Westerdahl, to prevent the Lane County Sheriff's Department from enraging the students with more tear gas assaults. "I sent the state police to escort [the sheriff] off campus," Westerdahl said later.[28] Westerdahl had, in fact, been authorized to make all the decisions regarding situations of campus violence, because McCall was a "hothead when it came to protestors. He realized he would not think logically when it came to handling these crowds."[29]

It must have burned McCall that his alma mater was in such a shambles, and that the target of the students' anger was the ROTC building where he, his son Tad, and generations of patriotic "Oregon Ducks" had trained for military service. McCall had been an early and enthusiastic supporter of the Vietnam War. Shortly after being elected in 1966, he sent a personal, hand-written note to President Lyndon Johnson, assuring him, "I have supported your policy every step of the way in southeast Asia."[30] Earlier that year, he savaged war opponents Senator Wayne Morse and Governor Mark Hatfield, who was then running for an open U.S. Senate seat, saying that he felt "contempt for the apologists who divide us, and the name callers who weaken our national purpose."[31] In September of 1967 President Johnson appointed McCall, who he sometimes called his favorite Republican governor, to a bi-partisan panel, along with other elected officials and dignitaries, to observe and certify that elections in South Vietnam were fair. Governor McCall met with South Vietnamese President Nguyen Van Thieu "several times and reported" to President Johnson "that his aspirations seemed to reflect those of the Vietnamese." Though McCall later observed, "As it turned out, he was too much of an authoritarian … most of his political rivals were imprisoned."[32]

In any case, although McCall, as a former newsman, believed in freedom of speech, he had little truck for the demonstrators' foul-mouthed antics and acts of vandalism. McCall announced through the press the day after the U of O riots that he was "appalled" by "the disturbance caused … by a small number of students and non-students at the University of Oregon." Referring to his call up of state forces, McCall said, "It is my hope their in-close availability will dissuade this tiny minority of anarchists from choosing to go to war against law and order again."[33]

Not having anything to add and not wishing to detract from the governor's role in a violent situation, Bob Straub chose not to issue a formal statement. However, a year earlier, the state treasurer had clearly stated his position on retaining limits on police authority on campuses. During the 1969 legislative assembly, Straub issued a statement in opposition to legislative efforts to allow the governor to empower police to seal off college campuses if he feared violence is imminent. "This bill gives additional authority, not to the institutions, not to the governor, but to the police," Straub claimed, in a letter to the Senate Education Committee, which was considering the bill, released to the press on April 29, 1969. "The bill directs the police to act on their own," Straub continued; "as … written, the police would even have to exclude the

governor himself from the campus if he came to look into the emergency."
Straub sided with civil libertarians, who were worried that an overreaction to
campus violence could lead to greater domination of civic life by the police
and military. He also refuted a common charge leveled at campus protests—
that "radical infiltrators" incited them; hence the supposed need to seal off
campuses—calling the bill "an insult" to college students since it presupposed
"outside agitators could somehow turn these thousands of good students into
a rioting mob."[34] A year later, as Straub had said, there wasn't much evidence
of the need for outsiders to agitate the students—the unpopular Vietnam
War, the draft, and an escalating alienation against authority supporting them
had accomplished that—and the state's effort at reestablishing order didn't
suffer from the lack of ability to seal the campus.

The sparse evidence of outside agitators didn't stop others, including fellow
Democrat, Congresswoman Edith Green of Portland, from calling for harsher
policing of the campuses. Green asked, "Why should a campus of 18,000
allow a group of 400 to run it? If we allow our schools to be formed into
battlefields, they are just going to be treated just like any other battlefield."[35]

Just as the state was recovering from the shock of the events at the U of O
campus, national and international events intervened. On April 30, President
Nixon announced that U.S. forces were entering Cambodia in support of
South Vietnamese forces that were attacking Viet Cong supply lines along the
border. This decision significantly widened the war without the authorization
of Congress. Anti-war demonstrators organized protests throughout the
country. On May 4, at one of these demonstrations on the Kent State
University campus in Ohio, national guard troops fired live ammunition at
a relatively small group of peaceful protestors, seemingly by order of their
commander and with the support of the state's governor. Four students were
killed and nine others wounded, one permanently paralyzed.

Across the nation, young people responded to the shootings, closing
hundreds of universities, colleges, and high schools in a strike of some eight
million students. At Portland State University, an upstart college founded to
serve returning soldiers after World War II and now rapidly expanding along
downtown Portland's tree-shaded South Park Blocks, students reacted, like
their counterparts in Eugene, by setting up road barricades along the park
blocks (which at that time were still open to through automobile traffic).
Hundreds of angry, striking protestors blocking roads and occupying buildings
made operating the university nearly impossible. PSU President Gregory
Wolfe closed the university, announcing, "after a day of intense deliberation
with students, faculty and administration, I have concluded that classes of the
university should be closed [Thursday and Friday] until next Monday morning

as elsewhere in the nation."[36] Tempers cooled, as the weekend passed, but the park blocks barricades remained in place, with the exception of a 3 a.m. breach of a blockade by a determined garbage truck driver.[37]

By May 11, the protest was losing steam, but Portland Mayor Terry Shrunk sent in one hundred fifty blue-helmeted officers who quickly, and without much resistance, removed all the street barriers and secured the corners. What remained was a large white medical emergency tent in the center of campus that protest organizers claimed had a city parks permit allowing it to remain standing for one additional day. The mayor and police saw this tent as a symbol of the protest and decided that removing it would re-establish their authority. As the elite police "tactical operations" (TOP) squad, with white helmets and long, white clubs, along with their blue-helmeted reinforcements, massed next to Shattuck Hall, psyching themselves up by pounding on each other's shoulders and shouting like linebackers before a big game,[38] two hundred students, "many drawn by curiosity," but a core of whom were prepared to be arrested defending the tent, waited.[39]

Suddenly, swiftly and efficiently, the police "struck with incredible speed." Rather than arresting students, the police chose to brutally clear the park blocks, hitting them with their clubs "indiscriminately" and "viciously," creating a "blood-spattered spectacle" that hospitalized twenty-seven people. Within three minutes the block was cleared, the tent was crushed, and the entire campus was furious. Even many who opposed the student strike were shocked and felt the police had gone overboard, "cross[ing] all logic by send[ing] helmeted police into what had been a waning protest."[40] As commentator Bruce Baer on KATU-TV news said in televised editorial, "there was no riot for the riot squad to quell. Students did not provoke or attack the police."[41] The following day three thousand people marched on City Hall demanding to speak to the mayor, who refused to meet with them.[42]

In the midst of this chaos making daily headlines, nearly unnoticed, Bob Straub was running against an anti-war challenger, University of Oregon Professor Arthur Pearl, in the May 26 Democratic gubernatorial primary. Pearl was mostly a one-issue protest candidate and Straub rather easily shrugged him off. Straub's political credibility was high among Democrats and people had no reason to reject his leadership because of nuanced differences on a national issue over which the governor had no control. Straub won with 66 percent of the vote, Pearl received 12 percent, and the remaining 22 percent was scattered among six other lesser-known candidates. Tom McCall also easily triumphed in the Republican primary over two unheralded opponents, receiving 74 percent of the vote. Interestingly, McCall's vote totals edged Straub's by less than a thousand votes: 183,298 to 182,683. Factoring in the wild card of the roughly twenty-three thousand Independent voters who were not allowed to vote in the partisan races, the results seemed in line with the April opinion polls. The governor's race in the November general election was, indeed, shaping up to be extremely close.[43]

It was not at all clear what effect continued clashes between war protesters and police would have on the campaign, and whether or not the governor's handling of these skirmishes would redound to his credit. After the Park Block riots, toward the end of May and into June, large gatherings of anti-war protestors met to decide what to do next. A national convention for the vigorously pro-war American Legion was scheduled in Portland at the end of August and some activists had already begun organizing a nationwide protest mobilization in Portland, calling their gathering "the People's Army Jamboree, a Festival of Life." They put out the call for a mass gathering that would include "rock concerts, speakers from the Chicago Conspiracy, and lots of people grooving on beautiful Oregon."[44] The American Legion announced that President Richard Nixon was invited to address the convention, making a national call to protest seem more plausible, and adding fuel to the coming confrontation.

McCall faced a threat that he had every reason to think could lead to a complete breakdown of public order—and with his poll numbers shaky in his race against Straub, a potential electoral disaster. Unexpectedly, he received an opportunity to take charge of the situation from an unlikely source.

The anti-war organizations in Portland were riddled with infiltrators and collaborators reporting to the Portland Police Bureau and the FBI, who regularly provided information to the governor's office on the progress of the protest plans. The paid infiltrator from the Police Bureau actually arranged for a $10,000 donation from Patricia Sabin, a young heiress of the Blue Bell Potato Chip Company, to help fund the protest jamboree.[45] It is not clear whether he did this to gain the trust of the group, or to sow dissention over how that much money (a great deal to the struggling anti-war movement of that day) would be divided. If it was the latter purpose, it worked.

At a fateful meeting at Centenary Wilbur Methodist Church on June 22, 1970, which, according to one observer, "resembled a theological dissertation on how many angels could dance on the head of a Marxist pin," a major division appeared between more militant protestors and those wanting to use the event to promote a peaceful, alternative lifestyle.[46] Members of the alternative lifestyle contingent became fed up with others' angry talk of "seizing the streets and putting themselves in front of the cops," and, after failing to steer the group toward their vision of "a free festival, a demonstration where we show how people get along in peace and share resources," staged a walk out. Meeting upstairs on the grass, and then in a series of meetings over the next few days, a core group of about twenty of these disgruntled peaceniks, calling themselves the Family, developed an idea for a free, "Woodstock style" rock concert, away from Portland, to provide an alternative to confrontation with the police and American Legion. They envisioned their gathering as a coming together of positive spiritual energies, a New Age energy vortex, and thus "Vortex I: A Biodegradable Festival of Life" was born.[47]

Looking around the Portland area for a place to hold their gathering, the Family was finding mostly dead ends. Woodstock-inspired rock concerts the previous year in Oregon and Washington, "Sky River" and "Bullfrog's I and II," on rural private land prompted local authorities to pass a rash of anti-concert laws throughout the region. They decided to see if the state would allow them to use a state park. Going straight to the top, five of the Family drove down to the state Capitol in Salem to talk to the governor. They met with Ed Westerdahl, the governor's chief of staff, who was struck with the audacity of the idea, and taken by the concept of keeping young people busy far away from downtown Portland, where they might tangle with police and legionnaires.

Governor McCall and his staff had a tough decision to make. Should they go along with the longhairs' plan and risk losing the election, or proceed in an ordinary law enforcement fashion and risk the trauma of a potentially bloody civil disturbance? "Hosting an official pot festival would probably cost him the election," Westerdahl recalls. "Tom knew that." Bob Oliver, the governor's legal adviser, remembers that "the staff was divided and then the state officials, like the adjutant general of the national guard, balked. We finally told them it would *not* draw out the hard core troublemakers, but get the casual bystander off the street, inducing them, entertaining them, and we would facilitate it … it was the lesser of two evils." According to Ron Schmidt, McCall's press secretary, McCall had the final word at a meeting with a half dozen key staff members, dramatically turning away from the group for a moment, then swiveling back to face them, saying, "I have just made my decision. I have just committed political suicide. We are going to have Vortex."[48]

As if the governor didn't have enough to worry about, July was the month that NBC News aired Sander Vanocur's national television special on teenage drug use, featuring Tom McCall and his heroin- and pill-addicted son, Sam. Fortunately for McCall, the portrayal was sympathetic and "won McCall praise for his public courage."[49] Straub had long known of Sam McCall's struggle with drugs and petty crime and had spent many hours personally counseling the young man when he appeared on Straub's doorstep on several occasions, almost as if he were wishing to cause embarrassment to his father.

Straub resisted any attempted to politicize the McCall family's personal tragedy, even when union leaders suggested it to him during the campaign.[50]

About this time McCall's team shrewdly decided to start sharing its intelligence reports with State Treasurer Bob Straub and Secretary of State Clay Myers, the other members of the board of control, presumably to show the severity of the potential threat of violence at the American Legion convention and to avoid criticism from the frequently aggressive Straub.[51]

Moving quickly, the state authorities decided that the just-opened McIver Park near Estacada, deep in rural Clackamas County, would be ideal, because "there was one way in and one way out," Westerdahl remembered. "We could control everything and shut it down immediately and keep everyone there if necessary. 'Corral' is the word I remember using at the time." Lee Meier of the Family recalls, "We met Ed and the next thing we know we're getting a call that McIver was ours."

McCall and his team decided to make the announcement of this cockamamie scheme without directly involving the governor. On August 6, they held a press conference with the stone-faced and properly button-downed Ed Westerdahl, along with Craig Berkman, a clean-cut young Republican businessman who headed a group raising money for alternatives to the People's Army Jamboree, sitting next to two members of the Family, represented by budding rock impresario Bobby Wehe, looking "utterly Christ-like" and hippie pottery storeowner Glen Swift.[52] It was a most incongruous picture to the gathered media, as they watched Wehe describe Vortex as "an example of sharing this planet in a spirit of harmony and purity, where brothers and sisters from all over the world can begin the self-education and self-discipline necessary to turn our isolated attempts at new-culture into a movement," and conclude his presentation with a poem describing a utopian future, ending in the lines:

...an abundance of organic vegetables and fruits and grains
were growing wild along the discarded highways
national flags were sewn together
into brightly-colored tents
under which politicians were allowed
to perform harmless theatrical games.
the concept of work was forgotten.

When asked by reporters if sponsoring the festival put the state in a "compromising position," Westerdahl answered with a single word: "yes."[53]

If Governor McCall and the State of Oregon were in a "compromising position," so was Bob Straub. The boldness of McCall's decision to sponsor

Vortex caught him and his staff off guard. An additional complicating factor was that, at about the time of the announcement, the police and FBI intelligence reports, which Straub was also receiving, indicated that the People's Army Jamboree was withering in the mid-summer sun. The disorganized group, broken into bickering factions, failed to secure outside celebrities or support. The galvanizing promise of President Nixon's appearance in Portland, the best chance local anti-war organizers had to draw people from other parts of the country, proved wishful thinking on the part of the American Legion organizers. Jamboree organizers put up a brave front for the media, including sending out an extremely ambitious multi-event calendar of events, but to those in the know, the much-ballyhooed confrontation with the Legion was shaping up to be more like the sound of one hand clapping.[54] Straub could not repeat to the media what he knew from these reports. It would have been irresponsible, Straub believed, and would certainly have been out of character for him to leak such privileged information. Instead, rather than publicly question the need for it, he criticized having the state sponsor the event in any case, saying that "giving in to people like that [is] a mistake—it [is] the wrong thing to do." Straub believed that the state should "just have enough national guard and police so that you could enforce the law."[55]

Straub was not alone in questioning the governor's judgment. An Estacada resident was quoted in the *Oregonian* newspaper as saying, "the Governor should get the chair for doing this," reflecting the opinion of many citizens who felt McCall was caving in to lawlessness. However, most of the news media were cautiously supportive of the attempt to divert young people from tangling with legionnaires in downtown Portland, eschewing the "easy political route," as KGW-TV news analyst Floyd McKay described it, which would have been "to do nothing about the upcoming convention, and have lots of police and National Guardsmen on hand." But, nearly everyone acknowledged, as Salem's *Capital Journal* newspaper editorialized, "if things go wrong either place, McCall is terribly vulnerable to the wrath of voters who will blame him for everything."[56]

August is normally a dead time in political campaigns, but in 1970, after the August 6 Vortex announcement, there was enormous interest in this story of impending radical confrontation, hippie hijinks, and McCall's political high wire act. Everyone in the state was paying close attention, waiting for the end of the month to see how it all turned out. Unfortunately for Bob Straub, he became just one of the many interested bystanders—perhaps just a little more interested than most in the outcome of McCall's risky strategy.

The McCall team left as little to chance as possible, quietly raising large sums of money, much of it through the behind-the-scenes advocacy of

Republican corporate fixer Glenn Jackson, to fund the Family's vision of hippie utopia. Jackson tapped, among others, Bob Hazen, President of the Benjamin Franklin Savings and Loan, and the Zidell family, maker of large marine barges in Portland. [57] The Family and a growing list of volunteers organized the event itself, engaging local bands, going to the site early to set up the stage, food, and medical tents and solve other logistical problems.

Meanwhile, Chief of Staff Ed Westerdahl organized the perimeter. On the days just before Vortex started Westerdahl even arranged for the state police to keep the Clackamas County Sheriff's deputies away from the event, where nudity, drugs, and rock and roll music amplified beyond legal sound limits would be an open invitation to a phenomenal bust. "My troops had the higher ground and we outnumbered them," Westerdahl remembers. [58]

As the on-the-ground decisions were being made, Governor McCall and his media wizard Ron Schmidt prepared a formal address to the people of Oregon. McCall delivered it on August 25, the eve of Vortex and the Legion Convention, at KOIN-TV studio in Portland, with a large, white peace symbol as a backdrop. It was a brilliant speech, fifteen minutes long, with just the right amount of sternness toward potential lawbreakers, expressions of concern for the safety of Portlanders—justifying his decision to endorse Vortex—and an appeal to the better nature of young Americans to live up to their ideals for a peaceful world by demonstrating it in the coming week. To say his speech was well received would be an understatement: one ecstatic letter writer told the governor his speech was in the same league as the best of "Churchill, FDR, and Abraham Lincoln." Even the national press took note, with syndicated columnist Max Lerner writing "it seems like a smart move—if it works."

At McIver Park, where some four thousand people had already arrived in advance of the official opening of the gathering, a few listened on transistor radios and shouted "right on" at appropriate moments. Other more conservative Oregonians, watching from the comfort of their homes, were apparently hearing something different in his speech, and thanked the governor for "cracking down on the hippies and preserving law and order." It appears that McCall's speech was the verbal equivalent of a Rorschach inkblot test, with everyone hearing what they expected to hear in it. [59]

When the concert officially opened on Friday, August 28, one thing that everyone across the state could see, on their TV screens or splashed across their newspapers, was a whole lot of naked or semi-clad, sweating young people dancing and bathing in the ecstasy of both natural and chemically induced highs. The local and national media swarmed both Portland and McIver Park, reporting the surreal happenings.

Doug Babb, the young editor of Portland State University's *Vanguard* newspaper, moonlighted for Portland's Channel Six television and was on duty almost constantly for the nearly weeklong series of events; for him, a couple of incidents stuck out as particularly strange. The first was an interview with local Damascus, Oregon, resident Frank Hanks, owner of the original Portland Kentucky Fried Chicken franchise, "The Speck" restaurant and, intentionally, a spitting image of Colonel Sanders. Though not wearing his white suit and bow tie costume that day, Hanks bitterly complained on camera about the bizarre behavior going on down at the park. The second was the only violence Babb witnessed during the American Legion Convention in Portland. Renowned CBS TV reporter and anchor Terry Drinkwater was filming while the American Legion paraded close behind him, when a passing legionnaire carrying an American flag on a long pole, apparently feeling crowded by the famed reporter, suddenly swung his pole, whacking Drinkwater hard on the back of his head and knocking him forward. Though caught on film and the source of much mirth in out takes at the Channel Six newsroom, this incident didn't make it on to prime time news.[60] Nevertheless it was the only incident of violence recorded by anyone during that fateful week.

With enormous amounts of free publicity, private and public funding, and a safety cordon of national guardsmen protecting their party from police busts, Vortex I was a howling success. Crowds reached thirty-five thousand by the second day. Meanwhile, the People's Army Jamboree consisted of two small marches attended by one thousand people. Other than a few shouted anti-war slogans, Portland remained quiet.[61] At the close of the week's events, kudos to Governor McCall began to steadily and overwhelmingly roll in, and Oregonians breathed a giant sigh of relief.

Reacting to the images of "bare-breasted women" and rampant drug use, State Treasurer Straub wrote a puritanical press release, criticizing McCall and the state for needlessly sanctioning illegal behavior at Vortex. He showed it to his deputy and political confidant, Ken Johnson. Johnson read it over and then threw it in the trash, telling Bob "there is no way I can let you send this out." In the end, both men agreed that it was the common belief that Vortex had saved Portland and trying to tell the public or the media otherwise would have been whistling in the wind.[62]

At this point, the race for governor was effectively over. McCall had overcome the major strike against him with the voters—that he was a ditherer, who was afraid to make decisions. On the issues, McCall and Straub were similar enough that the average voter did not find enough reason to change leaders. To illustrate this, a young, college-aged Earl Blumenauer asked them at a September Portland City Club gubernatorial debate the following question: "You're both in favor of the environment, you're both for tax reform, and you're both tall enough to start for any high school basketball team in the state. How are you different?" Current Oregon Congressman Blumenauer remembers that "following some laughter in the City Club audience, the two physical—and political—giants struggled for five or six minutes to distinguish their fundamental difference, to no avail."[63]

In the end, McCall's newly affirmed decisiveness cinched the victory. When the votes were counted in November McCall received 369,964 votes and Bob Straub received 293,892. The 56 to 44 percent margin was nearly identical to that of four years before. The press hullabaloo around Vortex helped further establish Governor McCall, and Oregon, as players upon the national stage, and Oregonians were pleased to have this charismatic, high-profile governor leading them. The enormous popular success McCall experienced at that time, after taking a huge political gamble, set the table for his very successful second term, for which he is now most remembered.

Bob Straub was left to trudge back to the state treasurer's office and lick his wounds. He had fought the good fight and come up lacking. He fought honorably, not seeking to smear or take down his opponent with unrelated issues like the governor's son's drug use. He had chosen not to take cheap shots at McCall during the perceived crisis over the American Legion convention. Bob Straub ran on the issues he believed in: good, honest, efficient government, protecting the state's natural resources, and taking care of the less fortunate. Straub and his supporters knew that they had pushed the popular McCall to become better, and to serve the people more effectively, and there was quiet comfort in that.

A Darkened Victory

In the place where you now are, there is much to be observed ... But what will you do to keep away the black dog that worries you at home? ... The great direction which Burton has left to men disordered like you, is this, Be not solitary; be not idle: which I would thus modify;—If you are idle, be not solitary; if you are solitary, be not idle.

—James Boswell (1740-1795), *The Life of Samuel Johnson* vol. 3, p. 414, October 27, 1779

Coming off the 1970 campaign thrashing by Tom McCall in their governor's race rematch, Bob Straub was at a curious moment in his career. He would still be state treasurer for two more years, but his political momentum was gone and the question loomed of where to go from there. He felt some wistfulness about the result, but also some freedom. After serving a four-year term as county commissioner, Straub had been campaigning for office every two years starting in 1958—once for state senator, once for state Democratic Party chairman (by vote of county party officials), once for Congress in the 4th District, two times for treasurer and twice for governor. Term limited by the Oregon Constitution against a third run for state treasurer and with no need to gear up for his next race in 1972, Bob felt a strange relief.

His rivalry with McCall was officially over—settled in Tom's favor—and Bob only interacted politically with the governor as a member of the State Land Board, where they were mostly in agreement. The state treasurer's duties had been diminished by the elimination of the board of control—Ed Westerdahl's proudest legislative accomplishment as McCall's chief of staff—during the 1969 legislative session.[1] Control of state institutions was now centralized in the governor's office. Straub was thus deprived of the official duty of making surprise visits to the state correctional facilities, mental hospitals, and the schools for the disabled, which he had done regularly as a board of control member. Any opinions he had about running those institutions were now just that. Straub did not oppose this centralization of authority to the governor's office, believing, as many did, that it would lead to great efficiency. "He kind of rolled with the punches on that issue and didn't make a fuss about it," recalls his personal secretary, Barbara Hanneman, but he missed having that direct engagement with state institutions and their policy decisions.[2]

However, Straub was left with one project that interested him a great deal: institutionalizing the new Oregon Investment Council, the first public investment system in the nation to use private firms as contractors to invest public monies in equities, including the stock market.

It became clear early on that a key ally for the state treasurer was fellow investment council board member Roger Meier, an heir to the Meier & Frank department store chain, which his family had sold to the May Corporation of St. Louis a few years earlier. The diminutive, sophisticated Meier could not have appeared more different than the lanky, unrefined Straub, but they shared a strong business sense and a sound, conservative philosophy toward investment. Meier, an arch-Republican, remembers greatly respecting the Democrat Straub as "an excellent businessman and a very good investor" and that they "had a wonderful relationship that I value highly in memory."[3] Meier had been appointed by Governor McCall to serve on the board of the Public Employees Retirement System (PERS) in 1970, and, after a vacancy opened up later that year, he became one of the two PERS representatives on the Oregon Investment Council.

Meier and Straub were both excited about doing all they could to improve the financial standing of their "customers," Oregon state employee pensioners and the state's disabled workers. With Straub taking the lead, they developed the early principles guiding the investment council, and had "the privilege and benefit of listening to the advice of some of the best investors in the world." Meier continued on the council as chair when Straub left office, serving until 1985, in tandem with Straub's initial staff hire, Jim George, whose conscientious work, good investment judgment, and charming personality proved invaluable.[4] George continued to serve after Meier left, until his retirement in 1992. During this time, the investment council made exceedingly wise choices with its money and thrived beyond everyone's most optimistic expectations.

Ironically, the worst years during that period came early, during the 1973-1974 recession, when PERS members who invested in the variable account, which emphasized investment in the stock market, suffered losses of more than 16 percent in 1973 and 18 percent in 1974.[5] Nevertheless, by 1992, both PERS and the State Accident Insurance Fund (SAIF) were so successful that nearly all government employees at every level of state and local government had joined PERS. The state legislature had even poached money from SAIF during the recession of the early 1980s, though this action was later ruled illegal by the state courts. The legislature felt comfortable enough to set an 8 percent guaranteed annual rate of return on PERS funds and traded increased support of pension investment in exchange for a multi-year salary freeze. Roger

Meier observed later that the investment council's biggest problem was that the legislature kept passing laws "requiring us to get better and better returns."[6]

In order to get solid and consistent returns, Straub and the Oregon Investment Council agreed from the outset on a basic principle—a common business rule in those days, which looks prescient in light of today's economic events: they would not invest in any business or contract with any investment company, no matter how tremendous their history of profits, if they could not understand how their money was made.

In addition, because Straub had given the investment council the duty of selecting the private investment managers who would invest money in the state's trust, they also agreed to a second principle to prevent cronyism: they would generally not hire investment managers from within the state, unless there was a truly compelling financial reason. Straub and the council wished to avoid a "'Keep Oregon Green' social investment policy," as Meier would term it later, that would keep state trust money in Oregon firms, potentially at the expense of the council's true legal responsibility to Oregon pensioners and Oregon's pension funds.[7] This policy created headaches, but proved its merit, for Straub and future treasurers, when they had to fight off the advances of investors who had been political campaign contributors. One political contributor, Lawrence Black, who owned Portland investment firm Black & Co., "was particularly insistent that Bob hire him," Ken Johnson remembers.[8] Black had a strong claim for serious consideration, having purchased and enhanced a financial research firm in New York that was one of the best in the country.[9] "Larry was upset that Bob wouldn't consider taking business from him, but, to his credit, he remained friends with Bob and continued to support Bob politically, showing that his support wasn't just about getting state business."[10]

A less savory example of how this policy helped avoid conflict of interest occurred after Straub left the treasurer's office. Jeffrey Grayson, chairman of Portland-based Capital Consultants, continued to contact the investment council, using Oregon political leaders to try to open doors for his firm. Roger Meier could never figure out how Grayson was making money and steered clear. Despite outside "suggestions," the Oregon Investment Council never hired Capital Consultants, and avoided the ruinous collapse of their Ponzi scheme in 2000.[11]

Because Oregon was the pioneer in this type of public investment policy, and an attractive client for the best investment management companies in the country, Straub and his colleagues were able to select an all-star array of investment talent and pick and choose the replacements if any of their initial choices faltered.

In fact, Oregon selected some very talented investment people before they were well known—"and how! Some of them hadn't been hired by anybody," Meier recalled. An early example of this was the one exception in which Straub overturned his own unofficial rule against hiring local investment managers— the selection of Columbia Management of Portland to carry a small part of the OIC investment portfolio in 1971. Loren Wyss, one of the partners, along with James Rippey and Norm Inskeep, had created a unique small capitalization company growth fund that was considerably outperforming the market. Straub, over Roger Meier's objections, felt this local fund was too good an option to pass up. Columbia Management was tiny at the time and the ten million dollars they would receive from the State of Oregon would exponentially increase their investment portfolio. Meier thought, "My God, what if they don't do well and we have to fire them? You're going to put them out of business and all their employees." Straub's confidence in Columbia Management proved well placed and the company served as able investment managers for the council for decades. "They were one of the best we ever hired," Meier remembers.[12]

Most of the work of the Oregon Investment Council was done behind closed doors. Because there was not yet an open meetings law, there was rarely, if ever, any press in attendance, though Straub did allow local brokers to attend the meetings, and an increasing number took advantage of the opportunity to learn from visiting investment managers.

With much of this important work taking place in quiet offices and hotel banquet rooms without benefit of press attention, Straub for the first time in a decade, essentially, dropped from the public view. Besides the relative diminishment of the state treasurer's position in state government with the abolition of the board of control, Straub was further eclipsed by Tom McCall's continued rising celebrity. Buoyed by his second election and risky but successful Vortex gamble, McCall seemed to give his natural interest in grand gestures a free rein. It helped that his new chief of staff, former Republican State Representative Bob Davis of Medford, a steady and well-respected man, was at least as talented at organization as Ed Westerdahl had been but also understood the value of "letting Tom be Tom." Instead of second-guessing McCall's liberal and visionary tendencies, Davis felt his task was seeing to it that the governor's ideas got as broad a buy-in as possible. "Bob Davis's big talent, besides his excellent judgment, was building up the relationship between the governor and the state agencies; together they began to problem solve," Ken Johnson, Straub's former chief aide, who served in the last two years of the McCall administration, fondly remembers. "Davis won the affection and support of the state employees and you had the most harmonious relations within state government that I ever saw."[13]

McCall had already become a national figure through his various attempts at publicity and his naturally quotable contrarian statements at Republican meetings. His belated full embrace of the Bottle Bill in 1971 had a surprising resonance throughout the country, and McCall took full credit for its passage, going on national speaking tours touting its effectiveness in curbing litter and recycling raw materials. McCall's crowning moment in terms of national publicity came in January 1971, just after he had been sworn in for his second term, when, speaking about Oregon's unique beauty on national television, he told CBS News correspondent Terry Drinkwater's national audience, "Come visit us again and again, but for heaven's sake, don't come here to live." The idea of opposing growth was truly radical for an elected official and delighted Oregonians no end. The statement, of course, had the opposite effect of helping create an Oregon mystique, as McCall no doubt knew it would, and actually spurred growth in the state while it further enhanced McCall's image in Oregon and around the country. It also spawned an endless number of comically xenophobic Oregon "ungreeting" cards and television advertisements, such as the local Blitz-Weinhard beer ad in which a Oregon State Police-costumed actor stops a couple of ugly mugs driving a "Schludwiller" beer truck at the state border, asking them in a friendly voice with a little edge to it: "Say, where are you fellas goin' with all that beer?"[14] The "visit but don't stay" message was now thoroughly embedded in 1970s Oregon culture.

As McCall's star continued to rise, Straub labored quietly, setting in place the foundation for decades of rapid and remarkably consistent growth in the state's pension funds while serving out his final two years as state treasurer. On January 8, 1973, with no fanfare, Bob Straub locked the door to the state treasurer's office one last time, left the keys with security for his successor, Democrat Jim Redden, to retrieve the next morning, and strode out of the Capitol building. For the first time in eighteen years, he was a private citizen once more.

This new stage in Bob's life started well. There was no political pressure, just the familiar hard work of managing his many business enterprises, with ranching, logging, and farming operations in the Willamette Valley and southern and eastern Oregon; rental housing in the Springfield area; and a growing portfolio in the stock market. With a loving wife and family delighted to have his full focus once again, Straub seemed to have plenty to do and to enjoy. The first thing Bob did was to go with Pat on a two-month-long trip to Kenya, Greece, and Spain—something they had planned to do for years, but could not do while the kids were young and his political career took precedence. "Pat and I traveled for the first time in our lives," Bob remembered.[15] She had "always wanted to see the wild animals" of East Africa, and the two of them climbed to the top of Mt. Kilimanjaro.[16] They had come a long way since the chance meeting on the trail on Mt. Moosilauke, but their passion for the outdoors hadn't changed. Much as he did on their annual Mexican trips, Bob enjoyed meeting people from different cultures and spending enough time on their journey "to learn about the people there—to drink and dance with them."[17] They savored the luxury of that varied international experience and returned to Oregon refreshed.

It was during this time that Bob and Pat began going on a large number of rafting trips down Oregon's many wild rivers, usually led by their friend, Dean Brooks, the director of Oregon's state mental hospital. Bob was something of a daredevil on rivers, taking routes not recommended by the guides. After a particularly scary spill on the Owyhee River in far southeastern Oregon, Brooks fished Straub out of the river. Later, with a serious look on his face, Bob told Dean, "Thank you, you saved my life."[18]

But Bob Straub's lifeblood was work, and at first he enjoyed the personal control and the concrete tasks of running his businesses. He decided not to go back to building houses in the Eugene-Springfield area, "mainly because I didn't want to compete with the fellow who had bought out my building

Bob Straub with his extended family in 1974. Photo by Gerry Lewin

Pat Straub in the kitchen. Photo by Gerry Lewin

business [Floyd Konold]. I just didn't feel it was right for me to compete with him," Straub recalled.[19]

He and Pat remained in their refurbished 1860s farm house perched on a hillside on the edge of West Salem where Straub augmented the daily brain work of running his businesses with the brawn of such physical tasks as putting in fence posts and baling hay. Too restless for idle pursuits, as he saw them, that others enjoyed in their free time, such as fishing or golfing, a good day for Bob Straub was getting his sons out to work. His youngest son, Bill, eighteen at the time and freshly back from an Arizona boarding school, was the only "lucky" son available for work in Salem by the summer of 1973. "One of my greatest regrets was that I could never get Dad to go out fishing with me," eldest son Jeff Straub remembers. "It just wasn't relaxing to him and he never saw the point of it."[20]

This lack of patience for sitting still did not apply to mental pursuits, obviously. In addition to his ability to focus when at work or studying his business options, Bob continued to have a voracious reading appetite. Former State Librarian Kay Grasing attests that "Bob used the state library more than any other statewide office-holder—he would come over himself, frequently, and not send a courier. He used Moody's and Standard and Poor's to read himself to sleep at night, but really had a very wide range of interests, from Japanese culture to how to make fig wine."[21]

Pat continued, as she had for years, to raise organic vegetables in their garden and keep a variety of hens for eggs. She cooked hearty meals for Bob and whoever else might drop by, on her old wood-burning stove in the kitchen. Visitors at night might have the rare chance to drink a little of their surprisingly dry homemade rhubarb wine. People loved to drop by and enjoy Bob and Pat's company, sitting on the back porch in the summer and admiring the view of the fields through the trees, the deep slope of the valley below and the mountains beyond. Whether it was a neighbor dropping by or a famous visitor, such as Bob's friend Eric Hoffer, guests were made to feel at home and took part in interesting and lively discussions.[22] These simple pleasures were already a basic part of the Straubs' good home life, which was modeled closely upon the life Bob had lived growing up on the Los Altos, California, farm. Now, with no politics to interfere, the hearty country life was once again central to him.

A tradition respected during the political years that continued afterwards was the annual December trek of the Straub family clan and friends to a small village on the Sea of Cortez, the little known and totally non-touristy Guaymas, Mexico, on the mainland side of the Gulf of California. Ike and Jean Russell, Bob's sister and brother-in-law, who lived in Tucson, Arizona, were the first to discover the little fishing village just south of the beautiful sandy beaches surrounding San Carlos Bay. A large contingent of Straubs and their friends caravanned down through California, camping along the way, and met up with the Russells and friends coming from Arizona for a ten-day fiesta—along the sandy Mexican beach. For Bob, and for many of the Straubs, this trip was the highlight of the year. Bob was at his expansive best—extremely active, attempting, with a horrifyingly poor accent, to speak Spanish and to interact with everyone he met. His enthusiasm was infectious both with his family and with the local people, many of whom became good friends as the years went by.

One year, the weather was terribly rainy for several days and the group abandoned the beach for a hotel in town. Bob spontaneously decided that they all should have a barbeque in the hotel's courtyard, and he invited the hotel's current inhabitants, notably including an extremely attractive hooker, to join them. Everyone had a great time cooking, eating, drinking, and laughing, while coping with the rain soaked conditions. It made for another in a long line of memorable trips.

Back in Oregon, Bob was more serious when it came to getting work done around the farm—and expecting his youngest son, Bill, then eighteen, to pitch in. Bill was a child of quite a different generation than his older brothers. Bill and his sister Peg, three years older, were the most laid-back and easy-going of Bob and Pat's six children. Growing up a later baby boomer, Bill and his generation were more inclined to seek pleasure first and work second, and, after the Vietnam conflict exposed generational rifts throughout society, to question authority. Bill was a tall, handsome free spirit, with an open heart and charming smile. He was physically fit, and though he thought his Dad was irritating at times in his insistence upon hard physical farm labor, he appreciated its value. As part of his generation, Bill experimented with drugs with no real sign of difficulty. Nevertheless, a few years before, an absurd series of events had nearly gotten him in trouble during the ninth grade at Walker Junior High in West Salem.

Uncle Ike and Aunt Jean Russell, along with Cousin Barbara Straub, while traveling in Ike's small airplane through South America, mailed Bill a leather pouch stuffed with what Bill called "cocoa leaves." Ike and Jean described them in an accompanying letter as a relatively harmless mild drug chewed by the Andean Indians to give themselves a euphoric feeling, and to fight the bitter cold and nausea of the altitude. Bill brought the leaves to school to share with his friends, truly believing, contrary to one young skeptic, that they weren't coca leaves, the raw material from which cocaine is made (which they actually were), but were, instead, legal cocoa leaves. He and a friend chewed a couple dozen of the mystery leaves in the back of shop class and soon were laughing uncontrollably—on the way to the principal's office.[23] Because of Bill's naiveté, the Straubs were able to avoid any police involvement, but Bob and Pat decided at the end of the school year to send Bill to Verde Valley, an exclusive outdoor-oriented prep school in Sedona, Arizona, believing it would be a healthy outlet for him.

Bill missed his parents and home life, but he loved the alternative feel of school and its beautiful setting.[24] After graduating from Verde Valley, Bill came back to Salem in the summer of 1973 in no hurry for college and planned to spend a year or so working and traveling before deciding his next direction.

Bill spent part of that summer working around the Salem farm, but also went down to Curtin in Douglas County to work on the Straub family timber property there with his sister Patty and brother-in-law Jay Thomas—and to get a little relief from his dad's more heavy managerial hand. Bill probably felt pressure from his father, since Bob thought people should have a direction in their life and work to achieve it.[25] Nevertheless, surprisingly, sometimes even Dad showed signs of coolness occasionally. Bob and Pat came home with the story of spending the evening with legendary novelist and counterculture hero Ken Kesey and his sidekick, Ken Babbs, at the home of their mutual friend, Dr. Dean Brooks, the director of Oregon's state mental hospital. Kesey and Babbs had broken open some of Brooks' glow-in-the-dark light wands and smeared their arms and faces with the phosphorescent "goo" from inside the plastic sticks. Bill was highly amused, but also somewhat awed, by the vision of his straight-arrow dad hanging out with the Merry Pranksters.[26]

By the beginning of summer 1973, the new freedom from the pressure of public life that Bob Straub felt was beginning to lose its savor. He became increasingly restless. For one thing, he knew he needed to make an important decision soon about whether or not to jump back into politics: the 1974 race for governor beckoned and Straub was again the best-known potential candidate for the Democrats. With Tom McCall term limited out of the race, Bob Straub would have an excellent chance to win, though his likely opponent in the general election, Secretary of State Clay Myers, would have the backing of the same wealthy campaign donors that had helped keep the governorship in Republican hands since the 1930s, except for Robert Holmes' brief two-year tenure in the late 1950s.

After returning from his extended trip abroad with Pat in March, Bob kept tabs from his Orchard Heights Road home on the doings of Governor McCall and the state legislature down at the Capitol. 1973 was a momentous year in Oregon politics—the last legislative session of McCall's tenure. With strong Democratic majorities in both the House and Senate, the Oregon State Legislature passed landmark environmental, women's rights, and tax reform legislation. It proved to be the high-water mark of Oregon progressive politics of the activist 1960s–1970s era, which Straub had helped start eight years before. Oregon's unique statewide land-use planning law was established, working from the logic that, if coastal and riverfront lands deserved public protection, and mountain areas deserved federal wilderness designation, the rest of the state, especially farm and forest land, should be given some chance to avoid the relentless sprawl of human habitation and commercial non-agricultural use. Straub endorsed this measure, and closely watched its progress and successful passage from the sidelines.

Straub also quietly endorsed McCall's new tax plan. McCall, working with Straub's old Dartmouth Business School classmate Dick Eymann, by now Speaker of the Oregon House of Representatives, crafted a plan to shift a large portion of the increasingly onerous burden of personal and corporate property taxes to a revamped, more progressively oriented, income tax system. As property values continued to climb in Oregon, the impact of property taxes on people with fixed incomes rose, along with pressure to revise the system. The McCall plan replaced property tax money directed to local schools with increases in statewide graduated income taxes, with the belief that a system based upon a person's ability to pay would be more fair for Oregonians, and that voters would agree. They did not. At a May 1 special election, voters decisively defeated the plan 358,219 to 253,682—a 59 to 41 percent margin.[27] Even the great persuader McCall could not convince Oregonians to trust their government to make major changes in the tax system, although this more progressively oriented income tax reform did better than any sales tax measure before or since.

Despite this setback, the 1973 legislative session was a love-fest between a liberal Republican governor, a liberal Democratic-led state legislature, and their mostly devoted scribes in the media. Bob Straub was left to observe these exciting happenings from the outside. Losing political relevancy with each passing day, Bob pondered his missed opportunities. He was becoming restless, searching for meaning, and slowly becoming preoccupied with the looming decision of whether or not to take the risk of running for governor one last time. He knew he had the name recognition and would most likely win if he ran. McCall's victories had said more about McCall's personal appeal than any negative attitude the public had toward Straub. However, losing twice to Tom had, not surprisingly, changed Straub, dampening the over the top political optimism of his early career. Bob knew losing a third time would be truly crushing; yet he felt the pull to run again. His life didn't feel big enough now, since much of its meaning was tied to his drive for public service. He knew his long-sought goal of the governorship was within reach, but he was starting to suffer from a cautiousness that had not previously been present in his political thinking.

Thus conflicted, bit by bit, Bob started to fall under the familiar cloud of depression that marked so many of the men in his family. The up and down mood swings were something Bob had weathered throughout his life, but had generally navigated fairly smoothly during his long run in public office. Another factor that didn't help was a recurring physical issue that began to bother him, a hernia that he repeatedly re-injured with vigorous work before it could fully heal, and this further darkened his mood. The physical limitation of the hernia stopped him from doing the one thing he had consistently been able to do throughout his life to fight depressive thoughts: work up a good sweat, and some healthy endorphins, with some honest outdoor labor. Anxious to feel better, Straub would then push himself to prematurely begin full physical effort, ignoring his doctor's advice and reopening his unhealed hernia once more, further frustrating his efforts to lift his mood.

Bob's political indecision about the governor's race was beginning to affect the plans of other ambitious Democrats interested in seeking the governorship. Potential candidates and supporters respected Straub's right to claim the nomination, but with no indication from Bob about his decision, they eventually wanted to know whether he was in or out. In late July of 1973, State Senator Betty Roberts, a rising Democratic Party star and local champion of the growing women's rights movement, met with Straub at her Salem condo and boldly asked him point blank what his intentions were. Straub's "response was evasive," according to Roberts' memoir, with Straub saying "Well, you do whatever you have to do," telling her that "he honestly did not know yet," whether he would run. She asked for his support if he did not run and Straub was "surprised," mumbling "something like, 'I'll think about it.'"[28] Roberts realized that as a lesser-known figure statewide, if she was going to run at all, she needed to move forward with her campaign without knowing whether or not Straub was in the race. She declared her candidacy in September and began building a statewide support network.

In addition, newly elected State Treasurer Jim Redden, who had served many years as a moderate Democrat in the House of Representatives, also seemed a likely candidate. Redden was building ties with Oregon's business community as state treasurer and had a strong reputation as a legislative tactician and crafty compromiser. Jim Redden was less certain about running than Roberts, and was spending much social time in Salem with Bob and Pat Straub. Redden had been Bob's favored successor as treasurer, and he and his wife, Joan, even regularly attended an intimate annual Christmas party at the Straubs' house along with a dozen or so other guests, but Jim never asked Bob directly whether or not he planned to run. Redden eventually came to the conclusion that, whether Straub ran or not, 1974 was a prime year for a Democratic victory in the governor's race and he had to take a shot at it.[29]

While other Democrats planned and speculated, summer bled into fall, and fall into winter, and still Straub struggled with his inner demons. He felt low and was becoming almost frozen in making a decision. Finally, in November, a crushing blow forced Straub to directly face his problems or perish from grief. While he was in the hospital in Portland recovering from yet another hernia operation, Pat came to his hospital bed accompanied by their daughter, Jane, and told him that Bill had died in a car crash while hitchhiking across the country. The driver who had picked up Bill on an interstate highway deep in the flat sagebrush country of west Texas had been sleepy and they had pulled off to the side of the road in the middle of the night, leaving their lights on so other drivers could see them. A tired trucker saw the lights, assumed they were moving on the long, straight roadway, followed them off the road, and plowed right through the car, setting it immediately on fire. Police told Bob and Pat that Bill was killed instantly.

Bob and Pat, with family and friends, scattered Bill's ashes on a hilltop on their farm near the community of Curtin in Douglas County—a favorite place for outdoor family gatherings and camping in the summer time—and held a chilly outdoor barbeque. Straub, already struggling with depression, fell, emotionally, into a deep, black hole. Parents facing the sudden death of a child, in the midst of their grieving, often feel irrationally responsible, but Bob may have had an additional reason to feel that way. Bill had been in Massachusetts visiting a girlfriend from his days at the Verde Valley School in Arizona. He had hitchhiked east after Thanksgiving, as he had done once before, but this time didn't find short-term work at the Mattel factory, extruding plastic into G.I. Joes and other toys, and decided to come back. It was becoming uncomfortably cold to hitchhike and while stopping to visit his cousin, Luke Russell, at his home outside of Philadelphia, Bill called home to see if his folks would send him bus fare to make the rest of the trip. Bob refused. He told Bill that if he had the ability to get to get out there on his own, he should be able to find his way back. This decision was in keeping with Bob's own upbringing. Rugged self-sufficiency was to be bred into the young Straub males. Bill hitchhiked south to avoid the cold and met his fate on that flat stretch of Texas highway.[30]

As strange as some people might find it today, at the time, many parents felt comfortable with their children hitchhiking around the country, even when they had any say in the matter, which they mostly did not. It was a common experience for many young people at a time when the communal spirit of the sixties was at its strongest, and when getting and giving free rides was considered part of the adventure of life. Thumbing rides and having road adventures fit in well with the Straub ethos, passed on from father to son, of breeding toughness in the young men. Just as his father had made him pay his way through college, working for a year after high school in a logging camp to save money, Bob hoped to keep his sons from going soft and for them to develop an appreciation of what it meant to get by with little money or advantage. He believed this was necessary for their growth and development.

Bob had been encouraging his two elder sons to hitch rides and ride freight trains for years, even supporting it one memorable time, when they were given the choice of riding with the rest of the family to Guaymas, Mexico, and missing several days of school, or hitchhiking after school finished, a choice that gave them the opportunity to have an adventure. It seemed like a grand journey at the time, but his elder sons had very different reactions when they reflected later about this particular hitchhiking trip, most notable for the hair-raising middle-of-the-night ride, on twisting northern Arizona roads, they were given by a drunken man who claimed to have been, as he repeatedly said, "good friends" with 1940s radio cowboy Tom Mix. A one-hour stop at Mix's gravesite seemed to sober their driver up enough to get them safely down out of the mountains. For younger son, Mike, this experience and his arrest and overnight incarceration for vagrancy while hitchhiking in Hawthorne, Nevada, on the same trip seemed like daring exploits to remember and savor. The elder, Jeff, in remembering it, thought his dad had been recklessly irresponsible in urging them to thumb rides.

When he returned home from the hospital, Bob was as low as he had ever been in his life. Pat and the rest of the family didn't know what to do to help him. He was lethargic to the point of nearly being immobile. But the coming decision of whether to run for governor again was forcing him to take action, and he sought out his old friend Dr. Dean Brooks, Director of the Oregon State Mental Hospital, for advice. In asking for help from a trusted friend, Bob wondered if his brother Jim's recent experience in receiving assistance with his own depression might be useful for him as well. Jim, who had suffered from a long series of psychological highs and lows, had been diagnosed with bipolar disorder. Jim had found an almost miraculous relief in recent years through a new treatment with lithium and anti-depressant drugs after moving to London with his new English wife, Daphne. Bob was impressed that his brother was doing so well and thought that perhaps, given the family history, his own suffering was more than a common depression; that he was in fact, like Jim, also bipolar and that he might benefit from similar treatment. This was a huge step for Bob; reaching out to Dean Brooks at this time was an acknowledgement of the severity of his problem and a courageous attempt to correct it.

At the time, "there was substantial disagreement on diagnosis" of bipolar disorder between British and American specialists.[31] According to current information distributed by the National Institute of Mental Health: "People with bipolar disorder experience unusually intense emotional states that occur in distinct periods called 'mood episodes.' An overly joyful or overexcited state is called a manic episode, and an extremely sad or hopeless state is called a depressive episode. People with bipolar disorder also may be explosive and irritable during a mood episode."[32] These symptoms fit Bob's brother Jim to a tee. In the United States, at the time Bob sought help, mania was commonly undiagnosed, whereas schizophrenia, which U.S. doctors believed Jim suffered from, "was very broadly diagnosed in the United States. Mania with psychosis"—in describing Jim's wild and out-of-control spells—"was more typically diagnosed in the United Kingdom."[33]

Jim Straub's physician, Dr. William Sargent, "was a leading British psychiatrist, noted for his enthusiasm for drug treatment in mental disorders and his criticisms of psychoanalysis." Dr. Sargent had been doing pioneering work with lithium and anti-depressants in treating bipolar disorder for many years by the time Jim first visited him in 1971. Bob marveled at how much more under control and happier his brother was after drug treatment, and his recent marriage to Daphne. Jim, always considered the flawed, but beloved, genius of the family, was beginning to get his life together. Bob wondered if he, too, might benefit from these drugs, which were just beginning to be used in treatment in the U.S. Though the efficacy of lithium in bipolar disorder mania was discovered in 1949, the drug was only approved by the Food and Drug Administration for treating it in 1970.[34] In the U.S., this was still considered experimental treatment.

Bob and Pat went over to visit their friends Dr. Dean and Ulista Brooks at their home in Salem in December of 1974. Bob asked Dean, in his capacity as a mental health professional, to investigate the work done by Dr. Sargent. Brooks agreed to quietly look into it for Straub, as a personal favor to his old friend. He telephoned Dr. Sargent in London shortly thereafter, and discussed the case with him and, after doing some more of his own research, quietly arranged with another physician at the state mental hospital, Dr. Thaddeus Furlong, to prescribe lithium and anti-depressant drugs to Bob under an assumed name, to keep Bob's diagnosis private. The anti-depressants were designed to treat the immediate problem of Bob's still deep and debilitating depression and the lithium, which takes up to a month to kick in, had the long-term effect of moderating the highs and lows common to bipolar disorder sufferers. Because lithium can build up in the kidneys and reduce their ability to function, people on lithium require regular blood tests to monitor its dangerous side effects. Every few months, Dr. Furlong would drive out to the Straubs' farmhouse in the West Salem hills to draw Bob's blood, label it under the pseudonym, and have it analyzed.[35] Adding a further layer of bizarreness to the situation, at same time that Dean Brooks was secretly assisting Bob, he was also hosting the cast and crew of the film "One Flew Over the Cuckoo's Nest" at the Oregon State Hospital, serving as the film's technical adviser, and even acting in the movie, as Randle McMurphy's (played by Jack Nicholson) psychiatrist.

Under no circumstances did the Straubs want word to get out that Bob Straub, a public figure, was receiving drug treatment for depression. The public memory was still fresh with the experience of U.S. Senator Thomas Eagleton of Missouri, who had been forced by George McGovern's presidential campaign to step down as the Democratic Party's nominee for vice president in 1972, after press reports revealed that Eagleton had received electro-shock therapy in previous years in order to treat depression.

When reviewing Bob Straub's career in politics and business, the description of bipolar disorder—characterized by periods of high functioning, elevated mood, and a flood of ideas, sometimes accompanied by irritability, alternating with periods of, sometimes deep, depression—explain the ebb and flow of his professional and personal life. The puzzle pieces seem to fit if one attributes to an extended time of 'hypomania' his prolonged energetic, creative periods, buoyed by an optimism bordering on grandiosity. The entire period from his running for state treasurer in 1964 through at least the 1970 governor's race appears to have been one long period of extreme activity and productivity. By today's standards, Straub would most likely have been diagnosed as suffering from the lesser bipolar disorder II, since his "highs" were functional and likely to result in a new political idea, or inspired purchases of land or farming and logging equipment. "I could always tell when Bob was on one of his up moods when he bought someone a new truck," Pat said later.[36] Bob's euphoric "highs" seem to have served as a source of insights, rather than a detriment. It is frequently amazing what people can do when they don't understand what other, impartial, observers might believe are their limitations. Many successful creative people credit bipolar disorder's manic periods as the source for their best ideas and work. In fact, among some professions, mood disorders seem to serve the role that advanced degrees do in other vocations. They are almost a prerequisite for great poets, for example.[37] As far back as Aristotle, observers of human behavior have noted "the link between madness and genius, not just poets and artists, but also political leaders."[38]

Bob Straub had several pronounced depressive episodes in addition to some less dramatic lows over the years. He suffered his three most noteworthy periods of depression during his year away from school because of a childhood eye infection; upon the eye infection's recurrence during the Second World War; and now, while grieving his son Bill's death. These experiences gave him empathy toward the suffering of others that was utterly personal, and which, upon his recovery, led him to strive to lift the burdens of others.

Many notable leaders have constructively harnessed their personal suffering into empathy toward others. Clinical studies show that depression correlates not just with empathy but with realism, making those who have experienced it more valuable as leaders in times of crisis.[39] Abraham Lincoln, for example, who famously suffered tremendous bouts of melancholy and in his youth wrote poetry "on subjects such as suicide and madness," eventually led the country with a depth of intelligence and compassion that can only have been understood by someone who had personally endured great misery.[40] It may very well be that those things that separate a person from the herd—whether they be through tragic or other outside circumstances, or due to genetic brain chemistry—these differences allow those individuals to contribute enormous innovation and value to the greater society. Finding themselves apart from society in some way, such people "consistently turn convention on its head," drawing their "values not from the dominant conventions of society, but from within."[41] Both he and his rival, Tom McCall, among their peer political leaders, had two of the more peculiar personalities in politics and were also, not coincidentally, two of the most influential politicians of their era.

Overcoming the shock of Bill's death took more than the normal strength Bob Straub had mustered to overcome past "down" periods. He was grateful that Dean Brooks agreed to help him and anxious to see whether drug therapy would work for him. Bob's mood improved fairly rapidly with the benefit of the anti-depressant elavil, allowing him to fully participate in the annual family trek to Mexico, while the slow-acting and persistent lithium treatment took hold.[42] The normality of the family's relaxed time on the beach of San Carlos Bay was reassuring to everyone.

When they returned to Oregon in January 1974, time was running out for Bob to decide whether or not to run for governor. He was still adjusting to his new drug routine, had no campaign in place, and State Senator Betty Roberts and Treasurer Jim Redden were both running hard in the Democratic primary. Straub knew he needed to act quickly to put a campaign together, if he was going to do it at all. His loyal crew at the state treasurer's office had moved on to new jobs. His long-time campaign manager and former deputy, Ken Johnson, was now serving as deputy director of the State Executive Department in the McCall Administration; despite Governor McCall's kind offer of a leave of absence, Johnson was not interested in climbing the steep hill of another campaign for the governorship. Barbara Hanneman, Straub's dynamic, hyper-efficient, executive secretary when he was state treasurer, had stayed on when Jim Redden took office, putting the famously loyal Hanneman in a tough spot. "I didn't participate in any of the political stuff," Hanneman remembers. "I kept Jim's schedule and kept out of it."[43]

Lacking these former stalwarts, Straub's campaign would by necessity be quickly assembled. He spoke with a few key supporters from past campaigns—Janet McLennan, State Senator Keith Burns, R. P. "Joe" Smith, among others—to discuss his strategy and make the final decision. The feeling among his informal advisers was that he still had a lot of grassroots Democratic Party support from his years as the party standard bearer. Despite the fact that he had been out of the public eye for a while, his advisers believed he had relatively high positive name recognition, though they initially had raised no money for polling to test their theories. After these discussions, and, unbeknownst to his advisors, with enough time to make certain that his new drug regimen was working, Bob Straub filed in the Democratic primary for governor on March 11, 1974, a day before the filing deadline.

With Straub dropping in, a potential dark horse candidate, Multnomah County District Attorney Harl Hass, who was beginning to make a political name for himself, dropped out, and the 1974 Democratic primary shaped up as a three-way donnybrook between the insurgent feminist Betty Roberts, the wily downstate legislator and recently elected State Treasurer Jim Redden, and the battle-scarred veteran, Bob Straub. Roberts commissioned a March poll that showed Straub in the lead, 10 percent up on her, with Redden close behind. According to her poll, Straub had taken more votes away from her than from Redden, so his entry into the race was a real blow to Roberts' chances.[44] But both Roberts and Redden, as currently elected officials who were going to continue to hold office whatever the outcome of the primary, were able to raise money—Roberts from the more progressive, activist wing of the party and Redden, perceived as the most conservative of the three, from the business community.

Roberts and Redden had different strengths. One of Roberts' strengths was Portland name recognition for various reasons, not the least of which was that her ex-husband Frank Roberts was, like Betty Roberts, a state senator, and Frank Roberts' daughter from a previous marriage, Mary Wendy Roberts, was a state representative who was then (successfully) running for state senator—tripling the "Roberts" name familiarity in Oregon's largest metropolitan region. Of even greater importance was the surging women's movement. As the first woman running a serious campaign for governor, Betty Roberts was very appealing to progressive women and reached other progressive voters throughout the state, an important constituency in a Democratic primary. Roberts, with the help of Len Bergstein, an ambitious recent New York City émigré,[45] built an extensive statewide network from the ground up, traveling across Oregon, just as Straub had done years before. Redden, a Medford lawyer and former minority leader in the Oregon House of Representatives, had been elected state treasurer in 1972, crushing his Republican opponent, a young and callow Portland businessman, Craig Berkman. The fact that Redden had run for treasurer at all that year was a fluke. "I had given up politics after the 1967 Legislature," Redden recalls. "The financial pressure of trying to maintain a law practice and a family while taking off six months every other year was too much. My wife told me 'this is enough.'"[46] Redden didn't even run in the primary, but was selected as the Democratic Party's appointment to replace their primary victor, former State Senator Alice Corbett, who was ruled ineligible to run by the state supreme court.[47] Redden was pressed into service on short notice at a special convention in the summer of 1972. He was further boosted by the state's largest newspaper, the *Oregonian*, who went against their usual practice of supporting Republicans by printing a series of negative stories about Republican candidate Craig Berkman's lack of veracity in filling out his voter's pamphlet statement.[48] With a modest, competent, and *truthful* campaign, Redden won the treasurer's race easily.

Now, only a little more than one year later, Redden hoped to raise funds from the business community and run as the most moderate candidate.

But Straub's business credentials undercut Redden's appeal in the business community and Straub proved more centrist in his approach to the campaign, further reducing Redden's room to maneuver. In addition, Redden was ironically somewhat hamstrung by the poor returns of Straub's innovative new state investment plan. The recession of 1973–1974 meant a drop in the stock market and a serious hit on state investment earnings. Fortunately for Redden and the young investment program, business leaders and editorialists were convinced of the long-term wisdom of Straub's investment vision, but it didn't help Redden's chances that those investments were losing value while he was trying to run for governor.[49]

Against Roberts and Redden, Straub brought name recognition and his record of accomplishments and a well-developed, if now middle-aged, support network. Most of the people who had supported him in the past stuck with Bob again in 1974, even though the campaign had started slowly. Roberts drew strength from a younger generation of activists and state legislators, and recruited a number of new volunteers getting involved for the first time. Redden's volunteer effort lagged behind the other two, but was most loyal in his home territory in southern Oregon. Straub's campaign consisted primarily, as it had in years past, of campaign visits, organized by local volunteers, throughout the state and interviews with the local media at each stop.

As the campaign continued, the lack of independent polling and the three-way nature of the race made it unclear whether Straub would be as successful in the primary . In fact, young Ted Kulongoski, a Eugene lawyer who was being successfully wooed by Democrats to run for a State House of Representatives seat in rural Lane County, was told by political professionals in the know that "Straub doesn't have a chance. There's no way he gets more than 35 percent" of the vote.[50] There didn't seem much room for movement in Straub's direction, since he was already a known quantity, while all the upside was with the lesser-known challengers.

Nevertheless, despite these rumblings among expert insiders, Straub was confident he would win. He ran a positive campaign, talking about his accomplishments as state treasurer and expressing his desire to continue the fine work done by the McCall administration in protecting Oregon's environment, while applying a businessman's eye to better government efficiency, as he had clearly done as treasurer. In contrast to previous campaigns, Straub didn't emphasize new issues to champion. In part, this was because his agenda was far less ambitious and concrete than in past campaigns. Bob Straub simply thought he could win and looked forward to the challenge of governing. McCall had already begun much of what Bob had advocated and Straub wanted to bring these initiatives, such as the Willamette Greenway and the new law mandating statewide land-use planning, to fruition. Straub presented himself as the one with the best administrative experience and judgment to continue Oregon on its current path.

All the candidates mostly ran positive campaigns though Betty Roberts, toward the end of the primary tried to make an issue of Straub's business money support. At an April luncheon debate in a downtown Eugene restaurant, Senator Roberts, intimated that Straub must be getting special interest money. She demanded that Straub reveal who had been contributing to his campaign and in what amounts they had been giving—something he was not required to do at that point in the race.

Scott Bartlett, a young Straub advisor leaned over to Bob and whispered, "Bob, don't take the bait. Don't respond. Play your own game." When Bob took the microphone he did, indeed, decide to play his own game, though not in the way his aide intended. Stepping to the podium, Bob Straub grandly announced that, "Permission is now hereby granted to Betty Roberts, to Betty Roberts' husband, to Betty Roberts' campaign manager, and to Betty Roberts' dog, to look over my campaign books for as long as they like. I have an open record and I have nothing to hide."[51] With bold humor Straub blew that campaign issue away in one short statement.

In the primary election, on the third Tuesday in May 1974, the Democrats chose Bob Straub once more to lead them to a long-hoped-for gubernatorial victory in November. Ted Kulongoski's insider confidants had been right about Straub not breaking 35 percent—he received 34 percent, barely more than a third of the vote—but it was enough, as Senator Roberts took 31 percent, while Redden trailed further back at 28 percent. Minor candidates divided up the crucial remaining 7 percent of the vote in what had proven to be a very tight race. Roberts' polls indicated that she had gained the most during the campaign and the consensus was that she had run the best race of the three, but had too far to come to overtake Straub.[52] Betty Roberts later told Jim Redden that her polling indicated her presence in the race probably prevented Redden from winning—she took more votes from Redden than from Straub—but that she would have lost a head to head with Straub, due to sexism, she believed.[53]

As interesting as the Democratic primary was, the Republican primary was far more surprising. Secretary of State Clay Myers was the designated successor of Tom McCall, diligently waiting his turn in the Republican ranks and anointed by business insiders, but was unexpectedly bested by a low-key, fiscally conservative state senator from Washington County, Victor Atiyeh, a son of Syrian immigrants who had established a well-known carpet business in the Portland area. Myers' defeat was a surprise to many pundits, but reflected something of a conservative revolt within the GOP. Governor McCall was popular with most Oregonians, but Republicans, especially conservatives, were restive about what had been essentially a liberal coalition government of McCall and the Democratic-controlled state legislature. Senator Atiyeh, though a moderate himself on human resource issues, targeted those alienated voters, who felt that environmental regulations had become too intrusive toward private business and that state activities were requiring too many of their tax dollars to maintain. Atiyeh wanted to turn around what he felt was an anti-business attitude in Salem and had been a consistent opponent of McCall's plans on environmental issues and taxation.

Victor Atiyeh's victory made Robert Straub's path to the governorship much easier than it would have been had he been facing the establishment candidate, Clay Myers. Because Atiyeh was on record against many of the McCall reforms, McCall (not so secretly) threw his support behind Straub. In 1974, the broad electorate, which was still enamored with Oregon's newfound national prominence as a bastion of progressive thought and environmentalism, did not share Atiyeh's viewpoint. The press's affection for McCall led them to favor Straub, in what was seen as an effort to continue the McCall era. 1974 was also a terrible year to run in the general election as a Republican everywhere in the nation, as the country recoiled from the stench of corruption emanating from the Nixon administration's cover up of the Watergate scandal. President Nixon's resignation in August of that year and President Ford's rapid pardon of him made 1974 one of the best years to run as a Democrat in the twentieth century across America.

With the deck seemingly stacked for him for the first time in his political career, Straub was a strong favorite to win and received financial support from lobbyists and corporate interests of every stripe, seeking to cover their bets should he win. In addition, Straub's campaign organization was fully staffed and professionally run in line with the best campaign techniques currently available.

The day after the May primary, Bob Straub came by R. P. "Joe" Smith's law office in Portland and asked Joe to run his campaign. Straub had run his own race in the primary and knew he needed help. Smith, a lanky politico who was a direct descendant of Mormon Church founder Joseph Smith, was a former Umatilla County District Attorney who had run for attorney general against Republican Lee Johnson in 1972, losing by less than 1 percent of the vote. Smith was a decisive campaigner and immediately established ground rules if Straub wanted him to take over management of the campaign. He told Bob to cancel a trip to Mexico he was planning to take with Pat, and to immediately call all of Betty Roberts' and Jim Redden's supporters and ask for their help in the general election. He also required that Bob set up a campaign steering committee for focusing campaign strategy and create an executive committee that would make the ultimate decisions for the campaign. "You should consider yourself an employee of the campaign," Smith said. Bob agreed.[54]

The executive committee, notably dominated by two Tom McCall partisans—attorney and former McCall administrator John Mosser and Ed Westerdahl, Tom McCall's original chief of staff—hired Joe Smith as campaign manager and Len Bergstein, fresh off the Roberts' campaign, as Smith's assistant. Mosser was especially important, a one-man "directorate" of intellectual support and an *eminence grise* that campaign staff relied on for direction. That is not to say that Democratic stalwarts, such as Multnomah County Commissioner Don Clark and Portland's charismatic young mayor, Neil Goldschmidt, on Straub's expansive steering committee, weren't also extremely influential.[55] The committee also hired a young go-getter, Mitzi Scott, another newly proven veteran from the Roberts campaign, to organize fundraising and she began an aggressive round of coffees and social gatherings that netted large sums of money for the campaign.

That July, Oregon's "Tiger of the Senate," Wayne Morse, who had been nominated in May for a rematch with the man who defeated him six years before, U.S. Senator Bob Packwood, died on the campaign trail, of cancer. Joe Smith had told the Straub campaign that, if this happened, he would leave the campaign to attempt to have himself appointed by the Democratic State Central Committee as the nominee against Packwood. He left, leaving Bergstein in charge of the campaign, though Smith was ultimately unsuccessful in gaining the nomination, which went to Betty Roberts instead.[56]

Len Bergstein, Straub's new campaign manager, was a whirling ball of purposeful energy. Perpetually chuckling with good-humored malice, he was famously foul-mouthed in his Bronx accent. It was not much of an exaggeration to say that he couldn't get out a single sentence without using a swear word for emphasis. He once told Straub's former chief confidant Ken Johnson, whose wife, Sarah, was Straub's Mid-Willamette Valley campaign coordinator and was not likely to utter a phrase more colorful than "darn it," "Ken, your wife is a f#@%ing wonder." When it was suggested that some people thought he used perhaps a bit too much profanity in his daily discourse, Bergstein replied, "Where do they get that sh#t?"[57]

The stars were aligning for what was to be Bob Straub's best statewide political campaign. He was not as close personally with the newer folks, but they were capable campaigners. This represented a break with his past. Previously Straub built his campaign teams on personal connections and trust. Now he was turning things over to a new generation of professional politicos. With the campaign funded at levels beyond any he had run before, they could afford to saturate the airwaves with top quality television and radio ads, introducing Oregon to a tailored image of Bob Straub and featuring his wife, Pat, as Oregon heroes in the Tom McCall mode. In a sense, Bob Straub was running for the third term of Tom McCall—or the third term of the Tom and Bob Show, as it had once been billed. By the fall, Bob even had Republican Governor Tom McCall's official endorsement against his party's nominee. Senator Atiyeh ran a civil campaign and tried to downplay his conservative differences with Straub, in tune with the tenor of the times. His campaign slogan, "Atiyeh. Oregon's NEXT great Governor," implied a continuity with McCall's legacy that was not there.

Straub and Atiyeh had a series of debates around the state that were viewed as bland and lacking in drama, just as the frontrunner's campaign would have hoped them to be. As in the primary, Straub emphasized his support of existing programs that he had initiated, ones initiated by McCall, and others that he supported and wanted to sustain. He did not have many new initiatives on the environment as in years past, but talked about the need to run the state more efficiently during the economic recession, which was reducing state revenue, and follow through on the state's current course.

When the votes were counted in November, Straub defeated Atiyeh in the general election, 444,812 votes to 324,751.[58] The 58 percent to 42 percent gap was the largest margin of victory since 1950—larger than any of Straub's decisive defeats at the hands of Tom McCall. Bob Straub was in shock. He had finally attained the prize he been dreaming about since 1959, sitting around a pot-bellied stove in shack on his farm in Goshen with Ken Johnson, mapping out his strategy to become the State Democratic Party Chairman. All those years of hard work, triumphs, and disappointments and now his final success had almost been too easy.

Privately, Bob Straub still remained emotionally fragile and Pat remembers worrying about him looking vulnerable and awkward, nearly speechless, at one of the campaign coffees Mitzi Scott organized for him. "I felt so embarrassed for him, seeing him like that," she said.[59] Only she and the immediate family knew that Bob was getting treatment for depression; and Bob was already tinkering with the medication, trying to get the amount of lithium he used down to a lower level so that it didn't block his creative thinking. Bob described the lithium to Dean Brooks as providing "an emotional ceiling and floor," and like many patients, he bridled at the limitations it placed on him.[60]

The transition between the McCall and Straub administrations was as friendly as one could possibly hope for. Bob's growing group of advisors and

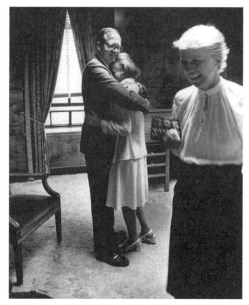

Bob and Pat Straub and Bob's sister Jean Russell celebrate the victory.
Photo by Gerry Lewin

Tom's departing staff met for a semi-public retreat at the Salishan resort on Gleneden Beach, complete with a friendly photo opportunity "walk and talk" along the beach of the incoming and outgoing governors. But as Bob began to anticipate his new job, a hollowness began to grow inside him—a sense of being overwhelmed by the number and scope of decisions he needed to make. Nevertheless, Straub persevered in making those difficult decisions despite his personal misgivings. Facing a downturn in the economy, the incoming governor was forced to consider what measures might need to be taken to turn things around for the state. He worked closely with his key advisors, especially attorney and former Legislative Ways and Means Chairman John Mosser, in developing his proposed budget for presentation to the 1975 legislature in January.[61]

Finally, on Monday, January 13, 1975, Bob Straub awoke for his inauguration. As the sun came up, brightening the frosty fields around their house, Bob was so depressed that he was almost completely immobilized. Pat, along with Bob's sister Jean Russell, accompanied him to the car, one on each arm, and drove him to the Capitol for his big speech.[62] Arriving and walking to the House Chamber, he warmed to the crowd of excited on-lookers: the state legislators, staffers, loyal campaign workers, and everyone who wished him well, and some who did not, but were charitable and smiling on that

Governor Bob Straub is sworn in by Oregon Supreme Court Chief Justice
Kenneth J. O'Connell, while Senate President Jason Boe (left) looks on.
Photo by Gerry Lewin

wonderful occasion of ceremonial transition. After his own formal swearing
in, Governor Straub gave a speech that was serious, well crafted, and well
received by listeners and the press.

Thanking the previous McCall administration for its help in a smooth
transition, Straub quipped that "the torch was passed and no fingers were
burned." The new governor quickly turned sober, observing that "there is
an economic chill across this land. And there will be no warming trend this
Spring unless we are prepared to act now." Specifically, Governor Straub told
the incoming state legislature:

> *This administration has prepared an employment stimulation package and
> I urge emergency action before February. With your approval, we can put
> 8,700 new jobs directly on line in necessary, productive work. When we
> apply the standard multiplier to those jobs, we can expect this program to
> result in general employment of another 10,300. I am asking the Legislature
> for an extraordinary response so we can put workers on the job before
> winter's end.*

Acknowledging that this bold plan would require "sizable allocations from
the State General Fund," and working closely with local government to seek
federal funding assistance, Straub outlined a six-point plan that would:

• use $20 million in state money to provide partial, interest-free financing
for a new multi-family housing construction program that would subsidize
low-income and elderly people;

• increase the state's Veterans Home Loan program loan limit by nearly 23
percent, stimulating further loans and home construction;

- create a small temporary employment program through the State Department of Forestry;
- address "long-neglected areas of need" in state infrastructure, spending $17.3 million on construction at the state's colleges and universities and the Oregon State Fairgrounds;
- shift state spending priorities at the State Highway Department from road construction to road "maintenance and state park projects"; and,
- use $1.3 million in state money to "underwrite 30 percent of the project costs" of a new state program for "stream bank erosion control."

In addition to this laundry list of projects, Straub proposed to recognize the increasing toll of financial inflation upon Oregon taxpayers by increasing personal income tax exemptions from $675 per dependent to $1,000. Straub told the assembled audience the budget he was presenting had been severely pared back by $377 million from agency requests in order to meet anticipated state revenues, claiming "we have been frugal. If any state agency is happy, we have not heard about it." This tough statement may have been to prepare listeners for his next revelation: that he would be requesting a phased-in 23 percent increase in state salary and benefits for state workers over the next two years in order to address inflationary income loss and settle an ongoing labor negotiation. Despite decrying rapidly increasing costs with no state controls, Straub also pledged a 25 percent increase in Basic School Support for the state's elementary and secondary schools, though he had "instructed a member of my staff to prepare an analysis of the disturbing increase in numbers of non-teaching school personnel and to provide me with appropriate recommendations."

Straub addressed major environmental programs by proposing to fund the state's new Land Conservation and Development program with enough money to complete local land-use plan reviews, covering 70 percent of local governments' costs in preparing those plans; consolidate the state's many energy programs into one new agency; and hinted at a new proposal to be revealed later to renew the Willamette Greenway Plan and "bring us back to the original intent of the program: to preserve this magnificent resource now and in the future."

The new governor promised to deliver further specific proposals for increasing dependent child welfare programs, address spiraling hospital costs, and require that public agencies implement strong "affirmative action to hire qualified applicants regardless of race, sex or disability." He wound up this comprehensive speech with a call to combat the growing inertia of a state bureaucracy that has brought "a justified frustration among Oregonians with delays in state service, delays in decisions, delays in rulings." Observing that "service delayed is service denied," Straub pledged that Oregonians would not be "stamped, computerized, filed and forgotten" but that his "administration will instill a new sense of urgency and visibility in delivering our one product: Service." Straub ended on a positive note, looking "to the future with confidence and enthusiasm," believing that "the new pages of the Oregon Story will … reflect not only our determination to prevail but that we did, indeed, prevail."[63]

After the applause died down and the reviews came in, Straub was credited with an unvarnished, fact-filled message and a solid performance by the pundits and state officials in attendance. He walked through the congratulatory crowd to his new office in the center of the Capitol for more ceremonial hoopla.

The next day, Bob Straub drove by himself to work. He was a new governor with a very full agenda. And now it was time to govern.

CHAPTER 11

Utopian Dreams, Economic Realities

*If you see a whole thing—it seems that it's always beautiful. Planets, lives
... But up close a world's all dirt and rocks. And day to day, life's a hard job,
you get tired, you lose the pattern.*

—Ursula K. LeGuin

Striding up the marble steps of the Capitol to the governor's office on Tuesday morning, January 14, the day after his inaugural speech to the incoming 1975 Oregon Legislature, Governor Bob Straub had a mix of proposals waiting on his desk intended to help the state's economic recovery, to provide human services to those in need, and to protect the state's scenic beauty and environmental heritage. Bob Straub began his governorship hemmed in by a recession, an energy crisis, and double-digit inflation. Governor Straub, by necessity, was forced by outside events to focus on efforts to stimulate Oregon's economy and deal with competing demands upon a financially strained state budget.

Straub's Natural Resource Advisor Janet McLennan remembers in the first weeks of the new administration "Bob invited me to come out with him for lunch at the farm, and the specific message which he delivered as we walked to his car afterwards was that, in light of the economy, we could not expect to undertake any new environmental initiatives. I didn't argue with it and kept it in mind."[1]

Much of the expansive nature of Oregon's governance that had made the 1960s and early 1970s such an exciting time for those in politics had been made possible because of a growing economy. Prosperity, and the expanding tax revenues that came with it, during those years, allowed for the creation of myriad new state commissions, blue ribbon panels, and programs addressing each new challenge the state leaders chose to engage. The expectation of the liberal Oregonians who favored improving environment quality, or improving care for the elderly, for example, was that existing programs would continue to grow and new ideas would continue to generate further innovations. This belief among activists, whose causes Straub had previously championed, that Oregon was a natural leader in unlimited governmental progress was beginning to crash into the reality of a severe economic downturn. The new governor would have to make uncomfortable funding choices between favored programs and among long-term allies.

According to Janet McLennan, Governor McCall "was addicted to executive orders setting up task forces, committees, and commissions he couldn't or didn't think he could get legislative approval on. Early in my career in 1975, I had the dubious pleasure of closing down the McCall Commission on Livability and the Willamette Greenway Committee," among others, McLennan recalls. "I am sure I did not do it with anywhere near the finesse the job called for."[2]

The recession had started with a sudden lurch in the fall of 1973, when Arab oil-producing countries established an oil boycott against the United States. At the time, Arab oil producers supplied most of the 28 percent of America's oil that was imported, and their shutoff was intended to punish President Nixon for supporting Israel in the Yom Kippur War. Through a combination of these oil-producing nations cutting back production by 20 percent and enforcing the new boycott, the price of crude oil on the world market quadrupled from $3 to $12 a barrel,[3] and the oil price shock sent the U.S. economy into the most dramatic nose dive since the 1930s, as measured by the stock market, which lost 45 percent of its value.[4] In the first quarter of 1975, the nation's unemployment rate reached 8.5 percent (up from 4.9 percent in the fourth quarter of 1973) and inflation, eating into everyone's budget, had peaked at 12.2 percent per year in the fourth quarter of 1974 and was just starting to ease downward.[5] By January 1975, Oregon was weathering a brutal unemployment rate of 12.1 percent[6]—much higher

Governor Straub looks over some papers with Pat. Photo by Gerry Lewin

than the national average—and the local annual inflation rate from the same period, though slightly lower than the national level, was still a crippling 11.5 percent per year.[7]

Coping with Oregon's hobbled economy gave Governor Straub plenty to worry about, but looming over the new governor, and further complicating his work, was the long shadow of his predecessor, Tom McCall, a man who was then, and is now, generally believed to be the most popular and remarkable governor in Oregon's history. With McCall's strong second-term legacy came the expectation that an Oregon governor should not only make wise decisions, but also inspire his people to greatness. Governor McCall was a hard act to follow and many political leaders, mostly McCall's Democratic allies, explicitly hoped that Straub would continue his good work, even if Bob couldn't hope to match Tom's showmanship. Because of Bob's affection and admiration for Tom, he, too, to a degree, saw himself in the role of maintaining what he felt were the ideals that both of them shared. Yet Governor Straub fretted that he could not equal his former rival's flair for the dramatic phrase or the ability to command the same clear, bold calls to action.

As if these burdens were not enough, Bob Straub also continued to have his secret struggle with depression due to bipolar disorder, which he managed with daily doses of lithium. Finding that the lithium drained his energy somewhat, Bob dealt with it by continuing to do what he had always done since moving to Salem—leaving the Capitol every day at noon for a home-cooked meal with Pat at their farmhouse and, often, a short nap, before returning refreshed to the governor's office. This habit was another sharp contrast to those of his predecessor, McCall, the former news reporter, who customarily had lunch every day at the press table in the Capitol Coffee Shop. Needless to say, the press loved McCall's personal attention and "after eight years of feeding like that, Bob preferring Pat's company to theirs was inexplicable," recalls Janet McLennan. "They marked it and resented it."[8]

Altogether, taking office as governor felt like stepping into a political pressure cooker and, by his own admission, it took a long time for Straub to become comfortable in his job. "I found it difficult to get on top of my work," Straub remembered later. "I'm the kind of person that has a keen sense of responsibility. And when I'm in a job I like to function and be in control of the job. The governor's job is big, because it involves thirty-five thousand employees, a number of state agencies, an innumerable number of problems, and it took me a long time to get personally in control so that I felt I was really running the ship."[9] Governor Straub's years running his own complicated business portfolio and the various projects and causes related to his time as treasurer, while challenging, had not prepared Bob for the complexity of a job as large as the governorship. His natural tendency for micro-management was not well suited for a position that required large amounts of delegation. Whereas McCall had been a quick study who left the details to his staff while he went out and sold his programs, Straub hunkered down in his office, read reports, and met with staff, trying to fully understand the government agencies he was responsible for, and to make sound decisions. Though Straub's intellectual capacity to grasp the issues facing the state was just as strong as ever, he was less prepared emotionally to take on the role for which he had battled for so many years. When it came to policy issues, his intellect and moral judgment served him well, but his multiple defeats at the hands of his rival Tom McCall caused him to doubt his judgment when it came to political matters. The new governor attempted, with the encouragement of aides who should have known better, to, at times, awkwardly mimic the flamboyant McCall style in conducting state business. In many ways, Governor Straub had taken too much to heart the advice he received from his 1974 general election campaign advisor R. P. "Joe" Smith. Smith had forcefully insisted that in the campaign Straub was to be an employee, rather than the employer, of his advisory team and that he needed to defer to their judgment. After he carefully followed this advice in the election campaign, the massive victory Straub achieved in November 1974 only vindicated this way of thinking, which then carried over into his governorship. As Straub buried himself in the policy details of understanding state government, his staff struggled to keep the political agenda moving forward. Straub's advisory team, when he began his term, lacked cohesion and clear strategic vision, and this became apparent to Capitol insiders and the media.

Chief of Staff Keith Burns, admired as a former legislator, labor and civil rights attorney, and Multnomah county prosecutor, had little administrative experience. Though Burns had been a long-time Straub loyalist, he had just left the state Senate after the 1973 session and remained caught up in the behind-the-scenes pursuit of his own personal legislative goals, mostly in support of organized labor. The new chief of staff, like Straub, seemed to suffer from the need to take a hands-on approach with the issues he cared about, and, consequently, neglected the task of managing the governor's staff, except to jealously guard Governor Straub's schedule and carefully screen who was allowed to meet with Bob.

Straub's bright young campaign manager, Len Bergstein, who became the administration's chief legislative liaison, was a neophyte in working the halls of the Capitol, and his sharp elbows and salty tongue didn't always charm legislators as much as it had his campaign staff. In addition, since neither the governor nor his chief of staff were providing the young Bergstein with regular legislative guidance, he fell under the sway of Oregon's other major Democratic office holder, Portland Mayor Neil Goldschmidt, a man who was, in 1975, at the height of his powers and a cyclone of ideas and schemes. This was not entirely negative, as Straub and Goldschmidt were close friends from many years back and were *simpatico* in their political philosophies, but it added to the confusion around the governor's office and in the legislature as to who was in charge.

Though it was a popular choice among many legislators, Straub's decision to reach across the aisle and hire Republican State Representative Stafford Hansell as the director of the State Executive Department—in charge of managing the state agencies—ruffled some loyal Democrats' feathers, who believed a liberal Democrat, rather than a conservative Republican, should have been hired. Straub, and many legislators, respected Hansell's strong understanding of the state budget from his years of service on the Ways and Means Committee, and Bob never forgot the help Representative Hansell had given him in orchestrating bipartisan approval of Straub's state investment program. Despite the early controversy, Hansell proved an able administrator and was in line with Straub's tight-fisted fiscal philosophy toward managing government.

From left: Press aide Ken Fobes, Chief of Staff Keith Burns, Governor Straub.
Photo by Gerry Lewin

Clearly the most problematic of all Straub's staff choices was the other Republican he chose for his cabinet, Ken Fobes, his new press secretary. Fobes had been brought on toward the end of the general election campaign at the suggestion of Ron Schmidt, Tom McCall's brilliant, legendary public relations man. Bob and Pat Straub were both convinced that the key to a successful governorship was good press, and who better to advise them on getting that than the McCall administration's press mastermind, Ron Schmidt? The slickly professional, sports-car-driving Schmidt was a competitive sort and never anyone's fool, so it seems plausible, as some Straub supporters believe, that his recommendation of the nervous and awkward Fobes was a joke or even an intentional attempt to sabotage the incoming Democrats, assuring that the public relations gap between the McCall and Straub administrations, which already promised to be large, would be enormous.[10] Even if that was not the case, Fobes, who had never held a position of such responsibility before, erroneously assumed it was his job to repackage Bob Straub as the next Tom McCall, with sometimes unintentionally hilarious results. The relationship between Straub and Fobes was an extremely poor fit, but it says something about the new governor's lack of confidence in his own judgment, and his political naiveté, that he and Pat stuck with this bad hire for his first couple of years in office, even though they had misgivings from the start. The Straubs innocently continued to believe that Ron Schmidt must know better than they what was best for Bob's press image.[11]

Within this mix of relatively new staff members, Straub retained two of his chief policy advisers: his old friend and confidant Janet McLennan, who became his trusted Natural Resources Advisor, and his former long-time campaign and policy aide Ken Johnson, who had been hired by Tom McCall as deputy director of the Executive Department in the last year and a half of his administration and retained the same position under Straub, as Stafford Hansell's deputy.

Also on the plus side of the ledger, engendering Governor Straub enormous amounts of good will, was his devoted and remarkable wife, who took an increasingly public role in promoting Bob's programs and giving the public a window into his life. Bob's strong bond with his wife, Pat, and his solid, outdoorsy life on their farm in the hills above West Salem, remained not just an antidote for him to the sometimes toxic political atmosphere at the Capitol, it was also a sound political asset—and he and Pat were not above using it for that purpose. Shortly before Bob's campaign for governor in 1974, Pat Straub wrote a short book entitled *From the Loving Earth* about organic gardening and healthy cooking, and, after he was elected, Ken Fobes arranged for Pat to write a weekly column that was carried by a large number

Pat Straub's garden was featured in a June 1976 *People* magazine article.
Photo by Gerry Lewin

of newspapers around the state. The column was called, "Letters Home," and was read and appreciated by many. People found Pat Straub's home remedies, recipes, nostrums, and gardening advice interesting and useful and the column helped people understand the loving, committed nature of the Straubs' relationship. In time, some politicos gossiped that Pat was more popular than Bob and that she should be the politician in the family—a notion she loyally, and vehemently, rejected. Her interest in the details of politics was minimal, though her interest in supporting Bob's career was intense, showing up in such ways as carefully combing through the governor's speeches. "She drove me crazy with her edits," one of Bob's speechwriters, Dick Sanders, remembered later. "I did everything I could to hide the speeches from her."[12]

In the Capitol, the Straubs' earthy lifestyle was a source of both admiration and mirth, depending upon the political sympathies of those observing it. For inside staffers and other Capitol denizens wishing to establish their proximity to the seat of state power, one of the ultimate status symbols was receiving some of the governor's own organic eggs from the farm. It began innocently enough when Bob began coming back from his daily lunch with Pat with several cartons of extra eggs tucked under his arms from the family's prolific hens. Of course, as would be expected with the notoriously tight Straub family, these eggs were for purchase. "Mom was the worst," son Mike remembers. "She even made family members pay for them."[13] Soon, demand in the Capitol for the eggs, which everyone claimed were "the best they had ever eaten—you can really taste the difference," was so great that Bob's executive secretary, Barbara Hanneman, had to keep a ledger to make sure that their healthy goodness was fairly distributed to those wanting them. "Senator Ed Fadeley [D-Eugene] especially loved those eggs when he found out about them," Hanneman recalls. "They were a real hot item, but I had to make sure there were still enough for my husband Gene and I to enjoy."[14]

Less charitably, some noted that Straub sometimes forgot to leave the barnyard behind when he came into the Capitol, as evidenced by his muddy shoes and pant cuffs, which even happened on his Inauguration Day.[15] The staff in Senate President Jason Boe's office loved to repeat the tale of a nearby barber who complained that he had even found chicken "leavings" in Bob's hair when he was cutting it one day—no doubt the result of his collecting some of the prized eggs for friends at the Capitol.[16] It all became part of the lore and charm, for his supporters, of Bob Straub, the unvarnished anti-politician, who couldn't remember a supporter's name to save his life, but was an honest, straight shooter. Stories like these convinced people that with Bob Straub there was no pretense. What you saw was what you got.

Straub began his relationship with the 1975 state legislature slowly. As with all new administrations, however, the governor wrong-footed a few of his early steps onto the statewide stage. The difficulties he would face with what should have been, for a Democratic governor, a friendly, Democratic-controlled House and Senate were apparent within the first week. Thinking that he would facilitate smooth relations, House Speaker Phil Lang (D-Portland) suggested weekly meetings between himself, Governor Straub, and Senate President Boe (D-Reedsport). Their first meeting was disastrous. The two presiding officers turned to Governor Straub, asking him to talk about his priorities for the session and Bob seemed ill prepared to discuss it with them. He seemed withdrawn and had very little to say about his agenda, leaving the Speaker and Senate President at a loss for words themselves. After the meeting, the somewhat imperious Boe told Lang, "I'll never waste my time doing that again," and Straub's relations with the most powerful senator were never very good from that point forward.[17]

Senate President Boe's agenda, which conveniently fit in well with his authoritarian personality, was to carve out a co-equal place for the legislative branch of state government. The legislature had long been by far the weakest of the three branches of Oregon state government and had become increasingly subservient to the growing power of the governor's office under the active governorships of Republicans Mark Hatfield and Tom McCall. The legislature was at a distinct disadvantage, meeting only for six months in odd-numbered years. Except for the presiding officers, nearly all Oregon legislators had no personal office and spent their working days at their desks on the floor of their respective chambers. Each legislator was allowed one secretary, who either joined them at the desk on the chamber floor or worked away in a large, central room that served as the typing pool. All this added up to a gross mismatch of power between the part-time legislature and the governor, with his thousands of full-time employees. Citizen legislators were, for the most part, reliant on either the executive branch or the omnipresent swarm of lobbyists to provide them the information they needed, making it difficult for them to come to independent legislative decisions.

Senate President Boe, with help from Speaker of the House Dick Eymann and then his successor Speaker Phil Lang, was trying to redress that imbalance. Boe was leading the effort to establish a beefed-up core of full-time professional staff to serve the presiding officers and ongoing interim committees. At the top of the Senate president's priority list for the 1975 session was securing funding for new Capitol office wings. The planned expansion, with Governor Straub's blessing, easily received approval that year. Construction of the new Capitol wings, which began shortly after the end of the legislative session in June, added several large hearing rooms, expanded space for the offices of newly hired permanent legislative staff, and gave each legislator a private office with an adjoining open staff and reception area. Legislators from both parties and all political persuasions were enthusiastic about these proposed reforms and appreciated the Senate president's leadership in promoting them, adding to Boe's clout in Salem. He continued to look for opportunities to increase his, and the legislature's, standing.

Away from the nuts and bolts of governing and political power plays, Oregon's innovative, gadfly reputation was still alive and well, and the 1975 legislative session bubbled with innovation, despite the state's economic concerns. A major reason was that the 1974 post-Watergate election had swept a number of left-wing Democrats into office in the heavy Democratic tide, some of whom pursued their activist interests, with support from Governor Straub.

Senator Walt Brown (D-Milwaukie), for example, was a happy liberal warrior with a laundry-list agenda, who managed to help wrangle two important Oregon innovations into law that session. The first was a *mandatory* automobile insurance law, which went through many careful drafts in the legislature's legal department before final passage, and survived a strong attack on the floor of the House by a young legal scholar, Rep. Dave Frohnmayer (R-Eugene), a University of Oregon law professor, who claimed the new law would be found unconstitutional. Frohnmayer eventually ended up voting for it. A mandatory automobile insurance law had previously only been established in Massachusetts and New York, but Oregon and several other states broke through in establishing similar laws during the 1970s, leading to its universal adoption throughout the country.[18] This bill was dear to Governor Straub, as he had attempted to pass something similar as a senator in 1961 and had even contemplated circulating the issue as an initiative petition for a public vote. Senator Brown recounts: "Bob Straub called me on the phone one day, out of the blue, to tell me that several opponents had been in to lobby him against it. Bob gave me a heads-up of who to look out for and encouraged me on."[19]

Another bill from Senator Brown was introduced with House co-sponsor Representative Pat Whiting (D-Beaverton), a strong-willed, diminutive woman who was also a self-identified "cause-oriented" liberal. The proposed law would ban the use of chlorofluorocarbons (CFCs) as a propellant in deodorant and other household items. The bill was truly cutting edge, as scientists were only just discovering the connection between these chemicals and the rapid depletion of the earth's atmospheric ozone, which protected humans, and all life, from cancer-causing ultra-violet rays. Representative Whiting recruited the help of Representative Ted Kulongoski, then a freshman Democrat from rural Lane County, who "proved crucial," according to Senator Brown. Kulongoski helped convince fellow rural Democrats, along with Democrats who, like himself, had strong labor ties, many of whom were environmental skeptics, that this innovative bill was not just the product of the feverish imagination of a few disgruntled and unhygienic hippies. Upon passage, Governor Straub proudly signed it into law, and in June 1975, Oregon became the first governmental body in the world to ban these destructive chemicals, followed shortly thereafter by the nation of New Zealand. Within a few years, it became the world-wide standard.[20]

Though it was more prosaic than saving the world's atmosphere from ozone depletion, the economic agenda took precedence over everything else in the 1975 state legislature. Governor Straub's economic stimulus plan included a modest cut in state income taxes, amounting to savings of "$91 a year for a family of four making $10,000"—figures that sound low today, but were significant in 1975. The state tax cut was almost certain to be matched by a much larger federal tax cut that the Democratically controlled Congress was negotiating with Republican President Gerald Ford. In addition, Straub hoped to bolster employment through low-income housing backed by state bonds and by beefing up, with a 20 percent increase, the amount veterans were allowed to borrow in the state's very successful veterans home loan program. He also included increases in his proposed state budget for construction at the state fairgrounds, and Oregon's colleges and universities, along with highway maintenance and park projects.[21] With unemployment high, and a sympathetic State Legislature controlled by Democrats, he wasn't getting any arguments on that part of his agenda.

Yet, despite believing he needed to focus on efforts to improve Oregon's economy and avoid new projects, Governor Straub was driven to follow up on one project with which he had a personal connection. No political goal was more deeply personal to Straub than attempting to renew his vision of a continuous parkway along the Willamette River, matching the effort to preserve the state's beaches along Oregon's coastline to the west and the growing series of Cascade Mountain wilderness areas, covering 577,000 acres of federal land by the time Straub took office, protecting a string of high volcanic peaks, forests, and mountain lakes to the east. Pursuit of the Willamette Greenway was frozen in place by the time Straub was elected governor in 1974. The voluntary approach taken by McCall in coaxing landowners to sell riverfront land to the state had yielded only two willing sellers among the six hundred property owners contacted between 1973 and 1975. Ignoring a parting warning from McCall that a more active approach would lead to "an uprising in the farming community," Bob could not resist taking up one of his signature causes, which he considered unfinished business.[22]

In March, only two months after taking office and after consulting closely with Glenn Jackson, the powerful, long-time chairman of the State Highway Commission, who agreed with Straub's more proactive instincts, Straub presented a detailed proposal to the legislature. The linchpin of the proposed legislation was granting to the highway commission's parks department broad property condemnation authority for a 500-foot strip along both sides of the river, not including farmland or developed land.[23] Despite this attempt to mollify farmers' fears, just as McCall had predicted, all hell broke loose.

When Straub publicly announced his new Greenway plans, opposing farmers, led by a firebrand named Liz VanLeeuwen, came to the Capitol in large, angry numbers. Liz and her husband, George, owned a Linn County farm that included Irish Bend on the Willamette River, a high scenic spot, perfect, highway commission officials thought, for a new state park.[24] They had been alerted before Straub's new plan by a flurry of parks department actions, pushed by Highway Commission Chair Glenn Jackson in late 1972, during McCall's second term, in which thirty to forty right-of-way agents were sent up and down the valley, attempting to purchase land. Catching wind of this activity, Liz VanLeeuwen called her neighbors, Charlie and Esther Jensen, urging them to beware of signing any land agreements too rashly, to which Esther replied, "It is funny you should call because they are sitting at our dining room table right now."[25] Some of the farmers felt that the state workers were particularly brusque in their early dealings with farmers, presenting the state park plans as a fait accompli. "These highway department agents were accustomed to using condemnation for new roads and weren't always very careful about hurting people's feelings," Ron Eber, a young Sierra Club activist at the time, recalls.[26] When the VanLeeuwens were approached, they refused to consider selling and soon they were uncompromising foes of any Greenway plan. Becoming nearly full-time legislative advocates, they founded a group with other likeminded farmers called the Willamette River Green Rights Association.[27]

Early on in the anti-land condemnation fight, the VanLeeuwens and other aggrieved farmers had key allies, chief among them McCall administration environmental advisor L. B. Day, who was helping to shepherd the proposed new statewide land-use planning bill. Day, who was also the leader of the Teamsters Union Agricultural Cannery Local, may have had multiple motivations for allying with the farmers[28] on what he perceived as a side issue, when compared to a statewide land-use system.[29] Another ally of the Greenway opponents was rising political star Representative Norma Paulus (R-Salem). Representative Paulus, another member of the liberal, McCall wing of the Republican Party, had taken the opportunity to make common cause with some of the more conservative farmers, and other defenders of private property rights, who had misgivings about the new land-use laws. Paulus had further political ambitions and was strongly rumored to be interested in running for secretary of state. "So many farmers were terrified of Straub's Greenway idea," Paulus recalls. "I had already carried a lot of water for Governor McCall on land-use planning, and I wanted to find a way to help the farmers that also preserved the riverbanks as they were."[30]

In the 1973 legislative session, L. B. Day and Representative Paulus had worked closely with the farming interests, creating a framework for dealing with the Greenway as part of establishing the Department of Land Conservation and Development, a new state agency, whose purview was nothing less than planning for the use of all lands in every corner of the state. The specific Willamette River Greenway sections of the bill, Senate Bill 100, protected farmlands along the river both from urbanized development *and* from condemnation by the state for parkland. In Paulus' view, these amendments were a compromise of continuing to allow "scenic easements, along the Willamette River, similar to those established along the Potomac River In Maryland," which would preserve the riverbank lands as farmland, but prevent the development of parks and footpaths. After the vote was over, then State Representative Stafford Hansell, a sage political observer, walked up to Rep. Paulus on the floor of the House chamber and shook her hand. "Congratulations, Norma," Hansell said. "You've just gotten yourself elected Secretary of State."[31] Bob Straub was very angry about the loss of condemnation rights along the Willamette for parks. He and Pat were out of the country in 1973 when the vote was taking place, but he made his feelings clear at a Willamette Greenway Committee meeting held the following year, in early 1974, on board the *River Queen* paddle ship on the Columbia River. Straub, once again running for governor, was given a chance to address the group and he chastised them heavily for, as George VanLeeuwen described it later, "allowing a bunch of dumb farmers to put this anti-Greenway law through."[32] It is doubtful that Straub, a farmer himself, would use such pejorative words to describe Greenway opponents, but it reflects the sense of grievance that some farmers felt against what they saw as urban interlopers.

The creation of a new state agency to oversee the use of land in the state was, in many ways, the culmination of the desire, expressed by Straub, and McCall, and felt by a majority of Oregonians, to prevent population growth and development from spoiling forever the beauty and productivity of Oregon's landscape. The sprawl of housing into rural areas, particularly farmlands, was a rising concern in Oregon. Interestingly enough, future Oregon governors and political rivals, then State Representative Victor Atiyeh (R-Washington County) and Senator Robert Straub (D-Lane County) had sponsored the Greenbelt Law in 1961 that attempted to preserve farmland by allowing counties to establish "exclusive farm use zones" to protect farming from urban encroachment. Unfortunately, only Polk and Washington counties made use of the law in any way.[33]

Eight years later, in 1969, the legislature, with Governor McCall's support, decided this voluntary program was not producing the desired results and passed Senate Bill 10, which "mandated that every city and county government produce and adopt a comprehensive plan, and zone its jurisdiction 'border-to-border.'"[34] Because many environmentalists and farm advocates still worried that this attempt to prevent unwanted urbanization might not be sufficient, the concept for the creation of the Land Conservation and Development Commission—a statewide land-use planning authority with the "teeth" to enforce its decisions—began to be debated by an interim committee on farm preservation created by the 1971 legislature, chaired by Republican Senator Hector MacPherson, a Linn County dairy farmer. MacPherson's committee, with quiet encouragement from Governor McCall, attempted to bring together in one agency all the state's efforts to protect state scenic resources, farmlands, and forests, and, above all, to control the sprawl of housing into rural areas. Senator MacPherson had personally experienced the problems of mixing suburban sprawl with farming, when new neighbors complained to authorities that his dairy farm produced too many flies. Farmers throughout the Willamette Valley were experiencing the squeeze of new suburban neighbors, rapidly changing the landscape and culture, and they provided much of the political push to move protection legislation forward. When concerned farmers witnessed the groundbreaking for the huge new housing development of Charbonneau, south of the Willamette River at Wilsonville, it stoked further fears that, unchecked, the I-5 corridor would eventually become one long city from Portland to Eugene—a strip of 120 miles.

"We were trying to make order out of chaos," Hector MacPherson remembers, trying to protect precious farmland from "people who looked upon land as a commodity that could be traded upon."[35] Senator MacPherson's committee produced Senate Bill 100, which created a commission to review and approve all local government land-use plans while taking into account prescribed land preservation goals and guidelines. Senate Bill 100 was radical in its concept of government control, at a statewide level, of the private use of lands throughout Oregon. In urging the legislature to pass the law, and Oregonians to rally to it, Governor McCall had to drill deep into his reservoir of purple prose, pronouncing "there is a shameless threat in our environment and to the whole quality of our life and that is the unfettered despoiling of our land. Coastal condomania, sagebrush subdivisions and the ravenous rampage of suburbia, here in the Willamette Valley, all threaten to mock Oregon's status as the environmental model of this nation."[36] Passage of the land-use laws in 1973 was the crowning achievement of Governor McCall and a bi-partisan coalition in the Oregon legislature.

Since this legislation from the 1973 session specifically prohibited the use of eminent domain on Willamette riverfront farmland, Straub's 1975 bill was intended to reverse that previous legislative decision. New Land Conservation and Development Commission Chairman L. B. Day furiously defended his agency's turf against Governor Straub and Highway Commission Chairman Glenn Jackson within the commission, among the farm community, and in the press.[37] Rep. Paulus was again at the forefront opposing state condemnation for parkland along the Willamette. She and Day were featured speakers at farmer rallies up and down the valley, organized by the VanLeeuwens and other opponents. Ken Johnson, who was shepherding the Greenway Bill during the 1975 session, represented the governor's office at several of these large, well-publicized meetings. The events sometimes reached such a pitch of rowdiness that Johnson had concerns for his physical safety.

Straub's bill remained stuck in Chairwoman Nancie Fadeley's (D-Springfield) Environment and Land Use Committee. For all the media attention and citizen commotion over the issue, the Greenway bill never left committee after Rep. Stan Bunn (R-Yamhill County) switched his position as the legislative session wound down, and supporters no longer had the votes to pass it. Demonstrating how badly the bill was trounced, opponents arranged for Ken Johnson, as Straub's representative, to be awarded the traditional Turkey Award for promoting the "worst bill of the session" at the end of the legislative session *Sine Die* party. The award was an actual turkey, thoughtfully pre-butchered and wrapped in plastic, which Johnson gladly took home to his family and ate.[38]

Surveying the situation after this legislative rejection, Governor Straub and Willamette Greenway proponents were forced to the default position offered by L. B. Day: regulating development along the Willamette River through the new system of statewide land-use planning. The most obvious way to codify the special importance of preserving the Willamette River for future generations was to establish it as one of the official goals of the LCDC. These goals, created by the commission under the mandate given it by the legislature, were to guide counties and cities in their planning for future land use, and to serve as a measuring stick by which the LCDC would decide whether local plans passed muster. The idea for creating a special Willamette Greenway Goal trickled up from the Department of Land Conservation and Development. "A number of us were sitting around talking about the problem and a light bulb went off," remembers Ron Eber, who was interning at DLCD by this time. The idea "ticked off" some of the Straub partisans at first, but they reconciled themselves to it fairly quickly.[39] Working with LCDC Chairman Day, Straub staffers organized more citizen meetings throughout the Willamette Valley and, by the summer of 1976, LCDC passed the Willamette River Greenway Goal.[40]

Thus ended Bob Straub's dream, imagined in his first campaign for governor ten years before, of creating a dramatic Willamette River Greenway that consisted of a series of large parks and a wide swath of public land hugging both banks of the Willamette, and linked Eugene to Portland and the Columbia River by trails and bike paths. Though some parks, large and small, and mainly in urban areas, were created along the river in ensuing years, the river was mostly preserved as it was and protected from further encroachment by human development.

A more successful venture for the new governor, though not without controversy, was his championing the creation of a new department of energy, in hopes of tackling Oregon's energy planning needs head on. The oil crisis of 1973 had made it clear that energy supply and planning were going to be critical factors in Oregon's economic development and would continue to have large environmental implications in years to come. The Straub administration inherited a body of work from the McCall administration and the state legislature dealing with this increasingly complex, and economically critical, field. An early task for the new governor's transition team was sorting through a large number of existing agencies, working groups, and programs and making decisions as to which of these to continue and which to cast aside.

McCall's early attempts at energy planning had begun accidentally. Attempting to make state government function more efficiently, Executive Department Director Cleighton Penwell had created a Special Projects Office in 1971, the state government's first general-purpose think tank, to "find a way to interrelate decisions and functions of state agencies."[41] Their job was "to peer into the future, and report back to the Governor, from time to time, with evolving social, economic and environmental trends, and to give him recommendations about policies favoring the best interests of the State."[42] Shortly after its founding, its young director, Joel Schatz, became enamored with a new field of study called "energetics," which attempted to break down "every human activity from eating to church attendance" and analyze "how much energy it consumes and produces."[43]

By the time the 1973 Arab oil boycott, and national gasoline rationing that resulted from it, hit the country, Schatz was well along in his research and quickly issued a report described later by McCall as filled with the "bold new ideas and ... innovative long-range planning" tools needed to cope with Oregon's "first dramatic energy crisis."[44] The report, entitled "Oregon's Energy Perspectives," was nationally recognized for its innovative thinking. In it, Schatz outlined the concepts of energetics, that is, the total energy needed to provide a unit of energy, including the energy cost of producing and transporting that energy. Such a method of determining energy cost gave priority to domestic, rather than foreign, oil, for example, or to conservation methods, which made the use of additional energy sources unnecessary. As an example of applying these principles, Schatz "calculated that to produce 1,000 BTUs of energy from the proposed Rocky Mountain oil shale plant would require 1,576 BTUs from elsewhere. The net energy produced would be less than zero."[45] Schatz' work was heralded nationally and internationally and a report he authored was adopted as energy policy by the 1973 Western Governors' Conference in response to the emergency of the oil supply crisis.[46]

The mustachioed, Einstein-coifed, countercultural savant Schatz became a favorite of McCall's, and the governor used to stop by, during cocktail hour on his way home, to the yellow and white state-owned bungalow on the Capitol Mall where Schatz and his staff worked, surrounded by a front yard vegetable garden. McCall and Schatz frequently engaged in animated discussions on esoteric topics into the wee hours of the morning at Schatz' home in South Salem. Schatz' small group of researchers continued to develop their theories and were reconstituted as the Office of Energy Planning and Research. Unfortunately for Schatz, Rep. Stafford Hansell, eastern Oregon hog farmer and the ranking House Republican on the state legislative Emergency Board was significantly less enamored with this new energy thinking. From his E-Board perch, Hansell tried, unsuccessfully, to pull the plug on Schatz's funding after the 1973 session, but did succeed the following year in blocking an additional grant of $133,000 that Schatz sought to "write an 'energy accounting' computer program for the 1975 Legislature." Schatz's goal was to create the "Oregon Resource Interaction Model" which he, perhaps immodestly, described as capable of evaluating "all the consequences of any decision the state or industry makes before the decision is made," based upon overall energy use.[47] Schatz's computer model inspired some forward-thinking opinion leaders, such as highly respected developer John Gray—who attempted to rally other business leaders to Schatz's cause—and left others, such as the leaders of Portland General Electric and Georgia Pacific, cold.[48] Even more threatening to utility companies was the report that the Office of Energy Planning and Research was preparing, at the request of Senator Ted Hallock (D-Portland), for the 1975 state legislature, applying OEPR's analysis to determine the optimal way forward in developing Oregon's energy future. This far-reaching report, in spite of a six-month funding delay by the Emergency Board, was poised for delivery just as Straub was taking office. Early drafts were circulating and there were clear danger signals to electric utilities.

As writer Phillip Johnson noted in his *Oregon Times* feature a few months later, "Among other things, [the report entitled] 'Transition' weighs heavily on the scales against nuclear fission, and in a chapter called 'The Solar Alternative' offers a detailed scenario by means of which EPR contends, the state could begin moving immediately toward solar power as a permanent alternative."[49] The conventional wisdom among utility executives, as expressed by Bonneville Power Administrator Don Hodel, was that the Pacific Northwest would need twenty new nuclear power plants by the year 2000. Oregon's electric utilities, both private and public, were moving aggressively to make this vision a reality. They and their supporters believed that meeting the region's burgeoning electric energy demand with energy conservation and new untested technologies, like wind and solar, was a dangerous, cannabis-scented pipe dream. These fears were reflected in the repeated reluctance of the E-Board to release funds for the various projects of the OEPR. "I think some of the members got influenced by representatives of the power company lobby," former speaker of the House Dick Eymann claimed, particularly highlighting the efforts of Pacific Power and Light lobbyist Jack McIsaac.[50]

These outside critics and some state administrators believed that the computer model "only distorts and simplifies problems by tracing them all to energy shortages." In the end, Schatz's computer model experiment, along with the Office of Energy Planning and Research itself, found its way onto the chopping block when Schatz's nemesis, Stafford Hansell, became Straub's director of the Executive Department. Hansell told reporter Dan Bernstein, "It [the computer model] could be a tremendous tool. But spending money on research to find more knowledge is not necessarily where the state should be."[51] Thus, despite national and international interest and acclaim, the OEPR stood little chance of surviving the transition into the new Straub administration. John Mosser, Straub's volunteer budget advisor, influenced by Hansell and other Schatz critics, made the formal recommendation to the incoming governor that he pull the plug. Mosser believed, incorrectly, that "their history was one of repeatedly coming in and saying, 'Just $100,000 more and we can produce something,' but they never produce anything." Bob Straub concurred with Mosser's recommendation, lamenting that "I couldn't understand what they were doing over there, and I couldn't find anyone who could tell me."[52]

In the aftermath of the decision to shut down Schatz's shop, Straub administration officials were so hostile to the content of 'Transition' that, initially, they told Schatz they would only print one copy of the report, and only because it had been mandated by the legislature. "They thought if they printed one copy they couldn't be accused of suppressing it," Schatz remembers. "It was so ridiculous. We had orders for the book from all over the world."[53] In the end the report was published and even had a second printing the following year, with a carefully worded letter from Governor Straub enclosed, disassociating the current administration from its contents. As Janet McLennan observed later: "People who were ideologically opposed to nuclear power lost an articulate spokesman, but providing one was not necessarily the best use of limited resources that Bob could deploy—and it was my impression that he was at that point ambivalent about nuclear power."[54]

In place of the Office of Energy Planning and Research, Governor Straub, his Natural Resource Adviser Janet McLennan, along with staff from a number of state agencies, plus the state legislature were channeling their desire to produce sound energy policy for the state in a new direction—the creation of a new agency that would combine many existing state functions and add some other ones under the title of the Oregon Department of Energy (ODOE). The new department had been in the works since the oil crisis, as part of the recommendations of an inter-agency study group led by the Public Utility Commission. It had been the subject of multiple hearings, with hundreds of witnesses, before the House Select Committee on Energy, created by House Speaker Dick Eymann in 1974. McLennan, who was at that time legislative staff to that committee, took responsibility for drafting the final language of the proposed legislation. The new agency would be responsible for energy facility siting, energy planning and forecasting, acting as a clearinghouse for information, and encouraging energy conservation.[55]

The Oregon Department of Energy consolidated a number of state agencies, incorporating energy plant siting previously done through the Nuclear and Thermal Energy Council into the ODOE's Energy Facility Siting Council (EFSC); the energy planning function previously done by OEPR into an ongoing public relations effort to encourage energy conservation; and, fatefully, a new energy forecasting staff, initially envisioned by OEPR's Dave Piper and Public Utility Commission staffer Lon Topaz to predict the rise and fall of gasoline supply with its price and access fluctuations. Significantly, the task force decided to include price, demand, and availability of all energy supplies in ODOE's forecasting unit, including electricity— which, unbeknownst to the drafters, to Governor Straub and his advisors, or to the vast majority of legislators who approved the new department in 1975, would prove to be the most controversial feature of the Oregon Department of Energy in the years to come.

In June of 1975, after the legislature had passed the enabling legislation for the ODOE, Governor Straub asked the PUC aide, Lon Topaz, to be its first director and he gladly accepted.[56] As the focus of the energy crisis debate shifted from concerns about access to gasoline supplies to the cost, supply, and source of future electricity, the Straub administration seemed to be off to a promising start.

More controversially, Governor Straub took a firm stand that first year in office, joining the opposition to yet another controversial highway expansion. On July 1, 1975, Straub announced he would "seek the transfer of $120 million in Mt. Hood Freeway funds for use in Portland-area highway construction projects," while allocating "the remaining $60 million the federal government has allotted" for the freeway "for various mass transit needs."[57] The Mt. Hood Freeway was plotted to veer off Interstate 5 on Portland's east side and head east, just south of SE Division Street to near 50th, where it would dip down and continue out SE Powell Avenue to meet the new ring road, I-205, which was under construction. With a spacious eight lanes, the Mt. Hood Freeway was intended as the new extension of I-84, replacing the narrow, twisting, and hazardous Banfield Freeway as the primary automobile access to and from downtown Portland. Straub's announcement had been in the works for months and was the fulfillment of one of Bob Straub's campaign pledges.

Gubernatorial candidate Straub had taken a position against the Mt. Hood Freeway proposal, at the urging of Portland Mayor Neil Goldschmidt and Multnomah County Commission Chairman Don Clark. In July of 1974, the Portland City Council had voted 4-1 to pull out of the contentious freeway proposal, following the lead of the Multnomah County Commission, which had voted 3-2 to do the same one month earlier.[58] These votes reflected several years of strong, grassroots opposition from neighborhoods that would be leveled by a new major freeway and a general belief among a growing number of Portland residents that freeway construction had already ruined enough of Portland's historic neighborhoods. The local governments' preferred alternative, beefed-up bus service through the newly formed Tri-Met regional mass transit district, was already underway. Goldschmidt, Clark, and other local leaders hoped that federal money already allocated for the freeway could be shifted to mass transit and other needed road projects in the area.

Convincing Straub to join their cause was not difficult. Starting in 1966, Bob had famously fought to prevent Highway 101, the Oregon Coast Highway, from despoiling Winema Beach, the Nestucca Sand Spit, and Cape Kiwanda. His success in defeating that proposed highway route played a little-known role in helping prevent Portland's Harbor Drive expansion, proposed by the state highway department a few years later. That saved a strip of land that later became Portland's iconic Tom McCall Waterfront Park. In 1968, during the Harbor Drive fight, Neil Goldschmidt, then a legal aid attorney envisioning a future candidacy for Portland City Council, organized a Portland press conference featuring State Treasurer Straub and local Harbor Drive opponents Bob and Alison Belcher. Less than a month after the press conference, not relishing another losing highway battle with citizen activists allied with Straub, Highway Commission Chairman Glenn Jackson and Governor McCall overruled highway department staff and began working with those who wished to create a park rather than expand a highway along Portland's Willamette River waterfront.[59]

The Mt. Hood Freeway battle of the early 1970s was a continuation of the struggle for an alternative vision of the Portland metropolitan area that imagined a more compact core, more urban housing, less sprawl, and greater mass transit use. Though "Bob wasn't a city guy, by instinct, his heart was in the Oregon landscape," as Neil Goldschmidt observed, these principles of orderly, controlled urban growth were all things that Bob Straub understood well and wholeheartedly supported—in part, to preserve the Oregon landscape elsewhere. "We knew that in order not to build the freeway, we had to have an alternative strategy that would use the same federal dollars,"

Goldschmidt recalls. "We were less anxious about stopping the freeway than we were about making the alternative work." [60]

Because federal money would be left on the table otherwise, "making the alternative work" required the State of Oregon to take the lead in lobbying the U.S. Department of Transportation and relevant congressional committees to allow that money to be transferred. Straub's July 1975 announcement of the state's intention to request a shift of allocated highway funds was the first time a state had tried to shift even part of designated federal highway money from highway to mass transit projects. This kicked off what Goldschmidt described as "a blood and guts fight," ultimately overcoming the opposition of powerful congressional committee chairmen and the administration of Republican President Gerald Ford. Straub's decision began to help turn Oregon's 3rd District Congressman, Bob Duncan, who represented the area, from a Mt. Hood Freeway supporter into an ally of transfer, along with the rest of Oregon's delegation in Congress. The Rubicon had been crossed and there was no turning back. In order to succeed, Governor Straub and his staff, working closely with Mayor Goldschmidt and his staff, developed "a consortium of people who helped work the terrain in D.C.," Straub's Legislative Affairs Director Len Bergstein remembers. "We used a number of consultants, several of whom had worked at the Federal Highway Administration. We needed to understand how we should approach repurposing the Highway money without losing it and having to reapply for the money along with every other jurisdiction in the country. It was such new territory, and they helped us navigate it." [61] As part of their strategy, they also built a coalition with other state governors who saw the wisdom of having this sort of flexibility. [62]

Meanwhile, back in Oregon, the Portland metropolitan community remained polarized on the issue, with strong partisans on both sides. Straub's decision to pursue fund transfer short-circuited a citizen's initiative, which had gathered forty thousand signatures to put an advisory vote regarding the Mt. Hood Freeway on the November 1976 ballot. "With the action I am taking, I assume no popular vote will be held," Governor Straub said at the time. "It wouldn't change what I have done or felt is the right decision." Given the votes in opposition to the freeway in the Portland City Council and the Multnomah County Commission, Straub believed that "voters would approve his action if it were presented to them." City Commissioner Frank Ivancie, an avid freeway proponent, said the governor had told the people, in effect, to "go to hell." [63] Regardless of Straub's intent, Oregon courts later backed his opinion that the advisory ballot had become moot and removed it from the ballot. The issue took on a symbolic quality in Portland's culture war, with each side fighting to determine the city's future path. The following story is illustrative of how deep the fissures were.

Representative Grace Peck (D-Portland) not only represented the district in the path of the freeway, but her beautiful, two-story, turn-of-the-century brick home, near the corner of 23rd and SE Ivon streets, would have been torn down in the process of constructing the freeway. Rep. Peck was a large, gregarious, grandmotherly woman, known in the Capitol for the multiple candy jars she kept filled on her desk on the House floor, free to all legislators and staff. With her house in danger, she seemed a natural ally when several of her neighbors approached her to oppose the freeway plan. After thinking it over, she told them, "No, I can't go with you on that. The freeway will be good for the neighborhood because it will clear out all the hippies and pot smokers that are living around here now."[64] Less subjectively based was the strong support the freeway had from organized labor, which expected to have jobs for thousands of unionized workers during construction.

Given the clear need for Straub to solidify his support with Oregon's congressional delegation, especially Republican Senators Mark Hatfield and Bob Packwood, Bob sought the help of Glenn Jackson, CEO of Pacificorp and legendary chairman of Oregon's Highway (now Transportation) Commission. Jackson understood the rationale behind the new vision of Portland's future, and believed, as a businessman, that he could work within it. He eventually threw his weight behind the transfer lobbying. "This was the genius of Bob keeping Glenn Jackson on as commission chairman after Straub became governor," Goldschmidt recalled later. Jackson traveled to Washington D.C. with the message, which had bi-partisan resonance, saying, in effect "we need to make this transfer or we risk being in paralysis" on Portland metropolitan transportation projects. This message, coming from someone as powerful and respected as Jackson, carried an enormous amount of weight.[65] "Glenn was on a first-name basis with the head of the Federal Highway Administration (FHWA)," Straub staffer Len Bergstein recalls. "He used to call him by his nickname, 'Nobby.'"[66] The FHWA director, a former Republican governor of Nebraska, Norbert T. Tiemann, was initially skeptical about repurposing highway funds, even partially, to mass transit, but warmed to the idea at Jackson's urging.

Less than a year after announcing the request for transportation funds transfer, Straub had won. On May 7, 1976, Governor Straub announced that "word of approval had come from the Federal Highway Administration." With the passage of the 1976 Federal Highway Assistance Act, signed by President Gerald Ford earlier that week, federal funds previously reserved for the Mt. Hood Freeway were now available for a variety of projects in the Portland metropolitan area. The new act also, importantly, included an inflation factor that allowed the value of the unspent funds to accrue higher, so as not to have lost their value during the previous planning dispute or due to any future delays during this time of high inflation.[67] Money now flowed into a substitute package to rebuild the Banfield Freeway, the Sunset Highway, Highway 217 at Allen Boulevard, SE Powell and SW Macadam boulevards, and Front Avenue, all important heavily used roads in the Metro area. In addition, the infrastructure was put into place for future light rail lines along the Banfield and Sunset corridors as a master plan of integrating Portland's new highly successful bus system with a grid of light rail lines that took shape in the minds of transportation planners and political leaders. Even additional rights of way were purchased along the I-205 construction corridor for a future light rail line that was not begun until thirty years later.[68] The defeat of the Mt. Hood Freeway settled the issue. The outline of the Portland metropolitan area's future transportation plan began to fall into place, securing another of Oregon's legacy cornerstones from the 1970s era.

Although not nearly as controversial or high profile at the time, Oregon's Project Independence was another first of its kind in the country. This innovative program made it possible for many elderly Oregonians to stay in their homes and avoid the indignity and expense of nursing home care. Governor Straub helped launch Project Independence, supporting and signing House Bill 2163 during the 1975 Oregon State Legislative session. The bill directed the Department of Human Services to develop and place in effect a program of supportive home services to people age sixty or older and required a fee for service based on the ability to pay. "At that time, there were no other in-home services available other than Medicaid. However, many people were not Medicaid eligible and were 'falling through the cracks.' The resulting program, Project Independence, has saved many seniors from premature institutionalization by providing a minimum amount of in-home services."[69] This program embodies Straub's core perspective that government should enable people to have the resources they need to control their own lives.

After what all agreed was very rocky start as governor—and a lamented departure from the love affair between the press and his predecessor, Tom McCall—the verdict on Straub's first legislative session from around the state was mostly positive. "He started out slowly," as the *Medford Mail-Tribune* noted in their June 11 editorial, "adjusting ... exploring ... self-examining" with "the giant figure of his predecessor ... in the background. But as the months went by, Straub gained in self-confidence," was "conciliatory and polite, but can summon up firmness and determination—and courage—

when it appears necessary." The *Mail-Tribune* editor, Eric Allen, seemed most positively struck that "Straub seems to have lost completely the querulousness that once marked many of his public pronouncements," noting with approval that Straub knows "he is not the phrase-making charismatic figure" and "isn't even trying to be. He is his own man, achieving respect in his own right and his own way."[70] While less expansive with their personal plaudits, the Portland *Oregonian* editorialists also judged Straub's 1975 session a success. Generally, "Governor Straub got most of the things he sought … He received less than he asked in some budgets and more in others, but his influence grew with the session. In the final days he was exercising strong leadership on such issues as employee salaries and field burning, while failing to get the Greenway bill he wanted." They also noted that Governor Straub "achieved his priority goal of … consolidation of the state's energy activities" in a "new department, whose director will be appointed by the governor." [71]

Consolidation of energy programs was one of the first obvious examples of Governor Straub moving toward increased executive authority for Oregon governors. Though his predecessor, McCall, had consolidated additional power to the governor's office by eliminating the board of control, the State Land Board remains to this day in the hands of a triumvirate of statewide elected officials. Straub had supported McCall's elimination of the board of control, though, as Treasurer at the time, it reduced his own personal influence. In addition to such power-sharing arrangements as the land board, Oregon had a tradition of strong, independent, appointed leadership on its volunteer boards and commissions, as evidenced, for example, by the power over transportation policy and state parks wielded by the highway, and then transportation, commission's long-time chairman, Glenn Jackson. One by one, Straub and his lieutenants sought to bring accountability for state agency actions back to the governor's office, and to reduce and simplify the large number of policy-making bodies in state government, as part of an overall attempt to centralize executive authority. "I doubt if Bob felt hampered by lack of power," Janet McLennan opined later, "but it is a fact that by constitution and law, Oregon had a very weak governor as compared with other states."[72]

As it stood, the governor could appoint members to a large number of state commissions, but many of those commissions had the power to appoint their department's administrative staff, and all had the final authority with respect to making administrative regulations spelling out implementation of state law. As a result, the governor frequently found himself having to mediate problems that he had not created himself, and suffering whatever political fallout transpired. The problem was not limited to dealing with holdover commissioners appointed by the previous administration. "Even after we had appointed the majority of most members of natural resources boards and commissions," McLennan remembers, "they were by no means subservient to the governor."[73]

It was these administrative battles that Governor Straub knew would be the most controversial, and would be the most essential to promoting his vision of Oregon's future. The governor's interaction with his appointed boards and commissions was critical to their direction and success. Even before the 1975 state legislative session began, Straub told county Democratic officials assembled for his coming inaugural that "the most important thing for the rest of this decade will be to do a wise, far-sighted, intelligent job of land-use planning."[74] Besides the coming fight in energy policy, most of the simmering environmental controversies in the state were not new initiatives but implementation of all the environmental laws that had been enacted in the McCall administration. This task fell to the Straub administration through its appointed boards and commissions, with rule making, reorganization of departments, hiring, and the myriad other duties involved in running government. The environmental success of the 1973 legislative session, Tom McCall's last session as governor, had essentially landed on Bob's desk—and on his shoulders. Unlike in years past, the risk of political damage sustained in carrying out these new environmental laws was substantially higher.

For the first time, many of these regulations applied to individual people not just some "polluting corporation." That was why the issue of field burning was so difficult, for example, and "especially difficult for Bob because his emotional sympathy was really with the farmer, though intellectually he perfectly understood the human health and safety considerations that made regulation necessary," according to his Natural Resource Assistant, Janet McLennan, "But this muted his message. And there were regulations requiring a permit to dig a pit toilet, and regulations requiring tail pipe testing to counter air pollution," a seemingly endless list of new intrusions on personal behavior.[75]

But none of the controversies over field burning, DEQ vehicle inspections, or homebuilding codes could compare with the imposition into personal property rights that was inherent in the state's new land-use planning laws. How to implement these laws was the Herculean task of the Bob Straub administration. Governor Straub, shifting his focus from legislative matters at the end of the 1975 session and feeling invigorated by his success, was ready to take the challenge head on.

Listening to the growing anger expressed by some timber, housing, and industrial interests, who were urging repealing the new land-use laws by an initiative petition and a public vote, Straub went to the September 19,

1975, Associated Oregon Industries annual convention at Salishan Lodge in Gleneden Beach and gave a "tough-worded speech," telling those assembled captains of industry that if they "attempted such a repeal action he would 'stand and fight.'" "'I will not yield an inch,' said the governor, 'and I will mobilize an army of good citizens who will stand behind us to protect what we have achieved.'" Assisting Governor Straub at the meeting was L. B. Day, still chairman of the Land Conservation and Development Commission, a staunch ally in this fight, if not the one over the Willamette Greenway. Day echoed the governor, reminding the convention, "We don't want to become a Los Angeles, or a Santa Clara Valley, or a bankrupt New York City—all because of a lack of planning."[76]

Bob Straub was back in full stride that day. He announced to reporters, "At this point in my administration, I think it is reasonable for Oregonians to assume that I will run again." This ended speculation in political circles that his low profile during the 1975 session and a reluctance to take charge of the public dialogue were an indication that he only intended to serve one term. Straub told reporters that "the job has settled down and I have settled into the job," but that he had not been coy when expressing ambivalence about his future during his first months in office. "Very honestly, I just didn't know at the time," Straub said. Now after nine months, Governor Straub believed that certain important goals for his administration had emerged, aimed at improving Oregon's future development and livability. Combating the naysayers on the left and the right, Straub vowed, "I now intend to remain in office, as long as the law and the people permit me to, in order to fulfill those goals."[77]

CHAPTER 12

Fighting Against the Tide

If it is dangerous to suppose that government is always right, it will sooner or later be awkward for public administration if most people suppose that it is always wrong.

—John Kenneth Galbraith

As the first year of Bob Straub's governorship was coming to a close, Governor Straub had reason to believe that his administration was gaining its footing and getting on track. Personally, he was now more knowledgeable about the functioning of the state bureaucracy and was, as he had been as an activist state treasurer, more comfortably engaged in expressing state policy in public. Nevertheless, governing remained extremely challenging. Oregon was changing and the changes were not favorable to Bob's basic values and agenda. The most dramatic and looming change to Oregon's economy was the growing knowledge that the state would soon be unable to rely upon timber as its only backbone industry. The early 1970s recession was just beginning to show some signs of recovery, but Oregon's economy remained sluggish and many in the state and in the nation remained dubious concerning government regulation and taxes. Opponents of activist government readily exploited this public shift in attitude.

By the end of 1975, despite the fact that the stock market was ticking upward, Oregon still struggled with monthly seasonally adjusted unemployment figures that stubbornly hovered above 10 percent.[1] The U.S. Labor Department put Portland on the national "critical list," along with New Haven, Connecticut, Wheeling, West Virginia, and Youngstown, Ohio. Oregon had "higher unemployment than at any time since the Great Depression."[2] This unemployment was also accompanied by persistent national inflation, creating a "stagflation" that haunted the entire American economy.

The ongoing rough economic situation fueled a second major problem confronting Governor Straub: a growing public disenchantment with government political activism. Paying for Oregon's activist policy making was pinching ordinary taxpayers. A variety of new regulations and laws, particularly environmental, meant individual Oregonians suddenly faced new limits on their rights to develop property or had to have their vehicles tested for pollution emissions. A new split was emerging in Oregon politics as blue collar and rural Oregonians developed powerful misgivings about regulation and taxation. These growing concerns were reflected in public opinion throughout the country and would help propel Ronald Reagan into the presidency in 1980. As a long-time advocate of government intervention on behalf of the environment and for the public good in general, Bob Straub faced a serious dilemma: how to maintain his political viability, while standing up for the things he had espoused throughout his career.

Oregon's greatest challenge and transformation was beginning to manifest itself in the area of timber policy. The lumber and wood products industry (including nurseries, tree farms, paper and allied products) was, by far, Oregon's largest employer, with over eighty-eight thousand workers and a payroll of over $1.2 billion dollars, around 10.6 percent of Oregon's covered workforce, earning nearly 14 percent of its wages.[3] The changing economic and environmental landscape of this major industry would require Straub to make some of his most difficult political choices. By the late 1970s, assumptions regarding the desirability of increasing timber harvest on the vast expanse of federally owned public forest lands in Oregon were colliding with a growing interest in preserving old-growth forests and adding substantially more acreage to wilderness areas. The employment implications were obvious. Oregon's timber harvest, post recession, was bouncing along at about 8 billion board feet per year between 1976 and 1979, down from pre-recession peaks of 10 billion board feet in 1972 and 1968.[4]

Four trends made long-term employment prospects poor: 1) increasing mechanization of lumber mills, vastly reducing the need for hands-on mill workers; 2) the over-harvesting of easily accessible, low-elevation timber, especially the high-value old-growth trees, which was exacerbated by; 3) the increasingly robust export to Japan of raw, unprocessed, old-growth logs from the Pacific Northwest; and, finally, 4) the prime reason given by the timber companies for economic distress in their industry—recreational and preservationist demand for expanding Oregon's wilderness and habitat protection.

The premise in Oregon's timber policy had been that the private companies would cut their own lands as demand required. The public lands would serve small mill owners who lacked private forest land holdings and be the reserve the larger companies could turn to while the newly planted private lands regenerated. By the mid 1970s, it was increasingly apparent that this policy had been flawed in its long-term assumptions. The multiple-use federal forests could not completely and sustainably meet the level of cutting the industry now desired. The groundwork and battle lines were being drawn for the "timber wars" of the late 1980s and early 1990s. The full magnitude of the conflict and the force of new environmental laws such as the federal Endangered Species Act and the Clean Water Act were just emerging and would balloon the conflict surrounding the industry.

Straub had sympathies on both sides of the battle over public forests. He initially supported both sides, pushing the U.S. Forest Service to increase its allowable cut to compensate for declining private harvests, while at the same time strongly advocating for a series of new and expanded wilderness areas throughout the state.[5] These issues were particularly difficult for Bob personally and politically. He had always had a direct connection to logging, having been a forest worker in his teens, working after college for the Weyerhaeuser mill in Springfield, and owning and harvesting timber on his own land in Curtin, in the southern Oregon forest of Douglas County. He maintained close connections with many in the logging industry and had regular meetings with Stub Stewart of Bohemia Lumber and other major timber company officials. Bob Straub also loved the hard, sweaty life of forest labor, yet pursued it in a sustainable way, replanting his own lands in Curtin and creating new forest acreage on land he purchased in Polk County, near Willamina. At the same time, from youth to old age, Bob always appreciated walking or horsepacking through unspoiled woodlands, or rafting the swift streams that flowed through them. As in all things, in forest policies he sought a balance between immediate economic demands and opportunities versus the long-term social values and needs.

Bob Straub recognized the challenge that evolving forest conditions and politics posed for Oregon. Scientific studies such as Oregon State University's Beuter Report of 1976 indicated that Oregon and the Northwest faced an imminent "timber gap" of at least twenty years when existing harvestable timber on private lands would not be adequate to supply existing demand and employment in the forest industry on a continual basis.[6] Having cut the prime lands, timber companies sought access to steeper, less stable hillsides and more inaccessible federal lands to maintain cut levels. This ran smack up against environmentalists seeking to preserve Oregon's wild places for wildlife, ecological health, and the enjoyment of Oregonians who loved outdoor recreation. An immediate question facing Bob was how much wilderness was appropriate on Oregon's extensive federal lands. Governor Straub had already demonstrated his care for selected wilderness areas when he sent Congress a letter strongly supporting the inclusion of the lower-elevation old-growth area of French Pete Creek into the Three Sisters Wilderness Area, along with other specific recommended inclusions in a wilderness bill, which Congress eventually passed in 1978. Yet he faced a much bigger philosophical and political question as the Forest Service inaugurated the "Roadless Areas Review and Evaluation, Number 2" (RARE II), a second effort to comprehensively identify the lands appropriate for wilderness designation.[7] RARE II provided states an explicit role in recommending the places and total acreage appropriate for wilderness within their boundaries, creating the opportunity for Bob to influence policy but also to take the political risks associated with his recommendations.

One of Bob's political strengths had been his interest in conferring with diverse people in making decisions, but in the RARE II situation he faced powerfully divergent advice. From his closest advisors on this issue Bob heard two radically different perspectives on how much wilderness was appropriate. As was his consistent perspective, Dan Goldy, director of economic development in the latter half of Straub's term as governor, recommended the more pro-business and, he believed, more politically safe position seeking to minimize the amount of land locked into wilderness. Goldy felt that the creation of extensive wilderness would mean an end to the high levels of harvests required to sustain Oregon's timber communities, especially in southern Oregon.[8] Bolstering Goldy's position were the state's powerful timber interests and the equally potent, especially for Democrats, forest products trade unions.

On the other side, Bob had his long-time natural resources advisor Janet McLennan (who saw herself as more of an "honest broker") and his friends and supporters from earlier environmental fights. In addition to the old guard of environmentalists there were a rapidly growing flock of newly emerging environmental groups and individuals, notably James Monteith and Andy Kerr from what was then the Oregon Wilderness Coalition (OWC),[9] who were pursuing a very different vision from those in favor of rapid clear-cut timber harvest. Straub met directly with groups such as the OWC even while maintaining close personal relations with Oregon timber executives, reflecting his belief that balancing these values was possible and desirable, and hoping to avoid the profound polarization that was beginning to characterize the debate.

Of the approximately two million acres of possible wilderness, Dan Goldy recommended that merely 20,000 acres near the Three Sisters Wilderness Area in Central Oregon be set aside, setting the stage for a major internal conflict. Janet McLennan disagreed, fearing that such a meager commitment would be very offensive to Bob's many environmental supporters, and would be a difficult position to maintain through an election campaign, given his former enthusiastic support for more wilderness areas. The office politics became byzantine, as the two principals maneuvered for position, with the aggressive Goldy, especially, seeking to be the last person giving Governor

Straub advice before he made his decision. At one point, Straub's legislative director, Len Bergstein, made a hurried phone call to Goldy, who was in his office in Portland, telling Goldy, "Dan, you might want to come down here." Bergstein laughingly remembers that he told Goldy, "Bob's sitting in his office with Janet and it looks like they are about to make a decision on RARE II." Goldy, oblivious to state traffic laws, made the trip to Salem in record time, charging into the governor's office in full lather, though it is unclear exactly how imminent any decision actually was on that day.[10]

Public hearings on the issue were just as divided and contentious, with hundreds of people showing up in Eugene (mostly in favor of additional wilderness area) and hundreds more showing up in Roseburg (mostly in favor of additional timber cutting on federal lands). Testimony at the hearings and in the press, on both sides, was dominated by angry, divisive talk.

In the end, Straub requested an extension of the deadline on the RARE II recommendation until December 1978. McLennan felt it was more prudent that any conclusive announcement be delayed while the state completed a ground-truth study of the land.[11] The study would provide more objective facts about the lands under consideration and delay the decision until after the 1978 gubernatorial election. Based on that study, Governor Straub signed a letter in December 1978 recommending that some 752,000 acres be recommended to Congress for wilderness designation. Straub said this represented one-half of one percent of the current potential harvest from federal forest, since much of the recommended acreage was at high elevation or in arid lands that produce little timber.[12] McLennan remembers Straub's sadness over the issue, probably believing, as Dan Goldy surely did, that "the pro-wilderness color of the process would contribute to his defeat." Wilderness advocate Andy Kerr notes that Straub still stands out for having made the largest wilderness recommendation by any western governor ever, and that his successor, Governor Victor Atiyeh, soon scaled back Oregon's recommendation to 60,000 acres. The final twist to the wilderness designation saga came when, after much high-stakes jousting between the widely admired timber industry favorite U.S. Senator Mark Hatfield (R-Oregon) and the irascible, but highly effective, environmental gadfly U.S. Representative Jim Weaver (D-Oregon, 4th District), Congress finally acted on a bill addressing the RARE II lands, approving 861,500 acres in Oregon as wilderness—more than Straub's 752,000-acre recommendation.[13]

Straub's efforts to insert environmental sensibilities to this critical part of Oregon's economy also included the regulation of herbicides, which were used to enhance forest productivity. The governor's office was heavily lobbied in 1977 and '78 by environmentalists, citing new scientific studies that implicated dioxin-laden herbicides, such as Agent Orange (which was used extensively by Americans during the Vietnam War) as both an ecological and human health risk. They strongly opposed the practice of spraying forests with the commonly used dioxin-containing herbicides 2-4D and 2-4-5T to kill competing vegetation around recently replanted tree stands. Initially Straub was hesitant to restrict chemicals that the timber industry and many other experts insisted were safe and crucial to speeding up the reforestation of cut areas.[14] While industry applauded, the unhappiness of environmentalists was vividly demonstrated at a Coos Bay meeting where Bob received a pie in the face.[15]

Environmentalists underestimated Straub, however. A state study and more personal analysis, including some lobbying from his wife, Pat, an ardent organic gardener, convinced Straub that the state needed more rigorous constraints on the chemicals, a decision reinforced by the United States Department of Agriculture's (USDA) adoption of very stringent regulations on the use of the 2-4 D family of pesticides. Although Straub's proposal did not go as far as the USDA's temporary action, he faced a difficult challenge in convincing the pro-timber-industry State Board of Forestry to *reverse* their strong support of spraying, especially since he faced the ardent and public opposition of the state forester, Ed Schroeder.[16] The high point of this conflict occurred at a board of forestry meeting on September 22, 1978. Having used the Oregon State Police to deliver to board members a two-page governor's letter telling them to ignore Schroeder's recommendation, Straub made a strong, emotional argument in person at the meeting. His 6'4" frame towering over the cramped meeting in the narrow upstairs conference room of the Salem State Forestry Building, Straub passionately and forcefully convinced the board[17] to require 200-foot buffer strips from waterways when these herbicides were to be sprayed by plane, plus more complete public notification of neighbors and interested parties when such spraying would occur.[18] Norma Paulus, who was the Republican secretary of state at the time, remembers that debate: "I was with Bob on that one. We were right but it wasn't easy to take on the timber companies."[19]

Straub fully appreciated the importance of timber and wood production to Oregon's economy. In a speech to the liberal advocacy group Oregon Student Public Interest Research Group (OSPIRG) in 1977, Bob noted: "Timber is still our number one economic resource," but then went on to identify how he would promote "the wilderness we want and the work we need to enjoy it." He had a three-fold plan to counter the projected declines in traditional timber sources: 1) higher forest productivity, 2) restrictions on log exports, and 3) increased production on small wood lots.[20]

Although he often addressed the forest productivity issue in general terms, Straub was more explicit in his criticism of log exports. The export of raw, unprocessed timber to foreign countries, primarily Japan, enabled those countries to keep their sawmills humming with the Pacific Northwest's timber while American mills faced log scarcity and high prices. Private companies, notably Georgia Pacific, were rapidly clear-cutting their own lands for this export market and shipping the prized raw logs out of the ports of Coos Bay and Astoria, and then turning around and complaining that federal lands were not available to make up the slack in their local mills. The organized-labor movement was split between the unions representing declining numbers of mill workers, whose jobs were threatened with mill closures due, in part, to the lack of a ready timber supply, and those representing longshoremen, who loaded the raw logs on ships for export.- Straub had a long-standing opposition to log exports and promoted the policy of no export from public lands. With strong, united backing by Dan Goldy and Janet McLennan on the issue, Straub wrote John Ball, the Western Woodworkers Union Secretary, that he "would be glad to join with you in any way you desire to oppose exportation of these logs. You may use my name in ads or in any other appropriate way for this purpose."[21] Straub fought unsuccessfully in the state legislature to prevent log exports from state lands and repeatedly lobbied the Jimmy Carter administration for a ban on log exports from federal lands, but never succeeded in convincing either the legislature or the federal administration to change their laissez faire policy. The timber companies that profited from the practice simply had too much clout.

From personal experience, Straub strongly identified one relatively undeveloped source of timber that some estimates placed at 3.5 million acres: small woodlots from 10 to 5,000 acres in size. Straub felt the land in small ownerships was a very significant resource and yet was concerned that most of this acreage was either unmanaged or woefully undermanaged. The governor created a Task Force on Small Woodlands under the direction of Dick Abel to identify how to expand the timber potential of these lands.[22] The task force's report was not issued until October 1978, just before the gubernatorial election; its recommendations formed the basis of legislation enacted in 1979. Bob's personal interest in small lot production continued long after he left the governorship. By early 1984 he figured he had planted at least sixty thousand Douglas firs and ponderosa pines in the five years since leaving the governorship, commenting wryly, "Some people say that I've done more for Oregon since I left office than I ever did while I was there."[23]

Straub could not avoid the complex multiple issues arising from the decline of available high-quality timber, a much higher public appreciation of the ecological and esthetic values of the land, and the state's traditional timber dependency. His efforts to find a balanced path disappointed or even angered everyone at some point, demonstrating the sincerity and difficulty of his effort to find a moderate sustainable model. Guiding the governor in this and other resource matters, such as land-use planning, was his belief that sustainable models of economic growth were possible and were crucial to Oregon's future prosperity and quality of life. Governor Straub understood, as did most economic forecasters, that for Oregon to prosper economically during an inevitable decline in timber-based employment, the state was going to need to diversify its economy. A prime area for growth, all agreed, was the nation's rapidly expanding computer-based high tech industry.

Shortly after he was elected in 1974, Straub met with Intel Corp. chief executive Gordon Moore, as Moore weighed opening a manufacturing plant in rural Washington County. The two found they had a personal connection. Moore grew up in the small farming town of Pescadero, California, just over the mountains from where Straub grew up in Los Altos and just below La Honda, in the beloved redwoods, where Straub's family spent several magnificent summers. Robert Noyce, Moore's immediate predecessor, had already built a small plant near Hillsboro, but the oil embargo recession had halted its opening. Moore, finding the economic conditions improving, decided to open the plant. Moore said later: "Bob and I would meet every three months or so for a while, and it was very pleasant. We had full cooperation from the state, but that wasn't why we chose Oregon." The real reason, according to Gordon Moore, was "cheap housing in a relatively attractive place; cheap power (back then); clean water; and it was a short flight from our headquarters in Silicon Valley. The only reason we would not have built and then opened the plant in Oregon was if the state somehow fouled it up," Intel's Moore recalls. "Given the way government operates sometimes, that could be considered an accomplishment."[24]

It also probably didn't hurt that Oregon's homegrown high-tech company, Tektronix, was already well established, and that its former employees were beginning to develop spin-off start-up companies, creating a minor hub of bright engineering talent in the Portland metropolitan area. Other Silicon Valley-based companies were considering Oregon, as well, for expansion. High-tech heavyweight Hewlett-Packard, using the same logic as Intel, moved its Advance Products Division to Corvallis, Oregon, in 1975,[25] also taking advantage of the proximity of the Engineering School at Oregon State University. Seeing the opportunities for new, "clean" industry to create jobs in Oregon that did not create the volumes of nasty smokestack pollution of previous manufacturing,[26] Straub and his administration actively pursued additional high-tech manufacturers to the state. This marketing included trying to lure foreign companies here, which was sometimes controversial, both in terms of foreign business ownership and the tax subsidies businesses were demanding in order to woo their expansion to Oregon.

Working with Portland Mayor Neil Goldschmidt, Straub and his director of economic development, Dan Goldy, traveled to Munich, Germany, to meet with officials of Wacker Chemie, which was, among other things, like Intel, a manufacturer of silicon wafers. This was the state's first foray into directly pursuing international companies to locate in Oregon. Together with the City of Portland, the state established an attractive tax-deferral and land-transfer package in return for an agreement by Wacker to hire only workers from the City of Portland and Multnomah County and pay to train them for their jobs at Portland Community College. This resulted in the opening of a new $100 million silicon wafer production plant employing one thousand people.[27]

In a similar vein, toward the end of his term in office, while dodging charges of wasting taxpayer money on junkets, Governor Straub made Oregon's first trade journey to Japan, speaking with executives from several high-tech companies there. This trip did not immediately bear fruit, but Straub's successor, Governor Victor Atiyeh, aggressively continued the painstaking courtship of Japanese and other high-tech business, as did Governors Neil Goldschmidt and Barbara Roberts after him, resulting in the location of several new silicon wafer plants in the Willamette Valley. The trend Governor Straub began reached its peak in the early 1990s, helping to spark "a major surge in the state's economy. In 1994, Governor Roberts' last year in office, there was actually more foreign investment in Oregon than in all of China."[28] Governor Straub's economic instincts were the right actions at the right time and set the economic stage for Oregon's future.

The dance of locating land for new industry and new housing to accommodate Oregon's burgeoning population, without succumbing to the uncontrolled sprawl seen in rapidly developing areas in California and elsewhere in the country, was the job of Oregon's ambitious new agency— the Department of Land Conservation and Development (DLCD). Former Governor Tom McCall's appointee as chair of the Land Conservation and Development Commission (LCDC) was the flamboyant and controversial L. B. Day, head of Teamsters Union Cannery Local 670, and a former Democrat, turned Republican Party maverick legislator. As we have seen, in 1975, shortly after Governor Straub took office, Day had helped thwart Straub's attempts to develop a Willamette River Greenway series of state parks. Nonetheless, Straub did not immediately punish Day's disloyalty by removing him from the LCDC, since the two saw eye to eye about the necessity of establishing a strong land-use planning system through this fledgling agency—and Day was a masterful and forceful advocate in those early days. Establishing the administrative meat upon the skeletal framework of the 1973 legislation was hard and controversial work. Day's bullying ways were initially critical in constructing the idealistic goals and guidelines for protection of farm and forest land and developing the procedures for how they would be met by local planners with approval from state managers.

But by the summer of 1976, L. B. Day had angered a wide variety of people and interests around the state, and Bob Straub and his staff felt it was time for a change. Henry Richmond, the co-founder (with Tom McCall) and director of the new land-use watchdog organization, 1,000 Friends of Oregon, reflected later that "L. B. Day did a great job" as Oregon's first LCDC chairman. "No one could defend the goals the way he did, because he wrote them, but he tangled with Straub and somewhat reduced his effectiveness. L. B. would have been a problem for anyone other than McCall."[29] It became clear to Governor Straub, even to L. B. Day himself, that a change was needed. Anti-land-use planning forces were gathering signatures for a ballot measure, which they eventually qualified as Ballot Measure 10, threatening to undo Senate Bill 100 and the LCDC's groundwork, and Day had become a lightning rod for opponents to land-use planning. "L. B. had an ego bigger than the State Capitol and he and Bob got increasingly sideways," former Straub legal counsel Edward J. Sullivan recalls. "Bob suggested that L. B. might want to resign and he received his resignation letter that same day."[30]

In June of 1976, Governor Straub announced that Commission Chair L. B. Day, plus Commissioner Steve Schell, a Portland attorney, strong advocate for coastal conservation protection, and long-time Straub associate, would be stepping down from the commission. They would be replaced by new chairman John Mosser and board member Anne Squier. Day's voluntary resignation served to diminish the potency of the Ballot Measure 10 campaign, which he claimed was his goal in leaving. Former State Senator Hector MacPherson, father of Senate Bill 100, was quoted in the *Oregonian* praising Day's tremendous impact on the planning body and his "moderating influence," but he also said, "It was probably time for him to step down ... It will be some help to the movement by him leaving the position."[31] For some, this seemed a step backwards, away from the strong support of statewide land-use planning, but for those who knew better this wise move put two equally committed and dedicated people in place. Mosser and Squier had the advantage of carrying no baggage and were notable for their intelligence and adroit diplomacy, and were extremely hard workers. Mosser, a Portland lawyer, former Republican legislator, and confidant to both Governors Straub and McCall, was widely respected; Squier, an environmental attorney, was less well known, but rapidly proved to be a strong, intelligent land-use planning advocate.

Mosser was a particularly critical choice, 1,000 Friends' Richmond felt, "because Oregon history shows that LCDC has been particularly strong when they had a chair who was a former Republican legislator." Just as L. B. Day had been "crucial to our success in 1975 in the fight over the budget," Richmond recalls, "John Mosser was also someone who could talk to approachable Republicans in the legislature. He knew his way around the Ways & Means Committee," the committee that controlled the budgets of all the state agencies.[32] This was especially important at this time because no matter how well written the original land-use laws were, or how diligently those early commissioners had been in crafting the land-use planning system we recognize today, the whole system could be derailed if legislators withheld the funds needed to run it.

At the same time that Governor Straub was shuffling the LCDC membership, he, through his new commission, changed the leadership at the staff level, appointing one of his West Salem neighbors, Wes Kvarsten, as the new director of the Department of Land Conservation and Development. The jovial Kvarsten—a back-slapping wild man known for his love of rock climbing, fast driving, bad puns, and all things Norwegian—had just helped complete Oregon's first urban growth boundary as the chief of staff for the Mid-Willamette Valley Council of Governments. Kvarsten's cheerful persistence drove the regional government decision-making process that included the City of Salem, plus Marion and Polk counties. Wes Kvarsten's practical experience in getting all the competing players to the table and making a sound decision had been the perfect training ground for a director of this experimental agency. "Wes was a superb appointment," according to Henry Richmond. "He was solid all along, but he really proved his mettle later in 1979 when he backed his staff recommendation in rejecting the Portland metropolitan area's planned urban growth boundary. It established strict standards for what goal 14," the urbanization goal, "really meant, and they had to take on Neil Goldschmidt and the entire Portland metro political establishment. Wes Kvarsten is as responsible as anyone for the strong land-use policies we have today."[33]

After changing the guard on the LCDC in the summer of 1976, Governor Straub and his allies turned their attention to defeating the citizens' initiative looming on the upcoming November ballot—Ballot Measure 10, which asked Oregon voters to snuff out the statewide land-use planning law. Straub asked Bill Scott, who had most recently been Portland Mayor Neil Goldschmidt's chief of staff, to head up the campaign in favor of land-use planning. "I was in Connecticut visiting the in-laws, when I got a call from the governor asking me to serve as campaign chairman," Scott remembers. "My mother-in-law was impressed."[34] With Scott on board, and a variety of strong, politically savvy supporters—including Salishan and Sunriver developer John Gray and Pacific Power and Light Chairman Glenn Jackson—assisting, Governor Straub campaigned vigorously against the repeal, helping to defeat Ballot Measure 10 at the polls by a 57 to 43 percent margin.[35]

The public was still very concerned about the rapid paving over of farmland in the Willamette Valley and slogans like "Don't Californicate Oregon" struck a chord with many people who were concerned about what uncontrolled development could do to the state. No on 10 campaign director Bill Scott says, "I especially remember a graphic we used on newspaper ads, and billboards, I think, that had a map of Oregon with a big drop of blood coming off of it. The slogan was something like, 'Save Oregon, vote no on 10.' It got covered as news, including a front-page article in the *Oregonian*. Roger Bachman, our advertising man, took a lot of grief for it, but I thought it was great. It made people think. It framed this measure as an assault on our values and a mortal danger to our state."[36]

Encouraged by LCDC Chairman Mosser and other opinion leaders, the chief supporters of Measure 10, Oregon's homebuilders, after losing in their repeal attempt, began to see the advantages of orderly planning efforts. In the interpretation of goal 10, the housing goal, "the state agency became an ally, not an enemy," according to 1,000 Friends' Henry Richmond. "The state was telling local jurisdictions, 'No, you can't have building moratoriums or set subjective criteria to deny housing projects.' For example, only 7 percent of available land in the state was zoned for multi-family housing even though half of the housing demand was for apartments and condominiums. Allowing for greater density within the urban growth boundaries made the program work as far as many of the homebuilders were concerned." Establishing certainty and a level playing field throughout the state for homebuilders, and businesses in general, became a major selling point for Governor Straub and the other proponents of land-use planning. Over the next two years the homebuilders went from the largest financial contributors in opposition to statewide land-use planning to the largest contributors in favor.[37] This made a second ballot measure to repeal land-use planning—this time a constitutional amendment, also Ballot Measure 10—much easier to defeat in November of 1978. 1978's Measure 10 failed by 61 percent to 39 percent, an even more lopsided margin than the first measure.[38]

The only major industry that remained generally skeptical of statewide land-use planning was the timber industry. The Weyerhaeuser Corporation, Governor Straub's former employer, who originally brought him to Oregon fresh out of Dartmouth Business School, had a particular bone to pick with the statewide planning agency. Wishing to branch out from logging and milling operations, Weyerhaeuser proposed a large destination resort on some of its land along the McKenzie River in the Cascade foothills of eastern Lane County. Facing local government opposition, Weyerhaeuser's plan was ultimately rejected by the state, souring them on the land-use agency. Though a Weyerhaeuser vice president was actively involved in writing goal 4—the forestry goal—they, and most of the timber industry in general, remained skeptical about any government agency that put restrictions on what they could do with their land.[39]

Perhaps not coincidentally, resentment of statewide land-use planning was prevalent in rural areas outside of the Willamette Valley, especially in those that were timber dependent, as part of the backlash against perceived state interference in the local economy. Even in those counties that had previously been Democratic Party strongholds—like Coos County, which voted in favor of Ballot Measure 10 in 1978 by a 69-31 percent margin[40]—opinions were shifting away from those in the urban centers of the state. Local Democratic coastal legislators, Representative Bill Grannell (Coos Bay) and Senator Jack Ripper (North Bend), became angry and determined opponents of the statewide planning process.[41] Coastal counties had an additional concern about the loss of local control. The Oregon coast was the place where the first battles were fought in limiting Oregon's commercial development during the Beach Bill controversy of the 1960s. In 1973, when Senate Bill 100 passed, creating LCDC, a separate agency, the Oregon Coastal Conservation and Development Commission (OCCDC) was also founded to develop similar goals and guidelines for local development within Oregon's coastal zone, designated, basically, as the lands from the crest of Oregon's Coast Range to the sea. LCDC had no jurisdiction, initially, over the OCCDC areas. This separation was partly due to the availability of federal moneys from the newly created Office of Coastal Zone Management for state coastal specific planning programs.[42]

The OCCDC was a very different animal than the LCDC, consisting of commissioners appointed by the governor, who were required to be locally elected officials—one third from cities, one third from counties, and one third from port districts. Naturally, adopting overall goals and adapting local practices to fit them was going much more slowly with the OCCDC than it did with the LCDC, and, once again, the large persona of LCDC Commission

Chair L. B. Day stepped into the breach. In a series of joint meetings between the LCDC and the OCCDC, Day muscled through the final four land-use planning goals—for Estuarine Resources, Coastal Shorelands, Beaches and Dunes, and Ocean Resources—and in 1975 the Oregon legislature, with Governor Straub's approval, ended the short-lived existence of the OCCDC, folding its responsibilities formally into the LCDC. "The way that L. B. Day was dominating their meetings, the handwriting was on the wall," 1000 Friends' Richmond remembers, "it was just a matter of time before the big snake was going to swallow up the little snake."[43]

The formal adoption of the coastal goals by the LCDC occurred after the politically damaged Day had moved on, but locally elected officials on the coast, and especially the south coast, having been disenfranchised by the demise of the OCCDC, remained particularly furious opponents to central planning decisions coming from the valley, serving as focal points for anti-state government outrage. Curry County Commissioner Mike Fitzgerald, "a publicity seeker who enjoyed thumbing his nose at the state,"[44] refused to even allow his county to participate in the state-mandated comprehensive planning, choosing instead to unsuccessfully challenge its legality in court.

By being foursquare in favor of the statewide land-use planning approach, Governor Straub, while supporting the majority position statewide, was losing support in key rural areas where organized labor had previously helped elect Democrats. Between the state government's land-use and forestry policies, rural resentment was becoming an electoral problem for Straub and he knew it.

Besides bringing the welcome defeat of Measure 10, the 1976 election also provided Straub the chance to redefine himself in the public eye. Disparaged by some for his staffing problems and "bumbling" performance in his first two years, the governor now had a second chance if he could work well with the new legislature. The 1976 election had changed the legislature significantly. National trends against Republicans, partially fueled by Nixon's disgrace, and the cresting wave of Oregon's progressivism led to the election of twenty-four Democrats in the thirty-member Senate, while the thirty-seven Democrats held a smaller though still strong majority in the House. This powerful Democratic tide did not, however, bring Democratic unity to Salem. Just as newly-elected President Jimmy Carter was facing congressional unrest in Washington, D.C., Straub had to contend with a state legislature where the Democratic majority caucus in each house was restless and divided.

Liberal expectations were high, but many Democratic legislators were from moderate and even conservative districts, particularly outside the Portland area. Large majorities tend to foster factions and the 1977 legislature certainly had its share. In the overwhelmingly Democratic Senate, Jason Boe (D-Reedsport) was elected president for the third of his record four consecutive sessions in that role, but his victory required him to defeat a push by Portland-area Democrats to oust him, a victory that was facilitated by the conversion of independently elected Senator Chuck Hanlon (Cornelius) to Democrat. In a move that reflected Boe's willingness to exercise power harshly, the Democratic rebels were denied committee chairs.[45]

The House faced even more turmoil when Speaker of the House Phil Lang was challenged over his committee appointments, and his assignment of the preponderance of bills to committees controlled by a small group of mostly Portland legislators. Lang's troubles were sparked by four rural Democrats nicknamed the Hornets: Representatives Dick Magruder (Clatskanie), Jeff Gilmour (Jefferson), Curt Wolfer (Silverton), and Max Simpson (Baker). They initially threatened to join the Republicans to form a coalition government, but, lacking the votes for that, the Hornets institutionalized their influence by joining with Democrats Bill Grannell (Coos Bay), Ed Lindquist (Milwaukie), and Ted Kulongoski (Junction City). Together this "Sixpack" (as they were called, for the suite of six offices above the Speaker's office that the prime movers occupied), working quietly behind the scenes with Senate President Jason Boe,[46] engineered a thirty-two to twenty-eight vote granting extensive powers to the Rules Committee and stripping the Speaker of much of his power, though not his title. Commentators at the time said that the conservative, more rural Sixpack, who dominated the

Governor Straub and coach Jack Ramsey (in plaid pants) fire up the barbecue while Portland Trailblazer coaches and players look on. In 1977, the Blazers won their lone NBA championship and were celebrated throughout the state.
Photo by Gerry Lewin

Rules Committee, called the shots and Lang "was left with his gavel … and practically nothing to bang it about."[47]

The final straw, so to speak, that provoked the Hornet rebellion, was the issue of field burning, which Governor Straub and the Speaker planned to make a major issue of the session.[48] During the previous session in 1975, long-distance runner Steve Prefontaine, who was coughing up blood running in the field-burning smog-filled skies of Eugene, passionately testified to retain the law that was scheduled to ban the practice of destroying pests by burning grass seed fields in the Willamette Valley. "Pre," UO coach Bill Bowerman, and fellow runners, even with most of the other oxygen breathers of the southern Willamette Valley on their side, proved no match for agricultural interests that felt their livelihoods threatened.[49] The ban was removed and Governor Straub supported a compromise in which massive, wheeled, field-burning contraptions were to be tested to see if they could run properly and eliminate smoke.

The field-burning machines proved to be a bust. Environmentalists were ready to take another run at a field-burning ban. "Before the spotted owl and the salmon, field burning was *the* environmental issue in Oregon," recalls Tom Chastain, a plant physiologist at Oregon State University.[50] The grass seed farmers were up in arms, and rallied their rural base to stop the ban, which proved the nudge the Hornets needed to perform their *coup d'etat.*

In the end, the 1977 session was a success for the governor, despite the fractious nature of the legislature. After the field-burning road block, Straub had gone forward with a relatively limited agenda, and was successful in most areas. The governor and his staff appeared very competent and well prepared, especially compared with the divided Democrats in the House. One key improvement was the replacement of his chief of staff, Keith Burns, with Loren "Bud" Kramer. Kramer appeared to have a better sense of Straub's strengths and weaknesses and was particularly adept at finding ways to keep the governor's priorities alive in Salem. Straub's new top team, especially Kramer, had a rapid and well-received impact. Stan Federman of the *Oregonian* noted that the governor's very promising start in the 1977 session was due to a more united and politically adept staff.[51] According to one analyst, his predecessor was sometimes viewed as Rasputin-like for his influence over the governor. Burns had assembled a talented but badly fragmented team, with the conflicts between him and Press Secretary Ken Fobes being particularly intractable and often petty.[52] Even William Bebout of the *Capital Journal*, a relatively consistent critic of Straub, felt that appointing Kramer would help the governor greatly, especially if Fobes was also replaced—which Straub did a few months later, appointing Michael Hartsfield in his place.[53]

In addition to the legislature being in town, Straub and his new team were tested during 1977 by the driest year on record, recording only an average of 13.98 inches of rain in the state, about 12.5 inches lower than average. According to the National Oceanographic and Atmospheric Administration, Oregon was a -5.33 on the Palmer Drought Severity Index (-4.00 is considered the extreme drought range)—the worst drought conditions in the state's history, only rivaled by three years in the 1930s.[54] Month after eerie month passed through the winter with no rain and sunny skies. There were signs of spring in February, and other disconcerting oddities. Living through that time, people celebrated each day, even as they began to dread what the consequences might be.

In early March, Governor Straub held a televised press conference, similar to the one that Governor McCall held during the oil crisis of 1973. He urged people to conserve water by doing such things as "putting a brick in the toilet," only flushing when "necessary," and showering less frequently or "with a friend." While there was some snickering in the press about the governor's hygiene advice, and unfavorable comparisons with the stirring rhetoric invoked by McCall, the message seemed to be received by Oregonians, who became much more conscious of their water use.[55] Mercifully, it began to rain in the spring and, though getting through the summer taxed Oregon communities' abilities to manage their water, 1978 was a higher than normal year, replenishing the Northwest's reservoirs.

In the 1977 legislative session, Straub's ability to promote his policies despite political headwinds was demonstrated when he successfully persuaded the legislature to create the Domestic and Rural Power Authority (DRPA), which would establish a statewide public utility to deliver low Bonneville Power Administration electricity rates to Oregon's private utility customers. Work on this project began in March of 1976, when Public Utility Commissioner Charles Davis recruited young Straub staffer Roy Hemingway to assist him in developing strategies to deal with rapidly rising utility rates.[56] Electric rates were skyrocketing, especially for private utilities in the Northwest, due to growing demand and the decision to build expensive new power plants to meet it. A new advocacy group called Oregon Fair Share, trained in confrontational Saul Alinsky-style organizing tactics, was conducting a highly successful door-to-door canvass in many Oregon cities, advocating their "Fair Share rate plan" to reduce rates for residential customers and gathering signatures on an advisory petition to present to Commissioner Davis. This effort put huge grassroots pressure on Governor Straub to do something to give ratepayers relief.

Charlie Davis, Straub's appointee and a stalwart Portland liberal, felt hamstrung by state law, which required him to give utilities a guaranteed rate of return for their investments. The law actually encouraged private utilities to engage in large-scale, expensive projects, whose price inflated the amount of return they could claim in rate increases—and no project had greater potential for high-priced cost overruns, and resulting rate hikes, than nuclear power plants. Portland General Electric (PGE) had just completed and brought on line its Trojan Nuclear Power Plant on the Columbia River forty miles downstream from Portland and was in the process of getting approval for the twin Pebble Springs reactors for Arlington, at the eastern end of the Columbia River Gorge.

The nuclear power issue passionately divided Oregonians, just as timber and land-use issues had. Voters rejected, 58-42 percent, a 1976 ballot measure to establish a long list of safety requirements before new nuclear plants could be built.[57] Since that vote, a lone activist, Lloyd Marbet, had stymied PGE's Pebble Springs reactor plans by winning a state supreme court case, arguing that the state and PGE had not considered alternatives to the nuclear plants when authorizing their construction, something that was required under state law. A consultant to Marbet, J. Carl Freeman, had developed a credible scenario relying upon wind energy, which the court agreed should have been considered by the state. This sent the nuclear proposal back to square one in the lengthy state siting process.

In the meantime, high utility rates were beginning to affect the consumption of electricity, as utility customers found ways to get by using less energy. Exponential growth predicted by the utilities was flattening out, and this fact brought them into conflict with Oregon's new Department of Energy (DOE) forecasters, who were predicting a more modest 3 percent annual growth rate, while the utilities were projecting 7-8 percent. Such differences could decide whether costly (and lucrative) new energy plants could be justified and both PGE and Pacific Power and Light (PP&L) were furiously lobbying the Oregon DOE to change their report. Possibly in response to this lobbying in the summer of 1976, Governor Straub felt caution was needed. He asked Janet McLennan to tell Oregon DOE Director Lon Topaz to hold off on releasing the figures until she could have them looked at by other outside experts. The hotheaded Topaz released the forecast numbers anyway and was summarily fired for his insubordination, fueling the controversy around the competing energy forecasts. "In hindsight, I would probably have handled it differently if I had it to do over," Topaz said later. "I felt I was required by state law to release the data and didn't realize how they would react."[58] Though Straub suffered a public relations hit for seeming to side with the unpopular utility companies, Topaz' successor, Fred Miller, presided over a nearly identical forecast the following year without interference or controversy.

Unlike the new Washington governor, Dixy Lee Ray, a former chairwoman of the Atomic Energy Commission and red hot nuclear power advocate, Governor Straub continued to take no position on nuclear power, though, based upon what he was learning from his staff at the Oregon Department of Energy, he did question the need to build them as quickly as nuclear power enthusiasts were urging.[59] The governor withstood some passionate lobbying that included friends and family. "We could never get Bob to come out against nuclear power," his sister, Jean Russell, remembers, "He would just say that he thought it would eventually fail because of bad economics."[60] Straub was proven right much sooner than many people thought possible. The governor supported efforts to end Construction Work in Progress (CWIP) charges— charging ratepayers for expenditures for new power plant construction as the plants were being built but before they were on-line—which voters eventually ended by passing Ballot Measure 9 in 1978 by a whopping margin of 69-31 percent,[61] despite an expensive utility advertising campaign in opposition. This law pinched funding for the Pebble Springs reactors, and after the Three Mile Island nuclear accident in 1979, Oregon voters, in 1980, finished the project off entirely by passing a nuclear power moratorium (Ballot Measure 7) by a narrower 53-47 percent margin.[62]

If not interested in intervening on the nuclear power question, Governor Straub was prepared to act on the issue of electric rate fairness for Oregon ratepayers. He put together a group that included PUC Commissioner Charlie Davis, his assistant, Roy Hemingway, Janet McLennan, attorney John Mosser, and, unofficially, McLennan and Straub's old friend and political collaborator Myron (Mike) Katz, a Bonneville Power Administration economist. "It did not go unnoticed that a disproportionate amount of the cheap federal Columbia River power went to Washington State," Mike Katz remembers. "Sixty percent of Washingtonians were preference customers, with power reserved [by federal law] for publicly owned utilities, while in Oregon only 25 percent received that cheap power. It struck many people that it was unjust for citizens who had paid taxes to create this system to be getting such different treatment in their utility rates."[63]

For Democrats, the traditional method for attempting to address this disparity was to attempt to form new publicly owned utilities, but the state legislature, at the behest of private utilities over the years, had made such efforts difficult and no new public utilities had been formed since the 1950s. Straub and his planning group felt the public power route was not practical. They devised the clever scheme of creating a statewide public utility, the Domestic and Rural Power Authority (DRPA), which would purchase power at the preference rate from Bonneville and pass it on to private utilities, regulated by Oregon's PUC, giving rate relief to Oregon customers. "No court had said what you needed to be a customer," Hemingway asserted later. "We felt it would work." Straub announced DRPA in a May 1976 press conference, and the group continued to prepare legislation for the 1977 session to bring it into being. "We were well aware, by that time, that new federal legislation was coming," Hemingway recalls, "and we thought DRPA could serve as a lever to solve the problem federally, rather than through state law."[64]

Straub's initial effort to pass this act faced the very formidable political opposition of Senate President Jason Boe, who created a Senate Energy Task Force that seemed "intended to attack Straub as preparation for the upcoming governor's campaign." Members of the committee included Boe himself (a possible gubernatorial candidate), Vic Atiyeh (R-Beaverton, who would repeat as Straub's election opponent), Ed Fadeley (D-Springfield, chair of the committee, famously inscrutable, and an attorney representing a public power utility), and Ted Hallock (D-Portland, who, enamored with his former working relationship with Tom McCall, had by this time become a left-leaning critic of the governor).[65] "Ed Fadeley seemed to get a kick out of poking Bob, feeding the perception that Bob was weak," Roy Hemingway observed. "He would hold hearing after hearing, but never call a vote. He was toying with me." The breakthrough came when PP&L, after staying out of the fight, negotiated minor amendments with Straub's chief of staff, "Bud" Kramer, and let members of the committee know that they supported it. "Suddenly, the bill passed," Hemingway remembers. "Fadeley just made it happen."[66] Though President Boe never took a public position on DRPA, the bill never would have stalled to begin with, nor eventually have left the committee, without his agreement.

Another interpretation of Boe's sudden support for DRPA can be found in the Straub administration's acquiescence on one of the Senate President's top priorities for the session—a bill to short-circuit the legal process that was slowing Portland General Electric's siting of the twin Pebble Springs nuclear power plants in eastern Oregon. Freshman State Senator Jan Wyers (D-Portland), with singular focused intensity and careful vote counting, managed to swing enough votes to defeat Boe's bill on the Senate floor, much to the surprise, and fury, of his presiding officer.[67]

The passage of DRPA vastly strengthened Oregon's negotiating hand with the State of Washington's powerful federal legislators on the coming Northwest Power and Planning Act (NWPPA). Bonneville Power Administrator Sterling Munro wanted the regional act to pass. He urged compromise with Oregon, adding credence to the threat that DRPA would be implemented. The public utilities in the region bitterly opposed DRPA, but wanted the regional act as well, hoping to get federal relief for their financially disastrous nuclear power plant project—the Washington Public Power Supply System (WPPSS), which was given the unfortunate moniker "Whoops" and was attempting to build five nuclear power plants simultaneously.[68] Governor Straub agreed not to implement the DRPA law, pending federal action, which maintained the ambiguity as to whether it would be found legal in the court system. The dance between Oregon and Washington delegations continued into 1980, with Roy Hemingway now representing Oregon under the Atiyeh administration. The passage of the NWPPA that year included rate relief for private power customers, Oregon's DRPA law was made null and void, and private power ratepayers in the Northwest still can find a small credit at the bottom of their electric bills, courtesy of the Bonneville Power Administration and the efforts of Governor Bob Straub.

Though DRPA was modestly successful, it came too late to help with Governor Straub's popularity, and was too complex, bureaucratic, and embedded with benefits for private power companies to convey much credit to him among the general public. Roy Hemingway remembers, "Bob thought that it was power rates that cost him his reelection."[69] Yet, DRPA's passage in the 1977 legislative session felt to Straub and his team like a worthy, hard-fought victory.

Senate President Boe and Governor Straub continued to clash over the governor's powers of appointment, shifting their personal and institutional rivalry into the realm of constitutional authority.[70] The conflict began when Straub decided that a young activist, Ron Wyden, would bring a much-needed critical eye to the state Board of Examiners of Nursing Home Administrators. Wyden, who later became Oregon's United States Senator, had made a name for himself as a co-founder of Oregon's Grey Panthers, promoting various methods of empowering seniors in social programs, and vociferously chastening nursing home operators. Since the state Senate was in recess in November 1977, the Senate Executive Appointments Committee was empowered to vote on interim appointments by the governor. The committee had already approved 136 other appointees since July 1977, but rejected Wyden because of strong opposition from the nursing home industry, who attempted to portray him as an opportunistic whippersnapper with little prior knowledge or interest in senior issues.

Straub's response was immediate and forceful. That same afternoon he appointed Wyden to the board of examiners anyway, stating that his action "will show the legislature that it can't run the administrative part of government."[71] Disregarding the state Senate's decision on an executive appointment wasn't without precedent. A few years earlier, the governor's chief of staff, Loren "Bud" Kramer, had himself experienced first-hand this tug of war between the Senate and the governor's office when his own nomination to the Oregon Law Enforcement Council by former Governor Tom McCall had been rejected by the very same committee. McCall ignored the Senate decision and retained Kramer, whose appointment was ultimately approved by the whole Senate.

President Boe and eight other senators challenged Straub's action in the Oregon State Supreme Court, noting that the Senate's statutory power to review appointments dated back to 1875. Ultimately, in May of 1978, the state supreme court rejected Boe's case on a technicality, leaving the constitutional question unresolved.[72] Straub's victory in asserting the governor's executive appointment authority proved to be short-lived, however. The 1977 legislature had already voted to refer the question of Senate approval of appointments to the public as a constitutional amendment, and the voters supported legislative power, passing Measure 2 in November 1978 with 57 percent of the vote.[73] This was an electoral victory one of its state Senate supporters, Victor Atiyeh, came to later regret during his first two months in the governor's office, when the Oregon State Senate rejected W. Kelly Woods, Atiyeh's nomination for Director of the State Department of Energy on a fiercely partisan fifteen to fifteen tie vote on the Senate floor.[74]

In Straub's executive appointments fight with the Senate, one of the biggest winners was Ron Wyden. Ann Sullivan of the *Oregonian* described how the controversy had raised senior issues to a new level in the public eyes, but her article is even more notable for providing Oregon a detailed biography of Wyden, whom she described as "that articulate young man" who has "accomplished a great many things for the elderly in Oregon."[75] The controversy provided more fuel for the rocketing political career of the ambitious Wyden, a future Oregon congressman and U.S. senator.

More importantly, on the issue of oversight of nursing homes and the creation of viable alternatives, the Straub administration continued to build upon the initial success of the Project Independence experiment launched by the 1975 legislature. Sue Hill, from the *Oregon Statesman*, reported in August of 1978 that "Oregon's leadership in slowing the automatic push of seniors into nursing homes once they needed some assistance was validated when the federal government allowed Oregon to experiment in diverting nursing home funds to in-home services that would allow low income seniors to stay in their homes."[76] This was the first waiver program of this type allowed in the nation. Eventually the program switched back to running on only state money because "with federal money there were always strings attached," according to senior advocate Phyllis Rand, "even though it was always more cost effective than institutionalized care."[77] Oregon's Project Independence remains to this day one of the major success stories in the country for helping maintain a good quality of life for the elderly.

Less controversial, but of great importance was Governor Straub's appointment of state supreme court and appeals court judges. "Bob took judicial appointments very seriously and always read through the information we prepared for him thoroughly," remembers the governor's legal advisor, Ed Sullivan. "I believe he appointed a series of excellent judges to the bench."[78]

Straub's two most noteworthy appointments were his old friend Hans Linde, a former chief aide to U.S. Senator Dick Neuberger, as a state supreme court justice in January of 1977 and State Senator Betty Roberts as a state appeals court justice in September of the same year. Described as "a giant of an intellect,"[79] Justice Linde became a nationally recognized judicial theorist, taking the strong civil libertarian position that Oregon's state constitution was intended to give its citizens greater personal freedom than was granted by the U.S. constitution. His arguments persuaded his colleagues and have influenced all civil liberties questions before the court ever since.

Betty Roberts, a ground breaker her entire life, was the first woman appointed to the State Court of Appeals and was later appointed by Governor Atiyeh as the first woman on the State Supreme Court.[80] Though Bob occasionally caught grief throughout his life, like other men from his era, for politically incorrect comments with regard to women, Roberts' appointment reflected Straub's commitment to women's rights and to affirmative action in general. According to historian Richard Clucas, "By all accounts, Straub ... appointed more women, minorities, and the disabled to state positions than any governor before him."[81] The State Senate, to its credit, did not question these affirmative action appointments during Straub's time as governor.

Overall, in the estimation of prominent political commentator Floyd McKay, Straub emerged from the 1977 legislative session with his agenda pretty much intact and without having to swallow anything he really disagreed with, a very successful outcome considering the forcefulness of various legislators.[82] After the end of the 1977 session, Bob's political prospects looked better, but certainly not ideal. Almost universally the press recognized the improvement from his "bumbling" start and, particularly, his much improved staff. But even as he enjoyed these improved reviews, Bob recognized that voters had developed new concerns and he needed to get past the baggage created by his opponents since his 1974 election. To rehabilitate his image in preparation for the 1978 campaign, Straub again turned his campaign over to the professionals, hiring David Garth, who had recently been recognized by *Time* magazine as "the nation's hottest political consultant." Besides getting the governor to lose fifteen pounds in the first half of 1978, Garth sought to promote a positive image emphasizing Bob's key qualities with the theme: "Bob Straub. Quiet, hardworking, effective."[83]

In a feature article in the *Oregon Journal* entitled "Bob Straub: I Want Four More Years," the governor strongly and confidently asserted that too much had been made of his initial circumspection as governor and that his strong record of success would continue since he had now mastered the job. This interview showed a fiery spirit. When told that one of his declared Democratic opponents, Marv Hollingsworth, had said that Oregon voters "hate the governor," Bob retorted that Hollingsworth "is full of crap."[84]

Straub's confidence was tested in the early months of 1978 when his old electoral nemesis, Tom McCall, formally entered the Republican primary field. McCall's electioneering in early 1978 highlighted the contrast in the two men's styles, to the detriment of Straub. As early as April 1977, McCall speculated that his campaign slogan could be "Let's put Oregon back on the map again," contributing to the view that Oregon needed more vigorous leadership.[85]

The political pundits, and the Straub camp, initially assumed that the popular former governor would overwhelm his primary opponents and would be heavily favored in yet another rematch with Straub. But the three-way race between Tom McCall, Senator Victor Atiyeh (R-Beaverton), and Representative Roger Martin (R-Lake Oswego) soon developed a dynamic that favored Atiyeh. On the hustings and in the media, Martin and McCall, representing the conservative and the liberal wings of the party, fought ferociously. "I could afford to be magnanimous," Atiyeh remembers, "and watch these two go after one another."[86] In addition, McCall had relied upon a strong campaign management team during his two terms in office, keeping the famously emotional and undisciplined former governor in check, but they had moved on to other things and were savvy enough to know that Tom's time was over. His former chief of staff, Bob Davis, warned him, "You'll get your heart broken." This left McCall managing a small team of inexperienced, overly awed campaigners.[87] As the campaign progressed Martin's barbs unleashed a fury in McCall that did not attract the typical Republican voter,[88] who probably already believed Tom McCall was too liberal. In the end, McCall's basic error seems to have been that he was running in the wrong primary. The Republican electorate had moved solidly to the right and he would have been better served running as an Independent or even a Democrat.[89] Victor Atiyeh not only had $130,000 of campaign expenditures over McCall's approximately $90,000, the senator also had built an organization and alliances within the Republican Party strongholds such as the business community that McCall had not anticipated.[90] In the May primary Atiyeh won with 46 percent of the vote to McCall's 33 percent, with Roger Martin, his negative campaign backfiring, bringing up the rear at 17 percent.[91]

Vic Atiyeh's defeat of McCall in the Republican primary seemed like good news to the Straub campaign. Everyone, the candidate himself included, felt that Tom McCall would have been a much tougher opponent in the general election than Atiyeh.[92] Soon Straub would find that Senator Atiyeh, the second time around, would prove to be a difficult enough challenge as an opponent.

Although the outcome was attributed to light turnout and some confusion among voters about whether McCall could legally serve a third term, Atiyeh's victory made him a giant killer and greatly encouraged conservative voters and business groups. Straub received endorsements from timber industry executives prior to the primary, when it still appeared that McCall would win; they believed Straub was the lesser 'evil, ' but their support quickly evaporated afterwards,[93] and large amounts of corporate cash flowed into the victorious Republican's campaign coffers.

As the incumbent in the Democratic primary, Straub had the natural advantage in fundraising and campaign organization, but the primary vote indicated some weaknesses in his candidacy. Strong incumbents usually have no significant opponents, and the governor had two noteworthy, but lightly regarded, Democratic rivals.

The first was Emily Ashworth, from North Bend, whose campaign was mostly focused upon environmental issues, fueled by anti-nuclear activists, including the newly formed Trojan Decommissioning Alliance, which had, as part of a nationwide movement, organized protests in the summer and fall of 1977 and the summer of 1978 resulting in over six hundred activists being arrested at the Trojan nuclear power plant and temporarily jailed. "The Widow Ashworth," as she called herself, was a schoolteacher and labor organizer, and an imposing figure at more than six feet tall. At times, she traveled around the state in a hot air balloon, and she was always highly quotable. Her favorite quote, which she used at every stop, derided Straub for what she saw as his indecision on nuclear power and other issues of importance. "If you keep on straddling the fence, you'll get a splinter up your crotch," Ashworth would say, complete with a helpful hand gesture.[94] Despite more than a decade of very prominent and innovative environmental advocacy, Straub lost 49,201 (about 17.6 percent) of Democratic voters to Ashworth, who had only $26,412 in contributions compared to Straub's primary contributions of $184,006.

Straub's second opponent did even better. Marvin Hollingsworth collected nearly $21,000 in contributions and 52,901 votes, or almost 19 percent.[95]

Hollingsworth had served as a one-term Democratic state legislator and now staked out a strong position on the right as, according to the *Oregon Statesman,* he proposed to "strip government of most of its powers and would establish a Reno-style casino in the center of the state to produce enough revenue to get rid of the property tax."[96] These right-leaning Democrats were a prime target for Atiyeh in the general election.

Overall Straub had won nearly 52 percent of the vote in a seven-person field, but clearly a sizable number of Democrats on both the left and the right were dissatisfied with Straub. Noting that Straub had skipped all debates with his primary opponents, Emily Ashworth later reflected, "I personally believe that Bob Straub made a tactical mistake by ignoring the primary election. That action implied to the electorate a personal indifference to the political process."[97]

Within a month after the May 23 primary, two driving features of the general campaign emerged. First, polls indicated that Atiyeh was the favorite. Second, on June 6, 1978, Californians passed Proposition 13, which would roll back property taxes and slow their future increase dramatically. The groundwork for a similar property tax revolt was set in Oregon as well. By early July petitioners turned in over two hundred thousand signatures for a measure very similar to California's. Straub believed the initiative, designated Measure 6, would unacceptably cut education and other core public services, but he had to carefully consider his response to the mushrooming anti-tax movement.

Despite the polls, Straub had many reasons for optimism as he looked toward the general election. He faced a candidate he had beaten, press reviews of his governorship had become much more positive, he would be endorsed by many papers throughout the state, and he was well on the way to gathering the $250,000 he had estimated he needed for a victorious campaign. Perhaps most favorable were the economic conditions. Although inflation remained very high, Oregon was in the best economic shape of the past ten years, with employment having dropped from 12.1 percent in January 1975 to 5.6 percent in March 1978 and fallen below the national average of 6.2 percent for the first time in nearly a decade.[98] Still Bob lagged behind Atiyeh in the polls and had yet to create a clear identity with Oregon voters. Despite following Garth's plan, the slimmed-down Straub could not connect with his natural constituencies, such as the Portland plumber who said: "Straub seems like a nice guy, but he hasn't done anything." Meanwhile, his Republican opponent was using a growing campaign war chest to hone a populist image as a "prophet of the people ... bringing the message of Oregonians to the state government."[99]

Despite the apparent popularity, according to early polls, of Measure 6, Oregon's version of California's Proposition 13, the property tax limitation measure that was gathering adherents across the nation, and Measure 8, which would legalize the death penalty in Oregon, Straub did not waver from his liberal views. Unlike Governor Jerry Brown of California, also up for reelection, who was reaping high poll numbers partially as a result of his reversal from Proposition 13 opponent to a "born again tax cutter," Straub stood his ground against what he saw as a wrecking ball solution to voters' concerns. He did not hesitate to oppose measures on the 1978 ballot that could weaken land-use regulation, allow the death penalty, restrict abortions, and particularly cripple local government by choking their principal revenue source. He viewed himself as pragmatic, but he "would not turn back the clock" on such core values as environmentalism, women's rights, and core social services.[100]

In early August campaign consultant David Garth met with Bob and the core group of his campaign staff. The message was not good. He brought with him a thick book of polling numbers and analysis from Peter Hart Research Associates of Washington, DC, a top national polling firm for Democrats. The governor had only a 36 percent positive rating and a 61 negative rating, and the report bluntly stated: "There is no getting around the fact that a governor with a job rating like this is not going to be reelected unless (a) he improves his job rating significantly, (b) he can convince voters his opponent is even worse, or (c) his opponent makes a major mistake." Notably problematic were Straub's "especially bad job ratings from those groups caught in the middle—the family age, middle income, blue collar voters especially hard hit by inflation and taxes … In our judgment, the Straub campaign must make a special effort to relate the governor's policies and accomplishments to the special needs these groups in the middle have." Straub's one strength noted in the poll was that the voters "perceived (him) as being on the right side" on environmental issues, but that Governor Straub needed to "restore some of the optimism, even chauvinism, about life in Oregon which seems to be disappearing."[101]

"Garth told us these poll numbers were so bad for Bob that we ought to try anything to shake up the race," Len Bergstein, once again Straub's campaign manager, remembers. "We had nothing to lose with a bold strategy."[102]

Coming out of that meeting, Straub decided that he would target Measure 6 and use that issue to break the negative polling pattern and to demonstrate why he was the best leader for Oregon. Initially, his Republican opponent for governor, Victor Atiyeh, did not directly endorse Measure 6, but he argued that he had always favored property tax reform. Atiyeh told audiences that the initiative had flaws, but could be amended later and that the growing public support for it demonstrated the public's strong sentiment on this issue. Over the summer, Straub attacked Atiyeh for waffling on the issue, emphasizing the clarity of his opposition. To defeat Measure 6 and advance his own reelection, he had to promote an alternate, more reasonable, property tax reform. Straub convened the state legislature for a special session, with the purpose of creating a legislative referral for the November ballot that would present voters a more moderate and refined tax reform option. Trying something this risky so late in an election year was a courageous move. There was danger that the legislature would fail to deliver any alternative, that the public would see this as an effort to subvert their support for drastic tax reform, and that a measure referred by the legislature would simply confuse or anger voters. These risks were compounded by the weak position of Speaker of the House Phil Lang and the great attention the passage of Proposition 13 in California drew to the issue. On the positive side, Senate President Jason Boe had his committees in order and was committed to action, and the entire Democratic majority had an interest in producing an appealing but more manageable alternative to the strongly polling Measure 6. While declaring he would not be a "prophet of hysteria," the governor emphasized the need for an alternative to Measure 6.[103] With no veto for legislative referrals, Straub could only use his powers of persuasion and hope for the best.

While not rigid on these matters, the governor identified several key elements he hoped would be in the legislature's referral: 1) a direct break for renters and homeowners, 2) limits on state and local spending, and 3) clarity. The legislature delivered a ballot measure that incorporated all three of Straub's values. Measure 11 would require the state to reimburse property owners up to one-half of property taxes up to $1,500, provide renters similar relief, set limits on state and local spending tied to population and inflation, and freeze property taxes for one year. In contrast, Measure 6 limited the tax rate to a total of $15 per $1,000 assessed value and required state and local tax increases to pass by two-thirds vote. Straub embraced Measure 11 and made Atiyeh's relatively late endorsement of Measure 6 a centerpiece of his campaign.[104] Straub received wide praise in the press for his leadership. Although the election was far more than a one-issue affair, pollster Tim Hibbitts noted that "Bob Straub tried and succeeded in polarizing the voters on Measure 6… But he seems to be losing as many votes as he is winning because of it." At least partially because of his clear position on this issue and how it brought out his fighting spirit, even if voters didn't necessarily agree with him on the issue, Straub made up much ground in the polls, closing from a 20point gap in June 1978 to a 5 percent gap in late October.[105] One bizarre portent that Straub might pull out a victory was the very visible support he received from Dorothy McCall, mother of Tom. Despite having left messages in the governor's office for him to "go to hell" since his election, the fiery ninety-year-old supported Straub without compromise in the general election. Feeling that Atiyeh had bought the Republican nomination she threatened to "poke Atiyeh's eyes out."[106]

The campaign rhetoric and strategies became more negative as the race tightened and the vote approached. Straub ridiculed the Republican candidate for his commitment to Measure 6, noting that Senator Atiyeh had voted for Measure 11 in the state senate during the September special session, and mocked the senator's claim that he would correct the flaws of Measure 6 once elected. Straub attacked Atiyeh for his commitment to "big business" in his support for Measure 6. "Tax relief for the rich," Straub called it in one television debate. On the platform with President Jimmy Carter on November 2 at Mount Hood Community College, the aggressive Straub croaked out that: "I lost my voice answering all the lies my opponent has been telling about me."[107]

The Democratic candidate was particularly irked by public attacks by a familiar combatant, now state senator, L. B. Day, whom Straub viewed as Atiyeh's "hatchet man."[108] In mid-October L. B. Day accused Straub of ethics violations for using state employees for political purposes, citing the request by Chief of Staff Loren Kramer to agency heads to send him a list of Straub accomplishments and for the printing of a picture used in the campaign in the Consumer Services Newsletter. Democratic Attorney General James Redden cleared Straub of the charges.[109]

Senator Day made a more damaging attack in early November when he accused Straub of using his influence to enable political donor Harold Schnitzer to get a state contract for low-income housing without the normal federal loan insurance. Schnitzer objected to the added federal insurance expense, asserting that the Harsch Investment Company was adequately financed to self-insure in case of problems in constructing the two-hundred-fifty-unit Clay Towers complex for low-income seniors. They believed they should have the cost waived, since they were not likely to make much money for doing what they felt was a good deed for the city. Portland Mayor Neil Goldschmidt agreed, but the State Housing Division Administrator, Gregg Smith, strongly objected. A smoldering Smith was overruled directly by Straub's chief of staff, Bud Kramer. Kramer, a successful and experienced administrator, was used to operating under the old, unofficial, but practical administrative understanding that you could bend rules as long as the end result was positive. Bill Radakovich, Multnomah County's budget director when Kramer was the county's chief of staff, remembers, "We had a motto, 'nothing in writing,' and we followed it. It was all verbal—our budgets, everything. We got a lot done that way. We were the first county in the country to computerize our tax system and we did it without any memos."[110] In the post-Watergate era in

Oregon state government, memos were kept more assiduously. Gregg Smith let Senator L. B. Day know that a folder full of his written objections to the Clay Towers deal was waiting for Day or any enterprising reporter who wanted to have an interesting read during the fall election. Portland Mayor Neil Goldschmidt, as someone involved in the negotiations and Straub's most visible political ally, leaped to the governor's defense, stating that not only was the project guaranteed by an irrevocable letter of credit by the Schnitzers, but that this arrangement was what made it possible to build the housing project for elderly citizens. While Atiyeh declared this charge deserved a more direct response by the governor, Goldschmidt asserted the Republican challenger had voted against a program to help house the elderly and that Vic Atiyeh "to the best of my knowledge, is not aware of what it takes to get a project of this scale off the ground."[111]

Neither of these accusations seems to have deeply affected voters, but they distracted from a campaign built on the image of a governor who had competence and, especially, integrity. The Clay Towers controversy hit the news the weekend before the election, blunting Straub support just as his poll numbers inched to within the margin of error. As election day approached, political pundits increasingly saw the race as too close to call. Straub seemed to have strong momentum, and Measure 11 appeared to be sliding ahead of Measure 6.

Straub was confident as the votes started to be counted. But the numbers started coming in with him consistently behind Atiyeh and stayed that way and by ten o'clock in the evening, it was becoming obvious to Bob that the race had been lost. Straub tried to reach Atiyeh at 10 p.m. to congratulate the Republican for his victory, but the senator could not take the call because he was speaking to the press. The governor-elect would not get the satisfaction of the concession that evening. Goldschmidt and other Straub advisors would not give up hope, and despite the mounting numbers, they convinced Bob that he should wait until the votes from liberal Multnomah County were counted.[112] The next day's news clarified the grim truth. Despite the governor's great push of energy and optimism, Vic Atiyeh would become governor. The victory was decisive. Atiyeh won thirty-three of thirty-six counties, earning 54.7 percent of the votes.[113]

How can you explain the loss by an incumbent who had no major scandals, under whom seventy-five thousand jobs had been created and unemployment dropped by 7 percent to below national levels, and who had proposed a far-reaching property tax cut? Three categories of explanation stand out: 1) Straub lost because his positions on the issues did not correspond to those of voters, 2) Atiyeh won because he ran a better campaign and developed a better public image than Straub's, and 3) the election's outcome reflected large social and political developments that worked against the incumbent governor.

Clearly for some voters the issues mattered. Although Straub and others were able to convince a small majority of voters to defeat Measure 6 (which gained 48 percent yes votes), Measure 11 was defeated with only 45 percent support. Considered together, the votes indicate a strong anti-tax sentiment, especially since Measure 3, increasing vehicle registration and fees, had a 76 percent no vote and an advisory measure calling for a balanced federal budget passed by 82 percent. Fiscal issues were winners for Vic Atiyeh. He ran as a fiscally conservative tax cutter and as one *Oregonian* post-mortem notes, "Atiyeh did an effective job of pinning the 'big spender' label on the Democratic governor."[114] Another issue that may have helped the Republican senator was his support of Measure 8, to re-establish the death penalty in Oregon, which passed by 64 percent. Straub never hid his views on ballot measures. He felt public leaders should state their informed opinions, but in this case Straub himself said, "I think my strong position on several issues— abortion, capital punishment, Measure 11—was a factor."[115]

While other issues were noted as possible factors in his defeat, notably timber supply concerns downstate, and power rate hikes in the Portland area, Atiyeh's campaign was, as an editorial in *The Oregonian* noted, "forceful, well-funded and well-organized state-wide." Straub could not match Atiyeh's grassroots organization, nor his funding.[116] The Atiyeh campaign was better able to control the issues and define the candidates in the public eye, foreclosing Straub's strong effort to catch the Republican in the final polls. In the general election campaign, Atiyeh raised a new record of $521, 251 compared to Straub's $291,957. For the primary and the general campaigns together, Atiyeh out-raised the Democratic governor by $652,000 to $475,963 in the state's first million-dollar gubernatorial election.[117]

But there was more to the campaign than money. In this election year, there was a notable enthusiasm gap between the two camps, reflecting a changing political tide, not just in Oregon, but throughout the nation. Once McCall was eliminated, conservatives in Oregon had a sense of renewal and Atiyeh's organization mobilized them in dramatic numbers.

In late October, Straub's political advisor, Len Bergstein, declared that the Straub campaign had one thousand volunteers in the Metro area, plus twenty-five hundred canvassing across the state.[118] Led by Sharon Paige, the Republican candidate was to deliver fifteen thousand volunteers, who staffed extensive phone banks and mailed out hundreds of thousands of pieces in the closing weeks of the election. According to reporter Wayne Thompson, the Democratic candidate was overwhelmed: "He was outspent, outcampaigned, outmaneuvered, and his campaign badly outmanned."[119]

Regardless of the impact of specific issues, the state senator from Beaverton and his people had a well-conceived and flexible game plan. Atiyeh was a moderate Republican in some ways, since he supported abortion rights, land-use planning, and strong funding for schools, but he campaigned hard as the candidate for small government, tax cuts, and a restoration of citizen control over the government. Atiyeh's message that it was time to re-balance the state after what many voters perceived as an elitist liberal imbalance of recent years struck a chord with elements of the right wing that not had been enthusiastic about politics for years. Oregon and the country had changed.

The liberalism and support for government activism that dominated the 1960s and 1970s had run its course. Certainly Proposition 13 had sent a powerful signal, and in the 1978 November election nine states approved tax or spending limits.[120] The 1978 election, mid-term in Jimmy Carter's presidency, was a political bloodbath for Democratic governors. Governors Jerry Brown in California and Hugh Carey in New York survived, but "Republicans captured seven statehouses in their first gubernatorial gains in nearly a decade."[121] In two years Ronald Reagan would take the White House with an unabashedly conservative platform. The volunteers and money that the Atiyeh camp gathered and deployed were a resource that had not been tapped effectively by the Republican Party in recent years. Also, as an editorial in the Salem *Oregon Statesman* noted, "Sensing an opportunity in the changing public mood, business opened its pocketbooks to finance the efforts of Republican candidates who stood a chance of victory. The resulting barrage of advertising made an impact."[122]

Most telling was the shift by major timber interests in Oregon from support of Straub in the primary, to a very wholesale explicit support of Atiyeh in the general election. After having made a very strong speech endorsing Straub on April 28, 1978, Aaron Jones of Seneca Sawmills announced the creation of a political action committee that would support Atiyeh. Jones asserted that Straub had simply gone too far with the pesticide regulations, his failure to resolve the RARE II issue in a timely and favorable manner, and his support for Measure 11.[123] The list of contributors to the Atiyeh campaign includes at least eighteen from the timber industry of $1,000 or more, including $5,000 from Seneca Sawmills, $8,500 from Georgia Pacific, and $4,000 from Weyerhaeuser.[124] That timber companies supported Republican candidates was not new, but this was funding on unprecedented scale.

How much had the political enthusiasm gap shifted in the recent years? One indicator is that the Republican Tom McCall's endorsement of Straub late in the general election, which had been political gold in 1974, seemed to have no impact at all. Straub had some strong supporters, especially in Multnomah County, but his party would have lower voter turnout (61.7 percent) than his opponent's (70.1 percent) and campaign polling indicates that he lost far more Democrats than Atiyeh lost GOP voters.[125] All of these patterns reflect the re-emergence of the Republican Party following the dark years after President Nixon's Watergate disgrace. Although the social conservatism that marked Republican activism in other parts of the country was weaker in Oregon, the strong anti-government populist appeal resonated with many voters.

The 1978 election marked the end of one of Oregon's most progressive times. Atiyeh was not so much an instrument of change as an able surfer of the reaction to the liberal 1970s. Although Republicans held more statewide offices in the late 1970s and early 1980s than they have in the years since, the election did not constitute a revolution in party control. Democrats retained control of the House for another twelve years and the Senate remained in Democratic hands until the 1994 election.. Yet it became clear over the years that 1978 was the year that the bipartisan progressive movement was broken in Oregon.

Two things in Oregon politics were clearly different following the 1978 election. First, the initiative system had become a major tool of conservative populist interests, reaching its high point in the 1990s when property taxes were drastically reduced by Measure 5 and its successor measures, while income tax dollars became captive of anti-crime ballot measures requiring the building and staffing of an expanded prison system. All governors and legislators henceforth lived in the shadow of potential initiatives that would make sustaining new government activism very difficult. Secondly, although Vic Atiyeh walked the middle ground between Portland and the rural areas and their strongly divergent social and political perspectives, Oregon's long-standing geographical split took on a new dimension that remains a core theme of Oregon politics today. Since the 1978 election, major new progressive policies have faced periodic revisions and sometimes reversals due to the initiative system, fluctuating revenues during economic downturns, or divided state government. The liberal bipartisanship that marked the McCall era had atrophied under Straub, as Republicans and conservative Democrats walked away from activist government. With the exception of a concerted effort to diversify Oregon economy, something Straub had already begun, Atiyeh's eight years were marked by the struggle to balance budgets and protect existing programs and services rather than by revolutionary policy change.

Straub's disappointment with the loss was profound, and his staff felt the same way. The governor's personal secretary, Barbara Hanneman, noted that in her long service with Straub they had seen many defeats, but this was the worst. She also reflected the sentiment of Straub's loyal supporters that Oregon voters had made a mistake, commenting, "I think Oregon will be the loser for this ... I know I'm prejudiced, but I just credited the voters with better sense."[126]

Vic Atiyeh (center) shares a joke with Tom McCall (left) and Bob Straub (right),
prior to Atiyeh's inauguration, January 8, 1979.
Photo courtesy of Governor Victor Atiyeh

Some of the accolades that he received after the defeat must have made the governor rueful, especially the note from his erstwhile foe, Tom McCall. In a personal letter addressed to Bob and Pat dated November 9, 1978, the ex-governor wrote: "Lee Hess and I just glumly agreed in the Multnomah Club gymnasium that you, Bob, would have been Oregon's greatest governor, ever, in your second term." McCall went on to assert that if he "had not responded to the siren song of favorable polls a year earlier and charged into the election like an old fire horse who had to respond to a fire bell," Straub would have won. Apologetically, McCall stated, "I messed up everything," and concluded the missive by saying that "Oregon is a better state because of everything you two have given its people."[127]

Bob must have had some solace in how praise for his service flowed freely from nearly all quarters, although he had to feel the irony (if not hypocrisy) of *The Oregonian's* editorial appreciation. After endorsing Straub in 1974, the Portland paper came out for his Republican opponent in 1978, stating that the previous four years "have not been the capitol's most shining hours."[128] Two months later the same editorial page declared, "Oregonians can all hope that we have not seen the last of the 58-year-old Straub in the political trenches. Oregon needs more like him."[129]

Contrary to this sentimental statement, whether sincere or not, this was Bob Straub's final campaign. In the last days of his governorship, Straub showed the fighting spirit that had characterized the best moments of his political career. In the end, he had the satisfaction of knowing he had gone down swinging.

CHAPTER 13

A Graceful Departure

*I bequeath myself to the dirt to grow from the grass I love. If you want me
again, look for me under your bootsoles. You will hardly know who I am or
what I mean, but I shall be good health to you nevertheless, and filter and
fibre your blood. Failing to fetch me at first, keep encouraged. Missing me
one place, search another. I stop somewhere waiting for you.*

—Walt Whitman, from "Leaves of Grass," 1855

Bob Straub's political journey was over. It was now time to turn his full
attention to his wife, his family, and his business enterprises. As dispiriting
as it was to lose the 1978 election to Vic Atiyeh, Straub knew that no
longer would his daily habits, off-hand comments, or smallest decisions be
picked apart in editorials and poison-penned political columns. His political
opponents were now in charge, and would be judged as rigorously as he had
been. Straub was stepping back into a world that would now treat him with
loving kindness and respect—a family who loved him, and a public and press
who could now look back with appreciation on his accomplishments. He
could engage himself fully, knowing that he was more or less in control of the
outcomes of his decisions. He was his own man again.

"When I think about my personal situation, I feel very rich," Bob said
the day after his defeat, "I have a wife I love and enjoy being with, we have
a wonderful family living in Oregon, I have good health, and I have enough
money that I don't have to worry about the wolf snarling at the door."[1]

Straub's wife, Pat, recalled the transition from public life, beginning just
after the November 1978 election defeat, when everyone was generally still
feeling low about the results: "I remember clearly how touching it was at
a family gathering, it must have been Thanksgiving, that our son Mike
announced that he was thankful that they had their father back."

Straub's peace was reflected in an unusually candid interview he gave to
television reporter Ted Bryant as he left office. Bryant asked what his role would
be in the party now—would he be "a so-called kingmaker or manipulator?"
Straub laughed, "No, no, I'm not that kind of person." He said that he would
not be taking an active role in influencing the operations of the party. "I've
done my share of that," Straub said, "and I'm going to get back into private

life, and I'm going to get back into business ... this doesn't mean I'm going to be mute ... and I'll be very free to speak out ... but to formally be an activist in the Democratic Party, I don't envision myself in that role."[2] Asked if he felt bitterness about the lack of enthusiastic support from Democrats during the last election, Straub was philosophical. "No, I don't feel any rancor or bitterness toward anybody in the state," he said, "including Governor-elect Victor Atiyeh. I feel very fortunate about that because a person can waste a lot of energy carrying grudges. I don't carry any ... I feel very appreciative toward the people of Oregon in letting me have four years in the governor's office. They were four good years. I did some useful thing for the people of Oregon, and I'm very happy about it."

Did Straub think the state would suffer under the new governor? "No, I don't think it will suffer," Straub replied, "I think there may be a slowing down of the pace a little bit, just because of the nature of Senator Atiyeh. I think maybe this is what the people of Oregon want. And maybe it will be a good thing to slow down for a little while." Still he couldn't avoid feeling regret about what might have been had he had a second term. "I felt in the last year and a half of my administration that I really was on top of things. And that's one of the reasons it hurt me so badly to be beaten, because I felt that I was in a position to really do some good things for the people of Oregon. And to provide the kind of leadership that they were entitled to."[3]

Apparently, incoming Governor Victor Atiyeh thought that Governor Straub had done a lot of things right, as well. "My philosophy was 'if it ain't broke, don't fix it,'" Atiyeh recalls. "Bob was an excellent manager. I found state government in pretty good shape and didn't make a whole lot of changes in management. We mostly had very good people and well-run departments."[4] Despite finding himself working with solid Democratic majorities in both houses of the state legislature, Governor Atiyeh provided more continuity with previous state policy, established during the McCall and Straub years, than many liberals had feared he would.

One notable example was Atiyeh's strong support of the state's land-use planning system. In 1979, Governor Atiyeh actively supported the effort by a number of land-use advocates who saw the unworkability of leaving legal appeals of local land-use decisions in the "inexpert" hands of the Circuit Courts.[5] As proposed by former Land Conservation and Development Commission (LCDC) board member Steve Schell[6]—with the crucial advocacy of the shrewd former Oregon Attorney General Lee Johnson, now Governor Atiyeh's chief of staff—the Oregon State Legislature created a separate, specialized court to handle land-use cases, the Land Use Board of Appeals (LUBA).[7] In addition to helping sway Republican legislators toward voting to make the state's land-use laws work as they were intended, Governor Atiyeh later appointed former Republican legislator, and former director of the state executive department under Straub, Stafford Hansell, to chair the LCDC, putting his stamp on a bi-partisan majority that clearly favored a strong, statewide land-use planning system.[8]

The land-use fight came to head again during the 1982 election season, with a cancer-ridden, but reliably cantankerous and effective, Tom McCall leading the fight against those wishing to repeal Oregon's statewide land-use planning experiment. Bob Straub, so vital to the creation of the land-use planning system during his term in office, strongly supported the campaign and made appearances on behalf of it, as well. The two former governors presented a united, bipartisan front with the current governor, Vic Atiyeh, who was running for reelection, and his political opponent, State Senator Ted Kulongoski. They were joined by significant business and homebuilder backing in support of Oregon's innovative program, describing it as the way to encourage smart economic growth that is attractive to businesses and individuals who wanted certainty in their ability to use property, while maintaining the state's agricultural base and a high quality of life. Ballot Measure 6, to "End State's Land Use Planning Power, Retain Local Planning" failed by a substantial 56 to 44 percent margin, 565,056 no votes to 461,271 yes votes.[9] Oregon's system of land-use planning did not face a significant challenge on the ballot again for over two decades.

Barely two months after the November 1982 election, on January 8, 1983, Tom McCall, weakened by his battle with cancer, died in Portland's Good Samaritan Hospital of pneumonia. The entire state mourned his loss. At McCall's memorial service on January 12, among thousands of hushed mourners in the House of Representatives, where the service was taking place, and broadcast into the rotunda of the state Capitol, where the late governor's body lay in state surrounded by thousands more, Straub gave what may have been the best, most heart-felt, speech of his life. With warm anecdotes and self-deprecating humor, Straub's four-page prepared speech was a masterpiece—extremely personal, and delivered with raw passion. Giving McCall full credit for the environmental achievements of their era, Straub made light of the fact that his own "political life had to be under [McCall's] shadow," but generously added, "it was a shadow of sunlight and hope and optimism, woven of the fabric of joy and friendship between him and me."

Tom McCall's "sage voice was clear and strong," Straub proclaimed. "Bold, audacious, visionary, exciting. He was always fun to be around. I never met Tom at a meeting but that in two minutes we were laughing uproariously about something. I'll miss his great humor and sparkling asides." Recalling the courage of McCall's last campaign to preserve the state's land use planning system, Straub quoted Emerson:

> *He was willing to perish in the using.*
> *He sacrificed the future to the present—*
> *Was willing to spend and be spent ...*
> *He used every day, hour, and minute.*
> *He lived to the latest moment,*
> *And his character appeared in the last moments*
> *With the same firm control as the day of his strength.*

Straub closed with his own poetic comparison, inspired by a recent flight out of Portland shortly before McCall's death:

> *As we lifted up out of the clouds and broke into the early morning sun there was the mountain—Mt. Hood—in all its stunning, so familiar, beauty. Breathtaking, inspiring, enduring.*
> *I thought of my friend Tom McCall. He's like that mountain—standing out in time—a monument to Oregon. A monument of light and joy and visionary hope. A monument that casts no shadows, only light.*
> *Tom McCall's spirit is tomorrow's sun, and it lights our way to the future. Vast in expectations. Bright with possibility. And as free as the man was himself.*
> *He will endure, inspire, and symbolize Oregon. He is Oregon's second Mt. Hood.*[10]

Bob Straub at Tom McCall's gravesite. Photo by Gerry Lewin

It was fitting that the man who had lived in Tom McCall's political shadow stepped out of them to give him the most rousing and memorable tribute of the evening. Some in the Capitol Rotunda that night, especially those who had never really known Bob Straub well, were struck with how remarkably well Bob spoke. Jackie Winters, who was serving as Governor Atiyeh's citizens representative at the time, recalls, "He spoke with such passion. We were all thinking, 'if you had been doing that all along, you would have been reelected.' That's what I remember."[11] Barbara Roberts, House majority leader at that time, echoes Winters: "I don't think anyone who was there has ever forgotten it."[12]

But that time in politics had passed for Bob Straub, and most of his time was now spent with business, family, and friends. Straub had found, once again, a familiar rhythm—a daily work routine combining management of his farm and forest enterprises, checking stock prices and trends with his investments, putting in hard, physical labor on his farm in West Salem and his tree farm thirty miles away in Willamina. At this point, he shared many of the responsibilities of the Straub land empire (including ranches in Douglas and Wheeler counties, and large swaths of rental housing in Springfield) with his son, Mike, who had taken over the business while Bob was serving as governor.

Bob had his customary lunches, lovingly prepared by Pat, and their evenings were spent reading or enjoying meals and laughter with a kaleidoscopic variety of friends and family. They loved having friends over, especially in the summertime when Pat could serve delicious, organically grown dinners out back on the picnic tables. Bob was filled with good humor, relishing his role as host. "They always made those evenings at their house special," recalls their friend Sarah Johnson. "I remember one time Bob had these South American bird call tapes he played during dinner that were just beautiful. They were always involved in something different or interesting."[13]

Every summer night, just as they had done for decades, Bob and Pat slept under big blankets, outside on a huge bed on their porch, breathing the refreshing night air. Summers meant camping trips for the whole family to the ranches in southern and eastern Oregon, and in mid-winter, the annual familial trek to Guaymas, Mexico, on the eastern shore of the Gulf of California. Bob and Pat made several overseas trips, including a stop in Dijon, France, to revisit the city in which Bob served in the Quartermaster Corps during the Second World War. In France, a friend who was now a diplomat stationed there, got them into the Lascaux caves to see the famous prehistoric cave paintings—something that fired Straub's still inquisitive mind, causing him to read every book the State Library possessed on the subject when he returned.[14]

Don Griffith (left) and Bob Straub riding at the Straubs' ranch in Spray, Oregon.

In retirement, Bob and Pat, lifelong lovers and companions, were more entwined than ever, sometimes, it felt like, to the exclusion of the rest of the family. "We could never seem to break totally into their private world," their daughter Jane remembers. "They were so very close."

As time passed and their children's families grew, Bob and Pat along with cousin Jack Urner bought a condominium in Guaymas, which was expanding from the sleepy Mexican fishing village they had discovered into a town that also included a modest cross-border tourist economy. They were joined by Bob's sister Jean and several other family members and friends who bought another four condos in the same building. The annual December trek with the entire extended family changed into periodic visits with just a few family and friends. The annual family event, attended by everyone, was now a summer venture to their eastern Oregon ranch in Spray.

Bob and Pat deeply loved and appreciated their children as the adults they had become, each blessed with children of their own.

Their eldest son, Jeff, had been a traveler since leaving the Air Force, doing a variety of jobs in Alaska, ending up as a federal food stamp agent in Nome, before returning to the lower forty-eight to work on a public works crew for the street department in Ashland, Oregon, for thirteen years. After returning to college, Jeff taught 4th to 6th grade school students in the Ashland Public Schools for another twelve years before he retired. Jeff and his wife had four children. Like his father and grandfather before him, he remained an avid reader and armchair philosopher.

Second son, Mike, had been a store manager for his uncle Dixon Stroud's business in rural Pennsylvania, and later a carpenter and a builder in Springfield. He continued, after Bob's retirement, with help from his wife, Linna, to assist in managing the Straub family businesses from their home in Springfield, taking on more and more responsibilities as time went on. Together, Mike and Linna raised six kids, and over the years, they assisted around seventy-five foster children.

Bob and Pat's eldest daughter, Jane, like Jeff, was a schoolteacher, remaining in Lane County most of her life. She received her master's degree in education from the University of Oregon and she and her husband ran an organic farm on Fall Creek, with their two children.

Patty, Bob and Pat's middle daughter, fell in love with Jay Thomas, son of one of the close friends of Uncle Ike and Aunt Jean Russell in Arizona, who came to Oregon to work as a Straub farm hand. Jay was a pioneer in the revival of horse logging on steep slopes, to prevent the type of erosion common when using big trucks and roads. He first worked for Willamette Industries on one of three horse-logging crews out of Lebanon, Oregon, and then managed the Straub timber holdings in Curtin in Douglas County, where he and Patty settled and raised their two kids.

Bob Straub with his dog, Tupper. Straub kept dogs all of his adult life.
Photo by Gerry Lewin

Bob and Pat's youngest daughter, Peggy, also fell for the Thomas boy charm and married Jay's twin, Robin, who was horse-logging with his brother. Robin got tired of the mud, so they moved back to his home state. Robin's talent was in home building, and he and Bob developed a joint business building beautiful homes in Tucson. Peg and Robin raised their two children for a dozen years there and then came back to Springfield to be near Patty and Jay and the rest of the Straub family. Peggy was very active with elementary school tutoring and a wide variety of volunteer work. Altogether Bob and Pat had fifteen grandchildren, most of them born and raised in Oregon.

Bob's active work routine and family life didn't stop him from agreeing to a series of volunteer and political activities in his local community. The Straub farmhouse became an important mid-valley location for statewide and local candidates: Ted Kulongoski in his unsuccessful 1982 run for governor against Vic Atiyeh, and Neil Goldschmidt in his successful run for governor in 1986, held major, well-publicized fundraisers on the farm, as did Goldschmidt's successor, Barbara Roberts, in 1990. Democratic Presidential nominee Walter Mondale flipped pancakes and served breakfast to supporters and the press at the Straub farm during the summer of 1984. Receiving Governor Straub's blessing had symbolic value for Democratic candidates who wanted to tap loyal party members.

Straub was also recruited by the Garten Foundation to help them raise money for their program of training mentally challenged people to run their local recycling program, a program he had helped to greatly expand as governor. At the time, there was little in the way of recycling being done by local governments, so the Garten Foundation, a private, non-profit, organization, became the main avenue for recycling in the Salem area, including state government buildings. The fact that they also trained mentally challenged people made it even easier for Bob and Pat to get excited about supporting it. "I remember the day he came to Garten in 1975, as governor, and I met him for the first time," says former Executive Director Emil Graziani. "He was taking a tour and he was very complimentary and supportive. That was the beginning of his long relationship with us."[15] Straub's executive secretary, Barbara Hanneman, made the initial connection with Garten. Using a state law sponsored by Senator Hector McPherson (R-Linn County) allowing non-profits access to surplus state property, along with another ingenious law, devised by Representative Nancie Fadeley (D-Springfield), which designated government waste paper as "surplus property," the Straub administration signed contracts, on Christmas Day in 1976, with Garten to handle all recycling in state buildings in Salem.[16]

Bob and Pat decided to help with an annual fundraiser Garten was planning. It began as a breakfast of *huevos rancheros* (one of Bob's Mexican favorites) held at a Salem hotel and was co-hosted by retired Supreme Court Justice Edwin Peterson, whose wife, Anna,[17] served on the Garten staff. After a couple of years with modest results, Bob and Pat met with the Garten leadership because the event "didn't raise the money it should have." Graziani recalls, "We were in the Garten conference room and Bob suddenly slapped his hand on the table and said: 'We're going to raise $10,000 and we're going to have it at our house!' And Pat looked at him and said 'We are?'" They did, and it was a smashing hit. "Bob Straub had a heart that was amazing," said Graziani. "He was such a great guy." He invited Governor Goldschmidt and Secretary of State Barbara Roberts and they catered the event with rib restaurant owner and future State Senator Jackie Winters, who was there with her husband Ted, serving up her famous ribs for a large group of friends and supporters. It became an annual tradition.[18] "Bob Straub legitimized Garten with the high rollers in the community," Garten recycling coordinator John Matthews recalls. "He raised our profile considerably and set expectations higher. It was not always easy, but it was a very stimulating relationship."[19]

In 1986, Governor Victor Atiyeh's second term was ending. Neil Goldschmidt narrowly defeated the popular Republican former secretary of state, Norma Paulus, for the governorship, bringing the Democrats back into the executive suites after eight years. Straub received several honors and assignments from his friend and former protégé Goldschmidt.

Having served as the dynamic, greatly admired mayor of Portland, credited with leading a massive revival of a previously dull, gray city; as secretary of transportation under President Jimmy Carter; and in a brief stint as Nike's international vice president, taking advantage of China's new opening to foreign manufacturing, Neil Goldschmidt was a rock star among Oregon politicians. Though he could sometimes be unsentimental in dealing with former colleagues, Goldschmidt remembered and always valued Bob Straub, who helped introduce him to state politics, beginning with a summer internship in 1966, promoting the Willamette Greenway and sleeping over on a cot in the Straubs' backyard.[20]

"Neil used Bob when he had an issue where Bob could weigh in," recalls Floyd McKay, who served as Governor Goldschmidt's first press secretary. "Bob was an adviser he could trust. Neil never felt that Bob had any agenda."[21] It was an interesting relationship between a politician who was notably Machiavellian in his approach at times—Goldschmidt—and one well known for his lack of political guile—Straub. Bob Straub never wavered from his ideals or principles, nor would he have ever considered doing so for a

Private citizen Bob Straub with Governor Neil Goldschmidt, sharing a laugh.
The two men were very close.[22]

second. Straub, without knowing he was doing it, brought out the best in the younger man, reminding Goldschmidt of the original idealism with which he had begun his political career.

Straub was of immediate use to the incoming governor on an issue that was near to Bob's heart. The 1986 National Farm Worker Act, signed into law by President Reagan, was going into effect in 1987, just as Goldschmidt was taking office. For decades, farm laborers, many in the United States illegally from Mexico and other countries further south, migrated to Oregon for the agricultural harvest—and each year they faced a temporary housing problem and some pretty grim conditions in the housing they did secure. As governor, Straub had attempted to improve conditions for these workers by mandating better housing conditions on farms—another grudge that some farmers held against him at reelection time. The 1986 act, offering amnesty to long-time illegal alien workers, made this annual temporary housing problem much worse in 1987 because farmworkers came early to their traditional places of work in order to establish their work credential with their farm employer and to apply for citizenship. By January and February, Oregon was beginning to see a flood of workers seeking legal status, with no work, in the cold weather, and without adequate housing.[23]

Straub, concerned with these workers' ability to find shelter and stay alive, contacted Governor Goldschmidt, eager to help. Goldschmidt quickly convened an agricultural labor conference and put Bob Straub in charge of the emergency effort. Straub, working with state agencies and non-profits, explored a range of options, including purchasing a large number of tents, but found they were able to cobble together an adequate safety net for the early migrants without resorting to setting up government-sponsored camps.[24] Bob and Pat Straub did their part on their farm in West Salem. "They had several Mexican workers living in their barn that winter, as I recall," son Mike remembers. "They used to come into the house in the morning for coffee and breakfast."[25]

"One of things that I thought was interesting about Bob was how much he liked and admired Mexicans and Mexican culture," retired banker Bill Bales remembers. "He saw how hard they would work, which went a long way with Bob, and he would give them work on his farm."[26] There was something about the joyousness of Mexican culture that contrasted so much with Bob's Calvinist upbringing, which kept him traveling south to Guaymas for the winter, or perpetually attempting to learn the Spanish language with an enthusiasm that overcame his limited vocabulary and mangled pronunciation. There was also something about his appreciation of those who strove to overcome difficulties that were no fault of their own that captured Bob's spirit. Straub quietly helped members of Oregon's Latino community when they needed assistance.

"I will never forget one incident in which Bob was helpful," remembers long-time state administrator Danny Santos. "It was when I was working in the governor's office on education scholarships for Oregon Latinos. There was a shooting in Woodburn in which a stray bullet struck a young boy in the head. He had medical and developmental issues and there was some press coverage of it. The story in the paper talked about one of the sisters who wasn't able to graduate from high school because she needed to take care of her brother. She was not just upset because of his situation, but because she had to put off plans for going to college. Money was also an issue for that family. Bob called me on the phone and asked to set up a meeting with the family. He encouraged them to continue to send the girl to Chemeketa Community College and provided a scholarship for her. She was not eligible for any state money because she wasn't a U.S. citizen or a legal resident, which did not matter to Bob at all. He didn't want or get any public credit for any of this."[27]

Governor Goldschmidt thought it natural to appoint Bob Straub to the board of the Oregon Investment Council, which Bob had created nearly twenty years before. The investment council had done better than anyone had imagined. Jim George, originally hired by Straub back in 1966, was still serving as chief investment officer in 1986 when Straub rejoined the council. "He, obviously, was a wonderful board member to have," George recalls.

"There was no getting him up to speed since he created the whole thing to begin with. He was like other key board members who were along in their years and very experienced. Dean Pape, a Eugene businessman, was like that, as was Bill Hunt of Louisiana Pacific, Harry Kane of Georgia Pacific, Don Tykeson, who owned a Eugene television station, and Sid Leiken, who was a southern Oregon timber guy. These were some examples of the stronger board members who were experienced in years and business. The up and coming resume builders were less useful."[28]

George remembered a humorous story from Bob's second time on the Oregon Investment Council. "We were staying at the Stanford Court Hotel on Nob Hill in San Francisco and Bob had a headache and needed some aspirin," George recollects. "I appealed to his miser's heart by telling him, 'we can't buy aspirin here, it's too expensive,' so we walked down to the bottom of the hill to a drug store, to save two or three dollars, then had a pretty steep climb back, for an old guy with arthritis. We both had a good laugh about that at the time. At my retirement party a few years later, he remembered that story in his speech, illustrating just how tight I was—which, of course, he highly approved of."[29]

Straub was a fierce watchdog, jealously guarding the state's investment program after his retirement. In the early '80s, before he was back on the Oregon Investment Council, he publicly fought against efforts by activists and state legislators, including future State Treasurer Jim Hill—who became the first African American elected to statewide office in Oregon—to divest state pension funds from businesses that had dealings with the apartheid government of South Africa. To Straub, as important as social causes were, it was even more important to keep faith with the fund beneficiaries to maximize their investments. The state law he had created mandated that they follow the "prudent person" rule, which required the trustees to invest in ways that a prudent person would in order to yield the maximum return. In Bob Straub's mind, that did not include diverting money based upon any worthy cause.

Just as "almost all state treasurers after Bob Straub had the idea of being governor some day, though some of them got diverted by realizing there was more money to be made elsewhere," as Jim George relates it, "nearly all of them had plans to try to invest these large pension funds in Oregon businesses with some sort of 'Buy Oregon' plan. This, of course, was not necessarily in keeping with running the investment council for the beneficiaries of the trust. It wasn't supposed to be a state economic-development engine. In fact, we always *did* have quite a bit of state investment, especially in mortgages."[30] Bob Straub was dead set against any dedicated fund under the OIC purview being sidetracked for state economic-development purposes, as he demonstrated a few years later. After state voters elected a Republican-controlled state legislature in 1994, for the first time in over two decades, the incoming Republican leadership found that out the hard way when Straub, though retired from the investment council by then, ferociously attacked their legislation, SB696, in the press for a modest "Invest in Oregon" program. On this issue, he joined the state treasurer at the time, and fellow Democrat, Jim Hill, with whom he had previously differed on the apartheid divestiture question, in opposition.[31]

In a withering *Oregonian* opinion piece, published on June 22, 1995, Bob criticized the bill, which had, by then, passed both houses of the state legislature and was awaiting Governor John Kitzhaber's signature.

What is so bad about SB696? It starts to crumble away the protective wall that has shielded the investment in the retirement fund.

Probably the most important fault of SB696 is the statement, "Pension funds managed by the Oregon Investment Council constitute a major financial resource of the state of Oregon and that such funds may be prudently invested in start-up businesses in this state."

Wrong on both counts! The pension fund managed by Oregon Investment Council is not a major financial resource of the state of Oregon. These are funds that belong to the members of the Public Employees Retirement System and are held in trust and managed for the benefit of the retirees of PERS.

Also, investing monies in start-up businesses is not appropriate for trust monies. I have heard from knowledgeable investment people that the rate of survival of start-up businesses is less than 15 percent, a very high-risk type of investment.

Straub pointed out that existing law allowed for prudent investment in local business, should independent money managers believe it wise, but went on to warn that, while mandating investment for worthy purposes in the state sounded like a good idea on the surface, "nothing is more enticing to an elected official than to have a pot of money that can be made available as an investment to political friends." Straub did not want that to happen in Oregon, and gave examples from Connecticut and Kansas, where large sums of money had been lost making politically popular investments in local businesses, and from California, where investments now were required to favor real estate projects that used union labor, "a wise political move perhaps," Straub asserted, "but hardly appropriate as an investment criterion for retirement-fund money." Straub concluded by saying, "Let social or political programs deemed to be worthy be financed with general fund money, but let's keep hands off the money that belongs, by law, to the members of PERS."[32]

Governor Kitzhaber agreed and vetoed the bill. Clearly, in the summer of 1995, Bob Straub was still in fine form intellectually and tuned in politically, especially when it came to protecting one of the proudest policy achievements of his years in public office.

Goldschmidt honored Straub in another, symbolic, way in 1987. Former newsman Floyd McKay, Goldschmidt's press secretary, had an idea for honoring the former governor: why not rename the Nestucca Spit State Park after Bob Straub? McKay enlisted the logistical help of his friend Ken Johnson, Straub's long-time aide, who was now serving as a jack-of-all-trades for Goldschmidt. What would be more appropriate than honoring Bob on the piece of land he had fought so hard to save from the highway department's asphalt so many years ago?[33] "It really wasn't very complex to do it," Floyd McKay recalls. "Even though it wasn't usually done, I always thought that waiting until someone dies to honor them is kind of foolish, and there already were other precedents—we had already honored Mark Hatfield and with a number of buildings by that time."[34] McKay took the idea to Governor Goldschmidt and he said, "Yes, let's make it happen."[35] The department of transportation and "parks people were fine with it," McKay remembers, and even though there was "a little grumbling down on the coast from the few who were still upset with him," everyone else "felt really good about it. We got a high school band to play, and had a real nice ceremony" in Pacific City at the new Robert Straub State Park, "with Neil, Bob, and Pat down on the beach."[36] The event ended with the hundred-odd guests having a picnic lunch among the dunes and driftwood piles in a place where, but for the strong will of Bob Straub, a four-lane highway would have run.[37]

Governor Goldschmidt's appointment of Pat Straub to the Oregon State Board of Forestry was not of a symbolic nature. Pat was put on the board, along with long-time Straub natural resources aide Janet McLennan, and environmental attorney Richard Roy, to add some environmental heft to a board historically dominated by timber interests. "Under Neil's leadership, the Board was substantially reconstituted," Janet McLennan recalls, "and there were additional changes in the organic legislation for Forestry as well." On the new seven-member board, no more than three of whom could derive "any significant portion of their income from persons or organizations subject to forest practice act regulation." Though Pat and Bob were small woodlot owners, their income was not sufficient to disqualify her. With building construction company owner Tom Walsh—a close Goldschmidt confidant, as chair, environmentalists had hopes of improving forest practices on state forest land.[38] "I thought it was very interesting and I did like serving on the board," Pat remembered later. But she eventually tired of it.[39] While, on the surface, the board was much less dominated by the timber industry than in years past, Pat did not serve her full four-year term on the board, possibly due to her frustration with being outvoted on a revision of the rules on aerial spraying of herbicides, an issue of great concern to Pat, that she and Dick Roy felt was too weak.[40] "She took her service on the board very seriously, but I think Mom mostly ended up feeling like a token environmentalist on that board," son Mike remembers.[41]

In personal manner and in some of his beliefs, Governor Goldschmidt was not cut from the same cloth as Straub, though Goldschmidt's political orientation was similar in some ways to Bob Straub's in that he was both pro-business and pro-government. Goldschmidt once told Central Oregon lumber mill owner John Shelk, "I want to make you rich and then I want to tax the hell out of you," which Shelk thought sounded fair enough. But, unlike Straub, Neil Goldschmidt never felt the natural beauty of his native state in his soul. Former *Oregonian* editor and reporter Wayne Thompson liked to tell the story of inviting Neil to come to his beach house at Road's End, north of Lincoln City, which had a drop-dead beautiful view of the Pacific Ocean through its living room picture window. Everyone who visited always said, "Oh, my God, look at that view!" That is, everyone except for Neil. He came in, kept talking, and sat down with his back to the ocean.[42] Goldschmidt understood that difference between them. Goldschmidt recalled working with Bob Straub when he was state treasurer: "He was passionate about Oregon as a physical place. It really was the first time I was forced to stop and think about the blessings I'd had growing up in Eugene, I just kind of took them for granted. I fell in love with them again when I hitchhiked around Europe in 1960-61, and I came home just feeling terrific about my state, but I frankly had seen less of Oregon than I saw of Europe. My dad wasn't a fisherman or a hunter, and we weren't out exploring the whole state all the time. But when I was with Straub, there wasn't a corner of the state he hadn't been in or didn't intend to go to if he hadn't. It's just the way he was."[43] Straub could not help but get involved when issues came up locally that he cared passionately about. In 1988, the City of Salem was finally completing plans for a long-awaited—and long-delayed—downtown park on a large, unused plot of land on the banks of the Willamette River. The grassroots organization, Oregon Fair Share, spearheaded by a local activist couple, Jim and Lorraine Pullman, decided that Mayor Sue Harris' carefully crafted plan to combine a private hotel and convention center with a public park was a poor use for Salem's precious downtown waterfront. Their door-to-door signature-gathering operation confronted the city council decision authorizing the public-private development agreement by placing a measure prohibiting any city participation in a hotel/convention center on Salem's riverfront on the city ballot for the May 17, 1988, primary election.[44] Suddenly, Bob Straub barged into the conversation, letting the press know that he, too, was not pleased with the city's plan.

The plan, which had the support of local businesses and some local environmentalists, would have converted the industrially contaminated, concrete-strewn, blackberry-choked eyesore along Salem's downtown waterfront, using half the land for a "$15 million privately financed hotel and a $2.5 million publicly financed conference center" and leaving the remaining land for riverside public gardens. Already, years earlier in 1977, Straub had weighed in on Salem's efforts to bring in a flagship hotel to replace the fire-gutted historic Marion Hotel, when, as governor, he vetoed a bill that would have given a local developer "five years of property-tax exemptions" for a Hilton hotel and convention center.[45] Now Straub became the leading political opponent of Mayor Harris' plan, debating local attorney (and future Salem mayor) Mike Swaim, who represented the Sierra Club, at a combined Salem City Club/Chamber of Commerce meeting convened for the special election issue. Swaim characterized Straub as wanting to "keep it 'natural' and leave the blackberries there."[46] Straub saw it more as a missed opportunity for a simple, open park on scarce public land. In keeping with Straub's Greenway vision of public, rather than private, access to Willamette riverfront, the former governor said, "You're not going to destroy that precious downtown natural resource that can bring a lot of joy to a lot of people. I don't like to see it obliterated with a lot of concrete." That sentiment, along with the $25 million public price tag, swung public opinion[47] and the city plan was defeated by a 13,633 to 9,675 vote.[48]

It took six years and the election of a new mayor, Salem dentist and former city council member Roger Gertenrich, to revive plans to replace the blackberries and toxic debris with an attractive downtown park. Gertenrich was elected Salem mayor outright, with over 50 percent of the vote in the non-partisan primary, and used his time between the May 1994 election and his swearing in the following January to prepare himself for office. In looking into the possibility of reviving plans for a riverfront park, one of Gertenrich's first phone calls was to Bob Straub. "As a Republican, I wasn't sure whether it made sense to meet with him or not," Gertenrich remembers, "but within five minutes of conversation we were like blood brothers." Shortly after that phone call, Mayor-elect Gertenrich came up for lunch at the Straubs' farmhouse in the hills above West Salem, spending a couple of hours on the farm with Bob and Pat. "We really enjoyed each other's company," recalls Gertenrich. "He told me, 'I expected you to lose. All the money was against you.'"

"Bob became my mentor, sharing his philosophy about Oregon and the Willamette Valley," Gertenrich says. "Bob said that to understand Oregon you needed to realize the importance of the original immigrants who came here with seeds in their pockets. They weren't gold seekers like the immigrants to California. Although the soil was good, what made Oregon what it was, was the Willamette River." For Bob, "that was what made the Willamette Greenway so important—to protect the environment, as well as to provide recreation for its citizens. Bob's ideas stuck with me and I totally agreed with his philosophy on the riverfront park." Pushing his staff hard, Mayor-elect Gertenrich came up with a new riverfront park plan that accomplished the simple goal of opening downtown Salem's window on the Willamette with a long grassy expanse, similar to the popular Tom McCall Waterfront Park created in the 1970s on downtown Portland's west Willamette riverside. It was privately funded for $1.5 million, with help from his election opponent Dean Wallace and local business and arts groups.

"That lovely luncheon in which Bob mentored me had an impact," Gertenrich says. "We felt we could make the park something. I was leaning in the direction he wanted—a simple park, open to all the city's people—and he helped bolster my resolve. Later on, I was able to spend more time with him, and my wife and I took Spanish classes with him and Pat. He was such a colorful character and a thoroughly enjoyable guy."[49]

Besides public political advocacy, Straub continued quiet charitable activities for those less fortunate. A couple of years after helping Governor Goldschmidt with the migrant worker housing crisis in the winter of 1986, "Straub was very helpful at the beginning of our efforts to set up the Salem Outreach Shelter," local activist and future Salem Mayor Mike Swaim remembers. "It was a shelter for seventy to eighty homeless men and, when Wally Eubanks, who had done some timber cruising for Bob, enlisted him, Bob was instrumental in making it happen."[50] Understanding that people who had been chronically homeless needed assistance in renting their first home, Straub decided to create a transitional housing non-profit group in Salem. "Bob personally found four old houses and put the down payment on them," banker Bill Bales recalls. "They were really worn out and needing repairs. His idea was to make them available for low-income people, and that some of them would get compensated for helping fix up these houses."[51] Straub called the fledgling organization Salem Self Help Housing and "he went out and recruited an attorney, an accountant, some real estate guys, a banker," Bales remembers, "and everyone he was appointing was a volunteer. We started renting those houses to mostly single women with children, then other low-income people. We had an initial drive for money, with a letter of appeal and raised around $15,000 from maybe a hundred people, mostly in small gifts."[52] The group continued to buy old, dilapidated houses on contract and were assisted with government funding through their renters, most of whom were eligible for the federal Section 8 Housing subsidy. They also eventually branched out to include building an apartment complex for those with mental health and drug treatment problems and became large enough that they had to hire a general manager to run their operation.

"From the money we collected we paid Bob back," Bales remembers. "The non-profit corporation owned the homes, and slowly, over twenty years, we built the investment up. After Bob passed on, we found it was difficult to keep it going. We were all getting older, too." In 2008, Salem Self Help Housing turned over its forty-four units of housing, including two apartment complexes and several duplexes, to Catholic Community Services (CCS) with the understanding that they would continue to be run in the same manner and for the same purpose for which they were originally created—housing needy families and individuals. The total value that sprang from Bob Straub's $15,000 in seed money and years of personal advocacy was $3 million in housing assets given to CCS, and $400,000 donated to local charities including the Salvation Army, the Union Gospel Mission, and a $250,000 endowment held by the Salem Foundation to provide nursing scholarships for Salem Hospital. "Bob was very hands-on," says Bales, "and he was able to get us loans that didn't need guarantees because of his good reputation. He was thrifty and just hated to spend money, but he always found ways to thank people who helped out. He burned wood and he loved to cut his own wood; he had a splitter up there on the hill and he'd haul it on a wheelbarrow to his house. Whenever I'd done some bookkeeping for him, he'd always bring me some wood for my fireplace. He was a very educated guy, but he hid it from everybody. Bob loved hard, physical work. I remember him telling me that the most exciting job he ever had was fresh out of high school as an assistant faller in the forest. They would look at a tree and decide how to cut and then lay it down. Even in his seventies, Bob still thought it was a great day to get out and work in the woods."[53]

The Straubs' tranquil, yet vigorous, retirement life continued on through the 1990s, but almost unseen, a darkening cloud was forming on the horizon. Gradually, Bob and Pat began noticing that Bob was forgetting things. This was not too remarkable to friends and family, because of his lifelong difficulty in remembering names and other key facts at different times. In hindsight, it is obvious that Bob was losing significant amounts of his memory as early as 1991, when he was interviewed several times by the Oregon Historical Society as part of their oral history project. Listening to those tapes, it seems that there may already have been large gaps in his memories of his personal and professional life. By the end of the 1990s, these memory lapses were becoming more pronounced.

Nevertheless, the Straubs kept their social schedule active. Notable visitors included Neil Goldschmidt, who continued to visit through the years. "Goldschmidt used to come by and visit and laugh with Dad and hang out with him," son Mike Straub recollects. "He didn't have to do that." "Neil made you feel important when he was around you," daughter Jane Straub remembers. "He was not stuffy. He'd come over to Dad's place and get him laughing—him and Loren Wyss [a professional financial advisor and Straub friend]. I could always tell when they had been around. Loren bought him clothes—really nice things that he claimed he'd just picked up and 'got a good deal on.'"[54] The sophisticated Wyss and the studied rustic Straub were tremendously compatible intellectually and enjoyed each other's company immensely. Loren Wyss, with his wife, Judy, a Portland artist, remembers spending many good times with the Straubs during those years in the mid-1990s. "We formed a little group of friends [calling themselves the Gang of Five, as in five couples] who got together each couple of months in one another's homes," Wyss recalls. "Bob and Pat, Bud and Eleanor Forrester, Dan and Rusty Goldy, Sam and Mary Naito, and Judy and myself. We had some wonderful, almost boisterous, times reliving the previous twenty years in Oregon and the rise of its Democratic majority."[55] Bud Forrester, a legendary Oregon newspaper publisher who owned, among others, the Pendleton *East Oregonian,* the *Capital Press*, and the *Daily Astorian*, took the lead, with his trademark big cigar in his mouth.[56] "Bud was relentless in forcing us to consider uncomfortable issues," Wyss recalls, "and everyone was required to have their say. Bob came alive on those evenings and showed little effect of his mental decline." These happy times ended when Bud Forrester died one Sunday morning after one of their gatherings and Dan Goldy lost his mobility soon after.[57]

Bob and Pat continued to notice Bob's difficulty in remembering things, but resisted having him medically tested. "The Alzheimer's came along slowly enough that it seemed like the natural aging process," his son Mike remembers. "He kind of didn't believe it for a while. He made light of it." The key incident that triggered their seeking medical evaluation was in the summer of 1999 when, on a short drive to pick up some bacon, Bob couldn't find his car in the parking lot of Roth's IGA grocery store in West Salem. Someone who recognized him saw his confusion. "She said, 'Governor Straub, can I help you with something,' and he said, 'I can't find my car,'" Mike Straub recalls. After she helped him find his car, he reoriented himself and was able to drive home.[58] "When he heard Bob's story about not being able to find his car in the Roth's parking lot, Dean Brooks said, 'Pat, I want to see Bob,'" Pat Straub recalls. Dr. Brooks, former director of the Oregon State Mental Hospital and their long-time friend and, at times, personal physician, was concerned that the problem went beyond Bob's usual difficulty of remembering names. "When we went to visit Dean at his office, we couldn't find the building," Pat remembers. "We asked a woman smoking outside, and she said, 'I don't know which building it is, but don't go into THAT one, because they won't let you out.' She, apparently, had been in there, so we took her advice," Pat remembers, laughing.[59]

Dr. Brooks put Bob in contact with two local doctors who ran him through a series of tests. A magnetic resonance imaging brain scan showed no sign of strokes, but that there was "a small amount of brain atrophy … that usually indicates some form of dementia." Straub also took a standard mental acuity test. Surveying the results, his doctors concluded that they were "more than 90 percent sure he has Alzheimer's,"[60] and that his prospects were bleak. "He was told he had better get his affairs in order because he only had about two years to live," Mike Straub remembers. Facing this shocking diagnosis, in contrast to how they had handled the decision for Bob to receive treatment for bipolar disorder in 1974, the Straubs decided to go public with their information, hoping that they could help others with a public discussion of Alzheimer's disease and how to cope with it. "We went to see Sarah Bentley, the publisher of the local paper, the (Salem) *Statesman Journal*," Pat says. "Bob was very anxious to get the story published." But Bentley, a family friend, wanted to make sure that the featured story, as sensitive as it was, would be fully researched and presented tactfully, so the publication was delayed for what seemed to the Straubs to be a long time.[61]

At what ended up being the last of the annual Straub-sponsored Garten Foundation bashes, held in the summer of 1999 at Salem's Mission Mill Museum, "Bob wasn't able to keep his thoughts straight during his introductory comments," Emil Graziani, then Garten's executive director remembers. "Pat was there at his elbow, helping him through it. It was not long after our event that the official diagnosis of Alzheimer's disease went public."[62] Finally, to the relief of Bob and Pat Straub, on September 19, 1999, the story was published. Splashed across the top of the front page of Salem's *Statesman Journal* newspaper, under headline "Diagnosed with Alzheimer's disease, former Oregon Gov. Bob Straub faces … Another Campaign," was a long story and several pictures of Bob and Pat, taking up more than half the page and continuing on to a full page inside spread. The Straubs were extremely forthright in their description of Bob's disease, its symptoms, and their struggle to help him cope with the changes it was wreaking upon his memory. "You can't stand on the sidelines and hover," Bob was quoted as saying. "If you do, that's where you'll stay."[63]

The news quickly shot around the state, bringing in calls of support from friends and political admirers. Interviewed a day later by the *Oregonian* newspaper, Straub was equally feisty, saying "'I have the feeling that people who think they might have Alzheimer's kind of submit to it ... I won't submit to it,' he said, smacking the arms of his chair with his palms."[64] The *Statesman Journal* article compared Straub's announcement to one that former President Ronald Reagan made in 1994. Interest in information on Alzheimer's spiked after Reagan's announcement, and the Straubs hoped their public discussion would be useful to others as well. "It's like him," his daughter Peg Thomas said at the time. "He's doing it because he might help someone else."[65]

Part of Straub's message to others in his situation was to "encourage people to work with their doctors. There are so many wonderful things being done in research. We are making headway." *The Statesman Journal* piece detailed the steps the former governor's doctors went through in diagnosing and advising their new patient. The news article got into several personal details about the medical advice he received and changes he was making to improve his quality of life, including ceasing drinking alcohol, after having been a "'consistent' drinker ... for 35 years ... enjoy[ing] cocktails after work and during social occasions." It also briefly mentioned changing "the dosage of Straub's anti-depressant medication so it was more effective,"[66] a rare public glimpse of Bob Straub's treatment for depression. However, observant newspaper readers who understood treatment for bipolar disorder would have already known of Straub's treatment from an earlier embarrassing press report about a drunk-driving arrest in Bend, Oregon, in December of 1981.[67] The court dismissed Straub's case because his blood alcohol level had been below the legal limit, and because he told the judge, and the press reported, that he was taking a prescription for lithium, which can cause smaller amounts of alcohol to have a more powerful effect. Despite these reports, few people, including virtually none of his friends, knew of Straub's continuing treatment for bipolar disorder.

The *Statesman Journal* article was a high point for Bob and Pat in their coping with Bob's diagnosis. They were hopeful that the experimental drug, Aricept, while not a cure for the disease, was helping Bob by slowing down the progression. Pat said, "'He's felt so good. He's got his sense of humor back.'"[68] As with all people suffering from Alzheimer's disease, there were ups and downs as Bob's symptoms became more evident. "At first he was pretty feisty, and a little paranoid," Mike Straub remembers. "He would have trouble making the connection between his brain and numbers. He couldn't run an adding machine. One time he had an ad for a truck in a magazine to show me and pointed at the price listed next to it and said, 'What does this mean?' The price wouldn't work in his brain." Another time, "he was trying to draw a map to the airport for someone and he just couldn't do it," Jane Straub recalls. "It was heartbreaking." Through it all, Bob kept striving to be useful. "He would want to do things to be helpful, like check the oil in your car," Mike Straub recalls. "He loved to run the wood splitter and the chainsaw. I worried about him. He probably drove the bulldozer longer than he should have." Putting limits on Bob was a difficult thing to do in these circumstances and it often fell to Mike Straub to do it, as he took on more and more of the Straub family business. "Mike had to take a lot of grief from Dad," Jane Straub recalls. "He was there helping and Dad would lash out at him. He had to have one person to blame and he was becoming delusional. But that began to change as the Alzheimer's progressed. Dad got more gentle and loving and he began to talk about himself more. Something opened up that had been closed."[69]

On May 6, 2000, Bob Straub celebrated the occasion of his eightieth birthday with around a hundred friends and supporters joining him on the campus of Western Oregon University. There they acknowledged the new Robert W. Straub Archives being built as part of a spacious new library on the Monmouth campus. Straub's supporters had raised funds to make the new archives possible. Bob spoke very briefly at the event, with Pat close by his side, and then all the guests trooped over to the construction site for a third-floor tour of the concrete shell that would become the rooms that would house the WOU archives and the former governor's personal papers. From the future reading room of the Straub Archives, they were treated to magnificent views of the Willamette Valley. This was to be Bob Straub's final public appearance.

Bob's illness was taking its toll on Pat. Family members were now regularly staying over at the West Salem farmhouse, and friends were coming to visit with Bob, so that Pat could get away for a break from caring for and worrying about Bob. Loren Wyss spent a few afternoons with Bob during that time. "We always had plenty of investment talk to keep us busy," Wyss remembers. "At the same time, he was very frank about his declining memory: 'I get a thought,' he said, 'and halfway through it just scurries away like a little mouse across the floor.'"[70] It was hard to put Bob into the Gateway Living Residential Care Facility in Springfield, but it was really the only way to get him the care he needed without completely exhausting Pat. She was worn down physically and emotionally in looking after him and her family began to worry about her health. Mike Straub remembers the decision this way:

"A few months before we put him in the Gateway Care Facility, Dad called me into his office to talk in private. He said that he knew that he was going downhill and wouldn't be able to make good decisions sometime in the future. He wanted me to know that he was counting on me to take over and most of all to take care of Mom. With that directive, when the time came I helped expedite getting him into Gateway, both for his care and to relieve the strain on Mom." Once Bob was at Gateway, Pat visited him almost daily. "Bob was always glad to see me when I came," Pat remembers. "He always knew who I was until the end and was very loving."[71] A few selected friends, in addition to Bob's children and grandchildren, regularly visited Bob in the care facility. Loren Wyss recalls: "The last time, just a month before he died, he still knew me, and when I kidded him that I'd come for investment advice he said very clearly, 'I'm sure you'll do the right thing.' That's the last time we spoke."[72]

On the morning of November 27, 2002, the Gateway Living staff contacted Pat to let her know that Bob had gone into a deep sleep and was unlikely to awaken. It was three and half years after his diagnosis with Alzheimer's, a year and a half longer than the doctors had given him to live.[73] She rushed over and, seeing him lying there so serenely, "I asked if I could get in bed with him," Pat remembers. "They were wonderful and told me 'of course you can,' so I crawled right in with him."[74] That day, at around 2:30 in the afternoon, Bob Straub peacefully died in the arms of his loving wife, with a large group of his family surrounding his bed. Bob wouldn't have wanted it any other way.

Bob and Pat

CHAPTER 14

The Arc of Bob Straub's Life

It is not the critic who counts, not the man who points out how the strong man stumbled, or where the doer of deeds could have done better. The credit belongs to the man who is actually in the arena, whose face is marred by dust and sweat and blood, who strives valiantly, who errs and comes short again and again, who knows the great enthusiasms, the great devotions, and spends himself in a worthy cause, who at best knows achievement and who at the worst if he fails at least fails while daring greatly so that his place shall never be with those cold and timid souls who know neither victory nor defeat.

—Theodore Roosevelt, from a speech given at the Sorbonne, 1910

One of the marvelous things about Bob Straub was his persistence in the face of his vulnerability. Bob was a human being first and had the humility to understand and accept his own flaws—and frequently laugh at them. So many humorous stories have been left out of this book that it bears listing a few here.

There was the time that Bob was governor, and he and Pat were in Bandon on the Oregon coast, on the campaign trail, talking to the local people, and the reporters travelling with them, about how much they loved Bandon cheese—that it was the only cheese they served at home—and then realizing that they were visiting Tillamook the next day. Bob peevishly turned to an aide and told him, in front of the press, "It's your job to keep me from saying stupid things like that."[1]

Then there were the dozens, if not hundreds, of times that Bob flubbed a person's name—something that politicians are never supposed to do. Len Bergstein likes to tell a story about Bob seeing a prominent supporter walking down the marble corridor in the Capitol and, at first, trying to avoid him because he can't remember his name, then suddenly turning with a look of recognition and shouting out "Art!" This was not the person's name, unfortunately, but he was a well-known patron of the arts, so Bob was close.[2]

There was the time, as told at Bob's memorial service in the Capitol by Governor Kitzhaber, that, during his final campaign, Governor Straub held a press conference along the I-5 freeway near Roseburg. It seems that a small herd of wild goats living on nearby Mt. Nebo would stay high on the hill when the weather was fair but come down from the hill when it was about to rain. The local radio station used to do "goat weather forecasts," based upon what the goats were doing. Sometimes when the goats were down off the hill, they would walk across the freeway to eat the grass in the median strip, creating a traffic hazard. Highway officials had just finished a goat fence that would prevent them doing that any longer and Straub was there to dedicate it. In the middle of his talk three goats appeared on the other side of the fence and then wandered into the median strip and started grazing. Bob looked up from his notes and, without missing a beat, said "It looks like rain."[3]

Finally, there are many stories about Bob's 'lead-footed' driving, but the one he loved to tell was about being pulled over for speeding by a highway patrolman in California shortly after he left office. The officer asked him what he did for a living. Bob replied that he was retired. The officer asked him, "Well, what did you do before you retired?" Bob replied, "I was governor of Oregon." Looking at his disheveled hair and clothes and old car the officer shook his head and said, "Well, you sure don't look like a governor to me."[4]

***

As the manuscript for this book neared completion, curious neighbors watched the progress of earthmovers tearing giant orange scars in the sloping hayfields below the Straub farmstead, on Orchard Heights Road in West Salem, and leveling the land for two new public schools. The following year, as the book was prepared for publication, students and teachers were finishing their first year in the clean-lined, modern Robert W. Straub Middle School and its twin, the Kalapuya Elementary School, located just below it. These attractive new school buildings are named after a local resident of the most recent past—Bob Straub—and for the original human inhabitants—the Kalapuya tribes, who lived, hunted, and gathered food among the oak groves, meadows, and hillsides of the Willamette Valley for millennia—some of whose descendants now own the Spirit Mountain Lodge and Casino in nearby Grand Ronde.

The evidence of Bob Straub's determination to retain Oregon's scenic and environmental integrity is all around us, if you look for it. But in looking directly at the destiny of the Straubs' West Salem farm you see, ironically, the compromises that were required to allow for land development within urban growth boundaries to prevent further sprawl onto productive farmland. This was the same fate that befell Bob's parents' farm in Los Altos in the 1960s, though the elder Straub homestead in Los Altos was razed for a new elementary school; the Salem-Keizer School District has, so far, allowed Bob and Pat's granddaughter Mary Chamness, her husband, Paul, and their two children, Justin and Jenna, to keep the house and immediate environs, including Pat's beloved root cellar and chicken coop, though they have lost the ancient red barn. The house and its yard are still ringed by the stand of redwoods planted by Bob and his kids to mark the edge of their homestead. The Straubs had already left the adjoining ten acres of old-growth woods, land that had never been logged or farmed, to the City of Salem for a park, and the Bob and Pat Straub Nature Park, traversed by a wood chip trail, is now open to the public.

The hillsides leading up to and around the Straubs' farm had gradually been enveloped by winding subdivisions that eventually contained enough children to need new schools. Bob really hated those subdivisions, spoiling his view from his summer bed on the back porch and the night stillness, previously broken only by crickets, but there wasn't anything he could do about it, since the development was within the urban growth boundary.

As a statewide political leader in the 1960s and '70s, Bob was concerned with uncontrolled development that encroached upon farming and recreational lands. He supported setting aside lands along rivers and Oregon's majestic coastline—the Willamette Greenway Plan, the Beach Bill, and Ballot Measure 6 in 1968, to preserve recreational lands—and the land-use planning laws passed during the term of Tom McCall, his predecessor as governor. Straub's iron determination to make the new state land-use laws work set in place the framework that exists to this day of caging in development within urban growth boundary lines.

The fact that the new subdivisions were there, near his house, and not on the flat Marion County farmland on the east side of town, was a victory, of sorts, for the land-use planning policies that Bob Straub helped establish. The urban growth boundaries for Salem, as they eventually were for the entire state, were determined with the assumption that flat Willamette Valley farmland, with its thick, rich alluvial soils, was an agricultural resource to be preserved and treasured. In Polk County adjoining West Salem, berry farms and cherry orchards that swept the hillsides, broken by white oak and Douglas fir stands, were considered less arable and more suitable for housing development, so a portion of these hilly areas closest to the city was sacrificed for the homes of future Salemites. Nearly no one knew that these Willamette Valley hills would also prove to be ideal for growing high-value pinot noir wine grapes.

Furthermore, in yet another irony, Bob Straub was a man whose business success began by building tract houses—affordable, but clearly "little boxes, made of ticky-tacky," as derided in Malvina Reynolds' famous folk song—spread across the farmlands, expanding the edges of a growing Springfield. He was an active part of the same destructive process that swallowed up all the farmland of his childhood. In turn, his own farm in West Salem, once surrounded by fields and orchards and an unblemished view of Cascade mountain peaks, was in a hilly, sacrifice zone for an updated version of the very sort of tract housing he himself had built in his younger days in Springfield.

Truly, the arc of Bob Straub's life traversed and became entangled in much of Oregon's recent history, with all of its contradictions.

The progressive young businessman, blasting roads through riverside rocks as Lane County commissioner in the 1950s became the insurgent environmentalist state treasurer, marching to stop beach highways in the 1960s, who, in turn, became the calculating bureaucratic governor in the 1970s, gaining federal exemptions from highway funds to convert money to Portland area mass transit. As a respected senior statesman in the 1980s and '90s, Straub had to reflect on the strange twists and turns his life's road had taken. He certainly is one of the few people for whom both a state park—Bob Straub State Park in Pacific City on the Nestucca Sand Spit that he had protected— and a road—the Bob Straub Parkway cutting through the Thurston area of Springfield, which he helped to plat and develop—are named.

Here was the ultimate capitalist—yet always a common man at heart— trained at Dartmouth, with connections to multinational business through his wife's family and his old school ties. Straub observed his father's accession to the top levels of the legal department of the utility behemoth Pacific Gas &Electric, but he learned the value of working with his hands on the farms and in the forests, of sweating alongside people with less lofty financial expectations. Bob's afflictions, physical with his eye problems, and psychological with his bipolar depressions, made him sensitive to other people's suffering and made him love the underdog, the immigrant—the Mexican workers, whose respect for hard work was the same as his, but whose joy of living was so different from his own Germanic upbringing. It was this care for the less fortunate that led Straub to support efforts for improving the lot of prisoners, the mentally ill, and the elderly. Straub's innovative Project Independence, assisting seniors in living in their own homes as they grow older, is a model throughout the country and continues to this day in Oregon, despite seemingly annual budget scares.

While pondering the contradictions of Bob Straub's legacy, consider another major issue in Oregon during Straub's time here: managing and preserving forest resources … Oregon's primary industry for nearly one hundred years.

Having worked in a California logging camp as a young man, Bob Straub came to Oregon with his Dartmouth MBA to work as a manager for the new Weyerhaeuser mill in Springfield. Yet Straub had grown up in a family that spent summers camping in the redwoods, and spent his college summers hiking the forested mountains of New Hampshire, with a backpack he'd made by hand. It was there on a mountain trail that he met Patricia Stroud, the love of his life. He and his wife chose Springfield, Oregon, to live in because of its proximity to wild, forested lands. His ambiguous, nuanced—some would call it balanced—view of the forest continued throughout his life, as he logged his own private lands near Fall Creek and Curtin, replanting there and, later, on his land near Willamina. All the while, he continued hiking the Cascade mountain forests with his family and friends, swimming in alpine lakes, taking extended treks with burros, and, later, whitewater rafting all over the Northwest.

His public stance on forestry issues embodied the balance of his private life. Straub supported the forest industry as one of Oregon's most important economic pillars, but favored setting aside large tracts of less-valuable timber in higher elevations, and areas around lakes, rivers, and streams, for use for recreation by the public, earning the enmity of the timber industry that had once employed him. Straub also parted ways with the timber companies in taking the long view of public land use, favoring a sustainable cut, rather than a boom and bust "cut and run" plan that provided short-term jobs at the expense of long-term unemployment. Unlike the timber companies and ILWU longshoremen, Straub believed we should be using our precious raw logs in Oregon mills, creating Oregon jobs, rather than creating jobs in mills overseas.

Bob experimented with horse logging on his own land, with his son-in-law Jay Thomas, and supported efforts to log in a less destructive manner: eliminating clear-cutting to the extent it was economically feasible and avoiding steep slopes, excessive road building, and cutting near streams in an effort to prevent erosion and silting, which was devastating the land and the salmon fishery. And, under the influence of his wife, Pat, he came to oppose the use of toxic chemicals in the woods, favoring more labor-intensive methods of brush clearing.

Neither Bob Straub, nor Tom McCall, nor any of their successors resolved these conflicts. All of these Oregon forest issues are still with us today. Lane County, where community meetings are held in the Bob Straub Conference Room in the courthouse and where Bob served as county commissioner, along with several counties in Oregon, is rapidly becoming insolvent, due in large part to a lack of timber receipts from federal lands. These counties relied for many years on these federal timber payments as a major part of their revenue stream. They are now victims of the "timber gap"—the overcutting of forests, leading to a dearth of harvestable timber for future forest workers—and other long-term forest issues that Bob Straub and others foresaw in the 1970s.

Straub's legacy is incomplete in other ways. His vision of a clean Willamette River, connected by a series of parks for hiking and water recreation is progressing slowly. Park land is gradually accumulating along the riverbanks and, between the death of the pulp industry in Oregon and sewage-treatment improvements (culminating in Portland's recent huge achievement of near-complete containment of its combined sewer outflow with the "big pipe" project), the Willamette's waters are now mostly swimmable and salmon are reestablishing themselves in its tributaries.

Tom McCall and Bob Straub fought over the best way to preserve Oregon's beaches or establish a Willamette Greenway, and other issues affecting Oregon's natural heritage. Mostly their battles led to good policies. Echoes of the McCall-Straub rivalry still live on . Tom McCall got that larger-than-life statue that he referred to in his famous Studs Terkel interview, which *is*, on certain sunsets, etched against a red sky,[5] in Salem's waterfront park—a park that Bob Straub, so far, unheralded, kept from becoming a small grass strip next to a waterfront convention center. But, a living memorial, commemorating the Straubs' contribution to Oregon's environmental protection in the capital city, is the Bob and Pat Straub Environmental Learning Center, established by North Salem High School teacher Jon Yoder with local contributions, which contains an up-to-date environmental lab for students and includes a regular community-wide lecture program and alert network.

And what of the underlying economic issues of government funding and public investment policy into which Straub, with his business orientation, put so much effort? His innovations as treasurer in creating the Oregon Investment Council and investing the state's money in ways that vastly increased its yield were successful for several decades. Nevertheless, the bubble economy of the late 1990s and the early twenty-first century has proven too powerful for the structures that Straub created to protect state monies. Investment mistakes have been common, even among the most carefully managed public agencies, like Oregon's. Decisions by the Oregon PERS board and pension funds throughout Oregon, the nation, and the world created demands upon their funding sources that cannot be delivered without sacrificing existing services. The out-of-control cost of medical care is busting public and private budgets throughout the US, and Oregon, despite some innovative policies by some of Straub's successors, has proven no exception.

In spite of Straub's contributions to the long struggles to provide property tax relief to Oregonians—including creating an income tax rebate during his time as governor—Oregon succumbed in 1990 to the lure of property tax limitations. Predictably, this hamstrung state and local government's capacity to pay for services, notably public schools and universities, degrading service quality and angering the public on both the left and right of the political spectrum. The quest for the Holy Grail of perfectly fair, equitable, and adequate taxation continues.

Long-term prospects for the Oregon economy are dicey. The timber economy has struggled, as noted, but the expansion of high-tech businesses that Straub and his successors encouraged has also struggled at times, as businesses of all types, especially those involved in manufacturing, have found that it is cheaper to make things in countries that don't have inconvenient labor or environmental laws, and ship them to worldwide markets.

Environmental issues have gone global, too. Climate change due to the burning of fossil fuels, with resulting unprecedented CO_2 accumulation, along with vastly increased methane release, threatens to change everyone's environment in drastic ways, and on a time scale that is difficult to predict. Green technology advances are touted as economic and environmental liberators, and Oregon political leaders are striving hard to put Oregon in the vanguard. Yet, alternatives seem to be too slowly implemented, flawed, or ignored entirely by those with an economic interest in perpetuating the current carbon-based energy system.

All of these problems— economic, environmental, and social—are left for today's activists, policymakers, businesspeople, and citizens of all stripes to solve as best they can, just as Straub, McCall, and their many friends, allies, and rivals attempted to do in their day. In the end, we only have ourselves to rely upon as we look for clues from those who came before us.

***

What a fragile, brief, beautiful thing is a human life. We stumble forward, using our instincts, intellect, and best intentions. The better among us strive to improve their performance and standing. The very best strive to improve the performance and standing of everyone.

Bob Straub was one of those.

Photo by Gerry Lewin

Epilogue

PROFESSOR MARK HENKELS

WESTERN OREGON UNIVERSITY, MONMOUTH

Robert Straub embraced and sometimes created policies that ran against the grain of the state's existing political class, reflecting his lifelong propensity to cut his own path. The demands of the Depression and World War II may partially explain Straub's decisiveness and character, but he also faced specific challenges that required uniquely personal resolve and vision. His policy creativity and determination seem to reflect the repeated lesson of his private life and business career: things worked best when he avoided imitation. Despite years of partisan battling, Straub never really fit the "political insider" saddle comfortably. In an interview for this book, Straub's former chief of staff, Bud Kramer, noting his former boss' lack of political craftiness, remarked, "He was an unlikely politician." This prompted a comment from the other room by his wife Ann: "That's because Bob Straub WASN'T a politician."[1]

The Oregon legacy of the 1960s and 1970s remains distinctive and powerful, exemplifying what American democracy can produce when the public and their elected officials share a vision and the willingness to break free of old policy assumptions and constraints. Any history of Oregon would be remiss to overlook the creativity Straub brought to state government and his enduring contribution to the vision and values Oregon embraced so forcefully in his era. His mark is seen in small stories and large public policies, and in the names of local schools and parks and the beautiful state beach park on Nestucca Spit.

Governors are not presidents. Their public fame is rarely as bright and generally diminishes quickly once they leave office. Predictably, Bob's visibility has faded, yet his character and accomplishments remain crisp to those who knew him well. What difference can a one-term governor make that lasts beyond his generation? In his excellent overview of Straub's public career, Professor Richard Clucas of Portland State University asserts that "Even if Straub did not capture the public's imagination, he left an indelible mark on Oregon, from state investments to the hiring of women and minorities to programs for senior citizens. For almost twenty years, he played a central role in shaping Oregonians' attitudes and public policy on the environment and was the most important leader on several of the major environmental crusades of the time, from protecting beach access and bringing mass transit to Portland to shaping land-use rules."[2]

The tendency of analysts and writers to focus on his governorship leads them to undervalue the audacity of Straub's visions and his challenge of core policy patterns over his entire career. While his fellow one-term governor Oswald West is frequently credited with saving Oregon's public beaches, candidate Straub was instrumental in reaffirming that public value and his contribution to the modern Oregon identity is undeniable.

Oregon in the 1960s and 1970s was socially and politically turbulent and creative. The most visible politicians, notably Tom McCall, seemed to succeed because they could surf or sometimes guide the tide of openness and change. Outside of Oregon, McCall's iconic statements about wanting people to visit—"But for heaven's sake don't come here to live"—were and remain emblematic of the times.[3] Within Oregon, things looked a bit different. While McCall was a towering figure, it was the debates of the "Tom and Bob Show" that inaugurated the unparalleled public commitment to environmentalism. Straub's competition with McCall was not built on ordinary pandering. The ideas and visions he brought to the table often presented novel visions of possibilities. The term "radical" might even come to mind when considering the long-term implications of some of Straub's ideas.

Straub as a radical? As odd as that phrase may sound, Straub was notable for getting past the superficial level of issues to directly consider problems or possibilities at the root level. Three episodes exemplify this point. First, how else can you label a state treasurer who challenged prevailing wisdom and habit concerning the historically staid field of state government finance? Second, it takes an iconoclastic vision for an elected official to stand up against the social, political, and economic forces pushing to streamline the Oregon coast's critical tourist artery in the heyday of road construction. Finally, Straub's persistent promotion of the Willamette River as a centerpiece of new vision of the valley was built from a deep recognition of the uniqueness of place. Straub's (and McCall's) Oregon was more than "not just California"; he saw the state as a distinctive land of unique characteristics, to be stewarded with care and cherished and enjoyed by all.

Straub himself was not one to speak philosophically of his work. He simply stated he wanted to do what was right in a given situation. Yet there are two patterns beneath his actions: a consistent concern for the long-term implications of existing and potential policies and a value of egalitarian outcomes. It's likely that his Ivy League education gave him a natural affinity for the conservationist-progressive ideas of Gifford Pinchot, but Straub informed this value with a deeper and more modern understanding of the destructive possibilities of economics and technology. He wanted an Oregon that would provide all current and future Oregonians as many options as possible. He sought to create that state through the combination of optimal management of resources (land, timber, cash reserves) and the preservation of unique irreplaceable resources (public beaches as ecological as well as recreational resources).

Straub embraced the concept of progress; that things could and would get better if the right decisions were made and people properly followed through on their work. This progressive vision freed him from feeling committed to existing policy patterns. For example, he readily appreciated the value of Oregon Project Independence and programs that broke the automatic reliance on the old nursing home model. This former builder and developer also made tough decisions to provide the nascent state planning system a good start because he could envision what unrestricted development would do to his state. He bluntly stated that those who sought to repeal the land-use planning system established by Senate Bill 100 were promoting "their own selfish interests."[4]

There are risks in espousing radical ideas, even if you believe these make mainstream common sense. Straub's strong positions sometimes created space for McCall and others to take a more moderate and politically safe embrace of Straub's visions. As Richard Judd and Christopher Beach point out in their book, *Natural States*, Straub's strong positions on the Willamette Greenway and beach preservation created a subtle split in the environmental community, with McCall generally on the more traditional pro-property rights side of the issues.[5] Pushing these frontiers sometimes allowed Straub's political opponents to defeat his ideas, such as when his advocacy of a temporary penny per gallon tax on gasoline fell to fears of government overreach heightened by his opponents slogan "Beware of Tricks in No. 6."

Another risk of being so audacious is that truly successful policies might over time be pushed too far. After forty years, Oregon's state and local governments face significant shortcomings in their retirement funding, partially the result of the brutal investment climate.[6] Although Straub had a very cautious and pragmatic perspective on investing, it is tempting to hold that investment strategy partially accountable for the current troubles. That perspective misses both the precautions Straub placed in his system and practices of the managers long after Straub retired. What would Bob Straub think if he could see the retirement system today? Certainly he would have reasons to take pride in his work. In 2009, PERS beneficiaries received over $2.5 billion in benefits. The large majority of benefits are paid for by investment income, which accounted for 69 percent of the program's revenues for 1970-2009.[7] Overall Bob would probably note, in agreement with long-time PERS board member Roger Meier, that the modern public pension fund investment program he pioneered was a success, but that its very success may have led governments and union leaders to imprudently rely upon a continuation of the unsustainable extraordinary returns of the 1980s and 1990s. Without a doubt, Oregon's public employees have benefited and will continue to benefit greatly from Straub's financial insights, even if adjustments must be made to reflect the impact of the "Great Recession."

Discussions about the Oregon of the 1960s and 1970s typically center on Oregon's famed environmental policies, and Straub's most visible impacts are in that realm. His contribution here was a distinctive part of a larger movement that was both strongly bi-partisan and undergirded with a groundswell of local activism. Straub was not an isolated prophet, but he took some surprising positions for a former homebuilder and small-timberland owner. His sophisticated views on timber opened him to criticism from both sides at times. He was, in a sense, both a "tree-hugger" and a "tree-user," who sought to balance timber policy with values other than board feet and corporate revenue. He recommended to the federal government more acres be designated wilderness than any other governor because he felt no single generation should destroy irreplaceable places all might enjoy through time. He viewed the Willamette River, the beaches, and specific wilderness areas as a legacy his generation should pass to the next. These were things all should share, common goods that simply do not belong in the marketplace.

Bob's environmentalist views were complicated by his ongoing concern for the timber industry and its many jobs. By 1982 Straub's sense of balance led him to say that environmentalists were pushing things too far; legal injunctions were too absolute, and he felt the pendulum would sometime swing back and take from environmentalists that which they sought to protect.[8] In striking the appropriate balance, environmentalists should not delay established policy implementation when "protecting every mouse, squirrel and minnow." Still Straub understood that Oregon's reliance on timber would inevitably have to give ground. As an article *in Business Week* noted, "Straub's top priority is to make Oregon's economy, which is 43% dependent on forest products less vulnerable."[9] His efforts to convince California's high tech industry that Oregon would be a "solid state for electronics" opened a door that his successor Vic Atiyeh would use to powerfully diversify the economy in the 1980s.

Straub faced a tough reelection battle in 1978. In face of a national and state counter-mobilization against the liberalism of the 1960s and early 1970s, Straub stood strongly for progressive policies. He committed much of his precious attention and energy in 1978 working to defeat ballot measures that would eviscerate statewide land-use laws and reestablish the death penalty. Straub's views prevailed on the major ballot battles, save that of the death penalty.

The rising national conservative tide of the late 1970s through the early 1990s did not reverse Oregon's progressive policies as much as in many other states, even as a persistent deep regionalism developed, pitting the Metro area and the university towns against the balance of the state. Oregon's environmental programs basically survived the passage of various anti-government and anti-tax ballot measures and Ronald Reagan's electoral successes. Straub was among the most important political actors in the creation of a new vision of Oregon values and building supportive new policies in the 1960s and 1970s. His governorship helped stabilize the new environmental policies by reinforcing their institutional structure and public image so they could effectively resist political attack. To this day Oregonians and their political leaders view policies such as beach access, the Willamette River, and the management of state funds as the Oregon way to do things, appreciating values established four decades ago. The vision of "what makes Oregon Oregon" remains fundamentally the same in 2011 as in 1971, providing a powerful reinforcing image for these policies.

Straub also helped secure Oregon's new environmental policies by making them workable. Governor Straub diligently accepted the less celebrated tasks of defending McCall's legislative accomplishments against hostile public initiatives and making the complex vision work administratively. The importance of this work can easily be overlooked. By the time Straub became governor, the nation and even Oregon were moving away from the acceptance of progressive government activism. A governor with less commitment to protecting the Oregon environment might have made the McCall era appear more of an interlude than a re-defining chapter in the state's history. The Straub governorship secured the gains of the previous decade and reinforced Oregon's appeal to those seeking "smart growth" and "green" lifestyles, values that were central to Bob and Pat's sense of what makes a good life.

Bob Straub lost three gubernatorial elections and was not to see the completion of his full vision for other major goals, such as the Willamette Greenway. He suffered both privately and publicly from living a life of highly visible service. Oregon would never be the same after the 1960s and 1970s, and Straub was an essential element in the transformation. He created or promoted a world where highway plans were not inevitably completed, where money did not just sleep, where a public recreational area could stretch through the entire Willamette Valley, and where senior services did not simply reinforce existing patterns of care. And he pragmatically built alliances, goaded opponents, and negotiated with anyone who could help make these visions work.

It is tempting to say that a person with so many personal foibles and such outspoken commitment to strong values would not get elected today. Certainly Straub would not be an ideal candidate, since he was not a polished speaker or mistake-free campaigner. But he did have some strengths that would serve him well in the modern campaign context. First, he was consistent on big issues and could identify winning issues early, so he might have dictated campaign agendas towards his visions. Second, he earned and kept the loyalty of key people. Finally, although he was badly outspent in his final campaign, Straub was no amateur at collecting endorsements and money in his day. Straub also was able to build trust and develop support because people came to appreciate his character and ideas over time.   Charles Sprague, the powerful long-time editor of the *Oregon Statesman*, and a former governor himself, demonstrates how Straub could build trust and respect. Over time Sprague's editorials evolved from frequently condemning Bob for being too strident and partisan in the 1960s to fairly consistently endorsing Straub's proposals in the 1970s.

There is no reason to think Straub would not adapt to the contemporary political context, but the very complexity and originality of his policy ideas might not be appreciated in a campaign world defined by sound-bites and twenty-second images. Conceptual sophistication works better within Salem than on the campaign trail, but Straub's integrity and vision might still resonate well in Oregon.

Straub's personal contribution to the "Oregon Story" of the 1960s and 1970s is hard to distinguish in part because it was not always clear even during that era. Bob's contributions were overlooked sometimes, even in the 1970s. Straub enjoyed telling a story that illustrates this problem extraordinarily well. According to Bob, a young man, recognized as a local "character," used to come to the public area of the governor's office frequently. Whenever Bob would walk through, he would inquire about the young man and his family. After a few years of this familiarity, one day Bob was walking in the Capitol and this fellow and another came running up behind him. The young fellow turned to his companion and said, "I want you to meet my friend. This is Governor Tom McCall."[10] The irony of all the adulation of the leadership of Tom McCall from this period is that Tom McCall himself appreciated Bob's character and unique contribution as much as anyone. After Bob's reelection defeat, McCall wrote in consolation, "Bob, you would have been Oregon's greatest governor, ever, in your second term."[11]

On December 18, 2002, all four living former governors, Governor Kitzhaber, governor-elect Ted Kulongoski, and a close group of friends and relatives gathered to recognize Bob Straub's life and work. Politically, Oregon state government remained a small world, one where Bob's humor, intelligence, and pragmatism earned respect and appreciation from all quarters. Before the final prayer at the memorial, Bob's wife, Pat, read from a letter in which Keizer city leaders stated, "We're constantly reminded of the saying that we can only see great distances because we are standing on the shoulders of giants who came before us. In terms of the Willamette River, Bob Straub was truly one of those giants." It's pure speculation, and sincere consolation, for McCall to say Bob would have become "Oregon's greatest governor." But it is not wrong to say he was truly a "one of those giants" of the era.

Reproduced by permission of the artist, Jack Ohman

Notes

Introduction

1. In conversations with author, 1997 and 1998.
2. Tom McCall interview, from *American Dreams: Lost and Found*, Studs Terkel, Knopf Doubleday Publishing Company, New York, 1980, page 335: "Heroes are not giant statues framed against a red sky. They are people who say: This is my community, and it is my responsibility to make it better."

Chapter 1

1. From "Bob Straub: A Personal Portrait." Interview of Governor Robert Straub by Ted Bryant, KATU, Channel 2, Portland, Oregon, January 6, 1979.
2. Author interview of Jean Russell and Barbara Straub, February 27, 2007.
3. Ibid., and author phone interview with Jean Russell, August 26, 2007
4. Author interview of Jean Russell and Barbara Straub, February 27, 2007.
5. Governor Robert Straub interview, Clark Hansen, Oregon Historical Society, 14 May 1991, Tape 1, Side 1. This "is one of the lesser attractive areas of Kansas," according to Bob Straub in an interview with Ted Bryant on KATU-TV Portland, in December, 1978.
6. Johann Jakob Friedrich (John Jacob Frederick) Straub, born in 1812 in Baden, Switzerland, married Anna Margarethe (Margaret Ann) Maichel (Michael), born in 1821, also in Switzerland, on November 7, 1841 in Coshocton County, Ohio. They had three children before moving to Jefferson County, Wisconsin, where Margaret gave birth to Francis Jefferson and six more siblings. By 1860, John and Margaret had moved to Grant Township in Caldwell County, Missouri, where Margaret bore two more children, for a total of twelve! *Sources: Marriage Index:* Ohio, 1789-1850 (Liahona Research, Orem UT); and Ohio, Wisconsin, and Missouri Census Indices (Ancestry.com).
7. Telephone interview of Alexander Russell III (Luke) by author on October 24, 2007.
8. Museum of the Kansas National Guard, Historic Units, The Twentieth Kansas Volunteers, Web site, <http://www.kansasguardmuseum.org/>
9. An indication of the common, openly racist and condescending attitudes among the new colonizers was the popularity of English writer Rudyard Kipling's poem, "The White Man's Burden," with the subtitle "The United States and the Philippine Islands." In it Kipling urges Americans to embrace the virtuous duty of colonialism to help civilize "new caught, sullen peoples, half devil and half child." "The White Man's Burden." *McClure's* Magazine 12 (Feb. 1899).
10. Museum of the Kansas National Guard, Historic Units, The Twentieth Kansas Volunteers, Web site.
11. From: Miller, Stuart Creighton (1982), *"Benevolent Assimilation": The American Conquest of the Philippines, 1899–1903,* Yale University Press; and Matthew Smallman-Raynor, Matthew (1998), "The Philippines Insurrection and the 1902–4 cholera epidemic: Part I: Epidemiological diffusion processes in war," *Journal of Historical Geography* 24 (1): 69–89. It was the Philippine-American War that introduced Americans to the form of interrogation and torture, developed during the Spanish Inquisition, that we now call 'water-boarding.' "Officers testified that the standard procedure when interrogating suspected insurgents was to use the 'water cure,' a method that had apparently been favored by Spanish officials. 'That torture,' occupation governor (and future U.S. president) William Howard Taft explained, 'involves pouring water down the throat so

that the man swells and gets the impression that he is going to be suffocated and then tells what he knows.'" "The History of Torture – Why We Can't Give It Up," by Colin Woodard, *Military History Quarterly*, On-line Edition, August 9, 2011, http://www. historynet.com/the-history-of-torture%E2%80%94why-we-can'tgive-it-up.htm/1.

12. Telephone interview by author of Alexander Russell III (Luke) on October 24, 2007.

13. The officer corps of Private Straub's Troop G from Independence had been particularly hard hit by Filipino sharpshooters, losing three, including, in their first major battle (Caloocan), the beloved Captain David S. Elliott, who had been editor of the Independence newspaper. *Correspondence Relating to the War With Spain (vol 1 p.593)*, Adjutant-General's Office, Walter Gentala, Kansas General Web. <http://skyways.lib. ks.us/genweb/archives/statewide/military/ks20.htm>

14. Telephone interview of Barbara Straub by author, September 29, 2007.

15. Governor Robert Straub interview, Clark Hansen, Oregon Historical Society, 14 May 1991, Tape 1, Side 1.

16. Though it was a good job to begin with, it became more lucrative when the well-known world explorers and photographers, Martin and Osa Johnson, came back to Kansas and began buying a great deal of property. Thomas received a percentage of each deed he recorded. Governor Robert Straub interview, Clark Hansen, Oregon Historical Society, 14 May 1991, Tape 1, Side 1 and telephone interview of Jean Russell by author, October 8, 2007

17. University of Michigan Law School Registrar's Office.

18. Telephone interview of Barbara Straub by author, September 29, 2007.

19. According to law school records, Straub entered the University of Michigan Bachelors of Law program in September 1907 and graduated on June 30, 1910. The Law School did not keep records of grades or law school rankings until 1912.

20. Author interview of Jean Russell and Barbara Straub, February 27, 2007; and Governor Robert Straub interview, Clark Hansen, Oregon Historical Society, 14 May 1991, Tape 1, Side 1. OHS interview: Robert Straub:- "That was the old tradition that the woman didn't chase after the man, and that was wonderful." Clark Hansen: "and he did it?" (return to Kansas for her). Straub: "Oh, yes. You bet he did it, or he wouldn't have gotten her."

21. William B. Bosley came to San Francisco fresh from Yale Law School in 1885 to teach at the University of California's Hastings Law School, which was independent from the rest of the University of California System. After leaving to join Pacific Gas & Electric, he remained a curmudgeonly force on the Hastings Board until as late as 1958. Writer Thomas G. Barnes dryly observed: "Bosley would just as soon have joined the Communist Party before he would let Hastings join the UC System." *Hastings College of the Law: The First Century,* Thomas G. Barnes; Hastings College of the Law Press, San Francisco, CA; 1978.

22. Tom Mooney was finally pardoned in 1938 (after twenty-two years in prison), when the first Democrat in forty-four years, Culbert Olson, was elected Governor of California.

23. Author interview of Jean Russell and Barbara Straub, February 27, 2007.

24. The Palmer Raids, named for President Woodrow Wilson's U.S. Attorney General Alexander M. Palmer, with future FBI director J. Edgar Hoover in the lead, from December 1919 to January 1920 resulted in the largest mass arrests in U.S. history, with over ten thousand people taken into custody. Over half of those arrested were members of the International Workers of the World (IWW) trade union organization. To give an idea of how viciously the state prosecuted Tom Mooney, this is what the prosecuting attorney, Edward Cunha, had to say about him and his associates: "If the thing were done that ought to be done, this whole God damn dirty low down bunch would be

taken out and strung up without ceremony. They're a bunch of dirty anarchists, every one of them, and they ought to be in jail on general principles. I'm not speaking now as an officer, I am just speaking as a man and a citizen, to show you my attitude … If I knew that every single witness that testified against [Mooney] had perjured himself in his testimony I wouldn't lift a finger to get him out. I told him to get out if he could." Edward Cunha interview by John A. Fitch, *Survey* magazine in July, 1917

25. Author interview of Jean Russell and Barbara Straub, February 27, 2007.

26. Nicola Sacco and Bartolomeo Vanzetti were anarchists arrested in Boston in 1920 on the charge of murder and armed robbery. After a long, controversial trial and series of appeals, they were executed in 1927, eliciting worldwide outrage in leftist circles. Many people believe the evidence and judicial procedures were fixed to prove guilt. Fifty years after their deaths, Massachusetts Governor Michael Dukakis signed a proclamation stating "that the high standards of justice, which we in Massachusetts take such pride in, failed Sacco and Vanzetti." (*Massachusetts high court puts Sacco & Vanzetti trial on exhibit*, Associated Press news, September 23, 2007).

27. Years later, when Robert Straub as a young Democratic politician from Oregon, met California Governor Edmund G. "Pat" Brown, Brown remembered taking classes from Thomas Straub in the 1920s.

28. Author interview of Jean Russell, February 26, 2007.

29. Ibid.

30. Ibid. and phone interview of Barbara Straub by author, September 29, 2007. Barbara Straub also said that Pat Straub used this same party technique for many years, and still does to this day, having learned how much fun it was from her mother-in-law.

31. Ibid. Jean Russell said, "I remember meat was 5 cents a pound."

32. Author interview of Jean Russell, February 26, 2007 and phone interview of Barbara Straub, September 29, 2007.

33, Telephone interview of Barbara Straub by author, October 22, 2007.

34. Author interview of Jean Russell, February 26, 2007.

35. Telephone interview of Jean Russell by author, August 26, 2007.

36. Author interview of Jean Russell and Barbara Straub, February 27, 2007.

37. Ibid.

38. Telephone interview of Alexander Russell III (Luke) by author on October 24, 2007.

39. Author interview of Jean Russell and Barbara Straub, February 27, 2007.

40. Telephone interview of Alexander Russell III (Luke) by author on October 24, 2007

41. Author interview of Jean Russell and Barbara Straub, February 27, 2007, and with Mike and Jane Straub, July 31, 2007. Family lore doesn't say how the date went, but it is the sort of thing a brother might never forget. This and other incidents like it may help explain some of the spiteful nastiness of Tom's later attacks on politician Bob Straub when Tom was editor of the *Lane Reporter*.

42. Interestingly, Ordway and Bob found themselves on the same army transport ship going to England during the Second World War. Ordway remained an adventurer and was lost at sea in the Pacific on a sailing voyage in the 1950s. Telephone interview of Barbara Straub by author, October 22, 2007.

43. On one or more occasions, Jim ducked behind a billboard when he saw his father's car approaching and then continued hitchhiking into San Francisco for a day of fun. Author interview of Jean Russell and Barbara Straub, February 27, 2007.

44. Ibid.

45. Ibid.

46. Ibid.

47. This problem recurred several times, leading to virtual blindness in one eye. Author interview of Mike and Jane Straub, July 31, 2007.

48. Thomas Straub knew little about his youngest son, and he was surprised to hear that he had trouble with stuttering when Bob talked to him about it when he was an adult. Jean said, "Can you believe that Dad didn't even know the number one problem in his life?" But Bob was very private about it. Author interview of Jean Russell and Barbara Straub, February 27, 2007.

49. Ibid.

50. Ibid. Cranston earned early notoriety when in 1939, as a youthful journalist, fluent in German, covering Berlin for the International News Service, he was sued by Adolf Hitler's publisher for publishing an unexpurgated version of Hitler's *Mein Kampf*, exposing the English-speaking world to the true nature of Hitler's plans. Straub was a freshman at Dartmouth by then, and quite proud of his fellow Mountain View High alum for making such a contribution in a critical cause.

51. Letter from Bob Straub to Mary Straub, July 27, 1936, on outside of letter is written in Mary's handwriting: "From Bob. To be kept." From the papers of Barbara Straub, Tucson, AZ.

52. Governor Robert Straub interview, Clark Hansen, Oregon Historical Society, 14 May 1991, Tape 1, Side 1.

53. Official Transcript of Robert William Straub, Mountain View High School, LaVonne Hand, Registrar.

54. School Records, Dartmouth College, Hanover, NH.

55. Author interview of Jean Russell and Barbara Straub, February 27, 2007.

56 Thirteen years older than Jean, Bernice Straub was Thomas' older brother Ivan's daughter. Ivan had moved to Baker, Oregon, to go into mining and had remarried after his wife died. The new wife had encouraged Bernice to live elsewhere and she came to live with Thomas and Mary in Los Altos. The cruise through the canal was very grand. Jean did a lot of dancing and in New York stayed one night at the Waldorf-Astoria. At $5 per night, this was quite a splurge. Author interview of Jean Russell and Barbara Straub, February 27, 2007.

57. Letter from Bob Straub to Mr. and Mrs. Thomas Straub, postmarked July 1938.

58. Jean was getting a new car and her father Thomas would not let her give Judy to Bob or Jim, as Jean wanted to do. Telephone interview of Alexander Russell III (Luke) by author on October 24, 2007.

59. Letter from Bob Straub to Jean Straub (Russell), postmarked August 12, 1938.

Chapter 2

1. Oral History Interview of Robert W. Straub by Clark Hansen, , Oregon Historical Society, Portland, May 14, 1991, Tape 1, Side 1.

2. Bob Straub conversation with author at his home in West Salem, some time in 1999.

3. Dartmouth College transcript, Robert W. Straub. From fall 1939 through fall 1943, Straub received 2.7468 GPA, which put him at 133rd in a graduating class of 489, almost in the top third of his class.

4. Dartmouth College Application, Robert W. Straub, 1938.

5. Oral history Interview of Robert W. Straub by Clark Hansen, Oregon Historical Society, Portland, May 14, 1991, Tape 1, Side 1.

6. Vox Populi, page 5, *The Dartmouth*, "The Oldest College Newspaper in America," October 29, 1940.

7. "Straub Sweeps East Debate Tournament," *The Dartmouth*, page 1, April 14, 1941.

8. "Stratton, '41, Brutschy '42 Win Barge and Class of '66 Prizes," *The Dartmouth*, page 1, May 7, 1941.

9. "Debaters Elect Straub and Oppenheimer," *The Dartmouth*, page 1, April 16, 1942.

10. "Dean's Office Warns 102 Upperclassmen," *The Dartmouth*, page 1, February 14, 1941.

11. Dartmouth College transcript, Robert W. Straub.

12. "Opposition to [Senator] Tobey," Vox Populi, *The Dartmouth*, April 26, 1941.

13. Author interview of Mike and Jane Straub, July 31, 2007.

14. New Hampshire Society of Sons of the American Revolution Web site, essay "The Founding of Dartmouth College," Compatriots Abe Weld and Hibbard Richter.

15. "Outing Club Names Eight Students to Ravine Camp Jobs," *The Dartmouth*, page 1, April 11, 1940.

16. "On Top of the World: Moosilauke Summit Camp on 'Dartmouth's Mountain' Again Operated by Crew of Undergraduates," Robert Straub '43, *Dartmouth Alumni Magazine*, June 1942.

17. Telephone interview of Lincoln Wales by author, January 8, 2008.

18. Telephone interview of Ellen Miller by author, January 9, 2008.

19. Author interview of Pat Straub, June 28, 2007.

20. "The Doc Benton Ghost Story," as told by Bill Thibault '64, June 1961, pp.1-12, Dartmouth College Archives. In addition to the Doc Benton story, the summit workers used to have great fun playing other elaborate tricks on their young guests. One involved getting the kids to "help" fill the water tank by having each of them climb a long ladder to throw fake "pills" into the rainwater tank on the side of the lodge before an expected nighttime rain. These "pills," painstakingly made out of small pieces of wood wrapped in gauze and thread, were supposed to "absorb more moisture out of the clouds." The next day, the workers would praise the youngsters for their fine work after the rain had filled the tank, telling them you "are the best group we ever had." Dave Heald quoted in *Reaching That Peak: 75 Years of the Dartmouth Outing Club*, by David O. Hooke, Phoenix Publishing, Canaan, New Hampshire (186-87).

21. Straub Autobiography folder, Robert Straub Archives, Western Oregon University, Monmouth.

22. Author interview of Pat Straub, June 28, 2007.

23. Oral history interview of Robert W. Straub by Clark Hansen, Oregon Historical Society, Portland, May 14, 1991, Tape 1, Side 2.

24. Author interview of Pat Straub, June 28, 2007.

25. Oral history interview of Robert W. Straub by Clark Hansen, , Oregon Historical Society, Portland, May 14, 1991, Tape 1, Side 2. In fact, in 1947, after receiving a silver star for bravery in Europe (and participating in the capture of Nazi leader Hermann Goering), Harry Bond *did* return to Dartmouth to a distinguished forty-year career as a professor of English.

26. Oral history interview of Robert W. Straub by Clark Hansen, May 14, 1991, Tape 1, Side 2, Oregon Historical Society, Portland.

27. Author interview of Mike and Jane Straub, July 31, 2007.

28. Saltus was an avid pilot and past-president of the Aero Club of Pennsylvania http://www.aeroclubpa.org/history/Presidents.html

29. Author interview of Pat Straub, June 28, 2007.

30. "Lana Stroud is Bride of Lt. Straub," *San Antonio Evening News*, page B3, September 15, 1943.

31. Obituary, "Dr. Morris Stroud, 76, Specialist in Geriatrics," AP wire story, *New York Times*, May 5, 1990.

32. Author interview of Mike and Jane Straub, July 31, 2007.

33. "Memorials – William Dixon Boulton Stroud," Princeton Alumni Weekly, October 5th, 2005 Renowned environmentalist Robert F. Kennedy Jr., founder and president of the national Water Keeper Alliance, credits the time he spent as a boy at the Stroud Water

Research Center with his lifelong interest in protecting streams and rivers. "Afterward," by Robert F. Kennedy Jr., from "A Portrait: 1967-2000," Stroud Water Research Center Web site "History" section.

34. Author interview of Mike and Jane Straub, July 31, 2007.

35. "Memorandum to the Trustees, Dartmouth Outing Club," Robert W. Straub, Hutmaster, June 22, 1942, Dartmouth College Archives.

36. Final report, Robert W. Straub, Hutmaster, Moosilauke Summit Camp, Warren, NH, September 15, 1942, Dartmouth College Archives.

37. *Reaching That Peak: 75 Years of the Dartmouth Outing Club*. David O. Hooke, Phoenix Publishing, Canaan, New Hampshire, pp., 190-91.

38. Author interview of Pat Straub, June 28, 2007.

39. Letter from John Dickerson, Office of the President, Dartmouth College, to John McLane Clark, Office of the Coordinator of Inter-American Affairs, Washington, DC, March 19, 1942.

40. Letter from Mary de Groat, Acting Director, Emergency Rehabilitation Division, Coordinator of Inter-American Affairs, Washington DC, to John Dickerson, Office of the President, Dartmouth, July 21, 1942.

41. Had he actually gone to Guatemala, Straub may have found that asking questions about the labor situation in the fall of 1942 could have been quite hazardous. By 1944, however, President Ubico was forced from power by popular pressure, led by the railroad workers, ushering in a decade of what "one Guatemalan scholar [called] ten 'years of spring in the land of eternal tyranny.'" In 1954, this brief period ended when President Eisenhower authorized a CIA-sponsored military coup of the elected government of Jacobo Arbenz (1951-54), leading to decades of oppression and bloody civil war. Arbenz' 'sin' was nationalizing some of the United Fruit Company's banana plantation holdings. From *Workers' Control in Latin America, 1930-1979*, edited by Jonathon C. Brown, The University of North Carolina Press, Chapel Hill and London, 1997.

42. Letter from Bob Straub, Hutmaster, Moosilauke Summit Camp, to John Dickerson, President Hopkins' office, Dartmouth College, August 1, 1942.

43. Oral history interview of Robert W. Straub by Clark Hansen, Oregon Historical Society, Portland, May 14, 1991, Tape 1, Side 2.

44. The bulk of his record as an enlistee was destroyed in a large fire in 1973 at the National Personnel Records Center in St. Louis, which burned a massive number of US Army records from World Wars I and II and the Korean War. Straub kept a copy of his discharge papers as an officer. Telephone call from National Personnel Records Center, St. Louis, September 22, 2011.

45. Telephone interview of Jeff Straub by author, August 26, 2011.

46. Telephone interview of Mike Straub by author, September 9, 2011.

47. Author interview of Pat Straub, June 28, 2007.

48. From "Record of Bob and Pat," a scrapbook made by Pat Straub of their sudden courtship, wedding, and early married life.

49. Bob also notes that "the bill came after we were married and I had to pay it anyway." Oral history interview of Robert W. Straub by Clark Hansen, Oregon Historical Society, Portland, May 14, 1991, Tape 1, Side 2.

50. Author interview of Pat Straub, June 28, 2007.

51. From "Record of Bob and Pat," a scrapbook made by Pat Straub of their sudden courtship, wedding, and early married life.

52. Author interview of Pat Straub, June 28, 2007.

53. From "Record of Bob and Pat," a scrapbook made by Pat Straub of their sudden courtship, wedding, and early married life.

54. "Lana Stroud is Bride of Lt. Straub," *San Antonio Evening News*, page B3, September 15, 1943.
55. Author interview of Pat Straub, June 28, 2007.
56. Army of the United States Separation Qualification Record, Robert W. Straub, signed by Captain William M. Shummers, April 29, 1946.
57. Author interview of Pat Straub, June 28, 2007.
58. Army of the United States Separation Qualification Record, Robert W. Straub, signed by Captain William M. Shummers, April 29, 1946
59. Oral history interview of Robert W. Straub by Clark Hansen, Oregon Historical Society, Portland, May 14, 1991, Tape 1, Side 2.
60. Author interview of Pat Straub, June 28, 2007.
61. Ibid.
62. Oral history interview of Robert W. Straub by Clark Hansen, Oregon Historical Society, Portland, May 14, 1991, Tape 1, Side 2.
63. Author interview of Pat Straub, June 28, 2007.
64. Telephone interview of Jean Russell by author, September 12, 2011.
65. Oral history interview of Robert W. Straub by Clark Hansen, Oregon Historical Society, Portland, May 14, 1991, Tape 1, Side 2.
66 Author interview of Pat Straub, June 28, 2007.
67. Army of the United States Separation Qualification Record, Robert W. Straub, signed by Captain William M. Shummers, April 29, 1945.
68. Letter from Francis H. Adler, M.D., to Dr. William D. Stroud of Philadelphia, 18 January, 1946, ccd: to Dean Harluf V. Olsen, Amos Tuck School of Business & Finance – from Dartmouth College Archives.
69. Author interview of Pat Straub, June 28, 2007.
70. Oral history interview of Robert W. Straub by Clark Hansen, Oregon Historical Society, Portland, May 14, 1991, Tape 1, Side 2.
71. Author interview of Pat Straub, June 28, 2007.
72. Oral history interview of Robert W. Straub by Clark Hansen, Oregon Historical Society, Portland, May 14, 1991, Tape 1, Side 2.
73. Author interview of Pat Straub, June 28, 2007.
74. Oral history interview of Robert W. Straub by Clark Hansen, Oregon Historical Society, Portland, May 14, 1991, Tape 1, Side 2.

Chapter 3

1. Oral history interview of Robert W. Straub by Clark Hansen, Oregon Historical Society, Portland, May 14, 1991, Tape 1, Side 2.
2. Ibid.
3. Michael O'Rourke interview of Mike Straub, August 30, 2005, Straub Archives, Western Oregon University.
4. Author interview of Pat Straub, June 28, 2007.
5. Michael O'Rourke interview of Mike Straub, August 30, 2005, Straub Archives, Western Oregon University.
6. Ibid.
7. Oral history interview of Robert W. Straub by Clark Hansen, Oregon Historical Society, Portland, May 14, 1991, Tape 1, Side 2.
8. Author interview of Mike and Jane Straub, July 31, 2007.
9. Michael O'Rourke interview of Mike Straub, August 30, 2005, Straub Archives, Western Oregon University.
10. Oral history interview of Robert W. Straub by Clark Hansen, Oregon Historical Society, Portland, May 14, 1991, Tape 1, Side 2.

11. Michael O'Rourke interview of Mike Straub, August 30, 2005, Straub Archives, Western Oregon University.

12. Oral history interview of Robert W. Straub by Clark Hansen, Oregon Historical Society, Portland, May 14, 1991, Tape 1, Side 2.

13. Michael O'Rourke interview of Mike Straub, August 30, 2005, Straub Archives, Western Oregon University.

14. Oral history interview of Robert W. Straub by Clark Hansen, Oregon Historical Society, Portland, May 14, 1991, Tape 1, Side 2.

15. Author interview of Jean Russell and Barbara Straub, February 27, 2007.

16. Author interview of Pat Straub, June 28, 2007.

17. Author interview of Mike and Jane Straub, July 31, 2007.

18. *Moses the Sassy; or the Disguised Duke*, Chapter 1: Elizy, by Artemus Ward begins thus: *My story opens in the classic presinks of Bostin. In the parler of a bloated aristocratic mansion on Bacon street sits a luvly young lady, whose hair is cuvered ore with the frosts of between 17 Summers. She has just sot down to the piany, and is warblin the popler ballad called "Smells of the Notion," in which she tells how, with pensiv thought, she wandered by a C beat shore. The son is settin in its horizon, and its gorjus light pores in a golden meller flud through the winders, and makes the young lady twict as beautiful nor what she was before, which is onnecessary. She is magnificently dressed up in a Berage basque, with poplin trimmins, More Antique, Ball Morals and 3 ply carpeting. Also, considerable gauze. Her dress contains 16 flounders and her shoes is red morocker, with gold spangles onto them. Presently she jumps up with a wild snort, and pressin her hands to her brow, she exclaims: "Methinks I see a voice!"*

19. Michael O'Rourke interview of Mike Straub, August 30, 2005, Straub Archives, Western Oregon University.

20. "McKenzie-Willamette History," McKenzie-Willamette Medical Center Web site, http://www.mckweb.com/About/Pages/History.aspx

21. Oral history interview with Clayton Anderson by Michael O'Rourke, September 16, 2005, Robert W. Straub Archives, Hamersly Library, Western Oregon University, Monmouth.

22. Author interview of Pat Straub, October 25, 2006.

23. Oral history interview of Robert W. Straub by Clark Hansen, Oregon Historical Society, Portland, May 14, 1991, Tape 1, Side 2.

24. "Charles O. Porter: Embattled Liberal," Robert E. Burton, M.A. Thesis, Department of History, University of Oregon, Eugene, OR, from Chapter I: A Political Prodigy, p. 16.

25. Oral history interview of Robert W. Straub by Clark Hansen, Oregon Historical Society, Portland, May 14, 1991, Tape 1, Side 2.

26. Ibid.

27. "Charles O. Porter: Embattled Liberal," Robert E. Burton, M.A. Thesis, Department of History, University of Oregon, Eugene, OR, from Chapter I: A Political Prodigy, pp. 16-17

28. "Voter Registration for General Elections, 1950-2006," *Oregon Blue Book 2008*, Secretary of State, Salem, 2007.

29. From *Adventures in Politics,* Chapter 5, "Two-party Blues in a One-party State," by Richard L. Neuberger, Oxford University Press, New York, 1954.

30. Oral history interview of Robert W. Straub by Clark Hansen, Oregon Historical Society, Portland, May 14, 1991, Tape 1, Side 2.

31. "Charles O. Porter: Embattled Liberal," Robert E. Burton, M.A. Thesis, Department of History, University of Oregon, Eugene, OR, from Chapter I: A Political Prodigy, p. 16.

32. Oral history interview of Monroe Sweetland, Oregon Historical Society, Portland.

33. "Oregon Commonwealth Federation," The Oregon Encyclopedia Web site: http://www.oregonencyclopedia.org/entry/view/oregon_commonwealth_federation/

34. Oral history interview of Monroe Sweetland, Oregon Historical Society, Portland.

35. *Oregon Voter*, Portland, December 1958, pp 58-60.

36. Oral history interview of Monroe Sweetland, Oregon Historical Society, Portland.

37. Author interview of Pat Straub, October 25, 2006.

38. Oral history interview of Robert W. Straub by Clark Hansen, Oregon Historical Society, Portland, May 14, 1991, Tape 1, Side 2.

39. Author interview of Pat Straub, October 25, 2006.

40. Telephone interview of Clayton Anderson by author, September 16, 2011.

41. From *Adventures in Politics*, Chapter 10, "It Costs Too Much to Run for Office," by Richard L. Neuberger, Oxford University Press, New York, 1954.

42. Oral history interview of Robert W. Straub by Clark Hansen, Oregon Historical Society, Portland, May 14, 1991, Tape 1, Side 2. Straub also said in the interview that after he won, "I sold that model 'T' for a hundred dollars. I thought I was just so smart to sell it for as much money as I paid for it. That thing would be worth ten thousand bucks now if I still had it."

43. Michael O'Rourke interview of Mike Straub, August 30, 2005, Straub Archives, Western Oregon University.

44. Telephone interview of Clayton Anderson by author, September 16, 2011.

45. Author interview of Pat Straub, October 25, 2006.

46. "Demo Candidate Raps Policies Toward Fair," Eugene *Register-Guard*, September 30, 1954, 1B.

47. "Harms Says Q St. Extension 'Wasteful,'" Eugene *Register-Guard*, October 7, 1954, 1B.

48. "Lane Political Pot Boils Merrily," Eugene *Register-Guard*, September 26, 1954, 1A.

49. "Victory May Go To Party Doing Best Job of Mobilizing Voters At Polls," Eugene *Register-Guard* Editorial, November 1, 1954, 14A.

50. "Summary of Register-Guard's Views on Candidates, Issues," Eugene *Register-Guard*, Editorial page, section 1, November 1, 1954.

51. "Skelton Objects to Editorial Choices," Eugene *Register-Guard*, October 31,1954, Op-ed page, section 1. Keith Skelton lost that year, but was elected in 1956 to the first of seven terms in the Oregon Legislature, representing first Lane County and later Multnomah County. He later married Democratic Party standard bearer and fellow legislator Betty Roberts.

52. Lane County, Oregon, Elections Office/Lane County Commissioner Bill Dwyer, March 19, 2008.

53. "Neuberger Holds Lead For Senate Post, Morse Vote to Swing Senate To Democrats," Eugene Register-Guard, November 4, 1954, 1A.

54. "Oregon's Votes Tallied," Eugene *Register-Guard*, November 4, 1954, 1A.

55. *Fire at Eden's Gate: Tom McCall and the Oregon Story*, Brent Walth, Oregon Historical Society Press, Portland, 994; paperback edition, 1998, pp. 100-12.

56. Oregon Secretary of State, Elections Division, telephone conversation with author, March 20, 2008.

57. Oral history interview of Robert W. Straub by Clark Hansen, Oregon Historical Society, Portland, May 14, 1991, Tape 1, Side 2.

58. Author interview of Pat Straub, October 25, 2006.

59. Michael O'Rourke interview of Mike Straub, August 30, 2005, Straub Archives, Western Oregon University.

60. Telephone interview of George Hermach by author, February 5, 2012. The new courthouse, located at 125 E. 8th, in Eugene, replaced an old brick structure built and

1898 and was completed in 1959. *Oregon Historical County Records Guide,* Oregon State Archives, http://arcweb.sos.state.or.us/pages/records/local/county/lane/hist.html

61. Ken Johnson, e-mail to author, December 16, 2009.

62. Michael O'Rourke interview of Mike Straub, August 30, 2005, Straub Archives, Western Oregon University.

63. Ibid.

64. Telephone interview of Clayton Anderson by author, September 16, 2011.

65. Author interview of Jane and Mike Straub, July 31, 2007.

66. As time went on, like those of the rest of America, Bob's attitudes on gender roles changed somewhat. "I loved working in the woods with my husband, Jay," Patty Straub said later. "I could actually join in and help. Mom and Dad would come to down to visit us and Dad seemed to enjoy watching both of us working out there." Telephone interview of Patty Straub by author, June 17, 2012.

67. Author interview of Jane and Mike Straub, July 31, 2007

68. *Backcountry Pilot: Flying Adventures with Ike Russell,* edited by Thomas Bowen, University of Arizona Press, Tucson, 2002. "Afterword: A Few Words About Ike," page 194.

69. Michael O'Rourke interview of Mike Straub, August 30, 2005, Straub Archives, Western Oregon University.

70. Ibid.

71. Oral history interview of Clayton Anderson by Michael O'Rourke, September 16, 2005, Robert W. Straub Archives, Hamersly Library, Western Oregon University, Monmouth. *Esta ciego?* means "Are you blind?" in Spanish, as in "blind drunk."

72. Ken Johnson, e-mail to author, December 16, 2009.

73. Association of Oregon Counties, History of AOC, www.aocweb.org

Chapter 4

1. "The 1958 Hatfield Campaign in Oregon," Travis Cross, *The Western Political Quarterly,* June 1959, Vol. 12 No. 2, page 568.

2. "Voter Registration for General Elections, 1950-2006," *Oregon Blue Book 2008,* Secretary of State, Salem, 2007.

3. Morse was by now a Democrat, after having been a registered Independent for two years after leaving the Republican Party in 1953. The maverick Senator Morse had left his party, three years into his second term in office, because of his opposition to the "red-baiting" tactics of Republican Senator Joseph McCarthy and President Eisenhower's selection of another "McCarthyite," Senator Richard Nixon, as his vice presidential running mate.

4. Governor Paul L Patterson Administration, Biographical Note, Oregon State Archives, Salem. http://www.sos.state.or.us/archives/governors/Patterson/Pattersonbiography.html

5. Governor Robert D. Holmes Administration, Biographical Note, Oregon State Archives, Salem. http://www.sos.state.or.us/archives/governors/Holmes/holmesbiography.html

6. Oregon Legislative Journal, 1955 Legislative Assembly, HB 694 and HB 709.

7. Oregon Education Association, 150 Years of Service to Public Education, OEA and Education History. http://www.oregoned.org/site/pp.asp?c=9dKKKYMDH&b=139662

8. *Wayne Morse: A Political Biography,* Mason Drukman, Oregon Historical Society Press, Portland, 1997, page 228.

9. Governor Elmo Smith Administration, Biographical Note, Oregon State Archives, Salem. http://www.sos.state.or.us/archives/governors/Smith/smithoverview.html

10. Distrust of the Republican legislature appears to have been a factor when one considers that Ballot Measure #1, a referral from the 1955 Republican-controlled legislature to allow tax laws passed by the legislature to take effect immediately failed by a whopping

487,550 – 175,932 margin! Oregon Secretary of State, Elections Division, telephone conversation with author, March 21, 2008.

11. *Wayne Morse: A Political Biography*, Mason Drukman, Oregon Historical Society Press, Portland, 1997, page 238.

12. Author interview of Pat Straub, October 25, 2006.

13. Author interview of Mike and Jane Straub, July 31, 2007.

14. Loren "Bud" Kramer, a future chief of staff to Governor Bob Straub, remembers that in 1959, when he was a fresh-faced kid working as a low-level aide to U.S. Representative Edith Green, during his first month in Washington D.C., he met Senator Morse in his office. Morse confided in him: "You know, I really need to try to work things out with Dick Neuberger for the good of the party. This just can't go on any longer." Not ten minutes later, he ran into Senator Neuberger, who, as they walked together across the mall toward the capitol, completely unsolicited, told him almost exactly the same thing. Their apparent mutual desire for reconciliation never bore fruit. Author interview of Loren "Bud" Kramer, May 7, 2007.

15. From *Wayne Morse: A Political Biography*, Mason Drukman, Oregon Historical Society Press, Portland, 1997, page 240.

16. Ibid., Chapter 9: "Dick and Wayne."

17. Ibid.

18. Author interview of Pat Straub, October 25, 2006.

19. See "The 1958 Hatfield Campaign in Oregon," Travis Cross, *The Western Political Quarterly*, June 1959, Vol. 12 No. 2.

20. Telephone interview of Robert D. (Denny) Holmes, Jr., by author, June 3, 2012.

21. See "The 1958 Hatfield Campaign in Oregon," Travis Cross, *The Western Political Quarterly*, June 1959, Vol. 12 No. 2

22. Oral history interview of Robert W. Straub by Clark Hansen, Oregon Historical Society, Portland, May 14, 1991, Tape 1, Side 2,

23. Author interview of Ken Johnson, August 23, 2007.

24. Author interview of Pat Straub, October 25, 2006.

25. Author interview of Ken Johnson, August 23, 2007.

26. Telephone interview of Floyd McKay by author, August, 31, 2010.

27. "Speech Expert Kenneth Wood Dies," Eugene *Register-Guard*, October 6, 1990, 3B.

28. Telephone interview of Margie Goldschmidt by author, November 11, 2011.

29. Telephone interview of Ken Johnson by author, March 13, 2011.

30. Observed by the author in fall 1966.

31. Telephone interview of Bob Buckendorf, PhD, speech therapist, Buckendorf Associates, Portland, by author.

32. Telephone interview of Floyd McKay by author, August, 31, 2010.

33. Author interview of Ken Johnson, August 23, 2007.

34. Author interview of Pat Straub, October 25, 2006.

35. Author interview of Ken Johnson, August 23, 2007.

36. "It Seems To Me," political opinion column, Charles A. Sprague, *Oregon Statesman*, Salem, November 26, 1960, 1A.

37. Author interview of Ken Johnson, August 23, 2007.

38. Author interview of Jane and Mike Straub, July 31, 2007.

39. "Demo Boss Straub Asks $50,000 For Revitalized Party," Tom Wright, *Oregon Statesman*, Salem, December 13, 1959, 1A.

40. "Straub Hailed By Neuberger; Gunnar Rapped," *Oregon Statesman*, Salem, December 13, 1959, 2A.

41. "Richard Neuberger," The Oregon Encyclopedia, http://www.oregonencyclopedia. org/entry/view/neuberger_richard_1912_1960_/ and "Richard Neuberger," The

Oregon History Project, http://ohs.org/education/oregonhistory/historical_records/ dspDocument.cfm?doc_ID=9CD888F2-1C23-B9D3-686DC973197F9ABD

42. Biographical Dictionary of the United States Congress, 1774 to present: Biography: Lusk, Hall Stoner (1883-1983) http://bioguide.congress.gov/scripts/biodisplay. pl?index=L000520

43. "Insults Traded in Sterilization Row, Straub called 'Liar,'" *Capital Journal*, Salem, March 4, 1960, 1A.

44. "Straub Quibbles at Dig-At-Mark Stress," Douglas Seymour, *Capital Journal*, Salem, February 26, 1960, 1A.

45. "Gunnar, Straub 'Stick In Knife' At WU Debate," Tom Wright, *Oregon Statesman*, Salem, March 26, 1960, 1A.

46. "Government Revamp Plan Gets Backing," *Capital Journal*, Salem, December 22, 1960, Sec.1, p.5.

47. "It Seems To Me," political opinion column, Charles A. Sprague, *Oregon Statesman*, November 26, 1960, 1A, 4A.

48. "Pearson Urges Party Chief Quit In Row Over Corbett," Tom Wright, *Oregon Statesman*, November 29, 1960, 2 (Sec. 1).

49. "Pearson, Straub Rift Widens," AP, *Capital Journal*, Salem, November 28, 1960, 10 (Sec.1).

50. *Natural States: The Environmental Imagination in Maine, Oregon and the Nation,* Richard W. Judd and Christopher S. Beach, Resources for the Future Press, Washington, DC, 2003, page 44.

51. Author interview of Ken Johnson, August 23, 2007.

52. "Straub Would Set Up Summer Work Camps," *Capital Journal,* January 13, 1961, Sec.1, p.8.

53. "Round Two: Patronage, Straub Claims He Got Cold Shoulder," *Capital Journal,* June 3, 1961, Sec. 1, p.1.

54. Oregon State Bar Bulletin, June 2006, Oregon Legal Heritage: "A Tribute to Sid Lezak: Oregon's Johnny Appleseed of Dispute Resolution," by Susan M. Hammer, Tigard. http://www.osbar.org/publications/bulletin/06jun/heritage.html

55. "Straub Seeks Vote: Driver Insurance Initiative Filed," *Capital Journal,* July 19, 1961, Sec.1, p.1.

56. "Bill Calls for Compulsory Car Insurance," *Oregon Statesman*, February 3, 1961, Sec.1.

57. "No Compulsory Insurance," Editorial, *Oregon Statesman*, February 6, 1961, Sec.1, p.4.

58. "Straub Defends Compulsory Insurance," *Oregon Statesman,* Letter to the Editor, July 26, 1961, Sec.1, p.4.

59. "Straub Charges Insurance Agents With Nit-picking," *Oregon Statesman,* August 25, 1961, Sec.1.

60. "Contrarian Congressman Charles O. Porter, 86," AP, Washington Post, January 6, 2006. http://www.washingtonpost.com/wp-dyn/content/article/2006/01/05/ AR2006010502166.html

61. "Charles O. Porter: Embattled Liberal," Robert E. Burton, M.A. Thesis, Department of History, University of Oregon, Eugene, from Chapter I: A Political Prodigy, pp. 19-21; telephone interview of Samuel C. Porter by author, June 14, 2012; author interview of Ken Johnson, August 23, 2007.

62. "In a mere four years in Congress, Democrat Charles Porter managed to do what it took his mentor, Wayne Morse, twenty-four years to accomplish: he rendered himself unelectable by the exercise of his big mouth. That he was unassailably and prematurely correct on every major issue of our times must be small comfort as he contemplates the wreckage of his career." From "Good Guy, Right Issues, Few Wins: Charles Porter,

smarter than hell, a political disaster," by Ron Abell, *Willamette Week,* Portland, March 22, 1976, vol. 2, no. 19, p.1.

63. Author interview of Ken Johnson, August 23, 2007.

64. "Demo Party Chairman in Congress Race," *Oregon Statesman*, August 22, 1961, Sec.1, p.1.

65. Author interview of Judge James A. Redden, September 2, 2010.

66. "Over 100 give views of Dunes and Wilderness," Tom Wright, *Oregon Statesman*, October 7, 1961, p1.

67. Telephone interview of George Hermach by author, February 5, 2012. The trip to Waldo Lake had been particularly harsh, with a freak summer icy rainstorm, leaving some guests who had come along less prepared "freezing and drenched despite a roaring fire." Bob had to cut the trip short, walking to a nearby road and hitching a ride to their vehicles to bring them to better shelter.

68. "Straub, Durno at Odds on Wilderness Area Issue During a Congressional Hearing Held in Portland," *Oregon Statesman*, October 7, 1961, p. 4.

69. "Hypothetical Prognosis Starts High Level Row," UPI, *Capital Journal*, October 26, 1961, Sec.1, p.5.

70. "Straub Asks Special Session on Colleges," UPI, *Capital Journal*, November 14, 1961, Sec.1, p.1.

71. "Research Center Plan Attacked," *Oregon Statesman*, January 10, 1962, Sec.1, p.1.

72. Oral history interview of Robert W. Straub by Clark Hansen, Oregon Historical Society, Portland, May 29 1991, Tape 3, Side 2.

73. Official Voters Pamphlet, General Election November 8, 1960, Ballot Measure No. 2, Explanation and Argument in Favor; and, Official Voters Pamphlet, General Election November 6, 1962, Ballot Measure No. 6, Explanation and Argument in Favor – Oregon Secretary of State, Salem.

74. "Sen. Straub Calling for Special Session," *Oregon Statesman*, March 30, 1962, Sec.2, p.12. Passage of a statewide ballot measure establishing Daylight Savings Time in November 1962 settled the issue. http://bluebook.state.or.us/state/elections/elections18. htm

75. Vote totals by county, Oregon Secretary of State, Elections Division.

76. Oral history interview of Robert W. Straub by Clark Hansen, Oregon Historical Society, Portland, May 29 1991, Tape 3, Side 2.

77. Author interview of Ken Johnson, August 23, 2007.

Chapter 5

1. Author interview of Ken Johnson, August 23, 2007.

2. Author interview of Pat Straub, October 2006.

3. Author interview of Ken Johnson, August 23, 2007.

4. Ibid.

5. Author interview of Governor Victor Atiyeh, July 30, 2007.

6. *Oregon State Employee News*, Vol. 6, No. 9, September, 1964.

7. Ibid.

8. Author interview of Loren Wyss, December 13, 2007.

9. *Dedication. Vision. Heart. The CalPERS Story*, CalPERS Board of Administration, The History Factory, Chantilly, VA, 2007. Chapter 4: New Benefits. New Leadership. New Name. Page 113.

10. "Robert Straub: Oregon's Trail-Blazing Treasurer," John S. DeMott, *Pensions* Magazine, Spring 1972, page 53, article copied in scrapbook of newsclippings, Robert W. Straub Archives, Western Oregon University, Monmouth.

11. *History of the American Economy,* "Railroads and Economic Change: Land Grants, Financial Assistance, and Private Capital," Gary Walton and Hugh Rockoff, South-Western/Cenage Learning, Mason, OH, 2010, page 286,

12. Author interview of Ken Johnson, August 23, 2007.

13. Ibid.

14. Telephone interview of Mike Straub by author, September 12, 2011.

15. Author interview of Don Clark, April 12, 2012.

16. "Straub Lashes Penal Theory," Joe Frazier, Eugene *Register-Guard*, July 10, 1964, page 1.

17. "Straub Stirs Up Campaign: Tight Race for State Treasurer," Douglas Seymour, *Capital Journal*, Salem, October 23, 1964, page 6, Sec. 1.

18. Political ad "For State Treasurer vote for Robert W. (Bob) Straub, A Stride Ahead for Oregon" Medford *Mail Tribune*, October 29, 1964.

19. "Straub Says GOP Policies Stagnate State Government," *Capital Journal*, Salem, July 20, 1964, page 16, Sec. 3.

20. "Straub Lashes Penal Theory," Joe Frazier, Eugene *Register-Guard*, July 10, 1964, page 1.

21. "Morse Boosts Straub at Picnic for Candidate," Eugene *Register-Guard*, July 12, 1964.

22. "Appling Laboring In Belton's Behalf," Zan Stark, UPI, Eugene *Register-Guard*, September 17, 1964, page 6B.

23. "GOP Going 'All-Out' for Salem Control," Doug McKean, *Oregon Journal*, August 30, 1963.

24. Appling Hits Straub Taunt As Ignorance," Douglas Seymour, *Capital Journal*, Salem, August 18, 1960, p.1.

25. "Officials Fire Back at Straub," UPI, *Oregon Journal*, Portland, August 6, 1964.

26. *Albany Democrat Herald*, "Big Rally Turnout Greets Mark, Candidates," by V. K. Sawhney, Septemberember 19, 1964, page 1.

27. "Officials Fire Back at Straub," UPI, *Oregon Journal*, Portland, August 6, 1964.

28. Author interview of Ken Johnson, August 23, 2007.

29. "Appling Doesn't Find Straub Letter Funny," Les Cour, *Oregon Journal*, Portland, August, 1964

30. Author interview of Ken Johnson, August 23, 2007.

31. "Mississippi led the nation in beatings, lynchings, and mysterious disappearances. Only 5 percent of black Mississippians [who made up 45 percent of the state's population] were registered to vote, the lowest rate in the United States. With majorities in many counties, blacks might well have controlled local politics through the ballot box. But segregationists were not about to let blacks vote; many would sooner kill them." From: *Eyes on the Prize: America's Civil Rights Years: 1945-1965*, Juan Williams, New York, The Viking Press, 1987, p. 208.

32. *In Struggle*: SNCC and the Black Awakening of the 1960s, Clayborne Carson, Cambridge, Mass., Harvard University Press, 1981, page 126.

33. *Pillar of Fire: America in the King Year, 1963-65*, Taylor Branch, 1998, Simon & Schuster, New York. p.465.

34. *Divided They Fell*, Ronald Radosh, 1996, The Free Press, New York; p. 9.

35. *Pillar of Fire: America in the King Year, 1963-65*, Taylor Branch, 1998, Simon & Schuster, New York, p.472.

36. Author interview of Ken Johnson, August 23, 2007.

37. *Capital Journal*, Salem, September 8, 1964, Sec. 1, page 5.

38. *Ontario Argus Observer*, "Belton Declines Comment on Fiscal Opinion," UPI, September 3, 1964, page 1.

39. Author interview of Ken Johnson, August 23, 2007.

40. "Straub Backer Called Violator of Liquor Laws," AP, *The Oregonian*, October 7, 1964, front page, above the fold.
41. "Straub Labels Raid 'Political Frame-up,'" Douglas Seymour, *Capital Journal*, October 8, 1964.
42. "Straub Backer Called Violator of Liquor Laws," AP, *The Oregonian*, October 7, 1964, front page, above the fold.
43. Ibid.
44. Author interview of Ken Johnson, August 23, 2007.
45. "Everybody's Laughing," *Albany Democrat-Herald*, Lead Editorial, October 8, 1964, page 18.
46. "Lane County D.A. Offers GOP 'Prosecution' of Liquor Case," AP, *The Oregonian*, October 8, 1964, page 17.
47. "A Tough Choice, But We Pick Belton," Eugene *Register-Guard*, editorial, October 28, 1964, 10A.
48. Mark Hatfield telephone conversations with author in 1998.
49. Dr. Dean Brooks eulogy at Governor Robert Straub memorial service, Oregon House of Representatives, State Capitol, Salem, December 18, 2002, Recording, Straub Archives, Western Oregon University Library, Monmouth.
50. *Fire at Eden's Gate: Tom McCall and the Oregon Story*, Brent Walth, Oregon Historical Society Press, Portland, 1994, page 158.

    In contrast to the state of the board of control and land board when Governor Hatfield, Secretary of State McCall, and State Treasurer Straub were on it, after the next election in 1966, the triumvirate of Governor McCall, his successor, Secretary of State Clay Myers, and Straub "were remarkably harmonious." Though "the political rivalry was unmistakably evident … the meetings were always friendly and unmarred by sniping or sarcasm." "Their chief assistants…were good friends and kept in close communication with each other," dubbing themselves "the 'Sub board,' and once or twice a month … made unannounced visits to the institutions." Their "snooping several times resulted in improvements in operation of a facility."

    Even the March 9, 1968, prison riot and fire, with a resulting prisoner stand-off, did not cause dissention among the three leaders, all of whom were away from Salem when it took place, leaving their deputies to working with Senate President Debbs Potts, temporarily serving as governor, in negotiating face to face with the convict negotiating team "in front of the TV camera and the press"… reaching an agreement over a sleepless night, which led to reforms to address the convicts' "legitimate complaints" about "neglect" at the prison. From: "Notes for Chuck Johnson on the Prison Riot," by George Bell, former assistant secretary of state for Clay Myers, August,15, 2011.
51. Telephone interview of Barbara Hanneman by author, September 9, 2011.
52. Author interview of Ken Johnson, August 23, 2007.
53. Oregon State Legislature, 1965 Legislative Session, Records, Senate & House Journal, State Archives, Salem.
54. Hearing of Full Ways & Means Committee, April 2, 1965, Oregon State Legislature, 1965 Legislative Session, Records, HB 1347, State Archives, Salem.
55. Telephone interview of Tim Hermach by author, January 19, 2012.
56. Telephone interview of Jeff Straub by author, June 17, 2012.
57. Author interview of Barbara Hanneman, June 30, 2007.
58. Ibid.
59. E-mail to author from Ken Johnson, December 16, 2009.
60. Author interview of James George, November 13, 2007.
61. Author interview of Barbara Hanneman, July 30, 2007.

62. "Straub to hire analyst to check on pollution," *Oregon Statesman*, sec.1, p. 10, February 3, 1966.

63. "River of Risk: It wasn't a healthy place to work," by Brent Huntsberger, *The Oregonian*, December 19, 2000; Oregon Live: http://www.oregonlive.com/special/river/index.ssf?/news/oregonian/00/12/rv_31health19.frame

64. "Straub's hat in; expects to row into a lot of 'heavy wind,'" *Oregon Voter*, February 12, 1966, p. 5-6, Portland, OR.

Chapter 6

1. Author interview of Jim Long, August 21, 2007. Long mused about how different journalism was in those days, feeding a quote to the person he was interviewing. This incident illustrates the huge gap in media savvy between Straub and McCall, who was a human quote machine. Long had just read the word "ecology" for the first time to his children from a new children's encyclopedia and thought it was an interesting concept. His editor cut the word from his story at first, saying, "That's not a word." Looking in a more recent dictionary than the one in their newsroom, Long proved his point and "ecology" stayed in.

2. Kathryn Straton, *Oregon Beaches: A Birthright Preserved*. Salem: Oregon State Parks and Recreation, 1977. Opening quote.

3. Also sarcastically referred to by their detractors as "Save Our Shacks"—author interview of retired State Parks Superintendent Dave Talbot, August 20, 2007.

4. Pat Straub, oral history interview by Michael O'Rourke, Robert W. Straub Archives, Western Oregon University, October 2, 2003; author interview of Ken Johnson, When Straub was State Democratic Chairman he'd seen Jackson's political horse-trading first hand, under the tutelage of another canny politico, U.S. Senator Wayne Morse.

In early 1960, Straub, Morse, and a couple of aides were touring southern Oregon supporting Democratic candidates and made a courtesy stop at Jackson's White City ranch. As they got out of the car, the slight, diminutive Jackson was dismounting from a fine gelding and Morse commented, "That's a good-looking horse, but I've got the perfect one for you back home at my ranch in Maryland." Jackson smiled and said, "No thanks, I like this one a lot." But Morse wouldn't take no for answer, bringing it up again and again as he and Straub toured the ranch. Each time, Jackson grinned at him and demurred. When they got back in the car and started to leave, Morse turned around in the front seat to Straub in the back and declared with a crafty smile, "I just sold a horse."

Straub couldn't believe his ears. "You did no such thing!" he said. "Didn't you hear him?"

Morse just looked back at Straub smugly. "I'm telling you, I sold a horse and I'll bet you a steak dinner on it," he said. Straub gladly took him up on it. When they arrived at the Medford hotel where they were staying, Morse had a phone call waiting. It was Jackson. When he returned to the group, Morse, looking very pleased with himself, said, "I told you I sold a horse." That evening Glenn Jackson, the CEO of Pacific Power and Light, purchased a horse and retained an old and powerful friend. Wayne Morse, in addition to getting a fair price for his horse, ate a steak dinner, courtesy of Bob Straub.

5. Interestingly, Clay Myers, Sr., chairman of the Tillamook County Commission, which came out heavily in favor of the beach highway, owned considerable land just north of Pacific City, along the new highway route. His son, Clay Myers, Jr., was Tom McCall's assistant secretary of state and was appointed as his successor after McCall was elected governor.

6. From *The People's Fight to Save the Oregon Beaches, 1965-1972*, pp 3-4, Catherine Williams, Oregon Environmental Council Collection, Oregon Historical Society, Portland.

7. From Folder #5, Forest Road 56, Oregon Coast Highway, Neskowin-Tillamook, 1966, Oregon Department of Transportation, Salem.

8. The anti-death penalty campaign, whose bipartisan co-chairs were activist lawyer Don Willner, a leading Democrat, and up-and-coming Republican Robert Packwood, was part of a national movement, which was also challenging execution in court as unconstitutional "cruel and unusual punishment." The Oregon ballot measure campaign won with over 62 percent of the vote, using the slogan "YOU are the executioner," plastered across billboards throughout the state.

9. Author interview of Martha McLennan, September 14, 2006.

10. A jealous Senator Morse had been thwarting it for years, and it never did come into being, though Honeyman State Park still exists in a portion of the proposed area, as well as a few areas included in the Oregon Dunes National Recreation Area under Forest Service management, established in 1972. "I never did understand why Senator Morse fought so hard against that one," said former Interior Secretary Stewart Udall in a telephone interview with the author, July 30, 2007.

11. Gordon Guild, whose vacation home was next to the highway path, was a particularly useful ally. Guild worked for Abbott and Lynn, a company in Portland, which rented mimeograph machines and other office devices. Now McLennan no longer had to reproduce flyers and pamphlets using hectographs, an arcane copying process that involved melting gelatin and duplicating jelly ten pages at a time in a pan of hardened gelatin in her oven. Today's political organizers have no idea how easy they have it compared to the labor-intensive practices of yore.

12. From *The People's Fight to Save the Oregon Beaches, 1965-1972*, pages 5 and 6, Catherine Williams, Oregon Environmental Council Collection, Oregon Historical Society.

13. Letter from Highway Commission Chairman Glenn Jackson to State Treasurer Robert W. Straub, dated June 1, 1966, Robert W. Straub Archives, Western Oregon University, Monmouth.

14. *Fire At Eden's Gate: Tom McCall and the Oregon Story*, Brent Walth, Oregon Historical Society Press, Portland, 1998, page 168.

15. "Reprieve for Beach." Editorial Comment, *The Oregonian*, Sunday, June 5, 1966, page 2F, Portland.

16. "The Political Legacy of Robert W. Straub," Richard Clucas, *Oregon Historical Quarterly*, 104.4 (winter 2003), pp. 462–77.

17. In addition to consulting Onthank, Straub worked with an architect to draw up the plan and consulted his Dartmouth college friend, Dick Eymann, who was serving in the Oregon House of Representatives. They explored precedents from California and New Hampshire to help craft Straub's plan.

18. Author interview of Ken Johnson, August 23, 2007, and "Straub aide claims 'censorship' by TV," Floyd McKay, *Oregon Statesman*, October 4, 1966, sec. 1, p. 1.

19. *Fire at Eden's Gate*, Brent Walth, Oregon Historical Society Press, Portland, 1994, pp 174-75, 1998 paperback edition.

Chapter 7

1. Author interview of Jim George, November 13, 2007.

2. Ibid.

3. Ibid.

4. Ibid.

5. Oral history interview of Robert W. Straub by Clark Hansen, Oregon Historical Society, May 29, 1991, Tape 4, Side 1.

6. Author interview of Ken Johnson, August 10, 2008.

7. Author interview of Jim George, November 13, 2007.
8. "The Political Legacy of Robert W. Straub," Richard A. Clucas, *Oregon Historical Quarterly,* 104.4 (Winter 2003) p. 466.
9. Oral history interview of Robert W. Straub by Clark Hansen, Oregon Historical Society, May 29, 1991, Tape 4, Side 1.
10. Author interview of Norma Paulus, May 14, 2007.
11. Case Summary Outcome, *State ex rel Sprague v. Straub*, Supreme Court of Oregon, 240 Ore. 272; 400 P.2d 229; 1965 Ore. LEXIS 493; February 25, 1965 Argued; March 22, 1965.
12. Author interview of Jim George, November 13, 2007.
13. Senate & House Journal, 1967 Legislative Session, Oregon State Legislature, Salem.
14. Author interview of Jim George, November 13, 2007.
15. Ibid.
16. Office of the Oregon State Treasurer's Web site: "About Us."
17. Robert Straub conversation with author, June 27, 1998.
18. Telephone interview of William P. Stalnaker Jr., by author, July 11, 2008.
19. Federal Reserve Bulletin, June 1951, Statement of the Voluntary Credit Restraint Committee, May 23, 1951, page 626.
20. Article XI, Sections 6 and 9 of the Oregon State Constitution.
21. *An Editor for Oregon: Charles A. Sprague and the Politics of Change*, by Floyd McKay, Oregon State University Press, Corvallis, 264-66.
22. Author interview of Jim George, November 13, 2007.
23. Ibid.
24. Ibid.
25. Telephone interview of Jim George by author, July 12, 2008.
26. *Sprague v. Straub*, Decree No. 64040, Circuit Court of the State of Oregon for the County of Marion, Val Sloper presiding, date July 29, 1968.
27. Telephone interview of Jim George by author, July 12, 2008.
28. *Sprague et al., Respondents, v. Straub et al., Appellants*, Supreme Court of Oregon, 252 Ore. 507; 451 P.2 d 49; 1969 Ore. Lexis 545, February 26, 1969.
29. Ibid.
30. Telephone interview of Jim George by author, July 12, 2008.
31. Author interview of Jim George, November 13, 2007.
32. "Straub Boldly Moves in Buying of Stocks," Gerry Pratt, *The Oregonian* business section front page, p. 7, May 7, 1969.
33. Author interview of Jim George, November 13, 2007.
34. Ibid. and telephone interview of Jim George by author, July 12, 2008.
35. Author interview of Ken Johnson, August 23, 2007.
36. Author interview of Jim George, November 13, 2007.
37. "Straub Boldly Moves in Buying of Stocks," Gerry Pratt, *The Oregonian* business section front page, Portland, p. 7, May 7, 1969.
38. Author interview of Jim George, November 13, 2007.
39. "Stock Rise Continues Despite Profit Taking," Phil Thomas, *The Oregonian* business section front page, Portland, p. 7, May 7, 1969.
40. "Straub Boldly Moves in Buying of Stocks," Gerry Pratt, *The Oregonian* business section front page, Portland, p. 7, May 7, 1969.
41. Historical US Inflation Rate 1914-Present, InflationData.com, Financial Trend Forecaster, a publication of Capital Professional Services. 2003-2004.
42. "Straub Boldly Moves in Buying of Stocks," Gerry Pratt, *The Oregonian* business section front page, Portland, p. 7, May 7, 1969.

43. Ibid.
44. Ibid.

Chapter 8

1. Author interview of Lawrence Bitte, August 19, 2007.
2. Email from filmmaker Tom Olsen, Jr. to author, February 20, 2011.
3. Author interview of Lawrence Bitte, August 19, 2007.
4. "Oregon's Highway Park System 1921-1989: An Administrative History," from *Personal Views on Development of the State Parks and Recreation Program*, by David G. Talbot, director, Parks and Recreation Department; Oregon State Parks, Salem, 1992, p. 97.
5. "The Beach Bill," written and produced by Nadine Jelsing, part of "The Oregon Experience" series, a co-production of Oregon Public Broadcasting and the Oregon Historical Society, DVD 2007, Oregon Public Broadcasting, Portland.
6. Telephone interview of Janet McLennan, by author, August 6, 2008.
7. *Natural States: The Environmental Imagination in Maine, Oregon, and the Nation*, Richard W. Judd and Christopher S. Beach, Resources for the Future, Washington, DC, 2003, page 118.
8. *The Park Builders: A History of State Parks in the Pacific Northwest*, Thomas R. Cox, University of Washington Press, Seattle and London, 1988, page 148.
9. Author interview of Dave Talbot, August 20, 2007.
10. "Oregon's Highway Parks System:, 1921-1989: An Administrative History," Oregon Parks and Recreation Department, Salem, 1992, page 88.
11. Author interview of Dave Talbot, August 20, 2007.
12. "Oregon's Highway Parks System:, 1921-1989: An Administrative History," Oregon Parks and Recreation Department, Salem, 1992, page 88.
13. *The Park Builders: A History of State Parks in the Pacific Northwest*, Thomas R. Cox, University of Washington Press, Seattle & London, 1988, page 148.
14. Ibid., pp 151-52.
15. Ibid., page 152.
16. Ibid., pp 152-53.
17. Ibid., page 153.
18. Author interview of Dave Talbot, August 20, 2007.
19. *The Park Builders: A History of State Parks in the Pacific Northwest*, Thomas R. Cox, University of Washington Press, Seattle & London, 1988, page 155.
20. *Tom McCall: Maverick*, an autobiography with Steve Neal, Binford & Mort, Portland, 1977, page 186.
21. Telephone interview of Janet McLennan by author, June 24, 2008.
22. From "The Beach Bill," written and produced by Nadine Jelsing, part of "The Oregon Experience" series, a co-production of Oregon Public Broadcasting and the Oregon Historical Society, DVD 2007, Oregon Public Broadcasting, Portland.
23. Author interview of Bob Bacon, August 5, 2007.
24. Ibid.
25. Ibid., and author interview of Larry and Diane Bitte, August 19, 2007.
26. Author interview of Bob Bacon, August 5, 2007.
27. Author note: "to table" can mean different things in different legislative bodies. In the United Nations, for example, "tabling" means to put forth a resolution for consideration by the General Assembly or its committees.
28. Author interview of Bob Bacon, August 5, 2007.
29. From "The Beach Bill," written and produced by Nadine Jelsing, part of "The Oregon Experience" series, a co-production of Oregon Public Broadcasting and the Oregon Historical Society, DVD 2007, Oregon Public Broadcasting, Portland.

30. *Fire at Eden's Gate: Tom McCall and the Oregon Story*, Brent Walth, Oregon Historical Society Press, Portland, 1994, page 188.

31. Author interview of Lawrence Bitte, August 19, 2007.

32. "The Beach Bill," written and produced by Nadine Jelsing, part of "The Oregon Experience" series, a co-production of Oregon Public Broadcasting and the Oregon Historical Society, DVD 2007, Oregon Public Broadcasting, Portland.

33. "Historical perspective" memo from the Papers of Janet McLennan, Robert Straub Archives, Western Oregon University, Monmouth.

34. *Fire at Eden's Gate: Tom McCall and the Oregon Story*, Brent Walth, Oregon Historical Society Press, Portland, 1994, page 188.

35. KGW TV-8 Editorial, May 10, 1967 (broadcast May 9, 1967), NBC Affiliate, 1501 SW Jefferson St., Portland, from the Papers of Janet McLennan, Robert Straub Archives, Western Oregon University, Monmouth.

36. Email from Tom Olsen, Jr. to author, February 20, 2011.

37. From "The Beach Bill," written and produced by Nadine Jelsing, part of "The Oregon Experience" series, a co-production of Oregon Public Broadcasting and the Oregon Historical Society, DVD 2007, Oregon Public Broadcasting, Portland.

38. "The Bazett House, Hillsborough," by Marty Arbunich, The Eichler Network Web site pp. 1-3, http://www.eichlernetwork.com/article/bazett-house-hillsborough

39. From "The Beach Bill," written and produced by Nadine Jelsing, part of "The Oregon Experience" series, a co-production of Oregon Public Broadcasting and the Oregon Historical Society, DVD 2007, Oregon Public Broadcasting, Portland.

40. Author interview of Lawrence Bitte, August 19, 2007; and author interview of Bob Bacon, August 5, 2007.

41. From "The Beach Bill," written and produced by Nadine Jelsing, part of "The Oregon Experience" series, a co-production of Oregon Public Broadcasting and the Oregon Historical Society, DVD 2007, Oregon Public Broadcasting, Portland.

42. *Fire at Eden's Gate: Tom McCall and the Oregon Story*, Brent Walth, Oregon Historical Society Press, Portland, 1994, page 189.

43. "The Beach Bill," written and produced by Nadine Jelsing, part of "The Oregon Experience" series, a co-production of Oregon Public Broadcasting and the Oregon Historical Society, DVD 2007, Oregon Public Broadcasting, Portland, -and "Timeline: The Beach Bill," OPB, "The Oregon Experience" Web site.

44. "The Politics of Sand," film by Tom Olsen, Cannon Beach Historical Society, 2008.

45. "The Beach Bill," written and produced by Nadine Jelsing, part of "The Oregon Experience" series, a co-production of Oregon Public Broadcasting and the Oregon Historical Society, DVD 2007, Oregon Public Broadcasting, Portland.

46. *Fire at Eden's Gate: Tom McCall and the Oregon Story*, Brent Walth, Oregon Historical Society Press, Portland, 1994, page 194.

47. "The Beach Bill," written and produced by Nadine Jelsing, part of "The Oregon Experience" series, a co-production of Oregon Public Broadcasting and the Oregon Historical Society, DVD 2007, Oregon Public Broadcasting, Portland,.

48. "Beach Bill Signed; McCall Clears His Desk," by Matt Kramer, AP, *Oregon Statesman*, Salem, July 7, 1967, section 1, page 7.

49. Janet McLennan, emails and verbal comments to Mark Henkels and Chuck Johnson in 2008 and 2010.

50. For those interested, an exhaustive discussion of this body of law may be found at *Environmental Law*, Vol. 4, No. 3, p. 383, "The English Doctrine of Custom in Oregon Property Law: *State ex rel. Thornton v. Hay*, Lew E. Delo (1973).

51. Janet McLennan, emails and verbal comments to Mark Henkels and Chuck Johnson in 2008 and 2010.

52. Ibid.

53. *Fire at Eden's Gate: Tom McCall and the Oregon Story*, Brent Walth, Oregon Historical Society Press, Portland, 1994, page 194.

54. "The one who was weird about beach front and what became of the Oregon Dunes was Wayne Morse. I never understood why he was so opposed to protecting them. I never really got along with him. I was disappointed in Wayne Morse. He was a quirky person. You could never tell where he'd come out on something." Stewart Udall comments in a phone conversation with the author, July 19, 2007.

55. *Fire at Eden's Gate: Tom McCall and the Oregon Story*, Brent Walth, Oregon Historical Society Press, Portland, 1994, page 196.

56. Phone conversation Stewart Udall by Author, July 19, 2007.

57. *Fire at Eden's Gate: Tom McCall and the Oregon Story*, Brent Walth, Oregon Historical Society Press, Portland, 1994, page 196.

58. Ibid., page 197.

59. "Historical Perspective" memo from the Papers of Janet McLennan, Robert Straub Archives, Western Oregon University, Monmouth.

60. Oregon State Highway Commission, Public Hearing, Social Hall, Tillamook Elks Club, Tillamook, Oregon, regarding Cape Kiwanda–Neskowin Section, Oregon Coast Highway, Tillamook County, November 29, 1967.

61. Ibid.

62. Ibid.

63. *Natural States: The Environmental Imagination in Maine, Oregon, and the Nation*, Richard W. Judd and Christopher S. Beach, Resources for the Future, Washington, DC, 2003, page 123.

64. Kathryn Straton, *Oregon Beaches: A Birthright Preserved*. Salem: Oregon State Parks and Recreation, 1977, pp. 51ff.

65. Ibid., p. 53.

66. "Historical perspective" memo from the Papers of Janet McLennan, Robert Straub Archives, Western Oregon University, Monmouth.

67. Ibid.

68. Janet McLennan, e-mail to author, December 28, 2009.

69. *Oregon Voters Pamphlet, 1968*. Oregon Secretary of State Office, 1968.

70. Ibid.

71. Kathryn Straton, *Oregon Beaches: A Birthright Preserved*. Salem: Oregon State Parks and Recreation, 1977, pp. 62.

72. Janet McLennan, e-mail to author, December 28, 2009.

73. Author interview of Lawrence Bitte, August 19, 2007.

74. Floyd McKay interview from "The Beach Bill," written and produced by Nadine Jelsing, part of "The Oregon Experience" series, a co-production of Oregon Public Broadcasting and the Oregon Historical Society, DVD 2007, Oregon Public Broadcasting, Portland.

75. Author interview of Ken Johnson, August 19, 2008.

76. Ibid.

77. Author interview of Dave Talbot, August 20, 2007.

Chapter 9

1. Oral history interview of Robert W. Straub by Clark Hansen, May 14, 1991, Tape 4, Side 1, Oregon Historical Society, Portland.

2. *Fire at Eden's Gate: Tom McCall and the Oregon Story*, Brent Walth, Oregon Historical Society Press, Portland, 1994, pp. 158-59.

3. "Straub Blisters McCall's Budget Ideas," Matt Kramer, Associated Press, *The Oregonian*, Portland, December 10, 1968, page 18.

4. "Robert Straub Suggests State Take Over Floundering Willamette Greenway Project," *The Oregonian*, Portland, December 11, 1968, page 29.

5. "Straub Says $43 Million Surplus Could Ease Tax Load," *The Oregonian*, Portland, April 10, 1969, page 34.

6. Bill Bradbury, *Oregon Blue Book, 2007-2008.* Salem: Oregon Secretary of State Office, 2007, p. 301.

7. "The Oregon Poll: McCall Grabs Hairline Lead for Governor," J. Roy Bardsley, *The Oregonian*, Portland, April 12, 1970, page 1.

8. Ibid.

9. Oral history interview of Robert W. Straub by Clark Hansen, May 14, 1991, Tape 4, Side 1, Oregon Historical Society, Portland.

10. Telephone interview of Ed Westerdahl by author, March 6, 2009.

11. Telephone interview of Ken Johnson by author, February 26, 2009.

12. "Starting Even," lead editorial, *The Oregonian*, Portland, April 14, 1970.

13. *Fire at Eden's Gate: Tom McCall and the Oregon Story*, Brent Walth, Oregon Historical Society Press, Portland, 1994, pp. 282-83.

14. Telephone interview of Oregon State Representative Vicki Berger (R-Salem) by author, March 12, 2009.

15. *Fire at Eden's Gate: Tom McCall and the Oregon Story*, Brent Walth, Oregon Historical Society Press, Portland, 994, pp. 253-62.

16. Telephone interview with Oregon State Representative Vicki Berger (R-Salem) by author, March 12, 2009.

17. http://bluebook.state.or.us/state/elections/elections07.htm

18. From "Local Color," documentary film by John Tuttle, Oregon Public Broadcasting, Portland, 1991, released in DVD in 2008.

19. *Packwood: The Public and Private Life, from Acclaim to Outrage*, by Mark Kirchmeier, HarperCollins West, New York, 1994, chapter 6, page 95.

20. Ibid, chapter 5, page 86.

21. O'Beirne, Kate, "Bread & circuses – Senator Bob Packwood's public and private stance on women," October 9, 1995, *National Review*, Washington, DC.

22. Author conversation with Andy Kerr, field director, Oregon Wilderness Coalition, spring 1980.

23. Oral history interview with Governor Robert W. Straub by Clark Hansen, Oregon Historical Society, Portland, Tape 4, Side 1, May 29, 1991.

24. The backlash could be as extreme, and surreal, as the rebellion, in some cases. The town of Hallandale, Florida, for example, took up town council time working on an ordinance to ban 'hippies' from its jurisdiction. Besides a few basic constitutional problems with such a law, the town's commissioners were having a hard time defining the hated 'hippies.' One defined them as "oddballs" with "bare feet, odd dress, and unkempt appearance crowned by long hair." Another councilman termed a hippie "a phony person belonging to the group which does not want to work or do right," while a third came up with "people who dress in clothing we don't accept, such as sandals, beads, large sunglasses, and one-piece pajama suits." From "What is a Hippie? Well if you don't know, just … just …" Jack Smith, The Oregonian, November 28, 1968, page 9.

25. Telephone interview of Dennis Stovall by author, March 10, 2009.

26. *"UO Radicals - 1970; the untold story,"* by Chad Sullivan, http://www.uoregon. edu/~insurgnt/closet/issues/12.6/radicals.html

27. Telephone interview of Dennis Stovall by author, March 10, 2009.

28. *The Far Out Story of Vortex I*, Matt Love, Nestucca Spit Press, Pacific City, 2004, page 60.

29. *Fire at Eden's Gate: Tom McCall and the Oregon Story*, Brent Walth, Oregon Historical Society Press, Portland, 1994, page 284.

30. Ibid., page 213.

31. Ibid, page 214.

32. *Tom McCall: Maverick*, Tom McCall with Steve Neal, Binford & Mort, Portland, OR, 1977, page 88.

33. "McCall 'Appalled' by Mob Action Against University ROTC Installation," Dennis Higman, *The Oregonian*, April 17, 1970, page 25.

34. "Straub Denounces Bill Aimed at Campus Riots," *The Oregonian*, April 30, 1969, page 13.

35. "Edith Green believes Douglas should be given day in court," Harold Hughes, *The Oregonian*, April 22, 1970, page 20.

36. "Wolfe stops classes; buildings stay open," *PSU Vanguard* newspaper, Portland, Vol. 25, No.63, May 8, 1970, page 1.

37. "Barricade people symbol of strike," Doug Babb, *PSU Vanguard*, Portland, Vol. 25, No. 65, 5/12/1970, page 6.

38. Telephone interview of Professor Joe Uris by author, January 21, 2009.

39. "Amid pleas for peace … Police attack hospitalizes 27," *PSU Vanguard*, Portland, Vol. 25, No. 65, May 12, 1970, Strike Special insert, page 3.

40. "Bloody spectacle; it couldn't happen here," Dean Smith, *PSU Vanguard*, Portland, Vol. 25, No. 65, May 12, 1970, Strike Special insert, page 3.

41. "Newsman blames City Hall for Monday's cop violence," transcript of television commentary by Bruce Baer, KATU-TV News, *PSU Vanguard*, Portland, Vol. 25, No. 66, May 15, 1970, page 6.

42. "3,000 march but mayor hides out," Stan Pusieski, *PSU Vanguard*, Portland, Vol. 25, No. 66, May 15, 1970, page 1.

43. Primary Election Results, May 1970, Oregon State Election Division Records, Secretary of State's Office, Salem.

44. "LA Free Press," Doug Weiskopf, June 1970, from *The Far Out Story of Vortex I*, Matt Love, Nestucca Spit Press, Pacific City, 2004, page 25

45. Telephone interview of Matt Love by author, March 6, 2009.

46. *The Far Out Story of Vortex I*, Matt Love, Nestucca Spit Press, Pacific City, 2004, page 45.

47. Ibid., pp. 52-53, 60-61.

48. Ibid., pp. 59-60.

49. *Fire at Eden's Gate: Tom McCall and the Oregon Story*, Brent Walth, Oregon Historical Society Press, Portland, 1994, page 239.

50. Oral history interview of Robert W. Straub by Clark Hansen, May 14, 1991, Tape 4, Side 1, Oregon Historical Society, Portland.

51. Telephone interview of Ken Johnson by author, February 26, 2009.

52. *The Far Out Story of Vortex I"* Matt Love, Nestucca Spit Press, Pacific City, 2004, pages 54, 60.

53. Ibid., pp. 70-71.

54. Telephone interview of Ken Johnson by author, February 26, 2009.

55. Oral history interview of Robert W. Straub by Clark Hansen, May 14, 1991, Tape 4, Side 1, Oregon Historical Society, Portland.

56. *The Far Out Story of Vortex I,* Matt Love, Nestucca Spit Press, Pacific City, 2004, pp. 72-74.

57. Telephone interview of Matt Love by author, March 6, 2009.

58. Telephone interview of Ed Westerdahl by author, March 6, 2009.

59. *The Far Out Story of Vortex I*, Matt Love, Nestucca Spit Press, Pacific City, 2004, pp. 93-96.

60. Author interview of Doug Babb and Dean Smith, March 17, 2009.

61. Vortex I, William S. Robbins, http://www.oregonencyclopedia.org/entry/view/vortex_i/, The Oregon Encyclopedia Project, Portland State University, 2009.

62. Telephone interview of Ken Johnson by author, February 26, 2009.

63. "Bob Straub: There's more to the story," by Congressman Earl Blumenauer, *The Oregonian*, Commentary section, December 26, 2002.

Chapter 10

1. Telephone interview of Ed Westerdahl by author, March 6, 2009.

2. Telephone interview of Barbara Hanneman by author, September 9, 2011.

3. Oral history interview of Roger Meier by Michael O'Rourke, January 19, 2004, Robert W. Straub Archives, Western Oregon University, Monmouth.

4. Ibid.

5. PERS Financial Reports, Web site http://oregon.gov/PERS/section/financial_reports/regular_and_variable.shtml. The variable account earned 19 percent in 1975 and 18 percent in 1976, regaining what it had lost in the previous two years. Over the long haul it has achieved spectacular returns.

6. Oral history interview of Roger Meier by Michael O'Rourke, January 19, 2004, Robert W. Straub Archives, Western Oregon University, Monmouth.

7. Ibid.

8. Telephone interview of Ken Johnson by author, February 26, 2009.

9. Telephone interview of Loren Wyss by author, November 10, 2009.

10. Telephone interview of Ken Johnson by author, February 26, 2009.

11. Oral history interview of Roger Meier by Michael O'Rourke, January 19, /2004, Robert W. Straub Archives, Western Oregon University, Monmouth.

12. Ibid.

13. Author interview of Ken Johnson, June 25, 2009.

14. "Blazing Trails in the 1970s," Brent Walth, *The Oregonian*, December 29, 1999.

15. Oral history interview of Robert W. Straub by Clark Hansen, May 29, 1991, Tape 4, Side 1, Oregon Historical Society, Portland.

16. "Straub Plans Trip Overseas, Uncertain of Next Undertaking," Charles E. Beggs, *Oregon Statesman*, Salem, December 3, 1972, Section 1, page 7.

17. "Straub's a rooster who doesn't crow about achievements," Larry Roby, *Capitol Journal*, Salem, December 9,1972, Section 3, page 30.

18. Author interview of Dean Brooks, April 11, 2007

19. Oral history interview of Robert W. Straub by Clark Hansen, May 29, 1991, Tape 4, Side 1, Oregon Historical Society, Portland.

20. Telephone interview of Jeff Straub by author, March 12, 2007.

21. Telephone interview of Kay Grasing by author, July 14, 2010. Grasing also noted that, in contrast, another governor she knew, who shall remain nameless, had only one personal request while she worked at the state library: "When he got into office, he requested a whole stack of books on Oregon that would look nice on his bookshelf."

22. Floyd McKay, then a reporter for the Oregon Statesman, remembers a night in the late 1960s when he and his wife, Dixie, who were Straub's neighbors in those days, met Hoffer at the Straubs and taking part in a fascinating discussion of whether the city or

the country was the place where the best ideas for human advancement came from. Hoffer, the field hand/longshoreman/philosopher known for his aphorisms and books like *The True Believer*, took the part of city dwellers and Straub, naturally, that of the country people. The two originally met when, after reading one of Hoffer's books, Bob decided to just call him up out of the blue and arranged to meet him. They remained good friends until Hoffer's death in 1983. Telephone interview of Floyd McKay by author, August 31, 2010.

23. The events described were personally witnessed by the author in the spring of 1970.

24. The school, in addition to strong academics, featured horseback riding and environmental seminars from such luminaries as Euell Gibbons, who instructed the students about harvesting the wild food of the mountains and the desert. Gibbons, did, in fact, show the students how to "eat a pine tree," since "many parts are edible" as he famously assured viewers in the Post Grape Nuts television commercial airing at the time. Telephone interview of Ann Frank, née Hawkes, by author, July 14, 2009, and Bill Straub conversation with author, summer 1973.

25. Mike Straub comment to Mark Henkels, September 2010.

26. Author discussion with Bill Straub in the summer of 1973, confirmed by author interview of Dean Brooks, April 11, 2007.

27. Bill Bradbury, *2007-2008 Oregon Blue Book*, Salem: Secretary of State's Office, Salem, 2007, p. 302.

28. *With Grit and By Grace: Breaking Trails in Politics and Law: A Memoir* Betty Roberts, Oregon State University Press, Corvallis, 2008, page 174.

29. Author interview of Judge James Redden, September 2, 2009.

30. Telephone interview of Luke Russell by author, May 2007.

31. *he Neuropharmacology of Psychosis*, Carol A. Tominga and John W. Davis, University of Illinois School of Medicine, Chicago, 2007, published by University of Oxford Press on behalf of Maryland Psychiatric Research Center, http://schizophreniabulletin. oxfordjournals.org/cgi/content/full/33/4/937

32. "What are the symptoms of bipolar disorder?" National Institute of Mental Health (NIMH), National Institutes of Health, US Department of Health and Human Services, http://www.nimh.nih.gov/health/publications/bipolar-disorder/what-are-the-symptoms-of-bipolar-disorder.shtml

33. *The Neuropharmacology of Psychosis*, Carol A. Tominga and John W. Davis, University of Illinois School of Medicine, Chicago, published by University of Oxford Press on behalf of Maryland Psychiatric Research Center, http://schizophreniabulletin.oxfordjournals. org/cgi/content/full/33/4/937

34. Ibid.

35. Author interview of Dr. Dean Brooks, August 11, 2009.

36. Author interview of Pat Straub, June 28, 2007.

37. Kay Redfield Jamison in her 1993 book, *Touched by Fire*, created a table of mood disorders in British and Irish poets born between 1705 and 1805 in which those exhibiting clear indications of mood disorder outnumbered those without such indications by a 27–8 margin. Table 3-1 pp. 63-71 Free Press Paperbacks, Simon and Schuster, New York, 1993.

38. "Depression in Command: In times of crisis, mentally ill leaders can see what others don't," by Dr. Nassir Ghaemi, Prof. of Psychiatry at Tufts University Medical School, *Wall Street Journal*, July 30-31, 2011, sec.C, p.3.

39. Ibid.

40. *Lincoln's Melancholy*, Joshua Wolf Shenk, Houghlin Mifflin Co., Boston - New York, 2005, Introduction, p. 8.

41. *The Intimate World of Abraham Lincoln*, C. A. Tripp, Free Press, A Division of Simon and Schuster, New York, 2005, inside jacket cover, hardbound edition.
42. Author interview of Dr. Dean Brooks, August 11, 2009.
43. Author interview of Barbara Hanneman, July 30, 2007.
44. *With Grit and By Grace, Breaking Trails in Politics and in Law: A Memoir*, Betty Roberts, Oregon State University Press, Corvallis, 2008, p.184.
45. Bergstein's New York University law school roommate, Steve McCarthy—a native Oregonian and another young political mover and shaker— recommended that Len come back to Oregon with him to seek his fortune. McCarthy told Bergstein, "Politics is different in Oregon, you can walk right into the governor's office, or meet a state legislator without an appointment. You will have opportunities from day one that you might never get in New York." Bergstein had been a legal aid attorney in Portland for a year and a half and now found himself in charge of a statewide political campaign. Author interview of Stephen McCarthy, March 25, 2008.
46. Author interview of Judge James Redden, September 2, 2009.
47. The Court had already prohibited her from holding office until January 8, 1972, for a previous offense of advertising a "re-election" campaign in 1968, two years after having left office. Corbett, had she been elected treasurer, would have taken office on January 1, seven days sooner than permitted by the previous ruling. "Alice Corbett not discouraged despite a series of setbacks," Ed Grosswiler, Eugene *Register-Guard*, Page 9A, September 29, 1972
48. Author interview of Judge James Redden, September 2, 2009.
49. Ibid.
50. Author interview of Governor Ted Kulongoski, December 7, 2007.
51. Telephone interview of Scott Bartlett by author, June 14, 2012.
52. *With Grit and By Grace, Breaking Trails in Politics and in Law: A Memoir*, Betty Roberts, Oregon State University Press, Corvallis, 2008, p.184.
53. Author interview of Judge James Redden, September 2, 2009.
54. Telephone interview of R. P. "Joe" Smith by author, August 31, 2009.
55. Telephone interview of Len Bergstein by author, October 28, 2009.
56. Telephone interview of R. P. "Joe" Smith by author, August 31, 2009.
57. Telephone interview of Ken Johnson by author, September 23, 2009.
58. General Election, 1974, Oregon Secretary of State, Elections Division.
59. Author interview of Pat Straub, June 28, 2007.
60. Author interview of Dr. Dean Brooks, August 11, 2009.
61. Telephone interview of Len Bergstein by author, October 8, 2009.
62. Jane Straub email to Mark Henkels November 21, 2009.
63. Inaugural Address of Governor Robert W. Straub, Oregon State Capitol, House of Representatives Chamber, January 13, 1975, Oregon State Archives, 800 Summer Street, Salem.

Chapter 11

1. Janet McLennan email to author, February 19, 2010.
2. Ibid.
3. "35 Years After the Arab Oil Embargo," Jay Hakes, *Journal of Energy Security*, IAGS, October 6, 2008, http://www.ensec.org/index.php?option=com_content&view=article&id=155:35yearsafterthearaboilembargo&catid=83:middle-east&Itemid=324
4. "Recession Cycles," by Bob Lotich, *ChristianPf*, October 2, 2008, http://www.christianpf.com/recession-cycles-economic/

5. "U.S. Recession 1973-1975," San Jose University Department of Economics, applet-magic.com, Thayer Watkins, Silicon Valley and Tornado Alley, USA, http://www.applet-magic.com/rec1974.htm#

6. "Oregon Resident Labor Force, Unemployment and Employment 1975," State of Oregon Department of Employment, Research, and Statistics, Salem, OR, January, 2010

7. Bureau of Labor Statistics Data, CPI All Urban Consumers – Portland-Salem SMSA, October 1974 – Jan. 1975, http://data.bls.gov/PDQ/servlet/SurveyOutputServlet

8. Janet McLennan email to author, February 19, 2010.

9. "Bob Straub: A Personal Portrait," television interview with Ted Bryant, KATU Channel 2 News, Portland, January 6, 1979.

10. Janet McLennan email to author, February 19, 2010.

11. Author interview of Pat Straub, June 28, 2007.

12. Author interview of Dick Sanders, January 17, 2005.

13. Mike Straub comment in meeting, February 19, 2010.

14. Author interview of Barbara Hanneman, July 30, 2007.

15. Telephone interview of Joel Schatz by author, January 5, 2010.

16. Author interview of Randy Stockdale, November 15, 2007.
    Once, when Washington Governor Dixy Lee Ray called the Capitol, saying she had not been able to reach Pat at home, Barbara Hanneman told her, "Oh, she's probably out feeding the chickens." That was not the sort of thing she had expected to hear about a governor's wife! Telephone interview of Kay Grasing by author, July 14, 2010.

17. Author interview of R. P. "Joe" Smith, September 7, 2009.

18. "History of Auto Insurance II, From Unsatisfied Judgment to Uninsured Motorist Coverage," Prof. Bill Long April 13, 2005, http://www.drbilllong.com/Insurance/HistoryII.html, Copyright © 2004-2007 William R. Long.

19. Telephone interview of Walt Brown by author, February 18, 2010

20. Ibid.

21. "Tax Cuts and Jobs Plan Top Gov. Straub's Priority List," Charles Beggs, *The Oregon Statesman*, Salem, January 14, 1975, page 1.

22. *Natural States: The Environmental Imagination in Maine, Oregon, and the Nation*, Richard W. Judd & Christopher S. Beach, Resources for the Future, Washington, DC, 2003, pp 138-39.

23. Ibid.

24. Author interview of Dave Talbot, August 8, 2007.

25. Telephone interview of George and Liz VanLeeuwen by author, March 3, 2010.

26. Telephone interview of Ron Eber by author, March 22, 2010

27. Liz VanLeeuwen's activism eventually led to a political career. In 1980, after several tries, she was elected a Republican state representative, serving for eight terms.

28. Janet McLennan email to author, February 19, 2010

29. L. B. Day conversation with the author, Charleston, OR, spring 1976

30. Author interview of Norma Paulus, Portland, May 13, /2007

31. Ibid.

32. Telephone interview of George and Liz VanLeeuwen by author, March 3, 2010

33. *Oregon Plans: The Making of an Unquiet Land-Use Revolution*, Sy Adler, Oregon State University Press, Corvallis, 2012, page 19.

34. Ibid., page 3

35. Author interview of Hector MacPherson, Corvallis, February 13, 2008.

36. http://www.onethousandfriendsoforegon.org/resources/mccall.html, from Governor Tom McCall's address to the Oregon legislature on January 8, 1973.

37. *Oregon Plans: The Making of an Unquiet Land-Use Revolution*, Sy Adler, Oregon State University Press, Corvallis, 2012,, pp. 147-48.
38. Telephone interview of Ken Johnson by author, February 27, 2010.
39. Telephone interview of Ron Eber by author, March 22, 2010.
40. Telephone interview of Roy Hemingway by author, March 22, 2010.
41. "Energeticist led state to become energy leader," by Ginny Burdick, *The Oregonian*, December 22, 1973.
42. Email message from Joel Schatz to author, February 17, 2010.
43. "Energeticist led state to become energy leader," by Ginny Burdick, *The Oregonian*, December 22, 1973.
44. *Transition*, Introduction to the 1977 reprint, by former Governor Tom McCall, Prometheus Unbound Specialty Books, Portland, 1977.
45. *A New Yardstick: The Science of Energetics*, by Harold Gilliam, self-published, 1974, page 22, available at Robert W. Straub Archives, Western Oregon University, Monmouth.
46. "Energy Office Unplugged: Power Lobby Re-calls the Schatz," by Phillip Johnson, *Oregon Times*, March 1975. p. 18.
47. "Energy wunderkind: genius isn't always enough," by Dan Bernstein, *Capital Journal*, Opinion, Salem, December 4, 1974, page 5.
48. Ibid.
49. "Energy Office Unplugged: Power Lobby Re-calls the Schatz," Phillip Johnson, *Oregon Times*, March 1975, page 18.
50. Ibid., page 20.
51. "Energy wunderkind: genius isn't always enough," Dan Bernstein, *Capital Journal*, Opinion, Salem, December 4, 1974, page 5.
52. "Energy Office Unplugged: Power Lobby Re-calls the Schatz," Phillip Johnson, *Oregon Times*, March 1975, pp. 18-20.
53. Telephone interview of Joel Schatz by author, February, 17, 2010.
54. Janet McLennan email to author, February 19, 2010.
55. Ibid.
56. Telephone interview of Lon Topaz by author, January 11, 2010.
57. "Straub expected to seek transfer of freeway funds," Stan Federman, *The Oregonian*, July 1, 1975, page 1A.
58. "Mt. Hood Decision," Editorial, *The Oregonian*, Saturday, July 27, 1974 Multnomah County and the City of Portland had been looking into whether or not they had the right to reverse their approval of the Mt. Hood Freeway, and their legal departments informed them that they could. The freeway required local government approval. Ron Buel, then a close confidant of Neil Goldschmidt, came to Don Clark and asked him to take the lead on pulling their support for the freeway. Clark asked him, "Why can't Neil do that?" Buel told him that Goldschmidt had other things to do. Clark introduced the resolution and found that with Mel Gordon, who was intrigued with the concept of a light rail network, and Ben Padrow, he had majority support on the commission for withdrawal of county approval of the freeway. After the hearing and the vote to withdraw, State Transportation Commission Chairman Glenn Jackson came up to Clark and said, "I certainly hope you know what you are doing." Author interview of Don Clark, April 12, 2012.
59. Author interview of Neil Goldschmidt, April 1, 2008.
60. Ibid.
61. Telephone interview of Len Bergstein by author, January 27, 2011.
62. Author interview of Neil Goldschmidt, April 1, 2008.
63. "Straub defends 'difficult' decision against freeway," Richard Colby, *The Oregonian*, July 2, 1975, 1A.

64. Urban Planner Richard Ross, a former neighbor of Rep. Peck, from comments of Richard Ross during presentation of "The Mt. Hood Freeway and the Preservation of Southeast Portland," recorded by author, by Richard Ross and Val Ballestrom, Architectural Heritage Center, Portland, November 8, 2008.

65. Author interview of Neil Goldschmidt, April 1, 2008.

66. Telephone interview of Len Bergstein by author, January 27, 2011.

67. "Fund Transfer OK kills Mt. Hood Freeway Plan," *The Oregonian*, May 8, 1976, A12.

68. Author interview of Stephen McCarthy, former Tri-Met executive director, March 25, 2008

69. "Oregon Project Independence, Protecting our Senior," Press release by the Oregon Department of Human Services, July 16, 2009.

70. "Straub's first six months," Editorial, Eric Allen, *The Medford Mail Tribune*, June 11, 1975

71. "The 1975 Legislature," Editorial, *The Oregonian*, Portland, OR, June 16, 1975

72. Oregon still has a slightly weaker than average governor, vis-à-vis other states according to "Politics in the American States: A Comparative Analysis, Ninth Edition," Virginia Gray & Russell Hansen, CQ Press, Washington DC, 2007, Table 7.6.

73. Janet McLennan email to author, February 19, 2010

74. "Straub Tags Land Plan Top Job In Next Two Years," UPI, *Statesman-Journal*, January 14, 1975

75. Janet McLennan email to author, February 19, 2010

76. "Gov. Straub warns industrialists not to block land use agency," Stan Federman, *The Oregonian*, September 20, 1975, page A 20

77. "Straub reveals he'll run again," Stan Federman, *The Oregonian*, September 20, 1975, page A 20.

Chapter 12

1. "Oregon Resident Oregon Labor Force, Unemployment and Employment 1975," State of Oregon Department of Employment, Research, and Statistics, Salem, OR, January, 2010

2. "Willamette Week: 25 Years; 1975, Events," http://wweek.com/html/25-1975.html, April 7, 2010

3. Oregon Statewide 1976 Covered Employment and Wages Summary Report, Oregon Labor Market Information System (OLMIS), Oregon Employment Department, Salem. http://www.qualityinfo.org/olmisj/CEP?action=summary&areacode=01000000&indtype =S&periodcode=01001976&submit=Continue

4. Oregon Harvest History, Excel graph of Oregon Timber Harvest from 1962-2009, Oregon Department of Forestry, oregon.gov/ODF/RESOURCE_PLANNING/docs/ OregonHarvest.

5. "Earthwatch Oregon," Oregon Environmental Council Newsletter, December 1976, p. 13

6. Beuter, J. H., K. N. Johnson, and H. L. Scheurman, *Timber for Oregon's Tomorrow: An Analysis of Reasonably Possible Occurances*. Oregon State University, Forest Research Laboratory, Bulletin 19 (1976).

7. "The Oregon Omnibus Wilderness Act of 1978 as a Component of the Endangered American Wilderness Act of 1978, Public Law 95-237." Author(s): Alan Tautges *Environmental Review*: ER, Vol. 13, No. 1 (Spring, 1989), pp. 43-61.

8. "Goldy, Straub still Planning to Review Economic Impact." Coos Bay *World* (September 3, 1977).

9. Founded in 1974, the Oregon Wilderness Coalition became the Oregon Natural Resource Council in the 1980s and is now known as Oregon Wild.

10. Author interview of Len Bergstein, October 3, 2007.

11. Janet McLennan, email to Mark Henkels and author, June 24, 2010.

12. Editorial: "Shorting the wilderness in Oregon," *The Oregonian*, January 7, 1979, p. C2.

13. "Oregon Wild: Endangered Forest Wilderness," Andy Kerr, Portland, Oregon Natural Resources Council, 2010, pp. 58 and 60.

14. John Hayes, "Straub Gives Go-Ahead to Spraying With 2,4,5-T." *Oregon Statesman*, February 25, 1977, P. A1.

15. "Coos Bay Women Decide Straub fit to be Pied." *The Oregonian*. May 5, 1978, p. A1.

16. John Hayes, "Schroeder Opposes Straub on Spraying." *Oregon Statesman*. September 22, 1978. P. A1.

17. Author interview of Andy Kerr, September 18, 2010.

18. John Hayes, "Forestry Board Limits Herbicide Sprays." *Oregon Statesman*, September 23, 1978, P. A1. "How Straub Put on the Pressure." *Oregon Statesman*, September 23, 1978. P. A8. "Muddling through the spray issue." *Eugene Register Guard*. (September 29, 1978)

19. Author interview of Norma Paulus, May 14, 2007

20. Robert Straub, "Straub: Even Flow Must Stay," Earthwatch Oregon, Oregon Environmental Council Newsletter (November 1977), p. 13.

21. Letter to John Ball, dated October 5, 1976. Memoranda from Janet McLennan and from Dan Goldy regarding log exports in Autumn 1976. Both in Straub Archives, Western Oregon University.

22. Janet McLennan, e-mail to author, May 3, 2010.

23. Larry Leonard, "Straub: Endings and Beginning." *The Oregonian, Northwest Magazine* (January 15, 1984). Pp. 7-8.

24. Telephone interview of Gordon Moore by author, February 20, 2008.

25. "How Corvallis Exceeds New York City: A View from Theoretical Physics," Joe Rojas-Burke, *The Oregonian,* 1/22/January 22, 2010, http://www.oregonlive.com/portland/index.ssf/2011/01/how_corvallis_ore_exceeds_new.html

26. Regulation of the toxic chemicals used in high-tech production was frequently overlooked in the early days of production. The groundwater under Silicon Valley, and in some hot spots in Oregon's Washington County, remains contaminated and not suitable for human consumption.

27. Author interview of Neil Goldschmidt, April 1, 2008.

28. "The Governor's Race: Let's not fear change more than the status quo," opinion column by Jack Roberts, *The Oregonian*, October 21, 2010.

29. Telephone interview of Henry Richmond by author, September 10, 2010.

30. Telephone interview of Edward J. Sullivan by author, September 16, 2010.

31. Craig Walker, "LCDC law originator supports L.B. Day's decision to resign." *The Oregonian* (July 4, 1976), P. c2.

32. Telephone interview of Henry Richmond by author, September 10, 2010.

33. Ibid.

34. Telephone interview of William C. (Bill) Scott, Jr. by author, September 29, 2010.

35. "Initiative, Referendum, and Recall, 1972-1978, Oregon Blue Book, Secretary of State, State of Oregon, Salem. http://bluebook.state.or.us/state/elections/elections19.htm

36. Telephone interview of William C. (Bill) Scott, Jr. by author, September 29, 2010.

37. Telephone interview of Henry Richmond by author, September 10, 2010.

38. "Initiative, Referendum, and Recall, 1972-1978, Oregon Blue Book, Secretary of State, State of Oregon, Salem. http://bluebook.state.or.us/state/elections/elections19.htm

39. Telephone interview of Henry Richmond by author, September 10, 2010.

40. Oregon Secretary of State, Elections Division records, September 9, 2011.

41. Telephone interview of Henry Richmond by author, September 10, 2010.
42. Ibid.
43. Ibid.
44. Telephone interview of Edward J. Sullivan by author, September 16, 2010.
45. Douglas Heider and David Dietz, *Legislative Perspectives: A 150-Year History of the Oregon Legislatures From 1843-1993*. (Portland: Oregon Historical Society Press, 1995). Pp. 185-88.
46. Telephone interview of former State Senator Jan Wyers by author, February 22, 2012.
47. Heider and Dietz, p. 190.
48. Telephone interview of Jan Wyers by author, February 22, 2012.
49. "Pre's Strangest Crusade: His Campaign Against Field Burning, Track Town USA, Eugene, Web site: http://www.tracktownusa.com/track.item.25/steve-prefontaine-crusade-against-field-burning.html
50. "Splendor in the Mass: The grass seed industry has moved past controversy to good times. Find out how." By Andy Duncan, *Oregon's Agricultural Progress*, College of Agricultural Sciences, Extension Service, Oregon State University, Spring/Summer 1998, http://oregonprogress.oregonstate.edu/springsummer-1998/splendor-mass. In the same article: "People chuckle about the research with field burning machines," says George Pugh, a third-generation grass seed farmer near Shedd in the southern Willamette Valley. "But I think it had to be done to show it wasn't possible."
51. Stan Federman, "Straub Shines in Legislative Work so Far." *The Oregonian* (February 28, 1977)
52. Ed Mosey. "News Analysis: Kramer must deal with tensions created by Burns." *The Oregonian*. (Nov. 26, 1976) p. C1
53. "Look out for Bud Kramer," "A Personal View" opinion column, William Bebout, *Capital Journal*, Nov. 11, 1976, page 4A, Salem.
54. National Oceanographic and Atmospheric Administration (NOAA) Web site: http://www.ncdc.noaa.gov/temp-and-precip/time-series/index.php?parameter=pcp&month=4&year=2012&filter=12&state=35&div=0 and http://www.ncdc.noaa.gov/temp-and-precip/time-series/?parameter=pdsi&month=1&year=2012&filter=1&state=35&div=0
55. "Straub's message getting through on drought program," *Oregon Journal*, Mar. 11, 1977, p.10.
56. Telephone interview of Roy Hemingway by author, March 22, 2010.
57. Initiative Referendum and Recall, 1972-78, *Oregon Blue Book*, Oregon Secretary of State, Salem. http://bluebook.state.or.us/state/elections/elections19.htm
58. Telephone interview of Lon Topaz by author, January 10, 2010.
59. "Straub seeks N-plant delay: Power needs unknown," *The Oregonian*, June 3, 1976, A1.
60. Author interview of Jean Russell, February 26, 2007.
61. Initiative Referendum and Recall, 1972-78, Oregon Blue Book, Oregon Secretary of State, Salem. http://bluebook.state.or.us/state/elections/elections19.htm
62. Initiative, Referendum and Recall, 1980-1987, Oregon Blue Book, Oregon Secretary of State, Salem. http://bluebook.state.or.us/state/elections/elections20.htm
63. Author interview of Myron (Mike) Katz, February 17, 2009.
64. Telephone interview of Roy Hemingway by author, March 22, 2010.
65. Stan Federman, "Task Force Puts political apple on Straub's head, takes shots." *The Oregonian* (April 25, 1977).
66. Telephone interview of Roy Hemingway by author, March 22, 2010.
67. Jan Wyers telephone conversation with author, February 12, 2012.
68. Only one of these plants, WPPSS 2 or WNP 2, was completed. Now called the Columbia Generating Station (CGS) it is the only nuclear power plant still operating

in the Northwest as of the printing of this book. WPPSS 3-5 defaulted on their bonds, resulting in what was at the time the largest municipal bond default in the history of the United States.

69. Telephone interview of Roy Hemingway by author, March 22, 2010.

70. Phil Cogswell, "News Analysis: Straub-Boe Relations more strained." *The Oregonian* (December 2, 1977), p. B1.

71. "Straub Defies Senate Panel on Appointee." *The Oregonian* (December 1, 1977) p. C1.

72. "Appointment Suit Dismissed." *The Oregonian* (May 24, 1978), p. D5.

73. "Initiative, Referendum, and Recall, 1972-1978, Oregon Blue Book, Secretary of State, State of Oregon, Salem, http://bluebook.state.or.us/state/elections/elections19.htm

74. As witnessed by the author in February 1979.

75. Ann Sullivan, "Elderly Reaping Harvest over Wyden." *The Oregonian* (March 28, 1978).

76. "Oregon Program may keep Elderly out of Nursing Homes," Sue Hill, *Oregon Statesman, Salem* (August 29, 1978), p. A10.

77. Telephone interview of Phyllis Rand by author, February 1, 2011.

78. Telephone interview of Edward J. Sullivan by author, September 16, 2010.

79. "The Legacy of Hans Linde in the Statutory and Adminstrative Age, Shirley S. Abrahamson & Michael E. Ahrens, Symposium, 2007, *Willamette Law Review*, 43 Rev. 175, p.1. "Hans Linde has been the poster child for state courts to interpret their laws independently of the U.S. Supreme Court's interpretation of parallel provisions in the federal Constitution, while still adhering to the doctrine of federal supremacy. State courts handle more than 95% of the court business in this country, and state court judges have, as Linde continually reminds us, the obligation to expound state law. When the banner of state constitutions was unfurled with new federalism, Hans's writings in the opinions of the Oregon Supreme Court and his law review articles gave theoretical and pragmatic bases to the movement."

80. *With Grit and by Grace: Breaking Trails in Politics and Law, A Memoir*, Betty Roberts, with Gail Wells, Oregon State University Press, Corvallis, 2008, p. 209. Part of the anxiousness of governors to appoint her to these judicial positions may be explained by her strong performances as a statewide political candidate.

81. "The Political Legacy of Robert W. Straub," Richard A. Clucas, *Oregon Historical Quarterly*, 104.4 (Winter 2003) p. 473.

82. Floyd McKay, News Commentary, KGW-TV Channel 8 News, Portland, July 5, 1977.

83. Jim Church. "Confidence is key to "new" Bob Straub." *Capital Journal* (May 30, 1978).

84. Douglas Yocum and Don Jepson. "Bob Straub: I Want Four More Years." *Oregon Journal* (November 4, 1977.

85. Robert Shepard. "McCall Slips in a Zinger." Capital Journal (April 19, 1977).

86. Author interview of Victor Atiyeh, May 30, 2007.

87. *Fire at Eden's Gate: Tom McCall and the Oregon Story*, Brent Walth, Oregon Historical Society Press, Portland, 994; paperback edition, 1998, pp. 420-21.

88. In a post-general election consolation note to Straub, McCall could not resist a woeful aside, writing: "Roger and his pubescent gnomes left me tarred as an old man, broken in physical and mental health. That smear was spread so thick across the state that some of it will never become unblotted." Letter from Tom McCall to Bob and Pat Straub, dated November 9, 1978, Robert W. Straub Archives, Western Oregon University, Monmouth.

89. *Fire at Eden's Gate: Tom McCall and the Oregon Story*, Brent Walth, Oregon Historical Society Press, Portland, 994; paperback edition, 1998, pp. 420-32.

90. Norma Paulus, Oregon Secretary of State. *Summary Report of Campaign Contributions and Expenditures: 1978 Primary Election*. Salem: Oregon Secretary of State, 1978.

91. *Fire at Eden's Gate: Tom McCall and the Oregon Story*, Brent Walth, Oregon Historical Society Press, Portland, 994; paperback edition, 1998, pp. 431-32.

92. Jim Church. "Confidence is key to "new" Bob Straub." *Capital Journal* (May 30, 1978).

93. Author interview of Len Bergstein, October 3, 2007.

94. Observed by the author in spring 1978.

95. Norma Paulus, Oregon Secretary of State. *Summary Report of Campaign Contributions and Expenditures: 1978 Primary Election.* Salem: Oregon Secretary of State, 1978. And: Norma Paulus, Oregon Secretary of State. *Official Abstract of Votes: Primary Election, May 23, 1978.* Salem: Oregon Secretary of State, 1978.

96. "Straub deserves Demos' big vote of confidence," *The Oregon Statesman* (May 2, 1978).

97. Telephone interview of Emily Ashworth by author, September 14, 2011.

98. "State economy looks better than in past 10 years, governor says." *Albany Democrat-Herald* (April 21, 1978).

99. Wayne Thompson. "Vic Atiyeh, Bob Straub: A Contrast in Candidates." *The Oregonian.* October 1, 1978.

100. Ibid.

101. "A Survey of the Political Climate in the State of Oregon," Peter D. Hart Research Associates, Inc., Washington, DC, July, 1978 – personal and confidential.

102. Author interview of Len Bergstein, October 3, 2007.

103. "Quickly Draft Fair Tax Plan." *Albany Democrat Herald,* September 5, 1978.

104. Quinton Smaith, "Straub ties campaign to No. 11" *Albany Democrat Herald,* September 28, 1978.

105. Douglas Yocom, "Governor's Race hinges on tax vote." *Oregon Journal* (November 1, 1978).

106. B. J. Noles. "Dorothy Lawson McCall Turns 90." *The Oregonian.* September 28, 1978.

107. Wayne Thompson, "Carter Urges Oregonians to cast votes." *The Oregonian*, November 4, 1978.

108. Michael Alesko, "Atiyeh, Goldschmidt clash over Straub's role in state loan." *The Oregonian*, November 6, 1978.

109. "Straub not in violation of state election laws," *The Oregonian,* October 31, 1978.

110. Telephone interview of William J. Radakovich by author, January 30, 2011.

111. Michael Alesko, "Atiyeh, Goldschmidt clash over Straub's role in state loan." *The Oregonian*, November 6, 1978

112. Dick Thomas, "Conceding Loss Poses Challenge for Straub." *The Oregonian* (November 8, 1978), p. C6.

113. Norma Paulus, Oregon Secretary of State. *Official Abstract of Votes: General Election, November 7, 1978.* Salem: Oregon Secretary of State, 1979.

114. "Inflation was major voter target." *The Oregonian*, November 9, 1978.

115. Jim Church, "Lame Duck Straub: I would rather be a soaring eagle." *Oregon Statesman* (November 28, 1978).

116. "The Candidates: Governor." *The Oregonian*, November 5, 1978).

117. Norma Paulus, Oregon Secretary of State. *Summary Report of Campaign Contributions and Expenditures: 1978 General Election.* Salem: Oregon Secretary of State, 1979. Norma Paulus, Oregon Secretary of State. *Summary Report of Campaign Contributions and Expenditures: 1978 Primary Election.* Salem: Oregon Secretary of State, 1978.

118. "Atiyeh, Straub gear for Race." *The Oregonian* (October 20, 1978).

119. Wayne Thompson, "Results of governor's race explode myths of soothsayers." *The Oregonian*, November 8, 1978.

120. Louis Cook. "Tax, spending limits approved in 9 states." *The Oregonian.* November 8, 1978.

121. "Brown, Carey win governors' battles," R. Gregory Nokes, AP, *The Oregonian*, November 8, 1978.

122. "State, local government new look is Republican." *Oregon Statesman*. November 9, 1978.

123. Clay Eals, "Timber Industry forms group to back Atiyeh." *The Oregonian*. October 1, 1978.

124. Norma Paulus, Oregon Secretary of State. *Summary Report of Campaign Contributions and Expenditures: 1978 General Election.* Salem: Oregon Secretary of State, 1979.

125. J. Roy Bardsley, "Atiyeh holds Narrow Lead," *The Oregonian*. October 16, 1978.

126. Sandra McDonough. "Defeat leaves Straub loyalists at loss.*" The Oregonian*. November 9, 1978.

127. Letter from Tom McCall to Bob and Pat Straub, dated Nov. 9, 1978, Robert W. Straub Archives, Western Oregon University, Monmouth.

128. "Atiyeh offers Oregon new beginning." *The Oregonian*. November 9, 1978.

129. "Bob Straub's Record." *The Oregonian*. January 9, 1978.

Chapter 13

1. "Straub surprised by defeat: 'people want change,'" Steve Erickson, *The Oregonian*, Nov. 9, 1978, C1

2. "Bob Straub: A Personal Portrait," Ted Bryant interview of Bob Straub, KATU Channel 2, Portland. January 6, 1979

3. Ibid.

4. Author interview of Governor Victor Atiyeh, May 30, 2007.

5. Henry Richmond comments to author by email, November 17, 2010.

6. Author interview of Edward Sullivan, September 16, 2010.

7. Henry Richmond comments to author by email, November 17, 2010.

8. Author interview of Henry Richmond, September 10, 2010.

9. Oregon Blue Book Web site, State of Oregon, Secretary of State's Office, Elections Division, Salem. http://bluebook.state.or.us/state/elections/elections20.htm

10. "Remarks by Bob Straub," Memorial Service for Tom McCall, State Capitol, Salem, January 12, 1983; 353 .9795031 Straub c.2, Oregon State Library, Salem.

11. Telephone interview of State Senator Jackie Winters, R-Salem, by author, September 2, 2010.

12. Telephone interview of former Governor Barbara Roberts, by author, October 16, 2010.

13. Telephone interview of Sarah Johnson by author, July 18, 2010.

14. Telephone interview of Kay Grasing, July 14, 2010.

15. Telephone interview of Emil Graziani, by author, August 30, 2010.

16. Telephone interview of John Matthews, former recycling coordinator, Garten Foundation, by author, September 24, 2010.

17. At publication time, Anna Peterson is currently serving as Salem's mayor.

18. Telephone interview of Emil Graziani, by author, August 30, 2010.

19. Telephone interview of John Matthews, former recycling coordinator, Garten Foundation, by author, September 24, 2010.

20. Neil Goldschmidt, oral history recording, Michael O'Rourke interviewing, June 23, 2005, Dundee, Western Oregon University, Monmouth.

21. Telephone interview of Floyd McKay by author, August 31, 2010.

22. Today Goldschmidt's legacy is overshadowed by appalling public revelations about his personal behavior—something that Bob Straub, mercifully, never knew about. It would have broken his heart.

In 2004, Portland's *Willamette Week* newspaper broke the story that Neil Goldschmidt had a lengthy sexual relationship with a girl, beginning when she was fourteen years old, while he was mayor of Portland in the 1970s. He had subsequently covered it up, paying his victim money in an out of court settlement and avoiding prosecution due to the statute of limitations. "The 30-Year Secret: A crime, a cover-up, and the way it shaped Oregon," Nigel Jaquiss, *Willamette Week*, May 12, 2004, p 1.

23. Telephone interview of Danny Santos by author, August 10, 2010.
24. Ibid.
25. Mike Straub comment at Straub Archives sub-committee meeting, September 1, 2010.
26. Telephone interview of Bill Bales by author, September 27, 2010.
27. Telephone interview of Danny Santos by author, August 10, 2010.
28. Telephone interview of Jim George by author, August 6, 2010.
29. Ibid.
30. Ibid.
31. Ibid.
32. "State Shouldn't Put Pensions in Peril," Robert W. Straub, opinion column, *The Oregonian*, Thursday, June 22, 1995, page D9
33. Telephone interview of Ken Johnson by author, July 15, 2010.
34. Telephone interview of Floyd McKay by author, August 31, 2010.
35. Telephone interview of Ken Johnson by author, July 15, 2010.
36. Telephone interview of Floyd McKay by author, August 31, 2010.
37. Telephone interview of Ken Johnson by author, September 20, 2010.
38. Janet McLennan comments, by email to author, November 22, 2010.
39. Telephone interview of Pat Straub by author, September 12, 2010.
40. Janet McLennan comments, by email to author, November 22, 2010
41. Mike Straub comment at Straub Archives sub-committee meeting, September 1, 2010.
42. Telephone interview of Andy Kerr by author, September 18, 2010
43. Neil Goldschmidt, oral history recording, Michael O'Rourke interviewing, June 23, 2005, Dundee, Western Oregon University, Monmouth.
44. Marion County, Oregon, Elections Department, September 24, 2010.
45. "Decades of Dreams Finally Come to Life: Several Previous Proposals Fell through the Cracks," by Toby Manthey, *Oregon Statesman Journal*, Salem, February 24, 2005, http://www.statesmanjournal.com/apps/pbcs.dll/article?AID=/20050224/NEWS/502250301/0/SS01#ixzz0yhj2fHtN
46. Telephone interview of Mike Swaim by author, September 23, 2010
47. "Decades of Dreams Finally Come to Life: Several Previous Proposals Fell through the Cracks," by Toby Manthey, *Oregon Statesman Journal*, Salem, February 24, 2005
48. Marion County, Oregon, Elections Department, September 24, 2010.
49. Telephone interview of Roger Gertenrich by author, August 6, 2010.
50. Telephone interview of Mike Swaim by author, September 23, 2010.
51. Telephone interview of Bill Bales by author, September 27, 2010.
52. Ibid. The Salem Self Help Housing Board included Bob Straub, Bill Bales, Walter Achterman MD, Bob Boldt. Earl Baumann, Larry Epping, Ed and Mike Fischer, Jim Kreitzberg, Bob Ohmart, and Bill Tourtellotte.
53. Telephone interview of Bill Bales by author, September 27, 2010.
54. Author interview of Mike and Jane Straub, July 31, 2007.
55. Email from Loren Wyss to Mike Straub, Mark Henkels, and Chuck Johnson, September 16, 2010.
56. Author interview of Mike and Jane Straub, July 31, 2007.
57. Email from Loren Wyss to Mike Straub, Mark Henkels, and Chuck Johnson, September 16, 2010.

58. Author interview of Mike and Jane Straub, July 31, 2007.
59. Author interview of Pat Straub, July 10, 2010.
60. "Diagnosed with Alzheimer's disease, former Oregon Gov. Bob Straub faces…Another campaign," *Statesman Journal*, Meg Walker, page 1A, September 19, 1999.
61. Author interview of Pat Straub, July 10, 2010.
62. Telephone interview of Emil Graziani, former executive director, Garten Foundation, by author, August 20, 2010.
63. "Diagnosed with Alzheimer's disease, former Oregon Gov. Bob Straub faces…Another campaign," *Statesman Journal,* Meg Walker, page 1A, September 19, 1999.
64. "Former Gov. Bob Straub battles Alzheimer's disease," *The Oregonian*, James Mayer, page E1, September 21, 1999.
65. "Diagnosed with Alzheimer's disease, former Oregon Gov. Bob Straub faces…Another campaign," *Statesman Journal,* Meg Walker, page 1A, September 19, 1999.
66. Ibid.
67. "Straub faces charge of intoxicated driving," Leslie L. Zaitz, *The Oregonian*, December 14, 1981.
68. "Diagnosed with Alzheimer's disease, former Oregon Gov. Bob Straub faces…Another campaign," *Statesman Journal,* Meg Walker, page 1A, September 19, 1999.
69. Author interview of Mike and Jane Straub, July 31, 2007.
70. Email from Loren Wyss to Mike Straub, Mark Henkels, and Chuck Johnson, September 16, 2010.
71. Author interview of Pat Straub, July 10, 2010.
72. Email from Loren Wyss to Mike Straub, Mark Henkels, and Chuck Johnson, September 16, 2010.
73. Author interview of Mike and Jane Straub, July 31, 2007.
74. Author interview of Pat Straub, July 10, 2010.

Chapter 14

1. Author interview of Mike Burton, April 24, 2007.
2. Author interview of Len Bergstein, October 3, 2007.
3. John Kitzhaber, Remarks at Robert W. Straub Memorial Service, House of Representatives, State Capitol, Salem, OR, December 18, 2002
4. Telephone interview of Clayton Anderson by author, September 16, 2011.
5. Tom McCall interview, from "American Dreams: Lost and Found," Studs Terkel, Knopf Doubleday Publishing Company, New York, 1980, page 335: "Heroes are not giant statues framed against a red sky. They are people who say: This is my community, and it is my responsibility to make it better."

Epilogue

1. Charles Johnson interview of Loren ("Bud") and Ann Kramer, May 7, 2007.
2. Clucas, Richard A. "The political Legacy of Robert W. Straub." *Oregon Historical Quarterly*. 104.4 (Winter 2003): p462.
3. Judd, Richard J. and Christopher S. Beach, *Natural States: The Environmental Imagination in Maine, Oregon and the Nation*. (Washington DC: Resources for the Future, 2003). P. 52.
4. Robbins, William G. *Landscapes of Conflict*. (Seattle: University of Washington Press, 2004)

5. Judd, Richard J. and Christopher S. Beach, *Natural States: The Environmental Imagination in Maine, Oregon and the Nation.* (Washington DC: Resources for the Future, 2003). Most notably, pages 117-123 and 138-142.

6. Sickinger, Ted, and Brent Hunsberger. "Can We Afford Public Workers?" *The Oregonian* (October 24, 2010).

7. "PERS By the Numbers – February 2011." Oregon Public Employees Retirement System, February 2011. P. 18. http://oregonpers.info/Library/Download.aspx?docid=1403

8. Sanders, Richard. "Bob Straub: Raising tress and capital." *Oregon Business* (January 1982)

9. "Wooing Business Instead of Chasing It Away." *Business Week* (March 29, 1976) pp. 76-77.

10. Telephone interview of Mike Swaim by Charles Johnson, September 23, 2010

11. McCall, Tom. Personal letter to Bob and Pat Straub dated November 9, 1978, in Straub Archives, Western Oregon University.

Acknowledgments

A number of people helped with this book at various stages of its inception, creation, and completion. Many sat for interviews, shared their materials, or provided sound advice on how to proceed with my work. If you are not named below, you know who you are. Please accept my sincere thank you.

This biography would not have been possible without strong support from the Straub family. From the start, Pat Straub, her son Mike, and the rest of the family made it possible for me to tell the true, complete story of Bob Straub. Their decision to share Bob's struggles as well as his successes was brave and rare. During the six years it took to write and publish this book, they responded quickly when called upon to review what I had written or to assist me in getting more stories and information to make Bob's tale more accurate and compelling.

From the formation of the Straub Archives Committee at Western Oregon University in the summer of 2000, Loren Wyss was determined that his friend Bob Straub, and the leadership he demonstrated for Oregon, should be properly remembered and studied by future generations in a biography. Whether my effort attains what Loren intended, time will tell. With Loren initiating, he and Mike Straub led the way in raising the funds to get the book written. They and the rest of the committee—including Jane Straub, Jim Straub, Governor Victor Atiyeh, Governor Barbara Roberts, Judy Wyss, Ken and Sarah Johnson (my parents), Janet McLennan, Barbara Hanneman, and Professor Mark Henkels—were invaluable with their insights into Governor Straub and their regular critiques of my writing.

Governor Atiyeh, who graciously agreed to write the foreword and was a kindly voice of wisdom throughout, joked that this experience would teach me not to write something this large by committee. He was right that it was difficult, but the committee's input made the book significantly better.

Of especial note was Janet McLennan, Straub's long-time natural resource advisor, who sometimes overwhelmed me with corrections, but never failed to guide me through the intricacies of state policy that she helped shape during her time in government service.

Then there was Governor Roberts—I would never have believed that I would be so honored as to have someone of her caliber avidly proof-reading my chapters as I completed them and cheering me on. She frequently shocked me by turning around line by line edits within two days of their completion, giving my rough work an instant polishing. This is something she did consistently through the various iterations of the manuscript.

Mark Henkels, also a published writer and a professional observer of Oregon politics, gave me insights into organizing and completing my work and served as my advisor and confidant. When I was struggling, two years before completion of the book, Mark took what I had written for what is now chapter 12, and completed its first draft. I have since added to and modified it significantly but if you notice the particularly nuanced analysis of the1978 political campaign, the 1977 legislative session, or Governor Straub's timber policy you will be admiring Professor Henkels' handiwork, or perhaps in his pithy epilogue, which places Straub's achievements into historical perspective.

Of course, this book never would have been attempted had I not already had the basic political story line thoroughly ingrained into me by my father and mother, Ken and Sarah Johnson. They were consistent contributors and gentle critics throughout. Dad didn't live long enough to see it published, but did get the pleasure of reading the completed manuscript, with its dedication, as accepted by OSU Press. Mom, with her copy-editing experience from the Oregon Legislature, was the last pair of eyes to look at the text before the indexing was completed. However, rest assured, all errors remaining in the text are mine, not hers.

In recognizing those who contributed to the completion of this book, I would be grossly negligent if I did not note my public sector patrons, as well. Western Oregon University and the WOU Foundation provided a home and a structure for me, and a primary source of material from the Straub Archives in WOU's Hamersly Library. Beginning with Library Dean Gary Jensen and Vice President for University Advancement Leta Edwards, the faith WOU showed in an untested writer is astounding. Gary and Leta's strategic vision, friendship, and consistent guidance were critically important in the early stages as I slowly learned what it took to organize a project of this size and began writing. Unfortunately for me, both of them retired during my writing process, but Gary's successor as Library Dean, Allen McKiel, assumed the leadership role and, a published writer himself, kindly encouraged and skillfully assisted me in completing my work.

Along the way, the Library and "the Cottage" made me welcome on campus and several people made significant contributions to my work, notably Librarian Camila Gabaldon, who was WOU's part-time archivist when I began, Roy Bennett who briefly took her place before he retired, and Archivist Erin Passehl, who has now taken charge. Oral historian Michael O'Rourke completed a tremendous series of interviews of Straub family members, friends, and associates that were an invaluable source. Camila's students Heath Wellman and Jackson Stalley (now on library staff) transcribed interviews and organized materials in the archives, building upon the original work done by Sharon Lehner, who received much of the original material while serving as the Straub Archives first archivist. Library assistants Jerrie Lee Parpart, Larry Bentley, Lori Bullis, and Lori Pagel were notably helpful at key moments of my work. On the administrative end, executive assistants Carol Tripp and Nora Solvedt calmly kept the library works rolling, and fiscal directors Jim Birken and Cara Groshong, along with executive assistant Sandy Newland, were especially helpful and supportive at the WOU Foundation.

As the book process progressed, the acquisitions editor at Oregon State University Press, Mary Elizabeth Braun, took this unpublished writer seriously from day one. Through the years, she encouraged and cajoled me, dispensing warm humor and good advice. The two commissioned critiques of my manuscript—especially the one signed by Professor Robert D. Johnston, of the University of Illinois-Chicago—were exceptionally instructive to my own editing of the book and led to significant improvements. Unofficial comments from Professor Floyd McKay of Western Washington University were extremely helpful as well, as were some notes from Professor Sy Adler of Portland State University. OSU Press managing editor Jo Alexander cheerfully wielded her sharp red font to cut out much that was extraneous—though I confess many, if not most, passages found their way back into the book, frequently in the end notes. Jo also managed to artfully squeeze a fair number of the excellent photos we had at our disposal, many courtesy of long-time political photographer Gerry Lewin, into the burgeoning text. Especial kudos go to David Drummond of Salamander Hill Design who created the cover art with one of Gerry's classic pictures of Bob, and to marketing associate Micki Reaman and associate director Tom Booth for orchestrating all the publicity and marketing.

Finally, I want to thank my friends and loved ones, who put up with a sometimes frenzied version of the person they thought they knew as I went through the personal changes it took to complete this work, especially my brother Bruce, who well understands the nuances of this tale, and sister Nancy who also lived and relived the world of Oregon politics at every family gathering; Nancy's delightful family - husband John Erickson and children Kayla and Trevor; and, last, but certainly not least, my son Mackintosh Rieder-Johnson—a keen political mind in his own right, who honors me by calling me out of the blue with witty and apropos analysis of the news of the day and has in recent years turned the tables on me by giving me political books to read.

Most of all I want to thank my dearest friend in the world, Rebecca Robinson. In the course of my writing, she reconnected with her Wales family cousins, after we discovered, with less than six degrees of separation, that they were close friends of Bob Straub's at Dartmouth College and afterwards. That happy rediscovery of long-lost cousins is only a small down payment on what I owe her. During my ups and downs in completing this project, Rebecca always made me feel loved and appreciated.

###

The research and writing of *Standing at the Water's Edge: Bob Straub's Battle for the Soul of Oregon* were supported by generous contributions from:

The Wyss Foundation • Mike & Linna Straub • Patricia S. Straub • Samuel T. & Mary K. Naito Foundation • Ken & Sarah Johnson • Herbert A. Templeton Foundation • Mike & Pam Forrester • The Bend Foundation • Bob & Geri Boldt • James & Lora Meyer • James & Shirley Rippey • James & Georgia George • Cheryl Meyers • Jonathan & Deanne Ater • Victor & Dolores Atiyeh • Len Bergstein & Northwest Strategies, Inc. • Lawrence & Susan Black • Brian Booth • Lucille Davis • The Samuel S. Johnson Foundation • Margery Bloomfield • Laura Meier • Jean Tate • Jean Russell • Barbara Hanneman • George & Frankie Bell • Kathleen Grasing • Gary & Afroula Jensen • Joe & Pat Kintz • Bill & Janet McLennan • Barbara Straub • Cliff & Joanne Trow • Blaine & Ines Whipple • Dr. Ray & Dorothy Brodersen • John & Sherla Collins • Nancie Fadeley • Robert & Mary Andrews

Index

Abel Dick, 226
Aguinaldo, 5
Albany *Democrat-Herald*, 99
Alinsky, Saul, 236
Allen, Eric, 217
Alzheimer's disease, 272-76
American Legion Convention, 160-66
Anderson, Clayton, 41, 46-47, 51, 54
Appling, Howell, 80-83, 86-88, 112, 114-15
Arab Oil Embargo, 195, 209
Arce, Jose, 24
Aristotle, 182
Ashworth, Emily, 244-45
Associated Oregon Industries, 219
Association of Oregon Counties, 54
Atiyeh, Victor, x-xi: 1974 election, 186-87, 189, 206, 224, 228, 239-42; 1978 election and aftermath, 243-56, 258, 261-62, 287
automobile insurance, 68-69, 202-3

Babb, Doug, 165
Babbs, Ken, 175
Bachman, Roger, 231
Bacon, Robert, 126-27, 129-30, 133, 140
Baer, Bruce, 159
Bales, Bill, 264, 270-71
Ball, John, 226
Ballot Measure 6 (1968), 140-44, 279
Ballot Measure 6 (1978), 245-50
Ballot Measure 6 (1982), 256
Ballot Measure 7 (1980), 238
Ballot Measure 9 (1978), 238
Bardsley, J. Roy, 150
Barker, Gordon, 89, 109-10, 113-14, 116
Bartlett, Scott, 186
Bateson, Cornelius, 90
Bazett, Sidney, 126-29
Beach Bill, 121-23, 126-34, 137-43, 148, 232, 279
Beaches Forever, Inc., 140-44
Bebout, Bill, 235
Belcher, Bob and Alison, 213
Bell, George, 305
Belton, Howard, x, xii, 77-82, 84-85, 87-89, 109-10, 113
Bentley, Sarah, 273
Berger, Vicki, 151-52
Bergstein, Len, 184, 188, 197-98, 214-15, 224, 246, 250, 277, 316

Berkman, Craig, 162, 184
bipolar disorder, and depression, xiv, 32, 40, 177-78, 180-83, 189, 196, 273-74, 280
Birrell, Jean, 91
Bismarck (the dog), 33, 35-36
Bitte, Diane, 126-27, 129
Bitte, Larry, 121-22, 125-26, 129-30, 133, 140-43
Bjurman, George, 118
Black, Lawrence, 169
Blumenauer, Earl, 165-66
Blyth and Company, 113
Board of Examiners of Nursing Home Administrators, 240-41
Boe, Jason, 191, 201-2, 234, 239, 240-41, 247
Boivin, Harry, 60, 62, 66
Bond, Harry, 20, 22, 295
Bonneville Power Administration, 56-57, 236, 238, 240
Bosley, William Bradford, 6-7, 292
Bottle Bill, 151-52, 171
Brandenfels, Martin, 86-87
Brooks, Dean, 89, 172, 175, 180-81, 183, 189, 273
Brown, Jerry, 246, 251
Brown, Walt, 202-3
Bryant, Ted, 254
Bunn, Stan, 207
Burns, Keith, 142, 183, 197-98, 235

California-Oregon Power Company, 99
CalPERS, 179
Cannon, Kessler, 137
Capital Journal, 163, 235
Capital Press, 63, 76, 79, 272
Carter, Jimmy, 226, 233, 248, 251, 262
Chambers, Richard, 151-52
Chamness, Mary and Paul, 279
Charbonneau development, 207
Churchill, Winston, 63, 164
Citizens to Save Oregon's Beaches (CSOBs), 130, 133-34, 140-41
Clark, Don, 80, 188, 213, 318-19
Clark, Robert, 156
Clay Towers, 248-49
Clucas, Richard, 242, 284
Coastal Goal (land use), 232-33
Construction Work in Progress (CWIP charges), 238
Columbia Management, 170

Cooper, Forrest, 101
Coos Bay World, 61
Corbett, Alf, 66
Corbett, Alice, 184, 316
Cordon, Guy, 45, 50
Cranston, Alan, 14, 294
Creswell, Oregon, 51, 57
Cross, Travis, 90
Curtin, Oregon, 52-53, 175, 178, 222, 260, 281

Daily Astorian, 272
Dargan, Tom, 106
Dartmouth College, 14, 17-25, 32-35, 42, 48, 76, 154, 176, 232, 280, 294-96, 307, 331
Davis, Bob, 170, 243
Davis, Charles, 236
Day, L. B., 205, 207-8, 219, 228-30, 233, 248-49
Daylight Savings Time, 73-74, 303
death penalty, 102, 246, 250, 287, 307
Democratic Party: Straub joins, 41-43; growth of 44-45, 48-49, 55, 58, Straub's leadership of, 61-68; 1962 primary, 70-75, 76, 81; 1964 National Convention, 83-84, 88, 102-3, 143, 147, 167; 1974 primary, 177-78, 181, 183-86, 189, 232, 255, 306
Dijon, France, 31-32, 258
dioxin herbicides, 224-225
Domestic and Rural Power Authority (DRPA), 236, 238-40
Drinkwater, Terry, 165, 171
drought (1977), 236
Duncan, Bob, 70, 73-75, 214
Durno, Edwin, 70-71, 73

Eagleton, Thomas, 181
East Oregonian, 272
Eber, Ron, 205, 208
economic development, vii, xiii, 57, 138, 189, 191-92, 194-96, 203-4, 208, 220-223, 225, 227-28, 245, 252, 256, 265, 281-83, 285
Eisenhower, Dwight, 56-57, 97, 296, 300
Eubanks, Wally, 170
eye problems (Straub), 13, 24-25, 32, 34, 182, 280, 293
Eymann, Dick, 48, 176, 202, 210, 212, 307

Fadeley, Ed, 201, 239
Fadeley, Nancie, 103, 207, 261
Fairview Home, 80-82
Fall Creek, Oregon, 40, 51-52, 260, 281
"Family, The," 161-64
Faust, Jack, 153
Federman, Stan, 235
field burning, 217, 218, 235, 321
Fitzgerald, Ken, 130, 133, 140, 142
Fitzgerald, Mike, 233
Fobes, Ken, 198-200, 235
Ford, Gerald, 187, 203, 214-15
forest policy: La Honda, 9-10; work camp 15-16; Weyerhaeuser job, 34-36, 39, 40, 51; Gov. Holmes, 60; youth camps, 62, 64, 67, 80-81; Waldo Lake, 71-72, 192, 221-27; Forestry Goal (LCDC), 232, 233; Pat Straub on Board of Forestry, 267-68, 271, 280-81, 287
Forrester, Bud and Eleanor, 272
Freeman, J. Carl, 237
French Pete Creek, Oregon, 222
Frohnmayer, Dave, 202
Frye, Bill, 87
Fultz, Lester, 139

Garten Foundation, 261-62, 273
Garth, David, 242-43, 245-46
George, Jim, 92, 111-17, 168, 264-65
Georgia Pacific, 210, 226, 251, 265
Gertenrich, Roger, 269-70
Gibbons, Euell, 315
Goldschmidt, Margie, 62
Goldschmidt, Neil, 188, 198, 213-15, 228, 230, 248-49, 261-64, 267-68, 270, 272, 325
Goldwater, Barry, 84, 88, 153
Goldy, Dan, 223-24, 226, 228, 272: and Rusty, 272
Gortmaker, Gary, 143
Goshen, Oregon, 51-52, 57, 63, 90, 189
Grannell, Bill, 232, 234
Grasing, Kay, 173, 315, 317
Gray, John, 210, 231
Grayson, Jeffrey, 169
Graziani, Emil, 261-62, 273
Green, Edith, 49-50, 57, 63, 67-68, 84, 143, 158, 301
Guaymas, Sonora, Mexico, 53-54, 174, 179: San Carlos Bay, 183, 258, 259, 264

Guild, Gordon, 98, 307
Gunnar, Peter, 65, 131

Hagenstein, W. D., 71-72
Hallock, Ted, 210, 239
Hanks, Frank, 165
Hanlon, Chuck, 234
Hanneman, Barbara, 89, 91: and Gene,
   Laurie, and Linda 93, 167, 183, 201, 252,
   261, 317
Hanneman, Paul, 129-30, 151-52
Hansell, Stafford, 109, 111-12, 198-99,
   205-6, 210-11, 256
Harbor Drive, 213
Harms, Ed, 41, 48
Harris, Sue (Miller), 268-69
Harsch Investment Company, 248
Hart, Peter, Research Associates, 246
Hartsfield, Michael, 235
Hass, Harl, 183
Hatfield, Mark, xii, 55-56, 60-61, 64-65,
   72-74, 79-82, 88-90, 98-101, 153, 157,
   201, 215, 224, 267, 305
Hay, William, 107, 121-22, 127, 131,
   139-40
Hazen, Bob, 164
Heald, Dave, 20, 295
Hemingway, Roy, 236, 238-40
Hermach, George, 50: and Ruth, 71, 299-
   300, 304
Hermach, Tim, 91
Hess, Henry, 45
Hibbitts, Tim, 247
Hicks, Jay C. "Doc," 42-44
higher education, 73, 110
highway development, vii, 48, 50: Highway
   101, 95-105, 107; beach as highway 121-
   22, 134-38, 142, 147, 192; Mt. Hood
   Freeway, 212-16, 217, 267, 280, 288
Hill, Jim, 265-66
Hill, Sue, 241
Hodel, Don, 210
Hoffer, Eric, 174, 315
Hoffman, Paul, 86-87
Hollingsworth, Marv, 243-45
Holmes, Denny, 60
Holmes, Robert, 55-57, 59-61, 68, 89, 149,
   176
Holmstrom, Bill, 129, 131
Hornets, The, 234

Humphrey, Hubert, 83-84
Hunt, Bill, 265
Huntington, Hallie, 47-48

Ingram, Charlie, 35
Inn at Spanish Head, 128, 131, 138
Inskeep, Norm, 170
Intel Corporation, 227-28
Irish Bend, Oregon, 204
Ivancie, Frank, 214

Jack (the dog), 2-3, 12
Jackson, Glenn, 99-101, 104, 123, 131,
   134-36, 138, 142, 148, 164, 204, 207,
   213, 215, 217, 231, 306, 318-19
Janovic, Helen, 12-13
Jensen, Charlie and Ester, 204
Johnson, Ken, v, xiv, 61-63, 76, 79-80, 82,
   85, 91-92, 99, 102-3, 117, 142, 144, 151,
   165, 169, 170, 183, 188, 189, 199, 207-8,
   267, 306
Johnson, Lady Bird, 91, 101
Johnson, Lee, 131, 143-44, 156, 187, 255
Johnson, Lyndon, 72-73, 83-84, 88, 134,
   157
Johnson, Sarah, 188, 258
Jones, Aaron, 251

Kalapuya Tribes, 278
Katz, Myron (Mike), 238
Keizer, Ennis, 72-73
Kennedy, Ethel, 139
Kennedy, John F., 66-68, 71, 134
Kennedy, Robert F., v, 67, 139, 155
Kerr, Andy, 154, 223-24
Kesey, Ken, 175
King, Martin Luther Jr., 155
Kirby, Robert, 118
Kitzhaber, John, 266-67, 277-78, 289
Konold, Floyd, 39, 173
Kramer, Loren "Bud," 235, 239, 240-41,
   248-49; and Ann, 284, 301-2
Kramer, Matt, 127
Kulongoski, Ted, 185-86, 203, 234, 256,
   261, 289
Kvarsten, Wes, 230

La Honda, California, 9-10, 52, 227
Land Conservation and Development
   Commission (LCDC), 192, 205-8, 218-
   19, 228-33, 255-56

land-use planning, xi, xiii, 176, 185-86, 205-8, 218-19, 227, 229-33, 255-56, 279, 286
Lane County Commission, 46-50, 51-52, 54-55, 79, 280
Lang, Phil, 201-2, 234, 247
Leiken, Sid, 265
Lezak, Sidney, 67-68
Lincoln, Abraham, 41, 164, 182
Linde, Hans, 242, 322
Long, Jim, 95, 306
Los Altos, California, 9-15, 32-34, 174, 227, 278, 294
Lusk, Hall, 65

Maclay, Robert, 47-49
MacPherson, Hector, 206-7, 229
Mahoney, Tom, 66
Manchester, Max, 90, 108-9, 112-14
Manning, Ordway, 11-12, 293
Marbet, Lloyd, 237
Martin, Charles H., 44-45
Martin, Roger, 149-50, 152, 243-44
Matthews, John, 262
McCall, Dorothy Lawson, 247
McCall, Sam, 161, 166
McCall, Tom, x-xi, xii-xiv, 49-50, 88-89, 94-95, 99, 101, 104-8, 112, 115, 120-25, 127-28, 130-32, 134-38, 141-44, 146-52, 154-57, 159-68, 170-71, 176-77, 182-83, 185-89, 191, 195-97, 199, 201, 204-9, 213, 216-18, 228-30, 236, 239, 241, 243-44, 247, 250-53, 255-58, 270, 279, 281-83, 285-86, 288-90, 291, 305-6, 323
McCarthy, Steve, 318
McGovern, George, 153, 181
McKay, Dixie, 62, 315
McKay, Douglas, 57
McKay, Floyd, 62-63, 242, 262, 267, 315
McKay, Mrs. Douglas (Mabel), 101-2
McLennan, Bill, 102, 140-41
McLennan, Janet, 102-4, 125, 131, 137, 140-42, 183, 194-196, 199, 211-12, 217-18, 223-24, 226, 237-38, 267, 307
Medford Mail-Tribune, 216
medical care for elderly, 72-73
Meier, Roger, 168-70, 286-87
Miller, Ellen Wales, 20-21
Miller, Fred, 237
Miller, Wally, 33, 40, 53

Mississippi Freedom Democratic Party, 83-84
Mix, Tom, 179
Mondale, Walter, 261
Monteith, James, 223
Mooney, Tom, 6-7, 292-93
Moore, Gordon, 227
Morgan, Howard, 43-45
Morse, Wayne, 49, 55-60, 73, 81, 84-85, 99, 135, 153-54, 157, 188, 301-3, 306-7, 311
Morse-Melanie, 84-85
Mosser, John, 188, 190, 211, 229-31, 238
Mt. Hood Freeway, 212-16, 318-19
Mt. Moosilauke, 17, 19-23, 25, 32, 172
Munro, Sterling, 239
Myers, Clay, 121, 162, 176, 186-87, 305-6

Naito, Sam and Mary, 272
National Farm Worker Act of 1987, 263-64
Neilsen, Kenneth, 47, 49
Nestucca Sand Spit, 95-104, 134-38, 147-48, 213, 267, 280, 284
Neuberger, Dick, 36, 43, 45-46, 49-50, 55-56, 58-59, 64-65, 102, 242, 301
Neuberger, Maurine, 43-44, 65, 67, 71
Nixon, Richard, 66, 69-70, 153, 155, 158, 160, 163, 187, 195, 233, 252, 300
Northwest Power and Planning Act, 239
nuclear power, 210-12, 237-40, 244, 322
Nunn, Warne, 65, 80

Office of Coastal Zone Management, 232
Office of Energy Planning and Research (OEPR), 210-12
Oliver, Bob, 161
Olsen, Tom, 131
"One Flew Over the Cuckoo's Nest," 181
Onthank, Karl, 105, 123-24, 133, 307
Oregon Coastal Conservation and Development Commission (OCCDC), 232-33
Oregon Department of Energy (ODOE), 211-12, 238
Oregon Dunes National Recreation Area, 71-72, 102, 307, 311
Oregon Education Association, 90, 108
Oregon Fair Share, 236, 268-69
Oregon Investment Council, xii, 90, 108-109, 111-19, 168-70, 264-66, 282

Oregon Journal, 95, 243
Oregon Liquor Control Commission: liquor raid (1964), 86-87
Oregon State Mental Hospital, 53, 80, 89, 167, 172, 175, 180-81, 273
Oregon State Parks, 100, 122, 123, 137, 144, 217, 228
Oregon State Supreme Court, 65, 69, 110-11, 113, 115, 117, 142-43, 184, 191, 237, 241-42, 262, 322
Oregon State University, 130, 222, 227, 235
Oregon Statesman, Statesman Journal, 65, 113, 129, 241, 245, 251, 273-74, 289
Oregon Student Public Interest Research Group (OSPIRG), 225
Oregon Welfare Commission, 72-73
Oregonian, 93, 101, 104-5, 117-19, 130, 150-51, 163, 184, 217, 229, 231, 235, 241, 250, 253, 266, 268, 274

Pacific Gas & Electric, 1, 6, 76, 280, 292
Pacific Power & Light, 99-100, 210, 231, 237, 239, 306
Padrow, Ben, 62, 318-19
Pape, Dean, 265
Patterson, Paul, 55-56
Paulus, Fred, 110-13, 115
Paulus, Norma, 110, 205, 207, 225, 262
Payne, Ancil, 128
Pearl, Arthur, 159
Pearson, Walter, 60-62, 66-67
Peck, Grace, 215
Penwell, Cleighton, 209
People magazine, 200
People's Army Jamboree, 160-63, 165
Peterson, Edwin and Anna, 262
Philippine-American War, 4-5, 291-92
Piper, Dave, 212
Porter, Charles O., 43, 57, 69-70, 73-74, 302-3
Portland General Electric, 210, 237, 239
Portland State University, 62, 158-59, 165, 284
Pratt, Gerry, 117-19
Prefontaine, Steve, 235
Project Independence, 216, 241-42, 280, 286
Proposition 13, California (1978), 245-47, 251

Public Employees Retirement System (PERS), 77-79, 90, 108-16, 118, 168, 266, 282, 286
Public Utility Commission, 211-12, 236
Pullman, Jim and Lorraine, 268

Radakovich, Bill, 248-49
Rand, Dewey, Sr., 63
Rand, Phyllis, 241-42
RARE II, 222-24, 251
Ray, Dixy Lee, 238
Reagan, Ronald, 153-54, 221, 251, 263, 274, 288
Redden, James, 70-71, 129-31, 171, 178, 183-87, 248
Register-Guard newspaper, 48, 51, 61, 88, 105, 318
Rhoten, Dave, 142-43
Richmond, Henry, 229-31, 233
Rinke, Ken, 49, 143-44
Ripper, Jack, 232
Rippey, James, 170
Roberts, Barbara, 188, 258, 261-62
Roberts, Betty, 177-78, 183-88, 242, 299, 322
Roberts, Frank, 62, 184
Roberts, Mary Wendy, 184
Robeson, Paul, 153
Rockefeller, David, 76
Rockefeller, Nelson, 23, 76
Roosevelt, Franklin D. (FDR), 14, 18, 35, 42, 56, 63, 97, 100, 164
Roy, Richard, 267-68
Russell, Ike, 29, 33, 52-53, 174-75, 260
Russell, Jean Straub, 1-2, 9-16, 29, 33, 40, 52-53, 174-75, 190, 238, 260, 293-94
Russell, Luke, 33, 47, 179
Rutherford, Bill, 115

Sabin, Patricia, 160
Salem Self Help Housing, 270-71, 326
Saltus, R. Sanford, 22-23, 28-30, 32-33, 295
Saltus, Willa Boulton Dixon Stroud, 22-23, 34-35
San Francisco, California, 1-2, 4-10, 129, 265, 292-93
Sanders, Dick, 200
Santos, Danny, 264
Sargent, William, 180-81

Sarofim, Fayez, 118
Save Our Sands (SOS), 98, 101, 103
Schatz, Joel, 209-11
Schell, Steve, 229, 255
Schmidt, Ron, 106-7, 130, 161, 164, 199
Schnitzer, Harold, 248-49
Schroeder, Ed, 225
Scott, Bill, 230-31
Scott, Mitzi, 188-89
Senate Bill 100, 205, 207, 232, 286
Shelk, John, 268
Shrunk, Terry, 159
Sisters, Oregon, 40-41, 52
"Sixpack," The, 234-35
Skelton, Keith, 43-44, 48, 299
Sloper, Val, 115
Smith, Elmo, 55-57
Smith, Gregg, 248-49
Smith, Joseph, 187
Smith, Robert E., 85-86
Smith, R. P. "Joe," 183, 187-88, 197
Sprague, Charles, 45, 110, 113, 115, 289
Spray, Oregon, 259
Springfield, Oregon, 35-41, 46, 48, 50-51,
    57, 171-72, 222, 258, 260-61, 275, 279-
    81
Springfield News newspaper, 62
Squier, Anne, 229-30
State Accident Insurance Fund, 112-13,
    115-18, 168
State Board of Control, 79-81, 88-89, 91,
    101, 121, 148, 162, 167, 170, 217, 305
State Board of Forestry, 225, 267
State Department of Transportation,
    Highway Department, vii, 48, 95, 97-101,
    104, 122, 130-31, 134-41, 148, 192, 204-
    5, 207, 213-17, 267, 278, 318-19
State Housing Division, 248-49
State Land Board, 79-80, 88-89, 91, 101,
    167, 217, 305
State Sanitary Authority, 67, 80, 89-90, 93
State Welfare Commission, 65, 72
Stevenson, Adlai, 57
Stewart, Loran "Stub," 122, 222
Stoll, Norm and Helen, 83
Stovall, Dennis, 156
Straub, Barbara, 175, 293-94
Straub, Bernice, 15, 294
Straub, Bill, 51-52, 86, 91, 173-75, 178-79,
    182-83, 315

Straub, Daphne, 180
Straub, Denny, 33, 40-41, 46, 53, 80
Straub, Francis, 3, 9, 291
Straub, Frank, 1, 3, 9, 11-15, 40
Straub, Jane, 35-36, 38, 51-52, 64, 86, 91,
    98, 178, 259-60, 272, 275, 293-294,
Straub, Jeff, 25-26, 31-38, 41, 51-52, 64,
    91, 173, 179, 259
Straub, Jim, 1-2, 9, 11-13, 33, 40-41, 46,
    52-53, 80, 180, 294
Straub, Mary Tulley, 1, 5-10, 12-15, 18, 29,
    33, 294
Straub, Mike, 26, 35-41, 47, 51-53, 57-58,
    64, 80, 91, 103, 179, 200, 254, 258, 260,
    264, 268, 272-73, 274-76
Straub, Patricia Stroud, 17-18, 21-24,
    26-38, 41, 46, 50-51, 57, 61-64, 76, 86,
    90-91, 93, 98, 171-76, 178, 180-82, 187,
    189-90, 195-96, 199-200, 206, 225, 253-
    54, 258-62, 264, 267-79, 281-82, 288,
    290, 293, 317
Straub, Robert W. "Bob," vii, x-xiv:
    childhood, 1-2, 5-16; meets Pat, 17-18;
    Dartmouth, 17-25; courtship/marriage,
    21-31; U.S. Army, 24-33; travels/graduate
    school, 33-35; Weyerhaeuser/Springfield,
    35-39; homebuilding, 38-41; enters
    politics, 41-46; county commission/land
    purchases, 46-54; state senate, 54-75; state
    party chairman, 63-70; runs for Congress,
    69-75; runs for state treasurer, 76-88; first
    year in office, 88-93; runs for governor/
    coast highway/Willamette greenway, 93-
    107; enacts state investment reforms, 108-
    19; Beach Bill/Measure 6, 120-44; runs for
    governor again/Vortex, 145-66; resumes
    treasurer duties, 167-71; "retirement" from
    politics, 171-77; depression/treatment,
    175-83; third race for governor, 183-
    90; inauguration and first year, 190-
    219; governing, 220-53; last campaign,
    243-55; goodbye to McCall, 256-58;
    activist retirement, 258-71; Alzheimers,
    271-76; recapitulation, 277-90; endnote
    comments/observations, 292-94, 296,
    299-300, 303, 306-7, 315, 323, 325-26
Straub, Thomas, 1, 29, 292-94
Straub, Tom or TJ, 293
Stroud, Cassie, 23
Stroud, Dixon (Dickie), 23, 29, 76, 270

Stroud, Morris III, 23
Stroud, Morris Wistar Jr., 22
Stroud, Pat. *See* Straub, Patricia Stroud
Stroud, Peg, 23
stuttering, stammering, xiv, 13-14, 19, 32, 62-63, 294
Sullivan, Edward J., 229, 242
Swaim, Mike, 269-70
Sweetland, Monroe, 43-45, 55, 62, 83-84

Talbot, Dave, 122-23, 125, 137, 144, 306
Task Force on Small Woodlots, 226
taxation: county fair tax, 48; sales tax, 56, 71, 148-50; gasoline tax, 124, 133-34, 140, 142-44, 282; property relief/tax limits, 148-50, 176, 245-52, 282; income tax, 148-50, 176; business inventory tax relief, 148; income tax exemptions/cut, 192, 203; tax deferral/subsidies, 228; developer exemptions, 269; income tax rebate, 282; emergency clause, 300-1
Teamsters Union, 205, 228
Tektronix, 112, 115, 227
Thomas, Jay, 52-53, 175, 260-61, 281, 300
Thomas, Patty Straub, 36, 38, 51-53, 86, 91, 98, 175, 260-61, 300
Thomas, Peg Straub, 46, 51-53, 86, 91, 98, 174, 261, 274
Thomas, Robin, 52-53, 261
Thompson, Wayne, 250, 268
Thornton, Robert Y., 82, 84-85, 90, 108, 113, 115, 139, 143-44
Thurston, Oregon, 36-52, 280
Tiemann, Norbert T. "Nobby," 215
Time magazine, 242
Topaz, Lon, 212, 237
trade: with Germany, 228; with Japan, 173, 221, 226, 228
Trojan Nuclear Power Plant, 237, 244
Tulley, Mark, 5
Tulley, Mary. *See* Straub, Mary Tulley
Terkel, Studs, 282, 291, 326
Tykeson, Don, 265

Ubico, Jorge, 25, 296
Udall, Stewart, 71, 134-36, 154, 307, 311
Ullman, Al, 57
University of Oregon, 58-59, 60, 62, 70, 85, 91, 105, 123, 126, 156-57, 159, 202, 260
Urner, Jack, 259

Urner, Sam and Margaret, 9-10
VanLeeuwen, Liz and George, 204-7, 317

Vortex I, 155, 161-66, 170

Wacker Chemie, 268
Waldo Lake, 71-72, 303
Wales, Donald, 20, 24
Wales, Lincoln, 20, 24
Wallace, Lew, 42-43
Ward, Artemus, aka Charles Farrar Brown, 41, 298
Washington Public Power Supply System (WPPSS), 239-40, 322
Watergate, 187, 202, 249, 252
Weaver, Jim, 224
West, Oswald, 46, 96, 121-22, 285
Westerdahl, Ed, 107, 151, 156-57, 161-64, 167, 170, 188
Western Woodworkers Union, 226
Weyerhaeuser Corporation, 35-39, 72, 222, 232, 251, 280
Whiting, Pat, 203
wilderness protection, 71, 154, 176, 204, 221-25, 287
Willamette Greenway (Willamette River Rediscovered), x, xiii, 105, 107, 122-25, 129, 133, 136, 147-49, 185, 192, 195, 204-8, 217, 219, 228, 262, 269-70, 279, 282, 286, 288
Willamette Greenway Goal, 208
Willamina, Oregon, 1, 222, 258, 281
Winters, Jackie, 258, 262
Wolfe, Gregory, 158-59
Wood, Kenneth, 62
Woods, Carolyn, 13-14
Woods, W. Kelly, 241
World War II, 19, 24-32, 36, 39, 83, 99, 108, 117, 158, 182, 258, 284, 293-94, 294-96
Wright, Tom, 65
Wyden, Ron, 240-41
Wyers, Jan, 239
Wyss, Loren, 170: and Judy, 272, 275-76

Yeon, John, 122
Youth Forest Camps, 67, 80-81